Solution-Focused Supervision

Frank N. Thomas

Solution-Focused Supervision

A Resource-Oriented Approach to Developing Clinical Expertise

Frank N. Thomas
Texas Christian University
Fort Worth, TX, USA

ISBN 978-1-4899-8693-1   ISBN 978-1-4614-6052-7 (eBook)
DOI 10.1007/978-1-4614-6052-7
Springer New York Heidelberg Dordrecht London

© Springer Science+Business Media New York 2013
Softcover reprint of the hardcover 1st edition 2013
This work is subject to copyright. All rights are reserved by the Publisher, whether the whole or part of the material is concerned, specifically the rights of translation, reprinting, reuse of illustrations, recitation, broadcasting, reproduction on microfilms or in any other physical way, and transmission or information storage and retrieval, electronic adaptation, computer software, or by similar or dissimilar methodology now known or hereafter developed. Exempted from this legal reservation are brief excerpts in connection with reviews or scholarly analysis or material supplied specifically for the purpose of being entered and executed on a computer system, for exclusive use by the purchaser of the work. Duplication of this publication or parts thereof is permitted only under the provisions of the Copyright Law of the Publisher's location, in its current version, and permission for use must always be obtained from Springer. Permissions for use may be obtained through RightsLink at the Copyright Clearance Center. Violations are liable to prosecution under the respective Copyright Law.
The use of general descriptive names, registered names, trademarks, service marks, etc. in this publication does not imply, even in the absence of a specific statement, that such names are exempt from the relevant protective laws and regulations and therefore free for general use.
While the advice and information in this book are believed to be true and accurate at the date of publication, neither the authors nor the editors nor the publisher can accept any legal responsibility for any errors or omissions that may be made. The publisher makes no warranty, express or implied, with respect to the material contained herein.

Springer is part of Springer Science+Business Media (www.springer.com)

*To the psychotherapy supervisors who labor for the good of the profession, who give themselves and their time (often without compensation) to support a new generation of competent clinicians ...
I salute you.*

Foreword

In the early 1980s, when I was a doctoral student in Iowa City, Steve de Shazer came to present on his solution-focused (SF) approach for the Iowa Division of the American Association for Marriage and Family Therapy (IAMFT). His first book (de Shazer 1982) was fairly new and the ideas that he, Insoo Kim Berg, and their colleagues at the Brief Family Therapy Center in Milwaukee, Wisconsin were developing were not well known. However, our supervisor and faculty mentor had introduced us to the book and we were experimenting with some of the ideas, particularly the Formula First Session Task (FFST; de Shazer et al. 1986). These kinds of experiments were not new to us: carrying out ideas that seemed to fit with systemic and constructivist thinking that were popular at the time was often our "therapy of the week." Because of its on-its-head similarities to MRI (Watzlawick et al. 1974) and Haley/Madanes Strategic therapies (e.g., Haley 1976; Madanes 1981), the SF approach intrigued us. We were already steeped in cybernetics (Watzlawick, Weakland, and Fisch 1974) and system thinking (e.g., von Bertalanffy 1968), and the idea of focusing on solutions rather than problems seemed an extension of those ideas. Because we typically used standard family therapy practices of assessing dysfunction and what maintained it, looking at what was going well relative to problems seemed a bit strange to us. Experimenting with the FFST was a relatively easy thing to do, however, not so different that we couldn't do it. When our clients reported change (as predicted by de Shazer), not simply what was going well or what they wanted to keep, we were persuaded to explore the approach further.

When Steve (in SF land, we tend to use first names) came to Iowa City for the IAMFT conference, we invited him to visit us and attend our clinic during practicum. We were a bit intimidated by the prospect of observation (and criticism?) by the originator of a family therapy approach, and were, at the same time, excited to see what he might say about our experimenting with his ideas, confident he would be impressed and amazed (little did we know that Steve seemed impressed and amazed at almost nothing unless it was related to his wife, Insoo). He watched a session I was conducting with a couple who were separating and who wanted to learn about patterns that negatively affected their relationship so that they could hopefully avoid similar patterns with future partners. I was using genograms to inquire about these patterns from their families of origin. Steve was behind the mirror and reportedly asked my supervisor what I was doing; Dave told him, and Steve reportedly said, "Well, I don't know why you would want to do that" and went to observe another student.

Of course, I was unsettled by this, but not crushed because my supervisor, without realizing he was doing it, used SF supervision principles to normalize my experience and compliment me on how well I was following my plan and correctly using Bowen principles. He then asked me how I might use some of Steve's ideas with the case. I don't recall what I said, but I do remember feeling validated and, at the same time, invited to examine my therapy from a different perspective rather than feeling shamed and defensive.

Over the years, I incorporated more and more SF ideas into my own practice, but not so much in supervision. I had been taught about the great responsibility of supervisors to "teach" therapy skills to trainees, and SF didn't seem to fit supervision as easily. At some point, I met Insoo and asked her how she applied SF ideas to supervision. In typical Insoo fashion, her eyes widened and with great animation she said, "Oh, it is so much fun! It is so much better than telling trainees what they are doing wrong, which is a great 'downer,' and sure to make everyone feel bad." I began to experiment with using SF practices in supervision and reading what I could find on it, which wasn't much. I found that the Miracle Question didn't work very well for me in supervision, but, as Stark reports (in this volume, Sect. 7.8), the SF stance of non-expert, not-knowing helped me put some of my love of being an expert and always being right aside, becoming more curious about my students' and trainees' desires and experiences in therapy and in supervision. I began enjoying supervision much more and even began using the ideas in the courses I was teaching. Whether working with trainees who are learning SFBT or some other approach, I find that I prefer getting out of their way of learning and "leading from one step behind" (Cantwell and Holmes 1995, p. 37) to directing them in ways that may not fit for particular situations (except, of course, in situations involving safety or ethical/legal issues). I have been rewarded with satisfaction in watching trainees learn and grow as therapists and life-long, collegial relationships with many who keep in touch with me about their work and their families.

One of the basic challenges of Solution-Focused Brief Therapy (SFBT) is that it is simple but not easy, and that is true for supervision as well as therapy, consulting, coaching, or any other activity that might use SFBT ideas. In this volume, you will see some of the clearest thinking and writing that deconstructs this difference about supervision in general and SF supervision in particular. Using his many hours of thinking, experience, research, writing, and self-observation, as well as conversations with Insoo (the epitome of SF supervision), and of observing her consult and supervise therapists, Frank Thomas gives us a solid text on SF supervision, its premises, and practices. These are built upon SF assumptions and practices as well as deductive observation of his own and others' supervision and recognize the differences between therapy and supervision. Using a systemic context, as did Steve and Insoo in their development of the approach, Frank gives us clear examples of SF supervision in both ordinary and so-called "difficult" situations.

Each chapter of this text, which should be required reading for all supervisors regardless of their therapy or supervision orientations, focuses on supervision and supervision examples, not simply pasting SFBT practices over supervision. I especially appreciated the many transcribed examples, thinking even more about how I can apply them to my own practices and self-reflection as a therapist and supervisor. I entrust this book to you, confident that you will learn as a supervisor, and that you will further recommend it to colleagues who are supervising. Who knows, you may even begin playing with the Miracle Question in supervision.

Santa Fe, New Mexico   Thorana Nelson, Ph.D.

Preface

Be an opener of doors.

~ Ralph Waldo Emerson

Acquiring supervision competencies is a life-long, cumulative, developmental process with levels of proficiency beyond competence.

~ Falendar, Cornish, Goodyear et al. 2004

Another Supervision Book … Why?

I would be the first to ask this question in a conversation about supervision among my peers. At the same time, a tacit understanding seems to exist in the psychotherapy world: good supervision is something experienced therapists can provide to students, novice therapists, and peers and requires little additional expertise, training, or education. I completely disagree. I believe that supervision is an art form, and the competencies required to be an exceptional supervisor have similarities to but are qualitatively different from the skills of an expert therapist (Casemore 2009). "Clinical supervision is more than an extension of counseling theory. It is a specialty in its own right, complete with established models, practices, and interventions" (Pearson 2006, p. 241).

In addition, I happen to be in agreement with Jeffrey Koob (2002) who wrote, "Solution-Focused Supervision is a viable construct, different from Traditional Supervision" (p. 177). His dissertation (Koob 1999) and subsequent research and writing based on his dissertation data (Baker 2006; Barrera 2003; Koob 2002) emphasize the differences between solution-focused (SF) supervision and traditional notions of supervision, and other competent researchers have contributed to this growing awareness (Berg 2003; Corcoran 2001; Cunanan 2003; Cunanan and McCollum 2006; De Jong and Cronkright 2011; Hsu 2007, 2009, this volume; Hsu and Sun, 2008; Hsu and Tsai 2008; Norman 2003; Pakrosnis and Čepukienė

2011; Roffman 2007; Rudes, Shilts, and Berg 1997; Strong 2007; Thomas and Shappee 2001; Trenhaile 2005; Triantafillou 1997; Wheeler and Greaves 2005). Therefore, I am committed to supervision as a distinct practice and SF supervision as a unique and worthwhile approach.

When prospective students apply to graduate programs, they often cite their excellence as psychotherapy clients as support for their future success as therapists—"I was in therapy and I did very well at it, so I think I'd be a good counselor." I often offer an analogy: Saying you'd be an excellent therapist because you were a good client is like saying you'd be a great pilot because you were a good frequent flyer. And although the categories may not seem as dissimilar to some readers, I believe the analogy fits for therapists and supervisors as well: Good therapists are not necessarily good supervisors. Epstein and Hundert (2002, p. 226) said it well: professional competence is "the habitual and judicious use of communication, knowledge, technical skills, clinical reasoning, emotions, values, and reflection in daily practice for the benefit of the individual and community served" (2002, p. 226). Effective supervisors are much more than good therapists; they are coaches, teachers, administrators, and mentors (Morgan and Sprenkle 2007).

So after well-respected colleagues[1] urged me to write a book on solution-focused (SF) supervision, I finally set aside time to compose a manuscript. Their sincere encouragement persuaded me that a book on SF supervision needed to be written. I believe the historical and professional connections I have to SF supervision give me unique perspectives on the topic. Also, I think the supervision legacy of the late Insoo Kim Berg, MSSW needs to be promoted. I completely agree with others in the field that Insoo[2] was the quintessential SF supervisor, and I have learned more about this art from her video examples, writings (both published and unpublished), and presentations than from any other person in the SF world. In addition, Insoo and I had several conversations through the years about supervision, including extended dialogues less than a year before she died when she came to Texas and enthralled large audiences of students and clinicians as one of my university's prestigious Green Scholars. As Archivist for the Solution-Focused Brief Therapy Association of North America (www.sfbta.org), I have exclusive access to video and audio recordings, unpublished manuscripts, personal correspondence, and other catalog items in the Archive. Because of a very cautious stance by the Association that safeguards confidentiality, I am among a handful of SF professionals approved to preserve, catalog, and finally review the contents of the Archive submissions. Many items involve SF supervision and consultation provided by Insoo as well as the late Steve de Shazer, MSSW, the two founders of the Brief Family Therapy Center of

---

[1] Janet Bavelas, Brian Cade, Peter De Jong, Yvonne Dolan, Michael Durrant, Harry Korman, Thorana Nelson, and Becky Taylor, colleagues I consider leaders in the SF world … I am grateful for their support.

[2] Insoo insisted on being called by her first name, whatever the context, and I believe referring to her as "Ms. Berg" or "Berg" in this book would disrespect her wishes to be known as the approachable colleague she was.

Milwaukee, Wisconsin (BFTC) and the originators of the SF approach.[3] Finally, research and therapist[4] views on supervision needed to be highlighted in a book on SF supervision. Although research involving SF supervision is still fairly sparse, related research, including that involving therapists' supervision experiences, can inform the development of the SF supervision approach and enrich our supervisory conversations. Also, given the SF community's strong commitment to collaboration, the book could not be written without advocating for research and practice that not only acknowledges therapists' experiences but requires it for optimal supervisory and clinical outcomes.

A quick glance at the table of contents will reveal this book is devoted to fleshing out a SF supervision tradition that is over two decades old, preserving the reputation of Insoo as its model supervisor and fostering research- and therapist-informed perspectives. Plus, compelling contributions from both established and emerging SF supervisors and researchers (see Chap. 7) provide multiple viewpoints on SF supervision to inform your reading and application.

What Makes This Different from Other Supervision Books?

> *You know more than you think you know, just as you know less than you want to know.*
>
> ~ Oscar Wilde

If you are picking up this book, I assume you are not yet satisfied with what you currently know or practice related to psychotherapy supervision. Most noteworthy supervision books are general texts, and these works have informed my own supervision practice, teaching, and research for nearly 30 years. However, this volume is dedicated to a single approach, Solution Focused Supervision. While a significant number of recent supervision books are edited volumes addressing multiple theoretical perspectives, they touch on many topics but lack detail in application. This book concentrates on practicality within one particular approach to thinking and acting as a supervisor. Also, many supervision texts are heavy on theory, ethical critiques, and general supervision-related research, all of which are valuable

---

[3] The fact that the originators insisted that SF be called an "approach" and not a model or theory has not clarified this for the profession or the general public. This single decision has probably done more to maintain the fluidity of change in this way of practicing than any other, perpetually preserving solution-focused as a "rumor" (see Miller and de Shazer 1998).

[4] Although it is common to use the term "supervisee" in the supervision literature, I have chosen to use "therapist" throughout this book whenever possible. My reasoning: I believe it is important to reduce hierarchy and share power in these relationships whenever possible. One way to promote mutuality and respect is through language. "Supervisee" is a diminutive term when paired with "supervisor," and I believe it is important whenever possible to promote collaborative concepts and relationships.

contributions to the psychotherapy supervision literature. In contrast, this book will briefly address research and outline assumptions that guide the approach, but since it is a largely inductive way of working, the emphasis will be on application.

Supervision illustrations and examples make up a significant portion of this book. Other supervision texts (Bernard and Goodyear 2009; Henderson 2009; Stoltenberg and McNeill 2010) contain supervisory vignettes and brief summaries of supervision interventions and dilemmas; however, I feel they are short on the "how to" aspects of clinical supervision. This book offers many examples of in vivo supervisory dialogue, sensitive to context and explanation. Whenever possible, I have created amalgamations of actual supervision sessions to illustrate concepts without disclosing details that could identify particular therapists with whom I have worked over the past 25 years. And there's an added bonus: this book offers a unique window into the supervisory style of Insoo Kim Berg by including transcriptions from her supervisory work largely unavailable to the public (Berg n.d., SFBTA Archives #10173-0092; Rudes 1992).

There is research support for the idea that some type of developmental process takes place over the course of supervision, so discussion of qualitative changes over and above mere skill attainment cannot be ignored (Inman and Ladany 2008). Some supervision texts emphasize a particular developmental theory (see Stoltenberg and McNeill 2010) while others survey the literature without highlighting any particular theory. Because SF supervision attends more to application than development, this text will emphasize systems thinking, a theoretical orientation that focuses on direct observation and action more than developmental concepts and has a long historical connection to SF approaches. I will briefly discuss developmental theory (Thomas 2000; Benner 1984), but therapist development will not be the focus. Instead, this text will address learning differences but allow the readers to hold to their own particular theories regarding therapist development and apply the SF supervision practices within their preferred developmental frame. I assume most supervisors will adapt, borrow, and revise this SF approach because … well, it's very adaptive and flexible.

Some supervisory texts and approaches emphasize isomorphism, the theoretical and technical fit (or even match) between the supervisor's supervision model and the supervisee's therapy model. This book will guide the reader in working as a solution-focused supervisor with almost any supervisee's therapy model. (The concept of isomorphism will be developed in Chap. 2, and I will make a case for a postmodern approach to supervision that does not depend on isomorphic assumptions.)

Finally, books on supervision tend to be stand-alone texts, attempting to address most theoretical approaches in supervision, research, culture, ethics, and other important aspects of supervision (Bernard and Goodyear 2009; Falender and Shafranske 2004; Pope-Davis and Coleman 1997; Stoltenberg and McNeill 2010). This book does not ignore the significance of these subjects of supervision but assumes that the readers/supervisors (1) have a desire to learn and practice a solution-focused approach in day-to-day supervision and (2) either already have a strong background in these other areas or will educate themselves through other sources.

This really is a unique supervision book. It will:

- Work within the assumptions that have historically guided SF practices
- Carefully document sources for further investigation
- Provide examples of supervision dialogue to illustrate assumptions and techniques
- Highlight the voices of therapists and clients in the supervision process
- Be informal whenever possible
- Emphasize the pragmatic more than the theoretical, and
- Supply hands-on materials for immediate SF supervision use

Brian Cade (personal communication, June 16, 2012) offered me his advice on writing this book: "Write it using straight-forward language; keep it practical and focused on pragmatics; avoid evangelising; and try not to mention Wittgenstein or any other philosophers." My intention is to keep as closely to his suggestions as possible. Enjoy!

Fort Worth, TX, USA   Frank N. Thomas

About the Author

Frank N. Thomas, Ph.D. LMFT-S is Professor of Counseling and Counselor Education in the College of Education at Texas Christian University in Fort Worth (Texas, USA). He was a professor and clinical graduate faculty in the Family Therapy Program at Texas Woman's University in Denton (1989–2001) and an adjunct faculty member and clinical supervisor at Brite Divinity School (TCU) in the Pastoral Counseling and Theology Program (1995–2007).

Frank's books include *Masters of Narrative and Collaborative Therapies: The Voices of Andersen, Anderson, and White* (edited with Tapio Malinen and Scot J. Cooper, 2011, Routledge), *Handbook of Solution-Focused Brief Therapy: Clinical Applications* (edited with Thorana Nelson, Haworth Press, 2007), *Tales from Family Therapy: Life-Changing Clinical Experiences* (also edited with Thorana Nelson, Haworth Press, 1998), and *Competency Based Counseling: Building on Client Strengths* (authored with Jack Cockburn, 1998). He has also written over 80 articles and book chapters and is amazed there were enough word combinations to accomplish it.

A Texas licensed marriage and family therapist and LMFT-approved supervisor, Frank was the inaugural Humor Editor for the *Journal of Systemic Therapies*. He has been a therapist for over 35 years, focusing on brief models of therapy in his teaching, supervision, and practice for more than 30 years. Frank serves on the editorial boards of five international journals and is a Clinical Fellow and Approved Supervisor with the American Association for Marriage and Family Therapy (AAMFT). He has presented over 210 workshops in 14 different countries, and his work has been translated into Spanish, Mandarin (Chinese), Swedish, Norwegian, Afrikaans, Japanese, and Finnish. Frank has published over 50 books, articles, and chapters and given over 100 professional presentations on solution-focused approaches. Additionally, he has written more than a dozen publications and given over 30 professional presentations on the topic of supervision (15 at international conferences).

People have called Frank "one who seeks clarity, not certainty," "a teacher who goes about making others' ideas clearer" for learners (and himself), and "a frustrated stand-up comic." He has achieved the rank of black belt in aikido, the "loving" martial art, and is a *sensei* (teacher) at Mizu Aikido dojo in Fort Worth. Frank is also an internationally-published amateur photographer and has been married to Lori, an attorney, for over 36 years.

Acknowledgements

Don't let what you cannot do interfere with what you can do.

~ John Wooden, former UCLA basketball coach

I stand on the shoulders of giants, and my success is dependent on the generosity of peers, family, and friends. So many have contributed to my life during this project ... with deepest gratitude, I thank:

Lori Thomas, my spouse, my greatest supporter, and my most dedicated editor ... I couldn't have done this without you;

Thorana Nelson and Michael Durrant, for your editing, wisdom, encouragement, and expertise;

Contributors to the "Applications" chapter in this book—Duane Bidwell, Jeff Chang, Weisu Hsu, Ben Kuo, Donald Lane, Teri Pichot, Jayson Pratt, Marcella Stark, Peter Sundman, Elizabeth (Becky) Taylor, Jay Trenhaile, and John Wheeler—you are all remarkable authors and dedicated supervisors;

Jim Rudes, for use of your transcription and for your insight into the supervision of Insoo Kim Berg;

Haley Bunch Cox and Kimberly Grigg, for permission to print your goal-setting and goal-progress projects in Appendix C;

Peter De Jong, Thorana Nelson, Harry Korman, the late Insoo Kim Berg, Yvonne Dolan, Janet Bavelas, Brian Cade, Michael Durrant, Bruce Gorden, and Becky Taylor, for encouraging me to write this book…without you, this project would still only be an idea;

the Solution-Focused Brief Therapy Association (SFBTA) Board, for permission to use transcriptions and unpublished documents from the Archive as well as for its commitment to preserving the Brief Family Therapy Center (BFTC) of Milwaukee and the origins of SF approaches;

SFBTA Archive Committee members Thorana Nelson (Chair), Cindy Hansen, Jeff Chang, Wendel Ray, and Joel Simon, for your efforts to make the Archive a success and your insights into the brief therapy tradition;

my current TCU teaching assistants Katie Parker Bowman and Olivia Scalf Wedel, for proofreading the final draft on a tight schedule and your dedicated work on the SFBTA Archive;

my past TCU teaching assistants Toni Haynes, Kat Deichler, Michelle Gaffney Miles, Christa Owen McCord, Lorna Runge, and Marcus Johnson, for your diligence and creativity working on the SFBTA Archive:;

TCU College of Education Dean Mary Patton and Associate Deans Kay Stevens and Jan Lacina, for the teaching assistants you so graciously assigned to me over the years and your support of my teaching and research;

Andrew Turnell, who manages to balance a resolute belief in solution-focused ideas with an uncompromising commitment to real-life best practices … I appreciate your encouragement through the years;

my daughter Allison … every challenge you take on makes me even more proud to be your dad;

Chris Green, Chris Hohmann, Fritz Ritsch, and the other *aikidoka* at Mizu Aikido for the much-needed distractions you provide by allowing me to throw you around (and tossing me about as well);

Tom Chancellor, Patrick O'Malley, Peter Kahle, Dennis Thum, and David Cross, men I trust who know how to laugh … thanks for humor and friendship;

my "Writing Support Group"—Duane Bidwell (Claremont School of Theology), Mary Moschella (Yale Divinity School), Tim Hessel-Robinson (Brite Divinity School/TCU), Allan Cole (Austin Presbyterian Theological Seminary), Emily Askew (Lexington Theological Seminary), and Janet Schaller (independent scholar)—for weekly affirmation and inspiration … keep your noses to the grindstone;

my first supervisors, including Bradford Keeney, Bill Quinn, Neal Newfield, Harvey Joanning, and Monte Bobele … you set the bar high;

all the therapists, students, clients, and peers who have taught me so much about supervision through the years;

the late Steve de Shazer, for rigor and stories, gone but not forgotten; and (last but not least),

the late Insoo Kim Berg, for inspiration and laughter…may you be honored.

Contents

1 A Solution-Focused Supervision Stance 1
   1.1 What Makes Something, Anything, "SF"? 3
   1.2 A SF Stance 9
      1.2.1 Pragmatism 9
      1.2.2 Tentativeness 12
      1.2.3 Nonpathology 19
      1.2.4 Curiosity 24
      1.2.5 Respect 26
   1.3 Concluding Thoughts on the SF Stance 30

2 Systems Thinking and Isomorphism in SF Supervision 31
   2.1 Systems: Conceptualizing the Supervision Context 31
      2.1.1 Historical Connections to the SF Approach 31
      2.1.2 Basic Systems Ideas and Their Fit with SF Supervision 34
      2.1.3 Multiple Systems and Mutual Influence 38
   2.2 The Idea of Isomorphism in Supervision and Therapy 47
      2.2.1 Isomorphic Applications: SF Supervision with
             Those Practicing SF Approaches 47
      2.2.2 Non-isomorphic Applications: SF Supervision with Those
             Practicing Other Psychotherapy Models and Approaches
             (Ungar 2006; Weir 2009) 54
   2.3 Concluding Thoughts on Systems and Isomorphism 58

3 The Supervision Approach of Insoo Kim Berg, MSSW 59
   3.1 Stance of the Supervisor 59
   3.2 Value of Ongoing Supervision 60
   3.3 Simplify 60
   3.4 Hierarchy and Becoming Co-learners 61
   3.5 "Leading from One Step Behind" 62
   3.6 Goal Orientation 63
   3.7 Process of Supervision 63

	3.8	Teaching/Education and Evaluation	65
	3.9	Assumptions About Therapists	66
		3.9.1 Therapists Have Resources from Which to Draw	66
		3.9.2 Therapists Have Positive Intentions	67
	3.10	Role of Language	67
	3.11	Therapists' Perspectives in Supervision	68
	3.12	Clients' Perspectives in Supervision	68
	3.13	Practices	70
		3.13.1 Highlighting Successes and Exceptions	70
		3.13.2 Scaling	70
		3.13.3 Complimenting	70
		3.13.4 Being Indirect	71
		3.13.5 Asking Questions that Consult the Client/Relationship	72
		3.13.6 Using Silence	73
		3.13.7 Hedging	73
		3.13.8 Using "Suppose…"	74
		3.13.9 Using "You Must Have Good Reasons to…"	74
	3.14	Concluding Thoughts About Insoo's Approach	75
4	**SF Supervision Practices**		**77**
	4.1	Goal Setting: Active, Responsive Goal Creation and Assessment	78
		4.1.1 Responsive with Supervision	83
		4.1.2 Interactive	83
		4.1.3 Challenging to the Therapist	84
		4.1.4 Responsive to Client and Other Systems: Creating a Supervisor/Therapist/Client Feedback Process	85
		4.1.5 Initial Goals	89
		4.1.6 Practice: Revisioning and Recalibrating One's Goals	89
	4.2	Highlighting Exceptions and Successes	92
	4.3	Scaling	95
	4.4	Hedging	98
	4.5	Complimenting	101
		4.5.1 Direct Compliments	102
		4.5.2 Indirect Compliments	104
		4.5.3 Self-Compliments	107
	4.6	Future Focus	108
		4.6.1 Future-Focused Question Examples	109
		4.6.2 Categories of Future-Focused Questions	109
	4.7	Utilizing the Indirect–Direct Communication Spectrum: Metaphor, Semaphore, and "Two-by-Four"	110
		4.7.1 Metaphor	111
		4.7.2 Semaphore	112
		4.7.3 Two-by-Four	113

4.8		Dilemma Talk	114
4.9		Promoting Self-Supervision: Ideas on the Self-Sustaining Therapist	116
	4.9.1	Embed Self-Supervision in Supervision	118
	4.9.2	Challenge Isolation and (Resulting) Insularity	118
	4.9.3	Be Transparent	118
	4.9.4	Set Goals Around Self-Supervision	118
4.10		Promoting Self-Supervision: Practices	119
	4.10.1	Goal Setting	119
	4.10.2	Highlighting Competence	119
	4.10.3	Identifying Challenges and Resources	120
	4.10.4	Deconstructing	120
	4.10.5	Being Temporarily Certain	120
	4.10.6	Contributing Without Imposing	121
	4.10.7	Keeping a Future Focus	121
	4.10.8	Teaching Therapists to Fish: Skills of Self-Education	122
4.11		Inviting Supervision Feedback from Therapists	122
	4.11.1	Formal Methods of Therapist Feedback	123
	4.11.2	Less Formals Ways to Invite Feedback from Therapists	123
4.12		Parting Thoughts on Practices	125

5 A Tap on the Shoulder: Supervision with Insoo Kim Berg 127
    5.1 Supervision Session 1: "Pain in the Butt" 128
        5.1.1 Supervision Transcription 1 and Commentary 129
        5.1.2 Observations on Supervision Session 1, "Pain in the Butt" 145
    5.2 Supervision Session 2: "One-Off Consultation on a Sad Little Girl" 147
        5.2.1 Supervision Transcription 2 and Commentary 147
        5.2.2 Observations on Supervision Session 2, "A Sad Little Girl" 158

6 Research and SF Supervision 161
    6.1 Psychotherapy Supervision Research 162
        6.1.1 Supervision Alliance and Interaction ("What Do Therapists and Supervisors Do Together that Is Useful for Therapists?") 162
        6.1.2 Client Outcomes ("What Do Therapists and Supervisors Do that Is Useful to Clients?") 165
    6.2 SF Supervision Research 166
        6.2.1 General SF Supervision Research 166
        6.2.2 "What Do Researchers Say SF Supervision Does that Is Useful?" 167

6.3	Researching Supervisees' Perspectives		169
	6.3.1	Key Non-SF Research ("What Do Supervisees Say Supervision Does that Is Useful?")	169
	6.3.2	SF-Related Research ("What Do Supervisees Say SF Supervision Does that Is Useful?")	173
6.4	Research-Related Guidance for SF Supervision		175

7 Applications ... 177

7.1	Introduction		177
7.2	Integrating Spirit: Solution-Focused Supervision for Pastoral Counseling		178
	7.2.1	My Supervisory Context	179
	7.2.2	"Greatest Hits": My Favorite (or Habitual) Supervisory Practices	180
	7.2.3	What Therapists Say Is Helpful	181
	7.2.4	"Not Doing Enough": An Example of My Supervisory Approach	183
	7.2.5	Contextual Challenges for Solution-Focused Supervision	186
	7.2.6	Conclusion	187
7.3	On Being Solution-Focused in Adversarial Places: Supervising Parenting Evaluations for Family Court		187
	7.3.1	Interpretation, Social Construction, and Context	188
	7.3.2	Family Court Processes as Language Game	189
	7.3.3	Competence in Parenting Evaluation	189
	7.3.4	Process: Being a Solution-Focused Supervisor	192
	7.3.5	Limitations of a Solution-Focused Approach	196
	7.3.6	Conclusion	196
7.4	Solution-Focused Supervision with School Counselors in Taiwan		197
	7.4.1	The Context	197
	7.4.2	Implementation of SF Supervision: Process and Outcome	197
	7.4.3	Supervision Review of the Video Recorded Role-Play Session in SF Group Supervision	199
	7.4.4	Team Case Conference as a Peer Supervision Approach	201
	7.4.5	Promotion of Team Case Conference	203
	7.4.6	Conclusion	204
7.5	Live Supervision-of-Supervision: Lessons Learned the Hard Way		204
	7.5.1	Roles and Rules in SOS	205
	7.5.2	Example 1: Building Collaboration with "Susan"	206
	7.5.3	Donald's Reflections on Susan's SOS and Our Debriefing	209
	7.5.4	Our Next SOS Session with Susan	210
	7.5.5	Donald's Reflection on SOS #2	213
	7.5.6	Final Note from Frank	214
	7.5.7	Final Note from Donald	214

7.6	Leading a Team from a Solution-Focused Perspective		215
	7.6.1	Systems Thinking and Acting in SF Supervision	216
	7.6.2	Application of SF Supervision with Those Within the Rest of the Work System	218
	7.6.3	Matching Supervision Style	220
	7.6.4	Favorite Solution-Focused Supervision Tools	221
	7.6.5	Summary	223
7.7	How Will They Know? Solution-Focused Supervision in Counseling Adolescents with Addictions		224
	7.7.1	Therapists Know What Is Best for Themselves	226
	7.7.2	A Small Change Is All That Is Necessary	227
	7.7.3	Supervision Should Focus on What Is Possible and Changeable	228
	7.7.4	Conclusion	229
7.8	Supervising Practicum Students: SF Supervision as a Cure for Negative Thinking		230
	7.8.1	Techniques	231
	7.8.2	Challenges of SF Supervision	236
	7.8.3	SFBT Versus Choose-Your-Own	237
7.9	Continuous Solution-Focused Supervision in the Workplace		239
	7.9.1	Continuous Supervision	239
	7.9.2	Solution-Focused Supervision	240
	7.9.3	Perspectives for the Supervisor	240
	7.9.4	Supervision in Phases	241
	7.9.5	Evaluation	247
	7.9.6	Positive Feedback and Ending Rituals	248
	7.9.7	Reflection	248
	7.9.8	Follow-Up	249
	7.9.9	Conclusion	249
7.10	Solution-Focused Supervision in a College Student Affairs Setting		250
	7.10.1	The College Student Affairs Professional (CSAP) Context	250
	7.10.2	Supervision with CSAPs	251
	7.10.3	CSAP Competencies	253
	7.10.4	Strength-Based Judicial Conversations (SBJC)	254
	7.10.5	Academic Action Meetings	257
	7.10.6	SF Supervision with Academic Actions	259
	7.10.7	Conclusion	260
7.11	Supervision Family Intervention Workers in the UK		260
	7.11.1	Historical Background	260
	7.11.2	Challenges Facing Family Intervention Workers	262
	7.11.3	What Does SF Supervision Have to Offer?	263
	7.11.4	Options for the Supervisor	264
	7.11.5	Conclusion	271

8 Concluding Thoughts on SF Supervision ... 275
8.1 Whither Supervision ... 275
8.2 SF Supervision and Ethics (See Sects. 3.5 and 6.2.1) ... 276
8.3 Cautions Regarding SF Supervision ... 278
8.3.1 "Delusions of Certainty" (Hubble and O'Hanlon 1992) or, "SF Is the Answer—What's the Question?" ... 278
8.3.2 "The Unsolicited Lecture (Especially When Given 'for Your Own Good!')" (Cade 1992, p. 30) ... 279
8.3.3 Minimalism Rules, Except When It Shouldn't ... 279
8.3.4 Therapy-Once-Removed Supervision ... 280
8.4 SF Supervision Research: What's Next? ... 282
8.5 What Matters in a SF Supervisory Relationship ... 283
8.6 Closing Thoughts ... 284

Appendix A Supervision and Informed Consent ... 287

Appendix B Systems/Cybernetics Reading List ... 293

Appendix C Goal-Setting Template and Examples ... 295

Appendix D Weekly Risk/Goal Chart Example ... 311

Appendix E Berg Japan Supervision Workshop ... 313

References ... 317

Author Index ... 335

Subject Index ... 341

Contributors

Duane R. Bidwell, Ph.D. The Clinebell Institute for Pastoral Counseling and Psychotherapy, Claremont, CA, USA

Jeff Chang, Ph.D. R.Psych. The Family Psychology Centre, Calgary, AB, Canada

Weisu Hsu, Ph.D. National Taiwan Normal University, Taipei, Taiwan

Ben C. H. Kuo, Ph.D. Department of Psychology, University of Windsor, Windsor, ON, Canada

Donald H. Lane, Ph.D. LMFT College of Education, Tarleton State University, Granbury, TX, USA

Teri Pichot, LCSW MAC LAC Denver Center for Solution-Focused Brief Therapy, Littleton, CO, USA

Jayson M. Pratt, M.Ed. LCDC TRS Behavioral Inc., The Right Step, Euless, TX, USA

Marcella Stark, Ph.D. LPC-S College of Education, Texas Christian University, Fort Worth, TX, USA

Peter Sundman, B.A. TaitoBa Network, Helsinki, Finland

Elizabeth R. Taylor, Ph.D. LPC-S LMFT RPT-S College of Education, Texas Christian University, Fort Worth, TX, USA

Frank N. Thomas, Ph.D. LMFT-S College of Education, Texas Christian University, Fort Worth, TX, USA

Jay D. Trenhaile, Ed.D. LP NCSP College of Education and Human Sciences, South Dakota State University, Brookings, SD, USA

John Wheeler, M.A. UKCP Tyne and Wear, Ryton, Tyne & Wear, UK

Chapter 1
A Solution-Focused Supervision Stance

Tell me to what you pay attention and I will tell you who you are.

~ Ortega y Gassett

Mitch entered the room with trepidation and a pile of case folders a foot thick. His head down, Mitch asked where he could sit.

"Put those folders down on the desk, man – this isn't the gym, it's supervision!" I said.

"Well…OK," he replied, carefully depositing the pile of paper on the furthest corner of my desk and slumping into a chair.

"How are you?" I asked.

"Not too good," said Mitch. "I didn't sleep well the last couple of nights."

"Why's that?" I asked. "You feeling OK?"

"Yeah," Mitch mumbled. "But…honestly, I haven't been looking forward to this…my last supervisor…"

"What?"

"…well, let's just say I didn't feel too tall when I left each time."

I paused, thinking about what he'd said. "Let's start with something different then," I finally replied. "Stand up for a second." Mitch complied, still slouched but now looking at me with curiosity. I rummaged through the middle drawer of my desk. (It's the one that usually has all the junk in it, right?) I found what I was looking for and slipped it into my pocket.

"Now, head over to the door," I directed. Mitch moved across the room. "No, stop in the doorway – don't leave," I said. "Now, put your head against the door frame and stand straight for a second." He looked straight ahead and put both heels and head against the frame. I pulled out the measuring tape, squatted next to him, and placed the tape container on the ground. Then I pushed the box against the frame with the toe of my shoe and extracted the metal strip until the tab was even with the top of Mitch's head. "Six feet, one and a quarter inches," I proclaimed with a smile. "Let's see if you are the same height when you leave today." Then I let go of the tape, which snapped into the case.

F.N. Thomas, *Solution-Focused Supervision: A Resource-Oriented Approach to Developing Clinical Expertise*, DOI 10.1007/978-1-4614-6052-7_1,
© Springer Science+Business Media New York 2013

Mitch burst into laughter! He doubled over and snorted, letting loose a real belly laugh. When he reached for a tissue to stem the tears, I said, "Well, you'll have to straighten up – all that laughing may have shrunk you already!" Then I joined him in laughter. I've always been accused of having a big laugh, and the noise we were making brought a couple of people from the agency out of their offices to see who was causing the ruckus. Mitch said, "You don't know how many times I heard a phrase in my head during my last supervision relationship: 'You'll have to straighten up, Mitch,' I would say to myself, over and over again. I felt like I couldn't do anything right, and nothing I did to correct things ever measured up."

"Well, as far as I'm concerned, you measured up to –
" – six feet, one and a quarter inches," he said, finishing my sentence. More laughter ensued.
"I think we're on a different page now," I said, returning to a moment of seriousness. "Let's start with something new…what do you do for fun?"

We spent the next twenty minutes getting to know each other—I would ask a question, and then Mitch would ask me the same question. We talked about favorite music, our work histories, even a bit about our ethnic backgrounds. (We found out we both like lefse, a Norwegian tortilla-like delicacy made from potatoes that you have to taste to appreciate.) Then I transitioned us to a different conversation.

"OK, what do you think I need to do with this pile of case files?" I asked. "I'm not going to read them right now – I know where the records room is and I can find them anytime I want, if you return a file each time you pull it."
"I thought you'd want to go through them one at a time; you know, check them for accuracy and then tell me what I should do in the next session with each client," said Mitch.
"Well, then we've reached a fork in the road," I said. "I'm not going to tell you what you should do. If that's the only option here because you believe I have to do that, then we'd better put our heads together and figure out another option."
Mitch stared at me, speechless.
"What do you think would be a good way to move forward?" I inquired.
"I don't have a clue," Mitch replied.
"OK, then for today… let's talk about any cases you feel need immediate attention, anything that's going on that might be dangerous or situations where you just feel stuck. Then, you've got some thinking and writing to do so you can tell me what it is you want from this supervision. Sound OK for today?"
Mitch sighed. "Whew," he said. "I do need some ideas on two cases."
"OK, let's get started! This'll be fun!" I exclaimed.

Mitch and I met for weekly supervision over the next nine months. He outlined his personal goals and shared his clinical case experiences, and I disclosed my ideas about supervision and good therapy practices. Through this time together, we laughed a lot and even shed a few tears. Mitch's skills grew, and with that came a renewed confidence in his abilities to counsel. And although there was an appropriate seriousness across the relationship, we both enjoyed the connection and conversations.

Solution-focused (SF) supervision isn't defined by frivolity, humor, or even particular techniques. For me, SF supervision is a stance, an approach one brings to a supervisory relationship that starts with certain assumptions, supports collaboration, notices and encourages particular ways of thinking and behaving, and inspires excellence in clinical practice and self-supervision. Any approach to supervision can have positive outcomes—SF supervision is not *the* way of supervising, only *one* way to think, act, and relate. But for supervisors who seek guidance on how to endorse strengths and take advantage of resources available in the clinical setting, SF supervision is a time-tested means to that end.

1.1 What Makes Something, Anything, "SF"?

The community of worldwide SF educators, trainers, supervisors, and practitioners who hold common ideas about the formation, structure, and practice of the SF approach diligently maintain conversations sustaining the viability and dynamic transformations of SF practices. This community, though ill defined and continually changing, lends authority when discussing what makes something "SF." Throughout the more than 30 years of SF practice, there has been general consensus regarding what is clearly *not* SF, although years of discussion on what constitutes a SF approach has been productive while managing to shun rigid conclusions. For example, it is clear that assigning pathologizing labels to people is outside the spirit of SF. In addition, most in the SF world would agree that centering on what the practitioner thinks is best or right for clients falls outside SF practices. Within SF approaches, the primary authority of "success" is the client, not the professional. Finally, being theoretically correct is less important than locating and practicing what works within the SF realm. Steve de Shazer, a founder of the SF approach, once said, "I don't want…anybody to develop some sort of rigid orthodoxies…(t)hat there is a right way to do this" (Hoyt 2001, p. 30). De Shazer clearly articulated his views on the ambiguity of "correct" SF practices in his article (with Gale Miller), "Have you heard the latest rumor about…? Solution-focused therapy as a rumor" (Miller and de Shazer 1998). They state it is not important that SF gets its story "straight" (p. 365) but that the focus remains on the pragmatic, on "what works." Still, this has not deterred attempts to clarify or qualify what is and is not SF. Beyebach (2000) wrote the research protocol guidelines for the European Brief Therapy Association (EBTA), widely recognized as an authoritative and respected body in the SF community. The protocol includes a clear focus on clients' goals, asking the Miracle Question, discussing exceptions, and other stances and practices. But while some have attempted to delineate a template for inclusion in SF research studies or within a particular context (Beyebach and Herrero 2004; Conoley, Graham, Neu, Craig, O'Pry, Cardin, Brossart, and Parker 2003), the consensus in the SF community seems to be to follow de Shazer's lead and focus on what works (description) rather than what "it" means (explanation) (Miller and de Shazer 1998).

Now, what follows may sound contradictory, but I think it parallels rather than undermines what I just wrote: I believe there is a community of long-term practitioners and proponents of SF approaches who have a common knowledge of what is and is not SF (see Bliss and Bray 2009 for a thorough discussion on this topic). This idea of common knowledge, which Gorsuch (2001) called "appropriate knowing," attempts to bridge the gap between notions of solipsism (where anything goes and all views are equally credible) and naïve realism (where everything *is* and can be accurately known by the individual). For even though there are significant variations among current SF practitioners and across more than 30 years of SF elaboration,[1] distinctions have been and continue to be drawn between what is and is not SF. For most with historical and clinical roots in the SF approach, the debates regarding what is or is not SF are frequent and not inconsequential. Plus, it is important to note that the SF community is fairly charitable, tolerating significant differences in theory, tenets, and techniques; it is also true that "anything goes" will never be acceptable. The collective wisdom of the SF community across time and geography continues to modify that which goes too far astray and reinforce important qualities of SF practice.

So if the target continues to move and change is constant, what ideas seem to endure across time when discussing what constitutes "SF practice"? Perhaps a metaphor from philosophy could assist in clarifying. The phrase "necessary but not sufficient" is common in discussions of critical thinking. We know what "necessary *and* sufficient" means in logic, as it is usually stated as an "if X, then Y" proposition. For example, "If it is a square, then it has four sides." But the reverse is not true; "if it has four sides, then it is a square" is an example of a "necessary but not sufficient" argument. This can be applied to varieties of human experiences as well. The proposition "if there is human life, then oxygen is present and available" is clearly true, but the reverse is not. Applied to "SF practice," one might say that the presence of certain techniques (Miracle Question, focus on exceptions, scaling, etc.) or even orientations (deferring to clients' understandings of their lived experiences, curiosity regarding clients' experiences, and so forth) *may* indicate an interaction is SF, but the presence of such techniques and/or suppositions cannot *define* an interaction as SF, for these techniques and orientations are also present in other psychotherapy models and approaches.

In summary, I believe the appropriate knowledge invested in the SF community is sufficient, weighing in on public conversations and articulating responses when questions are raised. This is most evident in what is commonly known as peer review for academic journals and professional conferences. Several journals publish SF-related articles, including the *Journal of Systemic Therapies*, the *Journal of Family Psychotherapy*, the *Journal of Marital and Family Therapy*, and *InterAction*. These journals choose or elect editorial boards whose members judge the value of the submissions and decide if they are appropriate for the journal. A rendering of these judgments must contain jurors' opinions of the content, including theory, practice descriptions, and research definitions—if something is not SF to the reviewers, then it simply is not SF. There are also professional conferences, including international meetings that limit program acceptances to a particular definition of what will be considered "SF." The annual conference of the Solution-Focused Brief Therapy Association of North America (SFBTA) is a clear example. The conference

---

[1] In keeping with a postmodern perspective, I purposefully try to avoid two commonly used terms here: "growth" (an organic metaphor invested in the idea of trajectory toward a supposed ideal) and "development" (a modernist concept assuming greater accuracy, improvement, or modification over time toward an evidence-supported practice that moves closer to perfection through scientific discovery).

proposal guidelines are clear: "In keeping with the original intention of SFBTA, only presentations that clearly demonstrate the basic tenets of solution-focused brief therapy (SFBT) … will be accepted" (SFBTA 2012). The list of "basic tenets" that follows is an articulation of appropriate knowing developed by the leadership of the organization and not a definitive list of tenets for the SF community outside of the conference context.

In spite of what I've written above (or perhaps because of it), I am going to propose my own summary list of *qualities or characteristics of SF practice* that may be necessary for something to be considered "SF." This list is quite limited, with no attempt to be comprehensive:

- The importance of exceptions in the SF process
- A focus toward the future
- The assumption that solutions are not necessarily connected directly to problems
- The assumption of each person's expertise regarding his/her experiences, including the evaluation of progress and conditions for terminating the SF relationship
- The belief in client resourcefulness
- The fluidity of language and understanding
- An emphasis on the pragmatic (focusing on what is possible and changeable and on "what works")

There are also *methods or techniques* I believe are commonly held as integral to SF practice:

- Questions eliciting client success and positive difference
- Consistently maintaining a future focus
- Goal setting, with the purpose of creating a preferred future rather than the absence of problems
- Inquiry into client resources that sustain change, including exceptions to problematic experiences
- Practices that bring attention to the possibility of personal agency (ability to choose and act) within an experience of positive change
- Compliments (direct, indirect, and/or self-compliments[2])
- Question types identified with SF practices, including exception, miracle, scaling, and relationship questions

While the majority of SF professionals across the world might agree with my list of both characteristics and methods, simply giving lip service to the tenets of the approach or using what have been called SF techniques might not be sufficient to actually *practice* the SF approach. That is, there is a gestalt that may be absent even though one uses SF techniques and claims SF orientation (Bliss and Bray 2009; Cunanan and McCollum 2006).

---

[2] See Sect. 4.5 for descriptions and examples of these types of compliments.

Few would debate the generally accepted idea that SF is a postmodern approach to supervision, therapy, or consultation (Carlson and Erickson 2001; Chang 2010). Postmodern, language-centered approaches to supervision such as SF (Philp, Guy, and Lowe 2007; Thomas 2012a, 2010a, 1996; Wheeler, J. 2007; see Chang 2010), narrative (Carlson and Erickson 2001; Crocket, Pentecost, Cresswell, Paice, Tollestrup, de Vries, and Wolfe 2009), and collaborative (Fine and Turner 1997; Gardner, Bobele, and Biever 1997; London and Tarragona 2007) differ from more modernist approaches in significant ways while retaining what I believe are the best features of traditional supervisory practice. Ungar (2006, p. 59) advises flexibility in supervisor roles to support therapists' experiences of "preferred identity conclusions." This parallels what he understands to be a process similar to postmodern therapy, supporting the idea of isomorphism connecting therapy and supervision. Ungar's proposals regarding supervisor roles are consistent both with postmodern assumptions and historical supervisory practice as he promotes the roles of supporter, supervisor, case consultant, trainer/teacher, colleague, and advocate.

Gardner et al. (1997) articulate postmodern assumptions that guide the supervision process that are similar to and different from Ungar's (2006) ideas. Their emphasis is upon the influence of social constructionist theory in supervision: there is no universal or cross-cultural truth, so conversation is the means to developing local knowledge and expertise. They propose supervision dilemmas that arise when one takes a postmodern approach to supervision, including the reexamination of "notions of hierarchy, expertise, 'truth,' classification, and evaluation" (p. 219). (I would add ethics to this list.) With regard to narrative supervision practices, Carlson and Erickson (2001) emphasize the person of the therapist with special consideration of the motivations, personal knowledge, and moral elements of practice. They also create "communities of concern" (p. 217) for new therapists, keeping with the narrative practice of witnessing communities and stressing ethics in retelling of storied experiences.

SF supervision has paralleled the changes experienced in SF clinical approaches over more than 20 years. Some articulations tie SF supervision to current supervision theory and research (Thomas 1996), while others attempt to outline a supervision approach reflecting general SF approaches (Juhnke 1996; Knight 2004; Marek, Sandifer, Beach, Coward, and Protinsky 1994; O'Connell and Jones 2001; Selekman and Todd 1995; Thomas 1996, 1994b). There are also professionals presenting ways to apply SF supervision in various contexts, including field supervision for social work and psychology (Bucknell 2000; De Jong and Cronkright 2011; Knight 2004; Nash 1999), school counseling (Hsu and Tsai 2008), agencies (Pichot and Dolan 2003), secondary schools (Franklin and Streeter 2003), university practicum supervision (Cigrand and Wood 2012), and (of course) psychotherapy training (Briggs and Miller 2005; Thomas 1996; Wetchler 1990; Wheeler and Greaves 2005).

The most common threads among SF supervision publications are contained in Tables 1.1 and 1.2. I have divided these into two categories: Table 1.1 lists the threads regarding supervisor assumptions, a part of their "stance" or orientation in supervision, while Table 1.2 lists the most common practices promoted or noted in the literature.

1.1 What Makes Something, Anything, "SF"?

Table 1.1 Assumptions of SF supervision from the literature

Commitment to amplification of successes	Koob (2002), Lowe and Guy (2002), Presbury, Echterling, and McKee (1999), Selekman and Todd (1995), Thomas (2012a), Waskett (2006)
Sharing power, flattening supervision hierarchy	Berg (2003, n.d., SFBTA Archive #10128-0064), Cunanan and McCollum (2006), Thomas (1996), Wheeler, J. (2007), Wheeler and Greaves (2005)
Change is constant and inevitable	Koob (2002), Thomas (1994b), Wheeler, J. (2007)
Commitment to the use of presuppositional language	Berg (2003), Berg and De Jong (2005), Presbury et al. (1999), Selekman and Todd (1995), Thomas (1996, 2012a)
Focus on language used within supervision context	Berg (2003, n.d., SFBTA Archive #10128-0064), Knight (2005), Rudes, Shilts, and Berg (1997), Strong (2007), Thomas (2012a)
Curiosity	O'Connell and Jones (2001), Thomas (1996, 2000), Waskett (2006), Wheeler, J. (2007)
Respect	Berg (2003), O'Connell and Jones (2001), Presbury et al. (1999), Thomas (1990), Wetchler (1990), Wheeler, J. (2007), Wheeler and Greaves (2005)
Assuming therapist competence, strengths, and/or resourcefulness	Berg (2003), Briggs and Miller (2005), Cunanan and McCollum (2006), Homrich (2005), Lowe and Guy (2002), Marek et al. (1994), Presbury et al. (1999), Roffman (2007), Rudes et al. (1997), Thomas (1994a, 2000, 2012a), Triantafillou (1997), Waskett (2006), Wetchler (1990), Wheeler, J. (2007), Wheeler and Greaves (2005)
Focus on therapist goals (development) more than client problems	Berg (n.d., SFBTA Archive #10128-0064), Briggs and Miller (2005), Koob (2002), Roffman (2007), Triantafillou (1997), Waskett (2006)
Importance of listening	Berg (n.d., SFBTA Archive #10128-0064); Rudes et al. (1997), Waskett (2006)
Goal setting and a future orientation	Hsu (2009), Juhnke (1996), Lowe and Guy (2002), Marek et al. (1994), Nash (1999), O'Connell and Jones (2001), Pichot and Dolan (2003), Presbury et al. (1999), Selekman and Todd (1995), Thomas (1996), Waskett (2006), Wheeler and Greaves (2005)
Attributing therapist's successes and exceptions (at least in part) to therapist agency (the role the therapist played in the success)	Homrich (2005), Hsu (2007), Juhnke (1996), Knight (2005), Marek et al. (1994), Nash (1999), O'Connell and Jones (2001), Presbury et al. (1999), Thomas (1996), Triantafillou (1997), Waskett (2006), Wetchler (1990)

Table 1.2 The most common practices in SF supervision

Amplifying therapist successes	Koob (2002), Lowe and Guy (2002), Presbury et al. (1999), Selekman and Todd (1995), Thomas (2012a), Waskett (2006)
Using presuppositional language	Berg and De Jong (2005), Presbury et al. (1999), Selekman and Todd (1995), Thomas 2012a; 1996)
Focusing on therapist goals (development) more than client problems	Berg (2003, n.d., SFBTA Archive #10128-0064), Briggs and Miller (2005), Koob (2002), Roffman (2007), Triantafillou (1997), Waskett (2006), Wheeler, J. (2007)
Initiating goal setting and maintaining a future orientation	Hsu (2009), Juhnke (1996), Lowe and Guy (2002), Marek et al. (1994), Nash (1999), O'Connell and Jones (2001), Pichot and Dolan (2003), Presbury et al. (1999), Selekman and Todd (1995), Thomas (1996), Waskett (2006), Wheeler and Greaves (2005)
Investigating therapist's successes and exceptions, including questions regarding therapist agency (the role the therapist played in the successes)	Homrich (2005), Hsu (2007), Juhnke (1996), Knight (2005), Marek et al. (1994), Nash (1999), O'Connell and Jones (2001), Presbury et al. (1999), Thomas (1996), Triantafillou (1997), Waskett (2006), Wetchler (1990), Wheeler, J. (2007)
Scaling questions	Berg (2003, n.d., SFBTA Archive #10128-0064), Briggs and Miller (2005), Homrich (2005), Hsu (2009), Juhnke (1996), Koob (2002), Marek et al. (1994), O'Connell and Jones (2001), Pichot and Dolan (2003), Thomas (2012a, 1996), Trenhaile (2005), Triantafillou (1997), Waskett (2006), Wheeler, J. (2007), Wheeler and Greaves (2005)
Complimenting and affirmation	Berg and De Jong (2005), Hsu (2009), Norman (2003), Waskett (2006), Wetchler (1990), Wheeler, J. (2007)
Miracle question	Knight (2005), Koob (2002), O'Connell and Jones (2001), Thomas (1996), Triantafillou (1997), Wheeler, J. (2007)
Relationship questions	Berg (2005, 2003, n.d., SFBTA Archive #10128-0064, n.d., "Hot Tips III," Berg and De Jong (2005, 1996); Homrich (2005), Nash (1999), Thomas (2012a)

1.2 A SF Stance

"In his last book, de Shazer and co-authors...set out the following as the major tenets that inform and characterize Solution Focused Brief Therapy" (Bliss and Bray 2009, p. 65):

1. If it isn't broken, don't fix it.
2. If it works, do more of it.
3. If it's not working, do something different.
4. Small steps can lead to big changes.
5. The solution is not necessarily related to the problem.
6. The language for solution development is different from the language needed to describe a problem.
7. No problems happen all the time; there are always exceptions that can be utilized.
8. The future is both created and negotiable (de Shazer, Dolan, Korman, Trepper, McCollum, and Berg 2007, pp. 1–3).

The set comprised of the first three tenets, a simple reordering of the Mental Research Institute's (MRI) assumptions about therapeutic change, remains one of the significant shifts from problem resolution to solution building within the SF tradition (de Shazer et al. 2007; see Korman and Söderquist 1999). Where problem resolution began with "do something different," the early articulations of the SF approach started with both the assumption that it is more important to focus on what is working ("if it isn't broken, don't fix it") and continuing the change process that is already in progress ("if it works, do more of it") (Cade and Korman personal communication, July 10, 2012). Of the eight tenets, de Shazer et al. (2007) identify the fifth, "the solution is not necessarily related to the problem," as the idea that most clearly separates SFBT from other approaches (for an extended discussion on this topic, see Miller and de Shazer 1998).

I have my own minimalist set of tenets or organizing concepts to apply to SF supervision, because supervision is *not* psychotherapy and requires different or additional assumptions and practices. I have organized my tenets under five categories: *pragmatism*, *tentativeness*, *nonpathology*, *curiosity*, and *respect* (see Thomas and Nelson 2007 for an extended development of the last four tenets in SFBT). These are not presented in any particular order of value or importance, as I believe all are important for the practicing SF supervisor.

1.2.1 *Pragmatism*

> *Do something. If it works, do more of it. If it doesn't, do something else.*
>
> ~ Franklin D. Roosevelt

This tenet returns to the roots of SF history. Both "if it works, do more of it" and "if it doesn't (or won't) work, don't do it" fit well within my pragmatic approach. This requires interaction and time, as one can only know what works in a relationship through experience. But supervisors begin supervisory relationships with some ideas on what never works for them or what never works for anyone (Cade 1992). An example from Cade's humorous article is the "be spontaneous!" paradox—one cannot demand a compliant attitude even though one can demand compliant behavior. One cannot legislate that a child must *enjoy* washing dishes, even though the child may be required to complete the chore. This is why most laws are written requiring behavioral compliance (you cannot do X or you must do Y), with some exceptions (e.g., laws defining the intent as part of the crime itself, such as racial discrimination). Along these lines, supervisors know their limitations. Some of these are legislated or required, while others are preferential but based on experiences in other relationships. For example, when I teach a university practicum class, I require that all students create goals for their practicum and write them in a particular format. I have come to this decision through trial and error as well as a great deal of personal reflection, and I know our relationships have the best chance of proceeding smoothly if students simply begin the process with this exercise. This does not mean that students have to enjoy the process, nor does it ensure progress toward students' goals—it is simply a limitation, resulting from university requirements and my personal philosophy of learning. Another pragmatic commitment in my supervision is transparent disclosure of client risk. I know a relationship requires time and interaction to create an atmosphere of trust, but I feel I must have immediate and continuous information on clients who take part in high-risk behavior, no matter how transparent my supervisor–therapist relationship may be. I have to live within federal, state, university, and/or agency policies, as I will be held accountable if harm results whether I was aware of the high-risk behavior or not.

In addition to ideas I hold, several practices fall under this tenet of pragmatism as well. I believe supervisors need to clarify personal and professional limitations (in writing whenever possible) at the start of a supervisory relationship. Much like the informed consent most states require that include (among other things) therapist qualifications, financial policies, and disclosures regarding the limits of confidentiality, I find that providing therapists with a "supervision informed consent" document creates a springboard for discussion and clarifies the "musts" and "cannots" defined by other systems for supervision as well as the supervisor's own philosophies and guidelines.[3]

Finally, there is the pragmatic side to the supervision relationship itself. I want to know the therapists with whom I work and learn, and I believe warm, supportive relationships are more generative in learning and result in better clinical work. In an effort to contribute to trusting collaboration, I strive to keep supervision relationships uncomplicated by openly disclosing my ideas and practices whenever possible. This sets the tone for relational transparency and models the type of behavior I believe is important to SF practice in any form.

---

[3] See Appendix A for an example.

1.2 A SF Stance

An example may tie these ideas together. Stephen, a student in a professional counseling program, has been assigned to his first practicum. This graduate-level course has a clear structure that program clinical faculty members have developed through the years. The semester before, Stephen completed the practicum application, proposing that his clinical practice take place at a local nonprofit counseling agency. This site application was approved by the clinical faculty after a thorough process vetting the agency, the clinical supervisor, the site administrator, and the student therapist. This vetting process includes (1) a criminal background check on the student therapist (required by law); (2) verifying supervisor licensure or certification credentials; (3) receipt of proof that the student therapist has purchased appropriate malpractice insurance; (4) securing site administrator signed permission for the student therapist's presence, clinical work, case documentation, and video recording; (5) and receiving the signed supervision agreement from the onsite supervisor. All of these practices are required for every student therapist and practicum site, keeping the agreement as clear as possible and maintaining a very pragmatic approach to what can become complicated. Although some student therapists and practicum site personnel have found the procedure arduous (i.e., they don't enjoy it), it is simply a requirement for all students—everyone's practicum application is put through the same process. Agreements, documents, rationale, and timelines are clearly articulated for students when they begin the counseling program, so when Stephen said he had been taken by surprise by some of the deadlines, limitations, and obligations of this application process, it created an opportunity for dialogue and clarification. It was obvious Stephen had been irritated at times, but it also became clear to him that most of his frustration was due to his lack of preparation and last-minute decisions. Through conversations, Stephen found his practicum professor Amelda to be understanding of his emotional responses and firm with regard to the requirements. This led to several discussions over the course of the semester about Stephen's "procrastination" (his term) and how it negatively affected his course work in the program.

Amelda distributed her personal "supervision informed consent" document[4] that outlined her philosophy and practices of supervision for all practicum student therapists when they submitted their practicum applications. This allowed Stephen a number of weeks to review the document and reflect on its effects on his goal-setting process and university supervision prior to the beginning of his practicum experience. At the start of the semester, Amelda scheduled initial meetings with each student therapist to discuss personal goals and begin the relationship-building experience. At their initial meeting, Amelda and Stephen agreed that one of his goals was the timely completion of required documentation and meeting other course deadlines, something he and Amelda both felt would serve him well as a professional once he completed the degree. The goal-setting obligation itself included submitting a draft of his initial course and supervisory goals by a deadline set in the course syllabus (yes, the circularity was apparent to both of them) in the requisite format, a

---

[4] See Appendix A.

requirement for all student therapists. During their biweekly supervision sessions, Amelda continued to be as vulnerable as possible by responding openly to Stephen's questions about clinical work and supervision. This included an extended discussion about the impact of Amelda's supervision consent document on Stephen's own clinical work, as the document itself served as a solution-focused prompt in areas of practice and personal growth. These discussions centered on Stephen's professional identity, intervention skill set, reflexive abilities, and self-supervision. When appropriate, Amelda disclosed details of her own change experiences, with the dual effect of fostering the relationship and modeling appropriate disclosure in clinical contexts. (By the way, Stephen did complete the work on time!)

1.2.2 Tentativeness

Hold on loosely, but don't... let go.
~ 38 Special, "Hold On Loosely" (Barnes, Carlisi, and Peterik 1981)

Although some may understand this term to include timidity or assign a negative valence to one's uncertainty, SF practice has long been defined by avoiding inflexible deductions and absolutes (Miller and de Shazer 1998). Being tentative includes believing in the imprecise nature of experience and language as well as holding lightly to conclusions one draws (what Herbert Anderson (2003, p. 157) describes as having your "feet planted firmly in midair"). The SF approach is centered on language, which can produce agreement but not certainty (Amundson, Stewart, and Valentine 1993; Gardner et al. 1997; Norman 2003). Therefore, the following fall under this category I call tentativeness and cannot be neglected if an approach is SF:

1.2.2.1 Recognizing the Potential Value of Exceptions in Experiences and Stories (De Jong and Berg 2012)

Awareness of exceptions is a hallmark of any SF approach, and it is difficult to imagine a SF approach that does not make use of these differences in client experiences. "Nothing happens all the time" (Durrant personal communication, October 4, 1994) is a cornerstone assumption of this approach, supposing differences in experience are always occurring and may be utilized. But all exceptions are not of equal value (Nyland and Corsiglia 1994). Tentativeness concerning exceptions is required so no one attends to a particular exception to the detriment of the change process or persons involved. Exceptions can be categorized in several ways, including deliberate and random (De Jong and Berg 2012) and may be considered positively consequential, negatively consequential, or inconsequential.

If the professional invests too much in one particular exception, it can lead to negative outcomes (Nyland and Corsiglia 1994). For example, I once had a client who told me that exercise reduced her anxiety, so I encouraged her to do more of it. The following week, she said, "I can't *do* more exercise! I tried, but I *can't*." Further conversation revealed that her *normal* exercise regimen included 250 push-ups, 1,000 sit-ups, running seven miles on a treadmill, and cycling an hour per day on a stationary bicycle; she said she simply did not have time in her day to exercise more. Clearly, I had not investigated the nature or extent of her normal routine or I would not have recommended increasing her exercise time, nor would I have endorsed the *current* amount of exercise without further questioning. (It turned out she was training for a triathlon, and this amount of exercise was typical in her training over the past several years and carefully monitored by her spouse/trainer).

1.2.2.2 Acknowledging the Risks of Imposing One's Will in Supervision Contexts and Taking Steps to Minimize such Imposition

No one should be forced to endure a particular approach in professional development. This includes pushing a SF approach on supervisees (Atkinson and Heath 1990). One of the ways I have organized my own supervision relationships is through selective admission into our university counseling program. It is clear to all applicants that our program emphasizes a SF approach. From the program brochures to live interviews, all applicants hear a consistent message: if a SF approach to therapy, supervision, and learning is not a good fit with how you see and participate in the world, then you should seek out a different program. My clinical colleagues and I are consistently SF in promotion of the program and in our teaching and supervision, so student therapists are well versed in SF approaches and expect SF supervision by the time they are enrolled in practicum courses. I imagine this expectation set is equally clear at other SF institutions around the world—it would be nonsensical for therapists to expect (or even demand) a psychodynamic or developmental approach from supervisors in a context that has plainly communicated their SF partiality in conducting supervision.

I have also supervised in other educational and agency contexts in which I had no say regarding the models therapists practiced nor influence on their theoretical orientations. In these contexts, I have worked hard to create relationships that allow space for negotiation of supervisory theory, style, and practice. I will develop these ideas later in the book, but here it is important to emphasize that *all* supervisory relationships and practices are negotiated to some degree and no supervision ideas or practices should be unilaterally imposed. Supervision relationships are more important than any ideals set by supervisors for therapists. "A key task in early supervision is building a strong working alliance…ongoing maintenance of the alliance should be the supervisor's responsibility throughout the course of the relationship" (Nelson, Gray, Friedlander, Ladany, and Walker 2001, p. 408).

1.2.2.3 Being Aware of the Limitations of Explanation Regarding Human Conditions, Actions, and Relationships

Every theory is partial; every explanation is incomplete. This concept includes SF assumptions and my own personal conclusions. A supervisee recently said to me, "How can you be confident without being cocky?" I hear this as a question about identity. Part of this question is, "How can you be confident in your ideas and actions and believe nothing is static at the same time?" This is a common experience when applying postmodern approaches like SF. Being continually informed moves away from certainty and conclusions, but the question remains: What do I actually know? Ken Stewart and Jon Amundson (1995, p. 70) once wrote, "not everything is relative all at once." They propose one hold differences in "dynamic tension" (p. 72) within a frame of ethics. For them, "the actual capacity to reflect upon problems between and within competing values or concerns is required" for postmodern practice (p. 72). A centrally situated power (see the discussion on systems thinking in the next chapter, Sect. 2.1) may regulate an activity that is counter to my own sense of what is fair or right, and this tension cannot be ignored whether one believes all views are relative or not. For example, the state licensing board may have created a policy on continuing education requirements with which I disagree, personally or professionally. Even if I teach a graduate-level course in psychotherapy (which requires dozens of hours of careful preparation, updating of materials, reading cutting-edge research and theory, and so on), I receive no continuing education credit; however, if I sit passively in a room with fifty people at a conference, e-mailing friends the entire time, and sign out after 3 hours, I receive continuing education credit. If I wish to remain a licensed marriage and family therapist, I must meet their requirements, so I do my best to engage the workshop leader and materials and ignore the temptation to e-mail. I maintain a dynamic tension between what I believe is short-sighted policy and my own standard of lifelong learning.

To address this continuous and unavoidable position of ambiguity, I practice Stewart's (2003) idea of "temporary certainty." This position allows one to hold firmly to his or her view in the moment, for the sake of argument or comparison. It is a momentary certainty, one that begins with "Let's assume for the moment that this is true…" and finishes with "Now, what *else* might be true here?" Stewart (2003) proposes questions for supervision that encourage dialogue on temporary certainty:

- "When you have this stance, what helps you remain there?
- What advantages does temporary certainty bring you?
- What experience have you had while using these practices?
- What is it that keeps you from slipping into permanent certainty?"

I would add my own questions to supplement Stewart's, including supervisor and therapist in the considerations:

- How can we act as if (this conclusion) were true and still return to other options later?
- What are potential downsides to believing and acting on this conclusion?
- If we're right, so what? If we're wrong, what's next?

1.2 A SF Stance

An example may illustrate the use of some of these "temporary certainty" questions. Supervisor Shari and therapist Chad are discussing a troubling development in one of Chad's couples therapy cases. Chad serendipitously observed the husband in public with another woman, and they were being openly affectionate.[5]

Chad:	This really bothers me…how can I do couples therapy when he's cheating on her?
Shari:	How do you know that?
Chad (somewhat taken aback):	What do you mean? I saw them!
Shari:	Could the hand-holding and cuddling have been anything *but* "cheating," do you think?
Chad:	Not that I can imagine…(long pause)
Shari:	OK, let's assume for the moment that the husband *is* cheating on his wife. How does that affect you? *(Discussion follows about Chad's personal distaste for infidelity in any form.)* Now, how would it affect *you* in your work with the couple? *(Discussion ensues about the difficulty Chad would have not confronting the husband or revealing what he saw to the wife; whether or not he would confront or reveal information to them individually; whether he would confront the husband and require him to reveal the infidelity to the wife before continuing their conjoint sessions; and other options resulting from the assumption of infidelity.)* Are there any "up" sides to this, in the way you're thinking about it?
Chad:	No…everything I can imagine will be unpleasant…for them *and* for me.
Shari:	OK, now…what *else* might be true here?
Chad:	What do you mean?
Shari:	What if what you saw isn't "infidelity" to *them*?
Chad:	Whoa! How could it *not* be?
Shari:	It might be tough to imagine…give me a couple of other possible understandings of what these two people were doing besides "infidelity," and then I'll chime in. Let your imagination go a little…like, "Could it be that…?"
Chad (after 20 seconds of thought):	Well…maybe *he* doesn't see it as infidelity…maybe they have an agreement in their marriage that he can flirt and stuff.

---

[5] Inspiration for this dialogue is drawn from a limited example in Stewart and Amundson (1995).

Shari: ...or...

Chad: ...or...maybe they *both* do stuff like this and it's OK with them.

Shari: Is it hard for you to imagine that could be OK within marriage?

Chad: Yeah—really tough.

Shari: But since we don't define what's right or wrong within others' relationships around what is or isn't infidelity, this has to be considered as possible.

Chad: What are some of your ideas here?

Shari: Well, it could be they are swingers...or polyamorous...or they just don't care; in other words, the couple might not have *any* definition of "infidelity" in their relationship and they're OK with that.

Chad: Wow...

Shari: Now, if we assume these other possibilities for a moment, assuming one of these is true about how they define and live with behavior like you witnessed, how might *this* affect your work with them? *(Discussion continues about Chad's immediate confusion and his desire to know more about their understanding of infidelity in their relationship. Shari asks Chad about the couple's goals in therapy and whether his curiosity about how they understand infidelity is related to their goals, and Chad admits he would be imposing if he brought up infidelity. Finally, Shari and Chad both talk about how some events can be disruptive to therapists' abilities to act in the best interests of their clients when certain information is disclosed or discovered, such as admissions of perpetrating abuse, illegal activities, and dishonesty in therapy.)*

Shari: Now, if we assume the couple is doing the best they can and both you and the couple believe things are better and they are making progress toward their goals, how might you proceed with them? *(The conversation turns to productively engaging the couple around their goals and how Chad might handle his own confusion and displeasure around the husband's behavior. Chad agrees to keep Shari up-to-date on his own experiences and monitor whether or not his responses in the case might be hindering optimal care.)*

1.2.2.4 Conceding the Transitional Nature of Goal Development and Problem/Change Experiences

Since language is imprecise and people are continually changing, it follows that how therapists define problems and measure success will change during the course of supervision. I contend that a qualitative research study tracing therapists' articulations of problems and successes would discover wide variations in both. So while initial goals are important, relationships and personal change experiences modify means and goals during the course of supervision.

Tim, a seasoned therapist, was assigned to supervision with Gabrielle when he began work at an urban mental health agency. Everyone at the agency was matched with a supervisor by design; that is, the agency's clinical director assigned supervision after careful evaluation of therapist strengths, level of experience, and limitations. Gabrielle was the senior bilingual, Spanish-speaking therapist and a gifted SF supervisor, but Tim resented this initial pairing because he felt his advanced clinical skills warranted assignment to someone who could help him learn more about his preferred model, structural family therapy. Since Gabrielle had less experience with the structural family therapy model, Tim had difficulty imagining supervision as a helpful exercise. At their first meeting, Tim outlined some of his professional goals: broader use of self, conceptualizing family structure patterns, and raising intensity to promote change. "All of these goals will help me be a better structural family therapist," Tim said. "How will you help me get there?" "Well, I have a lot of family therapy training and know quite a bit about structural family therapy, so I hope to be helpful in these areas," replied Gabrielle. "Also, the director has put us together to help you build cultural competence as well as team therapy skills because you have very little experience in these areas. So, how do we work together so you get all of it?"

Their discussion began to relax in part because Gabrielle was committed to collaborating and avoiding top-down goal setting. Additionally, she communicated this as clearly as she could in an attempt to build cooperation with Tim. As they talked about some of the founders of structural family therapy (many of whom are Hispanic) and Tim's desires to follow in their footsteps, Gabrielle took notes. At the end of their first supervision session, Tim asked about Gabrielle's notations, and she revealed that she was tracking ways she might help Tim meet his goals. Tim was surprised; he thought she was taking notes on his deficits or creating counterarguments to bolster her position as the supervisor. "I came in here thinking my goals were clear and I needed a different supervisor," Tim revealed. "Instead, I think my problem is that I am too short-sighted – I need to learn how to work with our client population, and you know way more than I do about that. I still want to get better at structural family therapy, but that won't happen without learning more about Hispanic culture." They began to forge an agreement toward goals that fit with Tim, Gabrielle, and the agency, plus their ideas about how they would work together toward these goals. This is a clear example of SF supervision that creates opportunities for therapists to refine goals and redefine success.

1.2.2.5 Respecting All Persons' Experiences in Relationship but Privileging Therapists' Accounts of Their Experiences Whenever Possible

If people are the experts in their lived experiences, as SF approaches argue, then professionals' views should usually be secondary to clients'. I believe this assumption is a guiding commitment in the supervision relationship as well. Keep in mind that I am talking about *respecting* experience, not *agreement*. Once a student therapist in his first semester of practice with fewer than 200 clinical contact hours of practice said to me, "I'm a better therapist than 90% of the therapists in the county" (there are over one million residents in our county, meaning there are hundreds of mental health professionals in this area). My response: "You haven't even *met* 90% of the therapists in this county," which led to an interesting conversation about hubris(!).

Some supervisors believe the only forms of legitimate supervision are live or video review. Listening to therapists' accounts of their work in case consultation allows supervisors the opportunity to hear how they are making sense of their overall performance. Paying attention as they talk about their conceptualizations, attitudes, and experiences will yield very different information than real-time or video supervision alone (McCollum and Wetchler 1995). This invites respect of a different kind, a witnessing of experiences sometimes diverging from single-session supervision that can inform goal setting, evaluation, and supervisors' understandings.

A clear violation of this idea of others as experts in their lived experiences is when SF professionals prematurely terminate psychotherapy when clients would prefer to continue (Metcalf, Thomas, Miller, Hubble, and Duncan 1996). If clear consensus has not been reached regarding termination, then the therapist should yield to the experience and opinion of the client unless there is a clear ethical question regarding continuation of services. I have often found that discussing termination is necessary and, at times, threatening to clients. Open discussion of progress toward client goals, especially when therapist and client agree that significant improvement has been made, often creates space for new goal setting with additional client struggles. The improvements clients experience may boost their confidence to address problems they had not yet considered.

Connecting this to supervision, the idea of privileging therapists' accounts has limitations. For example, there are occasions when supervisors must make judgments of therapists' competence or progress. These times call for open conversation when viewpoints differ and when they agree. Agencies, universities, and licensure boards often require supervisor evaluations that assume supervisors have the capacity to assess therapists' performance by measuring it against carefully crafted professional standards. There are times when therapists disagree with these assessments, which can lead to difficult confrontations. A SF approach would create open discussion about the standards, process, requirements, and expectations involved in evaluations *from the beginning*. If the therapist disagrees with the assessment, the conversation can focus on any aspect of the evaluative process, but the therapist's self-assessment does not trump the supervisor's simply because it differs. Both parties have views of the therapist's performance, and both can be respected; but valuing another's viewpoint does not require agreement.

1.2.3 Nonpathology

> *The map is not the territory.*
>
> ~ Alfred Korzybski
>
> *The name is not the thing named.*
>
> ~ Gregory Bateson

1.2.3.1 SF Supervisors Avoid Pejorative Labeling of Supervisees, Relationships, or Contexts

In a field filled with pathological distinctions, this is a challenge for many seeking to move toward a more SF stance. A major premise of SF approaches is they distinguish themselves from problem-solving models which are often dominated by a medical paradigm (De Jong and Berg 2012). In the typical medical model scenario, a problem may be understood through a process of comparison against a (supposed) standard of health. For example, "high blood sugar" is assigned to a test result above the maximum range of normal blood sugar readings. The medical paradigm would then treat the causes of the symptom, which could include an underperforming pancreas, obesity, or other physiological contributors. Successful treatment of the cause(s) of the symptom—in this case, high blood sugar—results in a return to normality, or blood sugar readings within the normal range. If treatment is required continuously, this person is usually called a "diabetic." Even if the person is able to manage blood sugar levels without medication, the label "diabetic" is still assigned, and an identity is often formed. The shift from "I have been treated for a physical condition called diabetes" to "I have diabetes" and ultimately to "I am a diabetic" is a process of reification, and few question the movement from treatment to label to identity.

In the mental, cognitive, emotional, and relational realms of human experience, many believe the medical metaphor not only fits but is as *true* as it is with physical problems. In this way of thinking, careful assessment and correct diagnosis based on the symptoms of one's distress leads to treatment, removing or remediating the causes of distress, and returning the person to normal functioning. One difficulty is the assumption that diagnosis equals reality. There is significant research supporting the notion that clinicians have inflated confidence in their ability to accurately psychodiagnose despite "numerous studies (that) have demonstrated the tenuousness of this kind of meaning-making and inferencing" (Smith and Dumont 2002, p. 297). Spiegel (2005, p. 62) has taken this a step further: "Reliability is probably lowest in the place where most diagnoses are made: the therapist's office." In addition, we contribute to the disease of the culture through the assignment of debilitating diagnosis.

> This infirming of the culture is progressive, such that when common actions are translated into a professionalized language of mental deficit, and this language is disseminated, the culture comes to construct itself in these terms. This leads to an enhanced dependency on the professions and these are forced, in turn, to invent additional terms of mental deficit. (Gergen 1990, p. 353)

Common uses among laypersons of terms like depression or acronyms like OCD or ADHD commandeer the terminology, taking over the mental health profession's control and creating identities with or without "proper" assessment. This results in the creation of additional categories of disability by the profession, and the process recycles again. (Gergen's argument is not without historical support. The DSM-V, due out in 2013, will more than likely add many diagnoses, expanding previous editions. In addition, despite its marketing as a scientific document, many disorders have little research corroboration.) All in all, the reification of deficit is one of the most difficult aspects to address in SF practice, as such beliefs often create significant barriers to goal attainment and personal agency.

How does this affect supervision? Therapists usually initiate conversations about weaknesses, limits, or insufficiencies with me in supervision. Sometimes it is as innocuous as new practicum student therapists saying, "I've never seen a client before," which they experience not as a simple fact in their lives but as a deficiency ("…so, how could I possibly help someone?"). On other occasions, therapists have introduced themselves to me as though I needed to know their every limitation before I could be helpful. As a professor, I know it is easy for students to compare themselves to others, which usually results in conclusions of deficit. I have heard therapists describe themselves as damaged, weak, obsessive–compulsive, anxious, and naïve. Many carry diagnoses from past or current psychotherapy with them wherever they go, defining both person and limitations. Time and time again I have found myself patiently listening to supervisees' self-descriptions filled with negative and derogatory labels, even if I ask about strengths or successes. In addition, many therapists assign negative labels to their past relationships and contexts, using concepts like broken homes, failed marriages, or toxic workplaces. Early conversations can often set understandings in concrete, making it more difficult to create differences as the relationship develops.

Therefore, it is important for the SF supervisor to demonstrate acceptance of the therapists' self-descriptions (see Respect below) as well as raise questions about possible alternative stories and understandings (see Curiosity below). When hearing a self-derogatory description, I often ask clarifying questions such as, "Is this how you would like me to understand you?" "How did you come to believe this is the best way to describe yourself to me?" "What descriptions have you left out that might counterbalance this?" "If you put your best foot forward and you gave me a list of your strengths and successes, where would you begin?" I don't assume that I know better (i.e., that my own conclusions about them are more accurate) or that their self-descriptions are untrue—that would not be in line with the postmodern concepts that guide SF approaches. Instead, I elicit additional (and just as true) terms and narratives that allow for different, less disparaging understandings. My supervision goal for every therapist is to build confidence and dignity; one of the means is countering self-deprecatory understandings.

This carries over to supervision discussions of clients. Many times, therapists are caught between philosophies; that is, they want to see the world and treat people as SF practitioners, but the language of their practice context dominates the descriptions and discussions. Case conferences are often filled with negativity and problem talk, with statements such as, "She's a borderline," "He's noncompliant," and "Her medication isn't right" ruling the conversations. One of the important practices in

SF supervision is to challenge such conclusions about people and guide conversations toward possibility. A favorite challenge of mine involves the diagnosis/treatment gap: "What seem to be the connections between these diagnoses and what people do in therapy?" The usual responses? "Nothing – the talk never gets to what to do about it." This usually moves the supervisory conversation away from (supposed) understanding and explanation toward action.

1.2.3.2 SF Supervisors also Strive to Avoid the Assignment of Blame, Cause, or Intent

Since postmodern thinking does not spend time speculating on causes, conjecture plays almost no role in SF approaches. There may be starting points in the history of a difficulty—after all, it's unlikely you have a problem with someone before you meet him or her!—but a chronological start is not necessarily a cause. There are times when an event marks the beginning of troubling experience. We all know cardiac surgery patients whose depression emerged in postoperative recovery, and there is little doubt that a life-threatening event such as a major automobile accident resulting in severe injuries can initiate new distress. But knowing "when" does not *predict* the "what"—it merely explains it. Every researcher knows that correlation is not the same as causation (and that coincidence is always a limitation of research, a factor that cannot be completely controlled). And the logic is flawed as well. It might be true that most heroin addicts began their drug use with marijuana, but that is not the same as saying the use of marijuana causes heroin abuse; if this were true, then the number of heroin addicts would match the number of marijuana users. Explanation is not prediction.

Happiness research illustrates this quite well. One study (Brickman, Coates, and Janoff-Bulman 1978) found that happiness levels of lottery winners and accident victims (which resulted in paraplegia or quadriplegia) were simply not that much different a year after the events. The authors emphasized the importance of these findings (p. 926): "severe outcomes do not have as great an impact as might be expected," whether positive or negative. Again, events are not necessarily predictive of individual experience in the future.

In the same vein, postmodern supervisors are skeptical of final explanations of anything, especially causes. And since we cannot discern absolute causes, blame cannot be easily assigned, and we should therefore move into conversations regarding change and resolution. SF supervision is a context that promotes responsibility rather than blame, a process of sorting and reflecting. Relationship researcher John Gottman (Gottman and Carrere 2000) has said that over two-thirds of marital arguments involve things that cannot be resolved. I take this conclusion regarding long-term committed relationships as guidance for discussions in less intimate relationships as well—what *can* possibly be resolved needs to be sorted from what *cannot* be, and discussions on topics that cannot be resolved need to be time limited. And all discussions need to be respectful of difference. For example, if a therapist says she needs to be "told what to do" with a client and I believe such an action on my part would violate important ideas I have about relationship, supervision, and clinical agency, then I will encourage a discussion. Part of the discussion will concern the process of supervision with the goal of open disclosure regarding expectations and limitations; in addition, we will talk about the case itself and how the therapist might act in concert with the client. Unless there are circumstances in the case requiring me to make a determination instead of the therapist, then my work is to assist the therapist in examining all possible clinical interventions as well as support his or her conclusions and subsequent actions. Why I did not make the choice for the therapist is open to time-limited discussion, which might include ideas around clinical judgment and responsibility as well as ethics; opinions we have about my making the decision *for* the therapist are open to dialogue but not to persuasion.

1.2.3.3 Therapists Are Doing the Best They Can Under the Circumstances in the Clinical Context

My fundamental belief in the goodness of people has been tested through experience, but it is how I have decided to approach interactions. I always remember that this belief is just that—a belief—and that I can be proven wrong. But it is a bias I choose, one that allows me to spend very little time speculating about intent and instead focus my thoughts and supervision time on goals and change. Judging intent is speculative and prejudicial, and most discussions regarding the "why" of a decision do not achieve different results. Instead of asking questions around "why," I tend to focus on the chronology of a decision, the thinking of the therapist across the chronology, and the possibilities that emerge from the discussion for the case and the therapist. For example, if a therapist was questioning his or her motives regarding a decision made during a session, I would begin with a careful mapping of therapeutic action—what was said by whom, from the beginning of the segment in question to the end. During this discussion, my focus is on challenging blame and certainty. Many therapists who feel they have made a mistake return to the memories of (or actual recording of) the session and second-guess everything they verbalized. They often ascribe ill intent or ignorance to their actions. Phrases like, "I shouldn't have said that," "Why in the world did *that* come out of my mouth," or "I should've seen that coming" are fairly common. Therapists often admit they feel guilt, embarrassment, and doubt, even questioning their competence. As supervisors, we have to take the short and the long view on cases when therapists "mess up." Reflecting on more than 25 years of supervising in a wide variety of contexts, only a handful of cases come to mind in which the therapist made inappropriate decisions based on bad intentions; nearly all of these decisions were simply mistakes, and few of the negative outcomes could have been predicted. People always have 20/20 hindsight: "I should have…" comes quickly after the fact. So my supervisory probing is often deconstructive, focused on raising doubt about certainty and questioning self-blame regarding intent. During the review, I ask questions such as these:

- When you asked that question, did you already know it was headed in a tough direction? What were you thinking about at that moment?
- Is it possible that others could have made that choice?
- Yes, I suppose that intervention could have been because you "weren't thinking"; how else could you understand it?

Some therapists even venture into explanations tied to the impossible-to-know, appealing to unconscious or subconscious reasons for their behaviors. "There must be some unconscious reason why I didn't hear the client hinting about suicide in that session." My commitment to building on successes and strengths leads me to challenge such statements: "That might be so – one can never know. But now that you *are* aware and see it on the video, what options open up for you?" I follow this with, "I think a lot of people would have missed that – I might have. Does that mean that I have an unconscious reason for missing it *or* could it be that sometimes people just miss things no matter how much experience they have?" Near the end of the chronological review, I ask about future options—what has the therapist learned during the conversation that might increase or improve clinical choices with this case and other cases? Since education has always been considered a part of SF supervision (Wetchler 1990), these critical events are often "learning moments" for therapists, followed by self-reflection, assigned reading, video review, and open supervisor sharing of possibilities. They also can help the therapist envision other possibilities of intent or action toward goals.

1.2.3.4 SF Supervisors Look for Resources, Assets, and Strengths in the Person, Stories, Skills, and Context of the Therapist and Client

Since SF approaches seek to create the presence of what is desired rather than the simple absence of problems, I will end this section on a note regarding presence. "Nonpathology" is a void, a concept defined by the presence of a negative (Gardner et al. 1997). Perhaps "health" or "normal" could substitute, but these are vague terms that imply some type of developmental or experiential standard. So, to take the initiative, I will simply quote the late physicist and constructivist Heinz von Foerster (1976, pp. 2–3): perception is "closer to an act of creation, as in *con*-ception, than to a passive state of affairs, as in *re*-ception (emphasis in original) (cited in Keeney 1983, p. 21)." What you look for, you find. As a SF supervisor, I *choose* to look for the good and the possible. An optimist sorts through a pile of manure saying, "There's got to be a pony in here somewhere!" One prominent SF practitioner has been called a "psychotic optimist," a label she heartily accepts (Weiner-Davis 1990). And although I have a skeptical streak in my worldview, I always seek alternative understandings whenever there is room for difference. One of the defining moments in my career took place during a qualitative interview I was conducting (Thomas 1994a) when the client told me, "You believed in me before *I* believed in me!" Taking this stance has been a deliberate practice of mine in all supervisory, educational, and therapeutic contexts ever since.

I often engage students in our program as well as workshop participants in an exercise I call "pathology talk/alternative talk." After dividing them into groups of three to five persons, I only distribute the "pathology talk" terms from the left column. They are to generate as many positive alternative terms for each negative construction as they can, and each group reports to the whole one concept at a time. The purpose of this exercise is to expand people's understandings toward resourcefulness, not to eliminate the more dominant interpretations. Table 1.3 gives some

Table 1.3 Pathology talk/alternative talk

Pathology talk	Alternative talk
Paranoid	Observant, sensitive, aware
Disruptive	Expressive, flamboyant
Depressed	Realistic, empathic, genuine, sensitive
Obsessive/compulsive	Thorough, detail oriented
Hyperactive	Full of life, energetic, creative
Resistant	Freethinker, holding back
Rebellious, argumentative	Nonconforming
Defiant, nonconforming	Individualistic, independent, unshakeable, mind of his/her own
Nagging	Persistence, having high standards
Acting out	Not easily controlled, age appropriate, expressive

examples of alternative understandings that are just as valid as the pathological understandings with which they are matched.

The alternative understandings are only limited by the amount of time spent on the exercise—creativity and hilarity abound! During postexercise discussions, many participants find their voice and talk openly about how the alternative understandings are usually neglected in the mental health profession. Nearly all agree that observations are influenced by vocabulary (and vice versa), and the feedback tells me they value the concept of "nonpathology" better after brainstorming and discussion.

1.2.4 Curiosity

> *Curiosity is lying in wait for every secret.*
> ~ Ralph Waldo Emerson

1.2.4.1 Not-Knowing

Curiosity involves sincere interest in the other (Anderson 2005). This requires a quiet center, controlling one's anxiety while remaining open to changing one's mind. One of the most prominent stances the SF world has embraced is the idea of not-knowing:

> The not-knowing position entails a general attitude or stance in which the therapist's actions communicate an abundant, genuine curiosity. That is, the therapist's actions and attitudes express a need to know more about what has been said, rather than convey preconceived opinions and expectations about the client, the problem, or what must be changed. The therapist, therefore, positions himself or herself in such a way as always to be in a state of "being informed" by the client. (Anderson and Goolishian 1992, p. 29) (cf. De Jong and Berg 2012; Gardner et al. 1997; O'Connell and Jones 2001; Thomas 2000, 1996; Waskett 2006)

Not-knowing is not the same as "know nothing." Bertrando (2000) explains the application of this stance:

> It is impossible to adopt a true not-knowing position, because the therapist cannot avoid knowing her own experiences.... Thus not-knowing risks either becoming a form of wishful thinking in which knowing simply sinks into the untold, or of becoming a strategic stance; pretending not to have an idea or a point of view is just a *simulation* of not-knowing. (p. 92, emphasis in original)

Each person brings knowledge and abilities to an encounter, but until the therapist begins to speak, I admit I am unacquainted with the events and possible understandings of the events. Supervisors bring a great deal to the supervision context—we are not ignorant. We have expertise in the areas of conversation management, research, common/appropriate knowledge about particular models and approaches to therapy, and experience with supervision itself. But the focus of attention is on what the therapist is asking for in the supervision context as well as what he or she believes is the most helpful way to interact. I hold myself accountable to pay attention differently, assuming that "believing is seeing" (attributed to Heinz von Foerster in Gergen, Hoffman, and Anderson 1996).

1.2.4.2 Therapists' Experiences

In addition, not-knowing privileges the therapists' and clients' experiences of the therapy over the supervisors'. I have commonly heard supervisors, team members, and professional associates in group supervision say, "I wasn't in the room, and you were," an acknowledgement of the therapist's unique experience and knowledge about a therapy session. Application of not-knowing is practicing what I call being "slow-to-know." Being slow-to-know is not pretending to be dense; it is a practice in patience. I find that people "re-act and re-search with me in hopes of re-creating some meaningful differences" from our supervision dialogues (Thomas 2007b, p. 14). Asking pointed questions as well as encouraging reiteration of the therapist's account allows me to slow down the inevitable arrival at conclusions, with resulting expansion of options and clear collaboration.

This benevolent desire to know more creates a bridled excitement, a generative tension that affects the telling and the tellers of the story. Therapists happily anticipate supervision when the supervisor brings the attitude of "Tell me more" (Ueland 1992). When curiosity reigns, possibilities become commonplace, and I become more informed about the therapist's style, actions, and creativity with every exchange.

1.2.4.3 Caring Curiosity

Curiosity does not indulge endless restatement or ceaseless questioning; there comes a point where temporary certainty may be reached, and the "what ifs" fall aside (Stewart 2003). But even those decisions are open to revision, should new information or ideas come up. And this type of "caring curiosity has benign intentions" (Stewart 2003)—it is not a series of questions attempting to change another's

Table 1.4 Comparing certainty and curiosity (*Italicize portions quoted* from Amundson et al. 1993, pp. 118–119)

A practice of certainty	A practice of curiosity
Is uncomfortable with ambiguity	*Can tolerate confusion and ambiguity without moving to premature closure*
Quickly insists on a diagnosis and adheres to descriptions from those diagnoses	*Moves more slowly in defining the problem, taking time to consider the experience in the room*
Relies on problem-saturated descriptions of behavior	*Takes care to discover exceptions to the problematic behavior*
Closes space by narrowing observations to one's constructions/predispositions	*Opens space by considering observations from many system levels*
Is concerned with teaching, explaining, disseminating "expert knowledge"	*Asks questions, looks for the special, indigenous knowledge*
Will tend to be more hierarchical	*Will tend to be more collaborative*
May inadvertently foster dependence	*May foster independence, a sense of competence, and self-confidence*
Will tend to create a context of passivity	*Will tend to create a context of discovery*

mind, nor is it an inquisition attempting to dig out the truth. Caring curiosity seeks to be informed and desires clarity, while certainty is the antithesis of curiosity. "Certainty is commitment to theory grounded only *outside* the room," and the more removed one is from an event, the more theory dominates one's understanding (Amundson et al. 1993, p. 115). These authors articulate a persuasive case for continuous curiosity, including the following points in Table 1.4.

1.2.5 Respect

> *Treat people with dignity and respect, even if you don't know them and even if you don't agree with them.*
>
> ~ Michelle Obama

One of the defining moments in most people's lives, I believe, is when one feels respected by a person who has power over him or her. An identification of respect can take many forms, but it is less about receiving something from a passive position than an active acknowledgement of one's own experience. People who have experienced oppression can often identify their first incident of oppression as well as their first experience of respect as indelible personal memories. And since supervision is a skill-building and a personal developmental experience, many therapists recall instances of insult as well as relational moments of respect as crucial in their identity formation.

SF supervision promotes respect as an important stance, and it is the supervisor's responsibility to initiate respect in word and action. "The (SF) supervisor fosters an atmosphere of mutual respect in which both parties celebrate skills, creative ideas, personal qualities and therapeutic successes" (O'Connell and Jones 2001, p. 402). The idea of mutual respect was found to be seminal from the therapist/supervisee viewpoint in Heath and Tharp's (1991) research, which has been cited multiple times in the SF supervision literature (Presbury et al. 1999; Thomas 1996; Wheeler, J. 2007; Waskett 2006). This should not come as a surprise to people in the field of psychotherapy: Carl Rogers (1951, p. 20) clearly stated his bias against neutrality when he wrote that his philosophy was "one in which respect for the individual is uppermost." Respect and trust are two sides of the same coin, a cornerstone in building the emotional bond between therapist and client and one of the factors most predictive of therapeutic outcome success (Horvath, Del Re, Flückiger, and Symonds 2010; Wampold 2001).

One particular aspect of this stance of respect involves the idea of "leading from one step behind" (Cantwell and Holmes 1995, p. 37), a prominent orientation in Insoo Kim Berg's work. Therapist expertise is validated, and supervisors purposefully limit the promotion of their expertise. Supervisors foster the idea that there are many ways to do good therapy and show respect for therapists' efforts, successful or not. Leading from one step behind assumes and supports therapist competence whenever possible, and "respect for what (therapists) have to say will enhance their receptivity to what their supervisors are teaching" (Wetchler 1990, p. 135). Responses from therapists complete this recursion: "Once I (therapist Greaves) felt my voice and opinions were valued and respected, I soon felt comfortable enough to contribute to the supervision agenda" (Wheeler and Greaves 2005, p. 267). John Wheeler (2007, p. 365) offers some wonderful contributions to respectful interaction: "contribute respectfully," "give people the benefit of the doubt," and remember that "ideas are an offering." How one contributes from a position of power may have greater impact than the words themselves, as using a tone the therapist considers courteous may convey more about the relationship than anything one says. "Ideas are an offering" creates a metaphor for me that I have often used when discussing power and respect. If I have an idea I would like to propose, I see myself placing it on a table in the presence of the therapist. I may wrap it beautifully with words of embellishment or I may speak plainly, but either way it is simply a contribution. If the therapist leaves one or more of my gifts on the table, that is her prerogative—once gifts are given, the one receiving has the right to treat them as she wishes.

I believe the following are incomplete but relevant relational values of SF practices related to respect:

1.2.5.1 Collaboration and the Valuing of Relationship

SF supervision does not claim to be unique in its relational values, but its commitment to building collaboration is unquestioned. Referring to previous discussion in this chapter, it is clear that forming relationships honoring persons and experiences is a prerequisite to learning and skill development under the umbrella of SF practices. The reduction of hierarchy and power is initiated and continually supported by the SF supervisor.

I looked up from my desk after catching an image in my peripheral vision. A young woman stood in my university office doorway, head bowed and eyes on the floor. After a few moments, I asked, "Can I help you?" The woman replied, "My name is

Ahsan, and I am here so you can tell me what courses to take in the program." She never looked up. "Well, I would like to help. Would you please step in and have a seat?" Ahsan hesitated, then walked gingerly to a chair far away from me. I dropped my gaze to the floor and said, "You and I can talk about the courses you will take, but in the end *you* will have to decide. Perhaps this is different from what you are used to?" Ahsan sighed and said, "Yes, in my country the professors just tell us what to take." I nodded, and waited a moment before saying, "Could we start with some conversation about other things? I would like to know a bit about you." What followed was a dialogue Ahsan has never forgotten. She has often told me that this encounter was the most liberating conversation she had ever had in an education setting. It opened up possibilities for her that she could not have imagined because a *professor* wanted to know about *her*. Nearly 20 years later, this former supervisee and I remain close colleagues, and I am honored to have been a part of the life of a therapist who introduced the SF approach to a part of the world devoid of postmodern approaches. We managed to reduce the power difference (although she says she will always call me "Dr. Thomas") and create a relationship that changed us both. This is the relational ethic of the SF supervision approach—mutual respect, collaboration, flattening of hierarchy, and the constant negotiation of relationship.

1.2.5.2 Cooperation/Flexibility

Selekman and Todd (1995) advocated a shift of supervisor interest from weaknesses and problems onto strengths and successes. They recommended that instead of drawing on their own knowledge of practice, supervisors should "identify carefully supervisees' unique cooperative response patterns" (1995, p. 22). Such a practice of cooperation requires great flexibility from supervisors (as well as pattern recognition skills). When one possesses power, those with less usually adjust to you.

I heard a story recently from a friend about inflexible power. His father, a Texas farmer, was walking down a New York City street years ago when suddenly the crowd ahead of him began to part. Not only had a 6-foot-wide path appeared, but everyone on the street was averting their eyes away from the path. About 20 yards ahead was a man in a Savile Row suit and fedora. He walked with purpose, his eyes straight ahead, swinging an ebony cane. The Texas farmer was no idiot—taking his cue from the crowd, he quickly moved to the side and looked away. After the man had passed, the gap disappeared and people assumed their normal direction and pace. "Who was *that*?" he asked a man next to him. "That was The Man," he replied. The Texan realized he should probably get more information from a trusted source, so he hustled to his hotel and spoke with the concierge about the incident with The Man. The concierge told him The Man was the leader of the local crime syndicate, a ruthless criminal who would not hesitate to strike out with his cane, without fear of reprisal, if someone impeded his path. The Texan counted himself fortunate that he attended to the crowd's behavior. I love this story because it illustrates the basest behavior from one with power. Cooperation was evident in this context—everyone did what the crime boss required—and he was able to maintain a position of complete inflexibility.

This goal of collaboration in SF supervision is not a form of cooperation resulting from simple compliance. Working toward a relationship of collaboration requires flexibility from both supervisor and therapist, as the default form usually favors supervisor control. In the illustration above regarding my relationship with Ahsan, cooperation required changes from *me* as well as from her. My endless struggle to be flexible in supervision is constantly informed by therapists who challenge me to fit with their cooperative styles—I am ever the learner.

1.2.5.3 Competence Is Assumed

> This new posture (SF) reduces the defensiveness of those being managed or supervised; thus, staff members rise to the challenge and start to think for themselves, taking actions based on this sense of competence, rather than always defending his/her (sic) position. Not allowing supervisees, staff members, clients, or even one's own children or partners to lower themselves to a defensive position is the most respectful, empowering, and yet demanding posture we can take. (Berg n.d., Hot Tips III – Supervision and Management)

Postmodern practices assume competence, emphasizing reflection and reinforcement more than instruction; SF supervision assumes the same competence of therapists. If (or when) deficits become evident, SF supervisors address them, but the emphasis is on future discovery more than present assumptions. Research by Heath and Tharp (1991) informed me on therapist's views of supervisors over 20 years ago. Soon after hearing of the results of their qualitative research with therapists on the topic (which was quite novel then), I was convinced this assumption was the most solution-focused position I could take regarding supervision—after all, as a SF therapist, it is what I assume about my clients.

Most supervision models assume therapists require supervision and guidance; in other words, supervisors assume a position of importance. The problem with this stance is that it attaches a great deal of significance to the person of the supervisor and the supervision process. This easily translates into deficit thinking and unilateral educational and clinical standards. I have written elsewhere (Thomas 2000) about this "guru" assumption and its negative impact on relationships: "Learners who are fulfilling their roles (for the gurus) sit at the feet of these experts and are filled with knowledge and wisdom as it falls from the mouth of the Learned One. Some supervisors view themselves as repositories of knowledge, dispensing wisdom to the ignorant and correcting the hapless" (p. 32). Effects of believing one holds such an elevated position can include impatience with therapist progress, inappropriate and groundless demands for compliance, and hubris. Since a tenet of SF practices is "leading from one step behind" (Cantwell and Holmes 1995), I have created my own version this stance tied to my martial art, aikido. The English translation of aikido is "the way of blending with energy." Instead of blocking or attacking, this "loving" martial art accepts and redirects the other's energy.

1.2.5.4 Caring for Persons, Relationships, and Process

Also discussed above under curiosity, what I call caring has been articulated in a variety of forms in the psychotherapy literature. Kitchener's (1984) classic articulation of therapeutic ethics includes the principle of fidelity, an element of practice emphasizing truthfulness, loyalty, and reliability in therapeutic relationships. Others have been bolder when discussing this contextual dynamic. Building relationships requires what Canadian psychiatrist and family therapist Karl Tomm has called therapeutic love or an ethic of caring, an opening of possibility that empowers all involved (Godard 2006; Tomm, Hoyt, and Madigan 1998). Chilean biologist Humberto Maturana (Maturana and Poerksen 2004) also calls this relational posture "love": "The only emotion not limiting but enlarging one's listening is: love" (p. 271). Here, he is talking about a "domain of relational behaviors" (p. 272) which is distinguished from the emotion of love. Although Maturana is speaking about therapists and not supervisors, the distinction is relevant: one acts in order to show acceptance of the "legitimacy of the other as a matter of course," with no personal gain or reward (Maturana and Poerksen 2004, p. 272). Regarding supervision, SF supervisor John Wheeler (2007, p. 345) places strong emphasis on the concept of "lovingness." Appealing to poetic expressions and biblical references, he stresses the importance of patience, kindness, and faithfulness in the development of supervisory relationships. And if one feels the positions taken above are still too distant, Debbie Horsfall (2008, p. 1) takes a clear stance on the use of the term love: "The emerging results of this inquiry are that self-consciously embracing a head/heart stance within the supervisory relationship is crucial in an environment where emotions and the body are often neglected or silenced." Working from author bell hooks' (2003, p. 131) definition of love as "a combination of care, commitment, knowledge, responsibility, respect, and trust", Horsfall (2008) presses teacher/supervisors forward by holding them accountable as responsive witnesses in the learning process we call supervision. I propose that SF supervision cannot simply be a mechanical, duty-driven activity that allows agencies or therapists to meet minimal standards of practice and legal requirements. Whether one adopts the concepts above or adapts these principles to decrease their somewhat radical nature, I believe caring for persons, relationships, and process is integral to SF supervision.

1.3 Concluding Thoughts on the SF Stance

I am a martial artist, a *sensei* (teacher) of the "loving" art of aikido. We get a fair number of new students at the dojo who have practiced other martial arts including tae kwon do, karate, and kung fu. I always tell new students, no matter their belt or rank in other arts, that all of the arts have value and limitations. Tohei Sensei, one of the original students of our art, articulated four aikido principles we all must master: keep weight underside (be "heavy"), relax completely, keep one-point (or center), and extend *ki* or energy (Bill Sosa Sensei personal communication, July 14, 1998). These are the four principles that guide our stance, and all techniques need to be in harmony with this stance. From sixth-*dan* (black belt) aikido masters to teenagers who have never before stepped into a dojo, the stance is the same.

Perhaps the stance I have outlined in this chapter—being pragmatic, staying tentative, avoiding pathologizing, maintaining curiosity, and nurturing respect—is a sketch from which this SF supervision approach can creatively evolve.

Chapter 2
Systems Thinking and Isomorphism in SF Supervision

> Lack of knowledge of interactional, systemic, and postmodern theories may ensure the practice of solution-forced (practices).
>
> ~ Nyland and Corsiglia 1994, p. 10 (emphasis added)

2.1 Systems: Conceptualizing the Supervision Context

2.1.1 Historical Connections to the SF Approach

Systems thinking[1] has been and continues to be influential in SF supervision conceptualization, development, and application. Some of the earliest publications on SF supervision reveal a close affinity to the systems paradigm. Wetchler's (1990) article was the first SF supervision publication in the USA, and his organizing ideas were based on systems. My early workshops on solution-focused supervision, presented about the same time as Wetchler's publication, were guided by systems thinking (Thomas 1990, 1992), and the usefulness of systems thinking has been a constant thread through the history of SF supervision publication and training, especially when applied to organizations such as schools, agencies, and universities. For example, Franklin and Streeter (2003) write about applying a SF approach within a large urban high school: "Solution-focused therapists have incorporated the systemic idea of wholism in their approach. Wholism asserts that by changing one part of a system, a ripple effect takes place which results in a change in the entire system" (p. 6) (see "small change" discussion below). Miller and McKergow (2012) promote the

---

[1] Although popularly known as systems *theory*, I generally refer to systems and cybernetics as paradigms or epistemologies. Thorana Nelson (personal communication, July 18, 2012) reminded me that she and I tend to avoid using the term system theory "because there are no testable constructs." Therefore, I will use the terms "systems thinking," "systems paradigm," and "systems" interchangeably.

usefulness of complexity theory and the place of systems thinking within it: "We see complexity theory as a useful framework for describing SFBT (solution-focused brief therapy) practices and their implications for clients' lives" (p. 164). Systems thinking is utilized in the description and understanding of the SF supervisory process in research as well (Rudes, Shilts, and Berg 1997; Smock, McCollum, and Stevenson 2010; Triantafillou 1997). So whether one sees it as a vestige of early SF development or a vital part of the approach's continued development, systems thinking is inextricably entwined in clinical, organizational, and supervisory approaches.

Since SFBT grew out of systems-oriented models such as MRI, early publications from Brief Family Therapy Center of Milwaukee (BFTC) had a distinctive systemic alignment. Steve de Shazer, Insoo's husband and collaborator, became the designated writer for the BFTC in its early years. De Shazer was educated as a social worker and studied at the Mental Research Institute (MRI) in Palo Alto, California, in the 1970s, where he was introduced to Insoo by MRI founder John Weakland (I. K. Berg, personal communication, September 5, 1998). After moving back to Milwaukee and founding BFTC, they organized an innovative team of clinicians and researchers and began to apply the MRI's ideas and their own innovations as they saw individuals, couples, and families in therapy.

While Insoo Kim Berg led the clinical innovations, Steve[2] documented and articulated the BFTC team's work. And when it came time to float their ideas in the professional world, it naturally fell to Steve to write for the group (Lipchik, Walter, Miller, Gingerich, Gallagher, and Cade 2010). For example, Steve described the BFTC's unique approach (simply called "brief therapy" in BFTC's formative years) in this way: "Brief therapy with families requires both theoretical and intervention tools which are based on the family systems as a whole rather than on the individuals or the discrete interaction between any two of the people" (de Shazer 1979, p. 83). His thinking and writing in the late 1970s was grounded in the strategic work of Jay Haley (1968) and MRI's Don Jackson (1968) and John Weakland, all of whom were involved in the Palo Alto group of Gregory Bateson (Kuehl 2008). Since Bateson was one of the preeminent cybernetician/systems thinkers of the twentieth century, it is unquestioned that the systems paradigm permeated the work of all of these brief therapy giants and was part of the BFTC development and reflection process.

Given the systems background of Insoo and Steve as they learned brief therapy, there is little doubt that the supervision and team training sessions were guided by systems ideas and practices in BFTC's formative years. This connection to systems thinking remained true to the end of Steve's life. In his final book, he and his colleagues wrote:

> For a number of reasons, the current SFBT approach can be seen as a systemic therapy. First, SFBT therapists routinely treat systems because couples and families – as well as individuals – come in for treatment… Second, SFBT is systemic because the solutions that are explored are interactional, that is, people's problems and their exceptions involve other people, very often family members,

---

[2] As with Insoo, nearly everyone involved in SFBT was on a first-name basis with Steve; therefore, I will try to consistently refer to de Shazer as "Steve" except when there is a risk of confusion.

colleagues at work, or relationship partners and friends. Third, SFBT is systemic because once small changes begin to occur, larger changes often follow, and those larger changes are usually interactional and systemic. (de Shazer, Dolan, Korman, Trepper, McCollum, and Berg 2007, p. 3)

It is also quite clear to most scholars in the SF community that ideas guiding SF practice have moved away from cybernetic/systemic thinking to constructivist (Miller 1997) and then to postmodern, social constructionist orientations (Bidwell 2007). Miller and de Shazer (1998, p. 371) said SF therapists avoid "metanarratives, or grand theories...that explain everything by reducing reality to a few foundational elements and principles." Some of the most recent articulations of the place of theory in the SF approach go even further. Although they do not speak for other practitioners of SF, two significant scholars, McKergow and Korman (2009, p. 34), make it quite clear that they believe SF therapists act "as if" there are no outside forces (i.e., systems) nor internal frameworks driving the individual human being. However, the usefulness of systems thinking within SF approaches is not dead. Miller and McKergow (2012, p. 164) tie the discursive orientation of SF to complexity theory: "A major emphasis running through this essay is 'narrative emergence.' We use this term to call attention to several interrelated aspects of SFBT as a distinctive form of discursive therapy and complex system." They articulate several systems properties that they find relevant in understanding SF approaches, including self-organization, synergistic characteristics of systems, and pattern. While some in the SF world of practice promote the idea of a theoryless SF approach, others continue to advocate for the inclusion of systems thinking. McKergow (Jackson and McKergow 2007; Miller and McKergow 2012) and Sparrer (2007) are among the most prominent proponents of the continuing need for the systems paradigm as a guide to understanding and practicing the SF approach.

The MRI approach was a formative model in the history of family therapy, and the field of family therapy has claimed SF as one of its models since it came on the scene in part because of its close connections to the MRI model (Kuehl 2008). Systems thinking has played and continues to play an important role in the development of family therapy supervision (Morgan and Sprenkle 2007; Todd and Storm 1997) and is thus influential in SF supervisory approaches.

While other theories have always been prominent within family therapy, systems thinking continues to be a core element of family therapy training (AAMFT 2005). The American Association for Marriage and Family Therapy (AAMFT) is the largest family therapy professional organization in North America, and this organization created the supervisor standards for family therapy licensure, registration, and certification adopted by nearly all 50 US states and other legislative bodies in North America. AAMFT Approved Supervisors "work from a systemic orientation" and must "be able to effectively apply a systemic perspective" in supervision as a requirement of both initial designation as an Approved Supervisor and in their ongoing supervision (AAMFT 2007, pp. 3, 13).

All of this is to say that systems thinking has a long and honored history with practitioners of SF therapy as well as within its conceptual and clinical development as a therapeutic approach, at least within the USA. Family therapy supervisors, including professors in many prominent programs granting degrees in family therapy, have always been at the forefront of SF development. Therefore, it is difficult (if not impossible) for me to write about SF supervision without integrating systems thinking into the discussion.

For those unfamiliar with systems thinking, what follows is but a quick overview of some of its primary ideas. For an in-depth study of the theory, I would suggest you start with the readings in Appendix B.

2.1.2 Basic Systems Ideas and Their Fit with SF Supervision

Most counseling supervision models are developmental or learning-based. At least in part, the supervisory processes in these models focus on the individual therapist–learner, and the supervision relationship is restricted and guided by the therapist's clearly identified and carefully assessed stage (Bernard and Goodyear 2009). Indeed, some models, including Stoltenberg and McNeill's integrative developmental model (2010), are rigorously organized by an individual developmental construct. There is an appeal to working exclusively within such a schema, as the supervisor's roles and techniques can be arranged to fit the therapist. At the same time, such models are built on linear assumptions of individual development more than relationship and interaction or supervisor expertise and education.

Joining a systems understanding to a SF approach to supervision creates a more inclusive and flexible process. Table 2.1 illustrates commonalities between systems thinking (applied as descriptive or formative) and SF supervision as I conceptualize it.

2.1.2.1 Interaction

Systems sensitivity in supervision requires (at least) two key abilities. First, *the supervisor must grasp the interpersonal and interactive nature of change*; that is, what defines a system is what emerges from the interaction of the members rather than from discrete knowledge or actions of the members themselves. This concept is probably a part of most people's day-to-day practice, but they "don't see that they see" (H. von Foerster, personal communication, October 12, 1997). And it is clear that supervision changes supervisors—at least good ones. The principle of mutual influence is embedded in this theory, whether one is attending to biological, ecological, or human interaction systems: one cannot not influence just as one cannot not be influenced.

A medical sales professional I know said it so well: "I am different with every physician I encounter; if I wasn't, I wouldn't make the sale." It was obvious from our conversation that she grasped this systems concept. She recognized that she needed to adjust herself in each potential sales relationship, showing keen attention to subtle differences in interaction as she moved from one physician's office to another. In one office she would approach the physician and extend her hand; in another she would wait for the physician to raise her eyes from her charting or computer and approach her, hand extended. In yet another relationship, the physician, a vascular surgeon,

2.1 Systems: Conceptualizing the Supervision Context

Table 2.1 Systems properties/SF supervision assumptions

Systems properties	SF supervision assumptions
Interconnecting parts function as a whole, relationship and interaction define the system, a change in structure changes interaction/behavior	Cooperation defines and is a primary goal in the SF supervision relationship; hierarchy is assumed and "flattened" whenever and wherever possible, creating greater collaboration
Change produces more change (reinforcing or positive feedback)	Ripple effect; change is inevitable
Systems seek to balance and maintain themselves (homeostatic tendencies, balancing or negative feedback)	Supervision adapts different goals through time, seeking the continuation of a productive and supportive relationship
Interdependence—influence on each individual/part in the system is inevitable	Mutual influence is expected and welcomed
Systems are not isolated, influence from the environment and other systems is inevitable	Therapists bring resources and influences into the supervisor–therapist interaction, including the influence of clients
Changes emerge from the interaction of the individuals/parts	Emergence is expected and cultivated
Context is critical	Context is critical
Hierarchy, embeddedness, and complexity are assumed	Hierarchy is recognized and addressed
Circular causality—focus on ability/responsibility, not blame/cause	Mutual influence is assumed; the supervisor's focus is on adjustment to therapist goals and resources, a recognition of shared purposes/responsibility
Established communication model	Grounded in language, communication
Equifinality—a system can reach similar goals through different routes	Unique nature of each therapist and supervisory relationship supports unique paths to therapist competency

was very cautious with his hands; a simple wave or nod was exchanged instead of a handshake. Although simplified by an example of business greeting behavior, she went on to talk about how this ability she had carefully developed, detecting key areas within a relationship in which she could adjust her behavior, set her apart from other sales representatives. "After I get to know the surgeons, I get access to them in ways my competitors could only dream of." Since neither supervision nor therapy should glorify sales techniques, it requires us to move beyond relationship manipulation (which is almost always a part of sales—see ChangingMinds.org 2005) to what we know about the importance of relationship building in supervision.

In systems thinking, mutual causality is more important than unilateral or linear causality; one simply assumes that a change in one part of the system causes a change in another part of the system. Even if one thinks the initial cause in a relationship can be identified, systems thinking would point out that the effect of that identified influence *plus* the interaction between the people involved in this exchange *after* any initial change is important. Insoo, as I will discuss in a later chapter, viewed supervision as a give-and-take, a mutually influencing relationship from which both benefit and within which both change. Jackson and McKergow (2007) said this: "Studying causes and postulating explanations is often unhelpful when seeking solutions" (p. 37). Within SF supervision, collaboration means mutual influence—the supervisor cannot not be changed by the relationship. Although she wrote little on the subject, Insoo agreed with this notion of mutual influence, even embracing it (Berg n.d., SFBTA Archive #10128-0064). Since social construction involves co-creation of meaning, Insoo believed the supervisor becomes part of this evolving process of change in supervision. "One's behavior is always in relation to the actions of others; we act or talk in relation" (Rudes et al. 1997, p. 212). It is simply this: I am different because we are different.

2.1.2.2 Context

Second, it is necessary for the supervisor *to be able to recognize the effect of context on behavior/interaction and meaning-making*. In systems thinking, context must be taken into account to understand and/or influence interaction. One can only appropriately understand and influence systems when they are viewed as a part of their interaction + environment.

Gregory Bateson wrote in his famous collection, *Steps to an Ecology of Mind* (1972), that "all messages…have 'meaning' only by virtue of context" (pp. 275–276). Further developed in *Mind and Nature* (1979), Bateson was emphatic that stories—at all levels—are generated and supported by particular contexts. "If the world be connected…, then thinking in terms of stories must be shared by all mind or minds, whether ours or those of redwood forests and sea anemones" (p. 14). So despite the criticisms of systems thinking being mechanistic, within the brief therapy tradition, it has always been organic. Bateson offered "the notion of context, of *pattern through time*" (1979, p. 14, emphasis in original). "Context is taken to include relationships as well as fundamental premises and habitual behaviors that are seldom questioned, all of which constrain action, and that are normally taken as a given" (Tognetti 2002, p. 183).

Few would disagree with the idea that SF approaches are best understood as postmodern (Mills and Sprenkle 1995). And although some—whether cybernetic (Keeney and Keeney 2012) or postmodern (Marovic and Snyders 2010)—might find systems/cybernetic ideas to be incongruent with a postmodern philosophy, others find common ground in that postmodern notions support the importance of context in the meaning-making process (Cullin 2005). In systemic or postmodern stances, Bertrando states that "confusion is generated when we forget such distinctions between contexts, and the fact that any context is in turn contained within a context, in a virtual *regressus ad infinitum*" (2000, p. 97).

Illustrations from SF practices may assist here. Most psychotherapy approaches assume that counseling with mandated clients requires modifications on the part of the therapist. SFBT has an impressive history of carefully accounting for the challenges mandated clients present and the special adjustments therapists must consider when working with those unwillingly engaging in therapy (De Jong and Berg 2012; Lee, Sebold, and Uken 2003; Walter 2006). Context-sensitive supervisors seek information from therapists about client background and service delivery contexts, seeking information from the therapists that might inform their consultations. This sensitivity to information is integral to both systems thinking and solution-focused approaches. While systems-only supervisors may ask about rules of disclosure, court involvement, or

2.1 Systems: Conceptualizing the Supervision Context

spousal differences in therapeutic investment, SF supervisors who ascribe to systems thinking may also inquire about indirect and less-obtrusive ways to engage the client and ways to carefully distance therapists from referral sources to cleanly separate the therapist from those in authority over the client. The content of the conversations may differ based on supervisor and therapist assumptions, but context is carefully considered.

A second illustration, using a case example, may further illuminate the importance of context within both systems thinking and solution-focused approaches: a male school counselor, Ramone, is frustrated with his inability to identify resources with Jesse, a 10-year-old female client. The client's English teacher has referred Jesse for counseling because of "test anxiety." During their weekly supervision session, Ramone tells his supervisor Linda his views on the situation:

Ramone:	Most of the time Jesse answers my questions, but when I try to find out what her strengths and resources are, she just goes "Ummm…" and looks at the ground. She says she really hates being so anxious, but when I ask about times when she's not as anxious or how she handles anxiety in other classes, she just goes into her "ummm" mode.
Linda:	How is that affecting you?
Ramone:	I'm getting pretty frustrated—not so much with her, but more with me.
Linda:	How's so?
Ramone:	I mean, by this point in my career, I should be able to…
Linda:	What—make people tell you things? (laughter)
Ramone (laughing):	No, that's not it! I should be able to do some work-around, something that will create a space for her to speak more freely.
Linda:	Let me ask you this: Who is important to Jesse?
Ramone:	Her mom's her best friend, for sure. And she really does like her math teacher. Let's see…she goes to lunch right after we meet, and her best friend Angela is right outside the door in the hallway to walk with her every time we meet.

(Now, there are two quite different conversations—one "systems-oriented-only" and the other "systems-sensitive SF")

#1 – "SYSTEMS"

SYSTEMS Linda:	OK…if we brought one or more of these folks into the counseling room for a consult, how might that affect things?
SYSTEMS Ramone:	Jesse might open up more, or she might not…I think having her friend there might ease things, but the other adults might bring even more pressure. Yeah, Angela might be a good choice.
SYSTEMS Linda:	And…how might having that teacher or Mom in the room affect what *you* do?
SYSTEMS Ramone:	Whoa…that would have a pretty big effect on me. I hadn't thought of that…I would ask Angela and Jesse to talk about Jesse's strengths—maybe ask Angela first, you know, some pointed questions about what Jesse's good at, and then see if the two of them could brainstorm about …

#2 – "SF"

SF Linda:	OK…how might you get the views of one or more of these folks into the conversation you and Jesse are having?
SF Ramone:	Yeah…relationship questions (De Jong and Berg 2012) – hadn't thought of that. I could ask Jesse, "If I asked Angela about your strengths, what would she say?"
SF Linda:	And how could you relate this to Jesse's goal of…what was it?
SF Ramone:	It was "less anxiety," but we've arrived at "more calm during tests," so it's really SF now…
SF Linda:	(waits…)
SF Ramone:	Let's see…maybe something like, "If I asked your mom about times you are 'more calm,' what might she say?"
SF Linda:	(nods…waits…)
SF Ramone:	Ah – then I'd ask, "what parts of Mom's 'more calm' stories about you relate to taking tests?"
SF Linda:	I like those. Now, how do you bring Angela's voice back into this?
SF Ramone:	Since Angela's in Jesse's English class, I could ask Jesse, "If Angela saw you 'more calm,' what would she see?"
SF Linda:	Nice questions! Now, how's your frustration level compared to when you came in here today?

2.1.2.3 Emergence

Solution-focused therapists began talking about emergence as part of their view of change quite early in the development of the approach; in fact, members of the BFTC team began writing about emergence within SF in a variety of ways. For some the concept was explicit (called the "ripple effect" by team member Michele Weiner-Davis [O'Hanlon and Weiner-Davis 1989, p. 42]), while for others the idea was implied. For example, de Shazer (1985) stated that following initial change, clients will create additional unintended and unanticipated changes. Often called the snowball effect (O'Connor and McDermott 1997), this reinforcing feedback is a defining feature of systems. Change leads to more change—it is how systems operate. The SF approach assumes the emergence of unique ideas, tasks, and suggestions from the client–therapist interaction and is clearly tied to this systemic tenet (De Jong and Berg 2012, p. 148).[3]

2.1.3 Multiple Systems and Mutual Influence

Marshall Fine and Jean Turner (1997) wrote a significant chapter on supervision that I have adapted to this discussion of systems in supervision. Although their

---

[3] See "small change is all that's necessary" below.

2.1 Systems: Conceptualizing the Supervision Context

conceptualization centers on power, their distinctions are relevant to systems thinking as well. First, whether systems thinking or some other conceptual frame is utilized, some explanation is required to grasp different types of influence among therapy, supervision, policies, and legal/ethical obligations. Supervision shares common characteristics with therapy and consultation, but there are additional controls, power, and responsibilities unique to supervisory relationships and practice in most contexts. For example, in most US states the supervisor assumes and is held responsible, at least in part, for the therapist's client relationships. If clinical lapses lead to harm or negative outcome, both the therapist and the supervisor are accountable to licensing and regulatory agencies. Supervisors must also meet requirements independent of their contractual supervisor/therapist relationships, such as continuing education. In addition to state/national/provincial regulations, the context of supervision is often embedded in an agency, university, or other local organization that has its own set of policies and procedures that must be observed. Therefore, for our purposes, four distinct units that overlap and interact will be discussed to illustrate the importance of contextual understandings and actions within supervision (see Diagram 2.1).

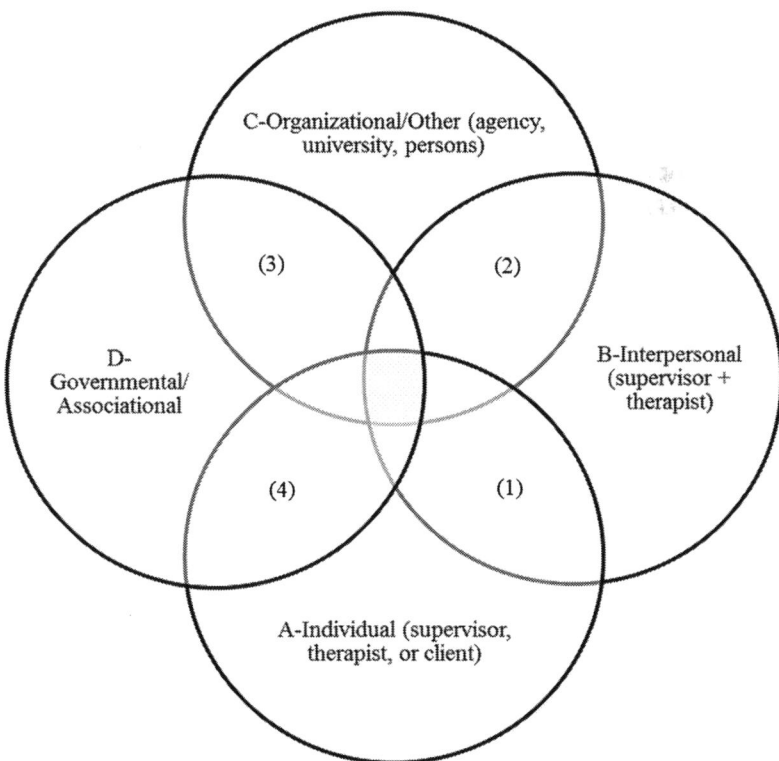

Diagram 2.1 Overlapping Systems of Influence in Supervision

- First, each person[4] is a system (Circle A); that is, each client, therapist, and supervisor brings unique experiences, expectations, and perspectives to the intersecting relationships.
- Next (Circle B), the interpersonal dyad of "supervisor + therapist" is an interactive system with special forms and patterns.
- In addition, the relationships among clients, therapist, and supervisor are influenced by organizational systems of rules and obligations (Circle C). Within this category, I include persons who have influence on both of the individuals involved (clients, therapists, supervisors) outside the interrelationships possible among the supervisor, the therapist, and the therapist's clients. These persons could be other therapists involved in supervision with the therapist, clients who influence the therapist/supervisor relationship via formal feedback, other supervisors in the organization, and administrators involved in the structure and process.
- Finally, governmental/associational entities (Circle D) often have authority among all the previous systems. Licensing and regulatory boards as well as professional associations with ethics codes that require certain member behavior would be included here. Accreditation organizations would also fall into this circle. Fine and Turner (1997, p. 233) state that these "centrally situated" entities are the "least flexible and most removed" from the persons involved in therapy and supervision.

Common metaphors used to describe influence among systems thinkers include Russian nesting dolls or onions. When thinking of systems this way, smaller systems are contained within and encompassed by larger systems. Lesser systems are subject to the rules of greater systems, and lesser systems are seen as unique systems and as parts of the larger whole. Although conceptually useful, I do not believe this metaphor accounts for the complexity of influence among the systems I describe here; a Venn diagram of overlapping influences among distinctive systems is a clearer illustration when discussing supervision. For example, few would question the systemic influence of B (supervisor–therapist) on all individuals in Circle A. However, it may be more difficult to imagine systemic impacts of Circle D (governmental/associational) on individual clients in Circle A, although there are some. For example, clients must pay appropriate compensation for services if required by the therapy contract they sign. If they do not pay for services they have received, therapists may have rights to pursue past-due fees via collection agencies and/or small-claims court. Also, clients cannot break the law and expect the therapist–client relationship to shield them from consequences. Examples include threatening or intimidating the therapist or demanding that certain information be kept private (e.g., insisting a therapist maintain confidentiality when child or elder abuse is suspected, which by law must be reported to authorities in most states).

To underscore the importance of systems thinking and acting within supervision, consider the following notions and examples. Although there are nine areas of overlap in this Diagram 2.1, I will only discuss four in order to keep distinctions clear:

---

[4] For simplicity, I will assume individual clients rather than couples or families in this section.

1. *Overlapping Influences of Circles A and B*
   Each individual (A) influences the supervisor–therapist relationship (B). While this may be assumed by some, there are supervisors who hold to a belief that they are *not* significantly influenced by the other persons involved in the clinical process of therapy plus supervision. Holding firmly to a belief in objectivity, some supervisors may even require that those they supervise embrace such beliefs and practice as though therapists merely act on clients and should not be affected by client experiences. No one from either second-order systems (Keeney and Thomas 1986; von Foerster 1990) or postmodern (Gergen 2001) perspectives would consider this possible. From a systems perspective, we cannot not influence and we cannot not be influenced. "No one can escape this fundamental subjectivity of experience, and the philosophers who purport to have access to a 'God's eye view' are no exception" (von Glasersfeld 1986, p. 72).

   Supervisor Angela has worked hard with therapist Matthew on a challenging case involving a Marine Corps sergeant returning from the war in Afghanistan. This military veteran presents significant challenges to the assumptions Angela and Matthew have regarding psychopharmacological intervention, multiple diagnostic labels, and larger system involvement. Louis, the Marine, has requested that both Angela and Matthew interface with Veteran's Administration (VA) officials who insist Louis receive particular "evidence-based treatment" and more frequent individual therapy sessions. Louis feels caught; his loyalties pull him in sometimes opposing directions. Louis feels he is improving in part because of Matthew's unique, solution-focused approach to his difficulties related to post-traumatic stress disorder (see Henden 2011 for an excellent resource). However, he is also appealing disability status with the VA, which requires frequent oral and written updates that take time away from Matthew's other clinical service and administrative time at the agency.

   Angela is affected by Louis and his special requirements in several ways. She has had to seriously question her commitment to supporting therapists in their choice of therapeutic models given the constraints of the VA. And while she firmly believes money should not override any clinical decisions, her administrator is losing patience with the case reimbursement and directing her to "move it forward." But these are multisystemic influences; let's restrict this to the Circle A–B overlap. First, she feels she is in a difficult position because the time demands imposed by those funding Louis' therapy are eroding the flexibility she has to assign new cases to Matthew. In addition, viewing video recordings of Matthew working with Louis has brought forth strong emotions of anger Angela has needed to process with her own therapist. Her anger, focused on the wrongs Louis has experienced at the hands of those supposedly in charge of his psychotherapeutic treatment at the VA, affects her own emotional responsiveness and her decisions regarding Matthew's supervision. Finally, Angela finds herself questioning the wisdom of supervisory involvement, in part, because she seems to be more negatively affected by the situation than therapist Matthew.

On the other hand, Matthew has felt caught between a rock and a hard place. He feels energized by Louis' gains in therapy; at the same time, he senses a negative change in Angela when their weekly supervisory discussion moves to this case. New to the agency, Matthew lacks a clear sense of the agency's politics and is uncertain whether vocalizing his discomfort with Angela could put him at risk in some way. Because of his apprehension, Matthew has withheld certain successes as well as setbacks from Angela on other cases, assuming that keeping a low profile and minimizing his contact with Angela would be the best route to take. He has begun to rethink his ideas about supervision–instead of seeing it as a safe, supportive context for open clinical discussions with a guiding mentor, his ideas drift toward negative associations from previous supervisory relationships that focused on compliance and administration more than clinical excellence and growth. The supervisory relationship has become strained.

Finally, client Louis has also been touched by the supervisor–therapist relationship, but his experience has been completely positive. Unaware of the politics tied to the VA/agency struggles, he has thoroughly enjoyed the therapy sessions with Matthew as well as the supervisory feedback Matthew brings each week after his meetings with Angela. Louis sees Angela as the platoon leader, the person in charge of Matthew (his "squad leader") who adds stability to his situation and offers additional knowledge and wisdom via Matthew. Because Matthew is highly complementary of Angela's input and direction, Louis has come to trust all involved at the agency in part because of Matthew's openness about supervisory oversight in his case. It is also clear that Matthew and Angela have appropriately shielded Louis from discussions taking place between the professionals and the VA that were policy-level decisions related to many cases and procedures.

2. *Overlapping Influences of Circles B and C*

Supervisors are not only accountable to regulatory or associational bodies that set and maintain requirements for supervisory status; they also answer to local entities that require more interaction than state and national boards. Anyone who has supervised within an agency, university, or training program has bumped up against policies and procedures that regulate goals and practices. The supervisor must practice within guidelines and requirements that serve to protect what I will call the local institution (whether agency, university or training program, or some other local entity) while at the same time supporting clinical service delivery and/or quality education and training. While state boards and national organizations may have conflicting stands at times, it is clear that none exist to protect the local institution's interests. To ensure continuous service delivery, the local institution must survive; to survive, it must create policies and procedures that protect it from financial and legal disasters while engaging in its important work. Most successful local institutions protect their interests and deliver quality clinical and educational services—their "P&Ps" have been carefully developed through trial and wisdom to create a delicate balance that serves institution, employee, and client. This being said, responsive local institutions influence and are influenced by supervisors.

Keeping with the scenario begun above, it is easy to see how Angela is influenced by the local institution, a nonprofit agency named Glen Rose Services that is dedicated to community mental health. Few nonprofit agencies have unlimited funds independent of revenue streams tied to the delivery of therapeutic services. In this situation, Glen Rose receives significant United Way funding but is reliant on VA reimbursement for services delivered to area active duty and retired military to meet annual payroll and expenses. Over the last decade, Glen Rose has become more and more dependent on federal funding streams, a natural outcome of quality service delivery and careful case supervision.

Angela reports to Leanne, an administrator who takes Angela's position and recommendations seriously. Leanne has two master's degrees, one in counseling and the other in management. She views problems that arise within supervision as indicators of systems adjustment. Because clientele change frequently, Leanne feels the most accurate barometer of agency health is the interaction among staff. She welcomes open communication with therapists while supporting the importance of the supervisor's direct influence on clinical decision-making by avoiding triangulation whenever possible.

Because of the collegial and accommodating relationships Leanne has worked hard to foster throughout the agency, Angela and Matthew seek her counsel. Neither supervisor nor therapist is aware that the other has sought out Leanne, and she maintains their privacy until both agree there is need for open discussion among the three regarding the supervision relationship. Leanne then sets a time for all three of them to sit down for a safe, collaborative conversation that focuses on supporting a more open supervisory relationship without negative repercussions. The result of this and subsequent meetings is a step toward a more positive supervisory relationship that benefits everyone—supervisor, therapist, clients, and agency. Both Angela and Matthew became more transparent. Matthew openly shared his apprehension and reticence to disclose in supervision, while Angela took a bold step to flatten the supervision hierarchy by sharing her personal struggles with anger around Louis's situation and how it has affected her supervisory relationship with Matthew.

The struggles Angela and Matthew experienced also affected Leanne and the agency's policies. The fact that conflicts existed was clear after therapist and supervisor contacted her for personal and administrative counsel. It was also evident to Leanne that the agency's policies dictating open disclosure between supervisor and therapist were paternalistic and outdated. Simply mandating therapist transparency was not sufficient; she saw that the culture and the policies needed to be reviewed with the intent of creating more open communication in supervisory relationships while decreasing fear of reprisal. This led to the formation of a committee that involved administrators, supervisors, and therapists, charging the group to elicit ideas and experiences with the goal of compressing the hierarchy and encouraging fuller disclosure within supervisory relationships.

3. *Overlapping Influences of Circles C and D*

The least flexible system in this schema is the entity I have called the governmental/associational. Few would disagree with the assessment that this theater grants the least input from individual, interactional/relational, and local systems; however, it is not above influence. Recent hiring policies within the VA in the USA (AAMFT 2012) suggest local institutions and individuals can impact a monolithic and seemingly impervious structure.

Leanne's momentum is carried over to this intersection in the diagram, the overlap between local institution and larger governmental/associational bodies. For her, the impetus for change within the agency was due in part to struggles with funding sources, including the VA. It was clear that supervisory relationships needed redefining to move toward greater openness and collaboration; at the same time, some of the strains within the agency, from clients to administration, were tied to no reimbursable time demands. Leanne recognized the importance of interfacing with VA officials was tied to the long-term sustainability of Glen Rose, so she decided to take a bold step. She requested meetings with local VA officials tied to the agency's case management as well as those connected to disability status changes. Her question that was to begin this conversation was quite simple: how can Glen Rose and the VA streamline communications to save agency and federal time and dollars? It was clear that the VA was working hard to communicate with the agency and that Glen Rose administration and staff were completely cooperative with the process, so the initial meeting was viewed as a start toward mutually beneficial adjustments. Over the course of the next year, monthly meetings were arranged, and through time, fewer and fewer staff from both entities attended as communication processes were streamlined. The results of this time-limited conversation were clearly win-win. The VA was investing fewer work hours in case management due to increased respect for Glen Rose's services. Billing was simplified because of enhanced relationships built on trust; short phone calls between colleagues at the VA and Glen Rose led to fewer redundancies. From the Glen Rose perspective, work hours were optimized as cooperation increased. VA case managers carefully considered the client outcome data Glen Rose had continuously collected on their mutual cases and began reconsidering their (unnecessarily) limiting standards of "evidence-based practices." It was clear that open access to client files, continuous consultation, and Glen Rose's use of standardized outcome measures providing evidence of efficacy swayed the case managers and decreased oversight. This reduced Glen Rose therapist work hours dedicated to case management and increased their ability to provide services to VA clients and to the community at large.

4. *Overlapping Influences of Circles D and A*

This overlap is perhaps easiest to conceptualize unidirectionally, with nearly all power of influence centered in the governmental/associational sphere and little to none with the individual. Government licensing agencies and professional organizations often elicit citizen/member input when policy decisions are made, and testimonies from some individuals have had significant impact. But the usual direction of influence is unilateral: if you choose to be licensed (government) or maintain membership (association), you must abide by the standards, rules, and regulations of these centrally located entities.

However, a quote attributed to anthropologist Margaret Mead comes to mind: "Never doubt that a small group of thoughtful, committed citizens can change the

2.1 Systems: Conceptualizing the Supervision Context

world. Indeed, it is the only thing that ever has" (Keyes 2006, p. xvi). Groundswell change is possible and even predictable. Single cases change national law, as in the US Supreme Court landmark decision *Roe v. Wade* (1973). In my home state of Texas, a single case set the stage for a significant Texas Supreme Court case regarding confidentiality for mental health professionals. In their decision on *Tharpar v. Zezulka* (1999), the court created a different standard for reporting dangerous behavior than the more widely known standard set by the California Supreme Court known as the Tarasoff decision (*Tarasoff v. Regents of the University of California*, 1976). Simply put, *Tarasoff* requires California licensed mental health professionals to report dangerous behavior; *Tharpar* allows the mental health professional latitude in the decisions surrounding potential threat of harm to another, as the Texas court ruled, in effect, that there is no duty to warn potential victims. The simple difference between "must warn" (Tarasoff) and "may warn" (Tharpar) creates a vast disparity. Both decisions hinged on single cases of individuals who sought justice, with resulting changes in precedent and current law.

Referring to the last elaboration of our extended example, Leanne and her VA counterparts managed to influence a small corner of a large federal bureaucracy by locating points of common interest, creating trusting and mutually beneficial relationships, and using existing ambiguities in federal procedures. In the end, all sought to benefit their clients; the outcome benefitted all parties. It is true that the VA and Glen Rose streamlined services without loss of quality or effectiveness. In addition, Marine client Louis was sought out by the local VA officials for consultation on the service delivery process. Though unexpected, Louis embraced the opportunity to openly discuss his struggles *and* successes, including Glen Rose case managers in the process. The results were impressive: Louis's therapeutic gains increased and his disability appeals met fewer roadblocks. His statements and ongoing consultation with local officials paved the way for other area veterans seeking assistance, a far-reaching outcome.

My intention in creating a story-based section on systems thinking is simple: for me, theory or paradigm without application is (at best) mere speculation or (at worst) mere mental exercise. Ways of thinking in the social sciences must include pragmatics if they are to be clinically relevant. It is not enough to have an understanding or explanation; we have too many nosologies classifying mental disorders and theories ascribing their origins and causes. The best theories in our field are constructive, leading one beyond explanation to action and change. Systems thinking is seminal to creating contexts of change and acting contextually.

Finally, I believe it is not enough to know about systems in the supervisory process; one must learn to participate systemically. Heinz von Foerster, a pioneer of cybernetic/systems thinking and application, often spoke of observer experiences regarding systems. He simplified the possible experiences to four states or abilities:

I see that I see (self-reflexivity)
I see that I don't see (self-awareness)
I don't see that I see (self-ignorance)
I don't see that I don't see (self-deception) (H. von Foerster, personal communication, July 27, 1997)

I call the first state self-reflexivity: "I see that I see." This acknowledges one's ability to perceive system organization and interaction. Whether one believes systems exist "in the wild" (independent of observers) or only in the experience of the observer, having this perceptual ability allows one to discern and participate systemically. If I see that I see, I can map a system's activity and influence it. At the same time, awareness of this ability allows me the opportunity to reflect on the system's influence on *me* and *my* experience—systems, by definition, affect all parts of the whole.

The second position, "I see that I don't see," is not a negative state. If I acknowledge that I am not able to discern/create pattern across time when viewing or participating in interaction, I can take steps to learn. I call this state self-awareness—I know what I perceive and I also am aware of what I do not recognize, opening the door for new possibilities in experience. Many have read about systems or sat behind one-way mirrors and observed interactional therapy, eventually coming to see systemic activity and influence. Not unlike learning how to see the hidden images within magic eye images (Magic Eye 2012), I believe most motivated persons can learn to perceive some types of systemic interaction.

I refer the third state as self-ignorance. "I don't see that I see" can be a common state prior to learning and/or experience in a context that identifies such abilities. My most frequent experiences with persons who come to identify that they already perceive systemically have happened with those from cultures in which the independence of the individual is emphasized less than familial or cultural identity. "Oh, you call it *that*!" is a familiar phrase I have heard spoken by students from Chinese, Taiwanese, Indian, Japanese, Nigerian, and other cultures when they encounter systems thinking. Many already perceive systemically because it is their culture's usual epistemology. Their commonality is that they already think, perceive, and participate in life as more than individual, more collectivist in their identity and interaction than many from Western countries. One student from Japan who had lived in the USA for more than 5 years said it brilliantly: "When one of you (European American peers in the class) fail an exam, the first thing you think is, 'How will this affect *me*?' The first thought I have is, 'How will this affect my *family*?'"

It is only this fourth state that holds peril. "I don't see that I don't see" is a denial of one's lack of ability to perceive systemically. I have experienced interactions with people who purport to have the ability to think and act systemically but simply don't recognize patterns other systemically oriented people identify. I believe this is a form of self-deception, compounded by the necessity for those persons to convince others that they *do* perceive interactional pattern and that no one *else* can see what they see. Unfortunately, I have experienced this phenomenon among those who choose to identify themselves as systemic supervisors and therapists, professionals who identify as systemic, teach systems orientation, and supposedly supervise from this epistemological stance. The confusion among students, trainees, and therapists is difficult to rectify when dishonesty is promoted by one in power.

Of course, I believe self-reflexivity is the desired perceptual ability. Awareness and deliberate practice can lead to shifts in perception, but such shifts do not come about simply by force of will or dedicated effort. Most pattern recognition is unconscious (Bateson 1979), so it cannot be directly addressed. However, changes in systemic perception are caught more than taught, so practicing one's viewing with other systems-oriented people often affords the best opportunity to nurture perceptual change from linear to systemic.

2.2 The Idea of Isomorphism in Supervision and Therapy

2.2.1 *Isomorphic Applications: SF Supervision with Those Practicing SF Approaches*

"As clinical training programs change, it is being discovered that a theory of therapy and a theory of training are often synonymous" (Haley 1976, p. 170). The primary source of this concept probably stems from the psychodynamic idea of parallel process and structure (Bernard and Goodyear 2009), but the most common use of the term within the field of family therapy was first developed by Liddle and his colleagues (Liddle and Saba 1985, 1983).

The idea of isomorphism was not invented by the field of mental health. It is a principle applied in many disciplines with actual and metaphorical applications. Physicist and cognitive scientist Douglas Hofstadter (1999, p. 49) articulates the concept.

> The word "isomorph" applies when two complex structures can be mapped onto each other in such a way that to each part of one structure there is a corresponding part in the other structure, where "corresponding" means that the two parts play similar roles in their respective structures.

When discussing family therapy supervision, White and Russell (1997, p. 317) define it this way:

> Isomorphism refers to the phenomenon whereby categories with different contents, but similar form, can be mapped on each other in such a way that there are corresponding parts and processes within each structure. When this occurs, these parallel structures can be described as isomorphic, and each is an isomorph of the other. Therefore, when the supervisory system is mapped onto the therapeutic system, the roles of supervisor and supervisee correspond to those of the therapist and client, respectively.

According to Liddle and his colleagues (1984), isomorphism is a systemic concept—each isomorph affects the other in a recursive relationship of mutual influence. White and Russell (1997) discuss the concept as having perceptual, conceptual, and participatory components.[5] Here is how they describe the "facets" of isomorphism:

- Facet 1: *Identifying Repetitive or Similar Patterns*. "This facet of isomorphism refers to the phenomenon of identifying similar patterns that occur across various systems," especially the supervisory and therapeutic systems that could include

---

[5] See Chap. 4 on practices for supervisory uses of these distinctions.

a practicum group or agency (p. 317). This notes the perceptual aspect within supervision and therapy (in this case, the ability to identify pattern).
- Facet 2: *Translation of Therapeutic Models and Principles into Supervision.* When therapists are learning SFBT, SF supervision is a clear fit with this facet. Most publications on SF supervision over the past two decades targeted this conceptual facet, seeking to translate the assumptions and practices of SF therapy to guide SF supervision (Marek, Sandifer, Beach, Coward, and Protinsky 1994; Thomas 1996; Wetchler 1990).
- Facet 3: *The Structure and Process of Therapy and Supervision Are Identical.* Supervision theoreticians, researchers, and practitioners have promoted this facet in family therapy supervision for many years. One might argue with the idea of a perfect one-to-one correspondence or match between the therapeutic and supervisory approaches, given the general agreement that supervision must include educational components, professional orientation, and other nontherapeutic requirements. However, SF supervision is usually an excellent fit for therapists learning the SF approach.
- Facet 4: *Isomorphism as an Interventive Stance.* White and Russell (1997) note the interventive nature of modernist supervision, identifying the intentionality of supervisors to direct changes in therapist behavior to improve skills and (supposed) client outcomes. As a postmodern approach, SF supervision is less impositional and more collaborative, focusing less on intervention and more on the identification and development of various participatory skills. However, since one cannot not influence, supervisory modeling, discussion, and instruction will have a direct influence on therapists' day-to-day practice.

If both the supervisor and therapist seek to apply SF assumptions and practices, the concept of isomorphism can be very useful for learning SF supervision. Identifying and applying SF assumptions plus practicing skills acquired as a SF therapist is a common path for SF supervisors.

2.2.1.1 Hierarchy

By definition, therapist and client roles contrast in the therapeutic context; in parallel fashion, supervisors and therapists have differing roles and responsibilities. Within a SF approach, both supervisor and therapist seek to flatten hierarchy and promote collaboration. Reinforcing SF supervision values articulated earlier in this chapter, this is perhaps the quintessential presupposition that distinguishes a SF supervision approach from modernist, hierarchical supervisory designs.

> Solution-focused supervision seeks to set up a cooperative, goal-oriented relationship that assumes that the therapist possesses strength, ability, and resourcefulness to resolve a complaint and achieve training goals. It naturally follows that the supervisor is not the expert on the therapist's situation—the supervisor defines the goals, directions, and options *with* the therapist to construct a participatory experience through consensus and teamwork. (Thomas 1996, p. 131, emphasis in original)

Differences in power do not disappear by defining or wishing them away (Bobele, Gardner, and Biever 1995). This is especially relevant when considering power in a supervisor/therapist relationship. Neither supervisors nor therapists unilaterally decide the nature and politics of the supervisory relationship. When both are in agreement that hierarchy should be reduced or even minimized, the next step is to discuss areas of concurrence and divergence. As much as supervisors may wish to create an atmosphere of collaboration, they still carry responsibilities therapists do not. Referring back to Diagram 2.1, Circles D (governmental/associational) and C (organizational) overlap the individual supervisor's personal system and restrict role definitions and behaviors. Therefore, SF supervisors create transparency in the supervisor–therapist system/relationship and expose the limitations imposed by larger, more encompassing systems within which both professionals work. Promoting transparency, for me, is not a declaration ("OK, we're going to be transparent now"). Openness is supported when supervisors initiate and demonstrate it. Most public information can be shared with therapists in written form, much like informed consent documents clients receive (see Appendix A for further discussion on and examples of transparent practices). In addition, periodic check-ins regarding clarity of expectations and requirements can be a collaborative experience if supervisors create an expectation set through initiating such conversations.

The following ideas, relationships, and practices are isomorphic when supervisor and therapist are working from a SF stance. Keep in mind that these are ideals, not absolutes; there are times when supervisor/therapist associations, like therapist/client relationships, do not fit the ideal. For ways to think and act from a SF approach when encountering obstacles, see the section on supervising non-SF therapists below.

2.2.1.2 Living in the Present While Utilizing the Past and Focusing on the Future

A SF stance holds to the importance of three distinct time periods—past, present, and future—but privileges a future orientation. While other supervisory approaches may focus on past events, motivations, and historical influences, SF supervision with SF therapists emphasizes current success experience and future activity based on recent successes. In addition, SF approaches are goal-oriented, so cooperative SF supervision should involve clear therapist goal setting. In addition, SF supervisors may choose to engage in an interactional focus on goals that addresses the process and desired results of supervision itself. Both therapist and therapist/supervisor goal setting reinforce the value of all three chronological categories: hindsight (drawing from past successes), insight (making sense of experience in the moment), and foresight (planning future actions).

2.2.1.3 Therapists Know Their Own Experiences Better than Supervisors

In cooperative SF supervision as in SF therapy, therapists are the experts on their experiences. In SF therapy, the therapist assumes the client knows herself better than anyone else, has the privileged position on the details and meanings of her experiences, and knows what is best for her. In parallel, SF supervisors assume the therapist is the expert on her own experiences, values, intentions, motivation, and abilities. While imposition is on a continuum, minimizing supervisory directives and declaratives sets SF apart from other approaches. Of course, there are moments when supervisors must insist on particular behaviors from a therapist or alter the direction of therapy, but such impositions are exceptional.

Supporting therapists as the experts on their personal experiences differs from the SF assumption that clients are the experts in their lives in at least one important way: therapists do not have privileged knowledge about *therapy* (Gardner, Bobele, and Biever 1997). While clients are assumed to have the final say on how they experience life and the meaning they have created from events, privileging therapists' views of the therapist/client relationship or allowing conclusions drawn by the clinician concerning the *relationship* diminishes the viewpoint of the client. Also, knowledge about therapy—its guiding ideas, assumptions, and practices—is not merely personal knowledge. When it comes to what *is* a SF approach, I return to the concept of appropriate knowing discussed in Chap. 1. And there is also the gestalt of what constitutes "good" when the therapist's performance and client outcome are assessed. Supervisors have views usually informed by practice, consultation, education, and research that cannot be subjugated by therapists' in-the-room experiences with clients. It is hard to imagine a supervisor who privileges a therapist's view that therapy "went well" simply because she or he believes it went well. Clients' views, first and foremost, hold primary importance regarding the outcome of therapy; if the client's view differs from the therapist's, one should assume the client is right.

2.2.1.4 A Small Change Is All That's Necessary

As in the systems discussion above, this assumption defines SF and systems viewpoints about change. Rather than rooting out causes or correcting erroneous thoughts or behaviors, the SF approach takes the view that a small change can (and usually will) result in larger changes. There is a parallel assumption: change in one context will often produce changes in another overlapping context. It is therefore necessary for supervisors to recognize the effects therapy practice has on therapists because change is multidirectional and nonlineal—changes experienced by therapists in the psychotherapy context may affect supervision (and supervisors) as much as differences produced in the supervision context affect the contexts in which therapists practice. These changes can be purposeful (such as progress therapists make toward their supervision goals) or nonpurposeful (including the effects of client tragedy on therapist and supervisor alike), and it is often difficult to gauge or predict the impact such changes will create (de Shazer 1985).

This assumption brings with it an ethic of caution: since everything that happens in supervision may create ramifying changes, all supervision practices should be carefully considered. I do not assume all changes will be favorable, as that would simply be Pollyanna thinking (Thomas 2007a). The best preventative measure to guard against unexamined change is supervisory transparency with continuous assessment. Within

2.2 The Idea of Isomorphism in Supervision and Therapy

the SF tradition, assessment is built into the goal-setting process, usually in the form of scaling personal goals (De Jong and Berg 2012). Openness about experiences of change outside of articulated goals should be a consistent aspect of supervision, with discussion of these unanticipated changes becoming a normal part of supervision meetings.

2.2.1.5 The Supervisor's Task Is to Identify and Amplify Desired Change

As stated above, the value placed on small changes that lead to larger changes is contextual. So part of supervision involves casting a wide net on change processes, identifying as many changes as possible without assigning relevance beforehand. Often novice therapists dismiss changes they have noticed or inflate the importance of other changes unless supervisors invite a more inclusive dialogue about what therapists have observed or experienced. To extend the fishing metaphor, the sorting of relevant from less relevant should take place after the entire haul is dumped on the deck and not prior to bringing the net full of sea life to the surface.

Several methods encourage such transparency, but the supervisor must avoid a solution-forced approach and seek out information besides discussions of "what's better." These are further developed in Chaps. 3 and 4, but one prominent SF technique is asking "what else?" (Iveson 2005) about areas besides positive exceptions, goal progress, and successes. In addition to asking about "what's better?", I ask about other changes regarding clients, contexts, and the person of the therapist that may be experienced as negative or confusing. After each therapist response I ask, "what else?" to invite thorough disclosure of insights or experiences. I have found this practice draws forth experiences and tentative questions from therapists better than any procedures that probe for specifics.

Once positive changes have been identified, the supervisor's charge is to amplify change. This is not cheerleading; it is a process that assists the therapist in making sense of these changes by investigating agency and meaning. Amplification is a process of calling attention to an event and reviewing it in the supervisory context. It involves questions around self-perception, other's perceptions of the therapist, and the significance of the change. Looking at one's role in the changes one experiences opens the door for the person to understand the role he or she played in the change process itself. One need not force significance in this process; originally tied to reinforcement, amplification has evolved into a more reflective practice in SF circles.

2.2.1.6 Curiosity Should Direct Supervisory Inquiry

Little more needs to be said regarding curiosity, as it has been thoroughly developed in the previous chapter. It is one of the central aspects of the SF supervisors' stance, guiding the structure and direction of supervision sessions.

An illustration may clarify several of these principles. Therapist James has been struggling with feelings of inadequacy related to a case he inherited from a therapist peer who resigned unexpectedly from the work setting. The client, Nancy, was well-known across the organization as one who demanded and took advantage of many services they had to offer, including legal assistance, social worker intervention with local and state agencies, access to the food pantry, and mental health services for most of her family members. James felt trapped in an advocate position at times, as Nancy appealed for him to persuade others to assist her when she was denied additional time or services, a role her previous therapist zealously accepted. Supervisor Claudia met with James at his request for special time to discuss this case:

James: I've been there…you know, where she's at. There was a time when I was the one needing services and pleading with anyone who would listen to me to intervene so I could get what I thought I needed. But the thing that changed *my* life and pushed *me* toward independence was when people stopped helping me and made me stand up for myself. I don't think it's good for Nancy when I become her "knight in shining armor" and ride to the rescue when people tell her "no." But since her last therapist did all this for her, she expects me to do the same.

Claudia: How do you know she expects this? *(This is a question from a position of curiosity, not a challenge or attempt to deconstruct James' experience or understanding.)*

James: Well, she calls me and demands or pleads with me.

Claudia: So, you know what she does and your reactions to it make sense to me… sounds tough. *(Claudia does not immediately begin processing James' feelings or question his conclusions about Nancy's expectations.)*

James: I don't have a clue what to do here…I know I'm not Nancy and how I got out of my hole isn't the way she'll do it, but…I don't know what to do here.

Claudia: Yeah, sounds messy and full of conflicts…Would it be OK with you if I asked you a few questions? *(Note: She seeks permission, promoting collaboration.)*

James: Sure.

Claudia: Some might not seem directly related to this thing with Nancy, but I'd like to know a few things that might be related. *(Curiosity)*

James: Fire away!

Claudia: Tell me about a time when you spoke openly with a client about your therapy relationship and it went pretty well. *(Exception talk—presupposes James has had parallel experiences with a greater sense of success in the past)*

James: (Talks about a recent case in which he felt progress had not been made and the client had not shown for several appointments; the in-session discussion with the client resulted in new goal setting as well as appointment times that fit better with the client's family obligations.)

Claudia: How did you do that? How did you start that conversation? *(Amplification—requesting reflective thought and conversation about a success)*

James: Well, I don't know…I guess I thought about his lack of progress and how his no-showing affected both progress and others on my calendar…

Claudia: And what came out of that? *(Curiosity)*

2.2 The Idea of Isomorphism in Supervision and Therapy   53

James: Part of the change was with me…I found out some of my assumptions were wrong. He no-showed because he had to take care of his kids last minute when his wife got called into work. And our goals were partly my goals, you know, him becoming more independent…

Claudia: OK, thinking about that success, are there parts of it that might relate here? *(Amplification—she asks him to consider possibilities of connections rather than telling him what might be common to both cases.)*

James: Yeah…maybe some of this is what I want for Nancy, like the way I kinda talked my other client into working on things that were more important to me than to him.

Claudia: How might that fit here?

James: It might be my goal for Nancy to be "independent" (makes air quotes with his hands).

Claudia: Might be… *(Remaining tentative)*

James: I guess maybe I need to start talking with her about my caught-ness rather than just continuing the way her last therapist did…and not assume she expects me to do it or that it's somehow getting in her way of becoming more independent.

Claudia: OK, maybe…if you *did* talk about this, what do you bring from that other client success into this situation? *(Collaboration—suggesting the possibility of change begets change or the ripple effect)*

James: I know I *can* have tough discussions with clients because I *have*. And, I know I need to put the client's goals ahead of my own ideas of what she should do.

Claudia: I like this. Now, if you were to take these ideas into a future therapy session with Nancy, how would you do that?

(Claudia continues a "what else?" conversation that draws from other success experiences in James' professional life in which he had honest discussions with clients and experienced positive change in the therapeutic relationship and in his own attitudes and behaviors with those clients. James leaves the supervision session energized, with personal experiences from which he can draw and ideas on how he might begin some difficult conversations with Nancy while remaining open to personal change.)

This conversation exemplifies several cooperative SF supervisory ideas including the focus on therapist knowledge of self, the optimal use of exceptions, a focus on future possibilities more than past failures, amplifying small successes, and supervisor attempts to work collaboratively and minimize hierarchy. But hopefully it also embodies Claudia's honoring of James' experiences and associated meanings. Claudia could have pointed out James' assumptions concerning his client Nancy and challenged his conclusions about her motivations. She also could have engaged James in a review of his own experiences as one receiving services, reviewing gender or cultural assumptions embedded in his viewpoints. Instead, in keeping with notion that "the therapist knows his experience best," Claudia became curious about other success experiences from which James could draw. She honored his conclusions in a way that did not say "It's good you arrived at the right understandings and learned the lesson here." She created conversational space in which James could safely contemplate future directions as well as consider ways he might adjust and change.

2.2.2 Non-isomorphic Applications: SF Supervision with Those Practicing Other Psychotherapy Models and Approaches (Ungar 2006; Weir 2009)

Some supervisors work in positions that allow them complete autonomy when choosing their therapist-supervisees. Others have fewer choices, including those who serve as supervisors for university practicum classes or clinics, mental health agencies, or government institutions and may be assigned therapists for supervision by someone higher on the organizational chart. Still others have the freedom to supervise only those who match with their philosophy or approach but choose not to exercise that freedom for a variety of reasons, including geographic necessity (e.g., few supervisors available in the area) or ethical positions (e.g., the ethical obligation to mentor new licensees).

One of the first questions facing the SF supervisor is, "Must the therapist be learning SFBT for SF supervision to be effective?" Some may believe therapist and supervisor models must match for optimal supervision outcome, but this is more of a philosophical stance than one informed by research. Wheeler and Richards (2007) reviewed one study (Steinhelber, Patterson, Cliffe, and LeGoullon 1984) that found an interesting association, concluding that in this research "congruence of theoretical orientation between supervisor and trainee supervisee was related to patient change" (Wheeler and Richards 2007, p. 63). On the other hand, researchers focusing more on the supervisor-therapist alliance point out that the strength of the alliance, a vital component in supervision success, does not require agreement on models or approaches (Cheon, Blumer, Shih, Murphy, and Sato 2009). Considering the scarcity of research, other paths to investigating this question need to be explored.

In an attempt to be sensitive to the "no cloning" preference expressed by supervisees (Thomas and Shappee 2001) and the ethical commitment to avoid imposing one's will on another (Atkinson and Heath 1990), I propose that understanding and awareness of the supervisor's authority plus acknowledging the unavoidable nature of influence may be the best protective measures for guarding against forcing one's approach on therapists. After all, SF approaches have a legacy of avoiding "solution-forced" practices (Nyland and Corsiglia 1994).

2.2.2.1 Coercive, Mimetic, and Normative Isomorphism and Supervisor—Therapist Model Incongruity

Weir (2009) provides an important conceptual tool for this discussion. He expands the concept of isomorphism in supervision while criticizing the narrow definitions created within the field. Weir explores different reasons for isomorphism's occurrence, including

2.2 The Idea of Isomorphism in Supervision and Therapy

coercive, mimetic, and normative influences, each allowing a different therapist agency. Coercive isomorphism occurs in part because of the psychotherapy industry's impact on education and training. The idea of evidence-supported practices (or EST) is often endorsed by people or movements in the field who receive the greatest research funding, and this unfortunately has replaced a broader pluralism in our approaches (Slife, Wiggins, and Graham 2005). Instead of a variety of practices and research regarding client outcome, empiricism and economics drive the field and eliminate diversity of practice. Supervision is affected by this push toward uniformity when funding sources require the practice of particular models rather than effective practices. What Weir (2009) calls normative isomorphism "stems from the professionalization of the field" (p. 70). Licensure, educational accreditation, and other influences pressure therapists to enter the field by meeting the same minimal standards, which directs and limits practice options. Finally, Weir writes about mimetic isomorphism, or the tendency for novice therapists to mimic supervisors' ways of thinking, perceiving, and acting. This is perhaps the dominant understanding of isomorphism within psychotherapy—as you learn, you practice, so the methods you witness are the techniques you will apply.

My reasoning for including Weir's (2009) distinctions in this section is tied to supervisor agency: even though supervisors cannot not influence therapists, *how* one influences can be modified. In my view, SF supervisors have options they can exercise in supervision regarding discussion of these three isomorphic trends and modeling practices related to these trends. Regarding coercive isomorphism, SF supervisors can stand against the pressure toward uniformity by assigning readings like Weir (2009), Slife and his colleagues (Slife 2005, 2004; Slife and Gantt 1999; Slife et al. 2005), and Wampold and his associates (Ahn and Wampold 2001; Wampold, Imel, and Miller 2009) as a part of therapists' education. There are also alternatives to the "party line" of EST (often invented and perpetuated by the non-professional media) featuring SFBT research that can be promoted in supervision, including the critically acclaimed research books by Franklin, Trepper, McCollum, and Gingerich (2012) and Macdonald (2007b).

Normative isomorphism can be openly discussed with therapists as a part of professional identity development (Weir 2009). When paired with a non-SF therapist, SF supervisors can practice their assumptions and techniques transparently. While some models of supervision stress parallel process (which is largely unconscious or assumed), SF supervisors work to flatten hierarchy and build collaboration, which opens up discussion and builds supervisory alliances while at the same time pushing against a passive process of cloning.

Encouraging therapists to set observable and measurable goals within their practice model means SF practices are additional rather than substitutionary or exclusive in the supervisor–therapist interaction. Mimetic isomorphism is unavoidable, but therapists may find certain questions or techniques in supervision useful with their clients. These would be adjunctive to therapists' primary, non-SF models, increasing therapists' choices for imitation or adaptation. Supervisors model behaviors that are atheoretical (such as active listening and purposeful use of silence in session), and therapists adopt and modify these practices whatever the supervisors' guiding theory is. Supervisors working from a SF approach offer alternatives to model-specific techniques that therapists may implement. Finally, following the SF assumption that supervisors should adjust to therapists' styles, needs, and goals, modeling non-SF techniques and role playing with therapists who are targeting specific non-SF skills will be met with enthusiasm.

2.2.2.2 Postmodern Supervisors' Roles When Supervisor and Therapist Approaches Do Not Match

In his 2006 article, Ungar outlined six role constructions performed by postmodern supervisors: supporter, supervisor, case consultant, trainer/teacher, colleague, and advocate. All of these roles deserve reflective thought, but I believe four of these are very relevant in this discussion, as a common mismatch between SF supervisor and non-SF therapist might also involve an incongruity between a supervisor using a postmodern approach and a more traditional therapist.

Supporter. Whatever the theoretical orientations of the participants are, supervisors assume a role of emotional supporter in the relationship.

> Within the bounds of the code of ethics, this role means that supervision explores emotional hurdles faced by a supervisee that relate to issues beyond his or her immediate work, without necessarily being so intrusive as to lead to the dual relationship of the supervisor becoming the supervisee's therapist. (Ungar 2006, p. 61)

Care and concern for the person of the therapist are vital in supervision. Since strong alliance is a key factor for supervision success, compassionate connections must be made and maintained without consideration of theory or model.

Supervisor. Ungar's emphasis on this supervisor role involves a focus on the supervisee's role as therapist. Supervisors are committed to helping the therapist become the "best clinician he or she can, drawing on the talents and abilities unique to that person" (p. 61). SF supervisors are at their best when functioning in this role. The SF emphasis on resources and strengths is atheoretical; in fact, those practicing this postmodern approach delight when therapists discover successes and abilities. In SF supervision, the relevance of a resource is connected to the therapist's goals; that is, resources do not exist apart from person and context. Helping therapists experience optimal performance is a primary focus of SF supervision, and theoretical congruence has little impact on supervisors' abilities to assist in this process.

Case Consultant. Ungar emphasizes the supervisor's role to provide "best practice options" (p. 61) when consulting on a particular case or session. Although therapists' models may guide conceptualization and intervention, additional options that were not obvious to the sole practitioner can be generated in conversation. SF supervisors need to develop the ability to shift between positions of expertise ("temporary certainty") and curiosity (Stewart 2003; cf. Stewart and Amundson 1995) when in case consultation, as they can alternately offer guidance on additional ways of intervening and remain curious about therapists' abilities to implement different practices plus the therapists' views on whether or not such practices would be appropriate with their clients.

2.2 The Idea of Isomorphism in Supervision and Therapy

Colleague. Ungar (2006) points out the obvious "share(d) clinical responsibilities" supervisors have with the therapist. Clients require and deserve the assistance this team approach can offer, and this common goal encourages a flattening of hierarchy and sharing of power (p. 61). Since both professionals in this relationship are concerned and committed to assisting clients, collaborating on methods and generating a united effort will provide the best results. The SF supervision tenet of respect is particularly relevant when one acts as a colleague. Assisting clients is not about models or theories, nor should it be. If mental health professionals practice as though they are in the therapy business and forget that they are actually in the helping business, clients lose (Miller and Hubble 2006).

Vicki is a therapist and supervisor who practices SF approaches in an agency that assigns supervision relationships. Policy states newly licensed therapists, novice therapists who are temporarily licensed, doctoral interns, and master's-level practicum students from multiple educational backgrounds must be supervised by more seasoned agency professionals, and the mixture is so diverse that theoretical orientations are not taken into account when supervisors and therapists are matched for the year. As a result, Vicki rarely works with therapists seeking to learn the SFBT approach. Her frustration could have created rifts, but instead she decided to adapt Unger's (2006) ideas and apply them in each supervision relationship.

Last year, Vicki was paired with three staff for supervision: a psychologist who practiced cognitive–behavioral therapy (CBT) exclusively, a master's-level social work practicum student who stated she used a client-centered or Rogerian approach, and a family therapy doctoral intern who practiced narrative and collaborative therapies (Anderson and Gehart 2006; Malinen, Cooper, and Thomas 2011). She met with each therapist individually and discussed her supervision philosophy while getting to know each of them as people and as mental health professionals. Vicki discovered in the first few weeks of meetings that there were more commonalities among and between the four of them than she had imagined. All the therapists had stated desires to become supervisors and wanted to learn about supervision from Vicki. Even though the three therapists had contrasting theories, many of their practice skills were similar. Also, all three were beginning therapists with little clinical experience (Dreyfus and Dreyfus 2005; Skovholt, Rønnestad, and Jennings 1997; Thomas 2000). Finally, there was a mutual commitment to clinical excellence and change that was sensitive to culture and family. Using Unger's (2006) role constructions to guide her own personal goal setting in supervision for the year, she decided to approach the three therapists with a proposal: in addition to weekly individual supervision, she proposed the four of them meet as a collaborative, multiperspective supervision team once a month for case consultation and once a month for supervision discussion. Vicki then asked each of them to read Unger's 2006 article and give her feedback on how she could best perform in each of the six supervisor roles.

The result could not have been better for all four professionals. From the creativity of the group emerged shared supervision desires that affected each supervision pairing as well as the group. Vicki's own goal-setting process was positively impacted as she worked to meet specific expectations and needs instead of general personal skill development. The group's thinking and conversation also moderated each therapist's goal-setting process. Listening to others' ideas and goals encouraged a more realistic individual goal-setting process. At the same time, goal possibilities were expanded because ambitions communicated by one person had not been imagined by others. The CBT-oriented psychologist set goals involving client–therapist relationship skills that he might have never considered without the group's discussion. While the social work practicum student had very limited exposure to approaches other than Rogerian, she established a goal to read, learn, and practice SF-related questions that she felt fit within her theoretical frame. Finally, the narrative/collaborative practices family therapist decided to team up with the psychology intern and learn possible uses for psychological testing and applying these ideas in postmodern ways.

Meanwhile, Vicki embraced emerging ideas she felt were particularly relevant to her practice as supervisor. Using Ungar's (2006) concepts, she articulated goals as supporter, supervisor, case consultant, and colleague to fit with each individual therapist's expressed needs and desires. Then she outlined goals and methods to address group supervision requests in the trainer/teacher, colleague, and advocate roles. Throughout the year, Vicki's goals shifted among role constructions in all relationship settings. But in retrospect, she found that her commitment to SF supervision principles and practices was even more profound as a result of her transparent, collaborative supervision experiences with these three professionals. Vicki found she could adapt SF concepts and methods without compromising her core assumptions. Her practice repertoire expanded, as she had to adjust to differing therapist approaches and skill levels. In addition, Vicki's commitment to openness and supporting the therapists' goals to learn about supervision forced her to rethink and more carefully articulate her own positions as she assumed the role of teacher. Finally, Vicki noticed she was actually *enjoying* the year's supervision. Although supervision meetings themselves and the preparation she required of herself taxed her schedule, the results were well worth the investment.

2.3 Concluding Thoughts on Systems and Isomorphism

This chapter covered basic systems thinking and many systemic applications related to SF supervision. While supervision has isomorphic connections to therapy, how such connections are created and sustained vary greatly from context to context. In an attempt to remain faithful to the SF legacy and my own systemic heritage, I decided to emphasize a way of thinking rather than create or articulate a theoretical model. As stated previously, this book is not intended to be a general supervision text. Instead, my purpose is to communicate and support a SF stance in supervision. Still, I could not write this book without including a discussion of systemic thinking and a re-examination of the concept of isomorphism in supervision.

There are some within SF circles who may discount the importance of exploring one's paradigmatic leanings, while other readers could not visualize a supervision book without some discussion of theoretical approach(es). I hope all readers found the discussion profitable.

Chapter 3
The Supervision Approach of Insoo Kim Berg, MSSW

Our job is to make them shine.

~ Insoo Kim Berg (Berg n.d.[circa 1997], SFBTA #10149-0074)

Insoo Kim Berg, MSSW (1934–2007) embodied the solution-focused (SF) approach. Her book with Peter De Jong (De Jong and Berg 2012) is one of the top-selling texts dedicated to solution-focused work, and few have traveled the globe providing training in this approach as much as she did over a nearly 30-year span. Videos of Insoo's therapy with individuals, couples, and families continue to provide illustration and inspiration for the current and future generations of mental health professionals, supervisors, business professionals, and educators.

In addition to her publications that address supervision and consultation, Insoo authored several unpublished manuscripts and handouts and provided workshops and in-house staff training on the topics. These documents and video recordings, contributions to the SFBTA Archive collection, provide additional information regarding her supervision ideas and practices that cannot be ignored.

3.1 Stance of the Supervisor

Insoo made it clear that one should take a modest, humble stance as a supervisor. She believed the very word "super-visor"…"denotes a relationship of expert and non-expert" and should be questioned (De Jong and Berg 2012, p. 280). At the same time, she promoted the value of supervision and supervisory relationships that "educate, mentor, nurture, and inspire" (De Jong and Berg 2012, p. 280). Insoo proposed that an isomorphic relationship exists between solution building with clients and SF supervision, stating that the assumptions and practices were "the same" (De Jong and Berg 2012, p. 280). Borrowing the phrase "parallel process" from the supervision literature, Insoo and her colleagues emphasized live, hands-on supervision practices (including shadowing therapists on home visits) that paralleled SF work with clients. Noticing successes and complimenting were specifically highlighted as valuable supervisory practices along with developing supervisory cooperation and focusing on therapist strengths and resources (De Jong, Kelly, Berg, and Gonzales 2012; Rudes, Shilts, and Berg 1997). "Insoo's guiding rule was this: 'Ask before you tell'" (Thomas 2012a, p. 347).

3.2 Value of Ongoing Supervision

> *Make sure that consultation and supervision is available to you.* The availability of formal or peer supervision/consultation on an ongoing basis is essential to you. Have brainstorming sessions with your colleagues on those "god-awful" cases and get someone else's opinion. Sometimes, it is reassuring to know that your colleagues or supervisors find these cases just as "awful" as you do (Berg 1994, p. 215, emphasis in original).

Insoo respected supervision as a lifelong practice. As a team member at BFTC, she was often the therapist everyone else observed from behind a one-way mirror or via a video feed. When sitting with her team of peers, she actively participated but was also very attentive to the contributions others made. Given the transitions the SF approach made from the late 1970s until her death in 2007, she showed a wide tolerance for differences of opinion, a clear agenda to assist clients, and continuous patience with the process of change. She consistently advised professionals to seek supervision or consultation on difficult cases and with "special problems" (Berg 1994, p. 19), which included (but were not limited to) sexual abuse, domestic violence, crisis management, multiproblem families, and alcohol/drug abuse. Insoo felt intrasession consultations with supervisors or peers were "helpful in enhancing the worker's objectivity by giving her some distance from the immediacy of the session." She also stated that consultations helped the therapist "recharge, collect her thoughts, and summarize her impressions" (Berg 1994, pp. 169–170).

3.3 Simplify

> *Out of intense complexities intense simplicities emerge.*
> ~ Winston Churchill

In an apocryphal story I have heard several times, Steve de Shazer was talking to a group about the SF approach's move to a more minimalist practice. To illustrate his point, he wrote Thoreau's famous phrase, "Simplify, Simplify, Simplify" on the whiteboard. Steve stood back and thought for a moment, focused on the words in front of him. Then he walked up to the whiteboard once more, crossed out the last two words, and said, "There."

Occam's Razor is a logical principle stating that "one should not increase, beyond what is necessary, the number of entities required to explain anything" (Heylighen

1997). This has been a major assumption of SF practices for many years and continues to guide changes in the approach worldwide (Thomas and Nelson 2007; see McKergow and Korman 2009). That Insoo subscribed to this principle is obvious from her writing on brief therapy and recorded statements about supervision. For example:

> What we do is so complex. But the more I work with (service professionals unacquainted with SF practices), the more I am realizing how you have to simplify it. And in order to simplify it, you really have to know what you're talking about.... You know, you really have to. It has to be in your bones...to be able to simplify for them.... They come up with these very complex situations they describe as, "Ah, this is not going to work, this postmodern stuff".... The longer I do this, the more I am appreciating the simplest, easiest way to explain things, absolutely jargon-free, so we're not using any big words but using the simplest words you can use, the most common words that you can use. (Berg n.d., [circa 1997], SFBTA Archive #10149-0074)

Insoo's conversation with this postmodern colleague discusses the need to teach and supervise using the simplest language possible. But she also states that learning the SF approach is *not simple*. Simplifying the notions and practices of the SF approach when supervising is not "dumbing it down." To the contrary, Insoo is proposing that SF trainers, educators, and supervisors appreciate the complexity of the application while communicating in the clearest ways possible.

While maintaining the assumption that one should keep it as simple as one can, Insoo also believed "simple" is not the same as "easy." She wrote, "Many people believe that because the basic premise of SFBT is so simple, it should be easy to do. They are surprised to find that a therapist must work very hard just to hang in there and not give up on clients" (Berg n.d., Hot Tips III, p. 2). When discussing therapists' abilities to notice positive exceptions and resources exhibited by acting-out adolescents, she offered this: "This ability to 'catch them being good,' sounds simple, but it takes a considerable degree of self-discipline and training" (Berg 2003, p. 56). Across time, Insoo taught and performed in a more minimalist fashion, adapting her style of practice to reflect her beliefs. At the same time, she recognized that some situations are more complex than others, requiring less-simple approaches. I think she would agree with Albert Einstein: "Everything should be as simple as it is, but not simpler" (Einstein 2012).

3.4 Hierarchy and Becoming Co-learners

Just like the relationship between client and therapist, Insoo recognized that the therapist/supervisor association is unequal and hierarchical. And while she placed some value on therapist motivation as a contributing factor, her major premise about learning in the supervision context was that reducing hierarchy created the possibility for better outcomes (Berg n.d., SFBTA Archive #10128-0064). Her style could be defined as learning through interaction, the creation of a co-learning environment in which curiosity drives the conversation and the context supports new possibilities and solutions (Rudes et al. 1997). Insoo would certainly agree with Bateson (1992, p. 41) that "participation precedes learning."

In one of her earliest recorded statements on supervision relationships, Insoo said, "some sort of negotiation would…be the beginning phase of a supervision contract… My first questions would be, What do you want to learn from me? What do you think you need (from me/supervision)?" (Berg, Friedman, Liddle, and Todd 1991). She advocated for supervisory relationships based on mutuality in most of her writing and speaking on the topic (Berg n.d., SFBTA Archive #10128-0064; Berg et al. 1991; Rudes et al. 1997) because she saw supervision as a reciprocally beneficial learning relationship.

Insoo related a story from early in her career as a supervisor that reveals a lifelong learner's orientation. In the early 1970s, she was approached by a male rabbi who wanted to learn more about psychotherapy:

> And here I was, a Korean lady. I don't know anything about Jewish culture or how to be a rabbi! I had a lot of nerve (becoming his supervisor)!…I just plunged right in and did it, and I learned more from him about Jewish culture. So in a way I see it (supervision) as an exchange of information. It's not just a one-way teaching…he taught me a great deal about how to be a rabbi…as well as what it means to be a Jew. And of course he learned a great deal from me about what it is to be a Korean in a white culture. (Berg et al. 1991)

3.5 "Leading from One Step Behind"

"Anybody can get concrete information (Cantwell and Holmes 1995). That's not hard. What's difficult is how to use the 'what,' the information you have…and that's where we are useful to the supervisee" (Berg n.d., SFBTA Archive #10128-0064). Insoo's approach to supervision created an encounter quite different from the experience of many therapists in supervision. A common supervision style that Insoo would oppose is what I call "therapy-once-removed." In this conventional approach to supervision, the supervisor requires a report from the therapist on a particular therapy session. During the therapist recitation, the supervisor corrects the therapist, stating what the therapist *should* have done to bring about a better outcome. At the completion of this speculative (and, for the therapist, often painful) dialogue, the supervisor directs future sessions with this client through suggestions and directives. This therapy-by-proxy style was purposefully avoided by Insoo whenever possible; instead of using the therapist as a middle person to impose an agenda, she led in a different way.

Continuing in the SF therapy tradition, Insoo stated that the best metaphor for optimal supervision was "leading from one step behind," a phrase adopted from Cantwell and Holmes (1994) and promoted in her work for more than a decade (Berg and De Jong 1996; De Jong and Berg 2012). Of course supervisors lead; most stakeholders (therapists, supervisors, accreditation bodies, etc.) hold this idea of leadership as a supervision expectation. However, Insoo's systems leanings are showing here: "when you lead from one step behind, then the therapist takes responsibility for his or her own learning" (Berg n.d., SFBTA Archive #10128-0064). She advocated for supervisors to encourage therapists to set agenda items and generate supervision topics. In this way, Insoo created a context of respect and shared power responsibility (Berg et al. 1991).

Insoo adopted many methods that contributed to collaboration in supervision. At times she was very frank in her directives to supervisors: "Avoid showing off how much you know" (Berg n.d., SFBTA Archive #10128-0064). But most of the methods she used when training supervisors and when conducting supervision were indirect and subtle as she attempted to create space for learning, differences of opinion, and respectful collegiality.

3.6 Goal Orientation

Insoo's commitment to therapists' goals in supervision is unquestioned. A natural parallel to setting client goals in therapy, she felt goal setting and cooperating with therapists' learning aims were crucial to supervision success (Berg et al. 1991). She also stated that while SF supervisors should form particular goals with each therapist, establishing and monitoring additional general goals for all therapists were the responsibility of the supervisor. Examples of general goals include boosting the competence of all staff members and developing therapist empathy for clients (Berg 2003, 199b; Berg et al. 1991; De Jong and Berg 2012).

In addition, Insoo wrote about administrative goals that supervisors set and monitored for the professionals they supervised:

> The supervisor focuses on worker's compliance with the professional, ethical, legal, and other standards that guide the practice of (the profession and context). The supervisor also ensures that standards are met in the worker's performance of duties in order to protect clients, workers, and the agency. The supervisor also must always consider the cost effectiveness of a decision, while being mindful of the unique needs of the clients. (Berg 2003, p. 16)

Seeing the larger context and safeguarding all involved—clients, institution, and therapists—was a goal-setting responsibility of the supervisor.

3.7 Process of Supervision

Instead of an emphasis on the "what," pay attention to the "how." Anybody can get concrete information. That's not hard. What's difficult is how to use the "what," the information you have.

~ Berg n.d., SFBTA Archive #10128-0064

Supervision theories abound. Most attend to therapist development, skill acquisition, and education. Consistent with her dedication to simplicity, Insoo focused on strengthening therapist expertise through particular practices and modeling those practices in supervision. She supported the knowledge and utilization of not-knowing skills, including empathy, exception exploration, complimenting, scaling and relationship questions, staying pragmatic, supporting *and* challenging, and collaboration (Berg 2003). Most of this book focuses on the skills a SF supervisor must acquire and practice to be successful in this process and are carefully developed in Chap. 4, so here I will simply quote Insoo in support of what I would include as SF supervision process methods:

Encourage empathy:
Teach your staff to learn how to put themselves in the other person's shoes, to develop empathy. (Berg 1999b)

The flow of conversation in sessions of solution-building supervision is organized around inviting workers to see clients through clients' eyes rather than their own. (De Jong and Berg 2012, p. 281)

Compliment:
The best way to build team spirit and increase a positive working atmosphere is the liberal use of compliments and of giving credit to workers, both in the presence of other workers and in private. (Berg 2003, p. 57)

Explore exceptions:
Because workers are not trained to look for exceptions, they miss a great many opportunities to enhance client motivation, to build a positive working relationship with clients, and even to see the successes in themselves. Therefore, it is imperative that supervisors get in the habit of not only seeing the exceptions to problems but also pointing them out to workers, so that they can apply this with their clients. (Berg 2003, pp. 54–55)

Ask Scaling questions:
Scaling questions indicate to workers and clients alike that problems and solutions are not an either/or proposition but are on a continuum…The flexibility of this scaling question means this can be a very useful tool for the supervisor-worker dialogues as well as the worker-client interviews. (Berg 2003, pp. 60–63)

Relationship questions:
Relationship questions alert the listener's views toward the need of the child. They nudge the parents toward looking at the world from the child's perspective (empathy)… The same principle applies to supervising workers. (Berg 2003, p. 65)

Stay pragmatic:
(Therapists/Supervisees) need to see some rationale behind (what they do). And what does that mean? You know, they have to sort of make the connection…You can explain until the cows come home about what the postmodern idea is, but unless you make a connection for them to a real-life situation, it doesn't make any sense…from the very unsophisticated, to interns, graduate students, to people who have been in the field for a long time and have moved up. I feel like I do a great deal more of making the connection between 'This is an idea they have no problem understanding' and 'This is the real-life situation that they can hook it up with.' (Berg n.d., circa 1997, SFBTA Archive Item #10149-0074)

Be Supportive and challenging (creating goals that require hard work):
Challeng(e) workers while being supportive…Being 'supportive' of workers comes in different shape and forms. It is a good idea to take an inventory of specific behaviors that you do to be 'supportive.' It is also very important for you to ask workers for a specific set of behaviors from you when they ask for your "support." Then you will be able to do the very things that the worker considers supportive. One person's definition of 'supportive" can be very different from another's. (Berg 2003, pp. 67–70)

The (supervision) group itself has its own culture…being supportive of each other and also challenging each other. And if the supervisor has failed to foster that kind of supportive and challenging atmosphere of the group, I would say, if I was their supervisor, I would consider myself having failed. (Berg et al. 1991)

Collaborate:
When supervisor-supervisee relationships are based on mutual respect, collaboration, and a willingness to learn from each other, the culture of the supervisor's unit is more likely to undergo positive changes. (Berg 2003, pp. 12–13)

Many of the qualities of this (supervision) approach are isomorphic to the theory/therapy of the solution-focused model. These qualities include (a) striving for supervisor/supervisee cooperation, (b) focusing on supervisee strengths rather than deficits, and (c) impressing on supervisees that they have the resources to overcome their therapeutic impasses with clients. (Rudes et al. 1997, p. 204)

3.8 Teaching/Education and Evaluation

Insoo was clear that at least two practices, teaching and evaluation, are essential to supervision (De Jong and Berg 2012). These fall outside the assumptions normally ascribed to SF therapy, setting supervision apart as a practice with distinct qualities and requirements (Berg n.d., SFBTA Archive #10128-0064). When discussing the formation of a supervisory relationship, Insoo said, "(I expect) the supervisee to have read some things about my work before he or she came to me and have some working knowledge of (SFBT) so they wouldn't have to start from scratch" (Berg et al. 1991). Whenever possible, Insoo would teach by indirect means, using relationship questions and other methods to draw forth therapists' curiosity to be involved in the learning process (Berg 2003; Rudes et al. 1997).

Insoo believed a good supervisor always gives a positive evaluation (Berg n.d., SFBTA Archive #10128-0064). Although this may seem incomplete or even naïve if taken as a stand-alone policy, she believed that evaluations are opportunities for teaching/learning. Criticism, or telling therapists what they do wrong, does not help this process. In addition to giving suggestions (another infrequent practice in SF therapy), she used evaluations to compliment and guide. "'Don't' is not a good way to teach. And 'stop' is not a good way to teach. So don't use these two words. Always use 'do this' or 'try this' or 'that was good,' 'that worked very well,' (or) 'so what do you need to do so that you can do that again?'" (Berg n.d., SFBTA Archive #10128-0064).

She also felt that evaluating a therapist's clinical work for the purposes of grades or promotions was a practice to be avoided whenever possible (personal communication, February 6, 2006). If it could not be avoided, she suggested that evaluation become a cooperative venture:

And he says, "And I have to evaluate them on how they are doing it." So I said, "You know, a better way might be why don't you have them pick out their own, they could review it, their best 10 minutes, that they thought was the best 10 minutes, and have them pick out their worst 10 minutes in the same session. And have them bring it to you and have them explain to you why this is the best 10 minutes and the worst 10 minutes." (Berg n.d., Archive #10149-0074)

In addition, Insoo promoted the idea that supervisees need to develop the ability to self-evaluate (Berg n.d., SFBTA Archive #10128-0064; De Jong and Berg 2008). Her philosophy of learning—including the eliciting of therapist viewpoints, sharing power, remaining tentative, and maintaining and promoting curiosity—took a long view of the therapists' career by encouraging self-evaluative practices. Ideas and practices that further develop self-evaluation are outlined in Sects. 4.1 and 4.9.

3.9 Assumptions About Therapists

> *I'm a dopeless hope fiend.*
> ~ Overheard at the SFBTA Conference, Toronto, Canada, November 2007

I think Insoo believed in the goodness of therapists—taking them one at a time, but assuming the best unless there was evidence to the contrary (Fowers and Tjeltveit 2003). Among the "core beliefs" (De Jong and Berg 2012, p. 280) Insoo assumed about therapists were that they:

- "Want to feel that their work makes 'a difference' in someone's life
- Want to learn the skills needed to achieve this motivation and commitment
- Want to be accepted and valued by the organization they work in
- Already possess problem-solving skills to some degree; thus, the task of supervision is to add solution-building skills
- Will, when they feel respected and supported by the organization and their superiors, naturally deal with their clients in the same respectful manner" (De Jong and Berg 2012, p. 280)

3.9.1 Therapists Have Resources from Which to Draw

For Insoo, SF supervision places a strong emphasis on recognition and development of therapist assets, and the sources were limitless. A supervision scenario posed in the "fielding supervision impasses" panel discussion included a question regarding the therapist's family of origin (Berg et al. 1991). While clearly a broad attempt to access multiple viewpoints from the panelists, Insoo stated that she would utilize the therapist's background and experiences whenever appropriate. "I would be asking a lot of questions about his own formation and what in his own formation (is) helpful or not helpful (in the case impasse)…if this (therapist's) family of origin issue came up, I would figure out how to use that (to benefit the client couple) rather than going back for more information, as a strength…He is certainly an expert in alcoholic families since he grew up in one – how can we use that? How can we use what he knows about these kinds of situations to the advantage of the couple?"

3.9.2 Therapists Have Positive Intentions

Whenever possible, Insoo assumed all parties had the best of intentions (Berg n.d., Archive #10149-0074; Berg et al. 1991). "And (regarding) their intentions, it doesn't always pan out as they intended, but their intention was very honorable" (Berg 1997, Archive #10149-0074). Part of her style of reducing hierarchy and establishing a positive atmosphere in supervision, her general orientation was to believe the therapist came to the therapy and supervisory contexts with altruistic and positive goals. Believing therapists held the Rogerian position of unconditional positive regard was a "basic ingredient" for creating the supervisory context in which everyone—clients, therapists, and supervisors—thrived and met their goals (Berg et al. 1991).

An example of how Insoo applied this approach is captured in the phrase, "You must have good reasons to…" (Berg 2003, p. 46ff). If a therapist was not meeting paperwork deadlines, she would suggest that the person was doing the best she or he could under the circumstances as a beginning posture or stance in the conversation. "'You must have a good reason for being late. How can I help?' And then I might say: 'What are some of your ideas about solving this problem?' So, by doing this, I am being understanding, helpful, and at the same time I am making my expectations clear…it is hardly ever necessary to be authoritative" (Visser 2004, p. 4). This approach often avoids the guilt and shame usually embedded in such conversations, allowing solution building to take place by assuming positive purposes.

3.10 Role of Language

"Just as in therapy, we are creating a whole different reality for the therapist. Our job is to change that reality so the therapist feels more in control, competent, and successful" (Berg n.d., SFBTA Archive #10128-0064). This reality creation in supervision is mediated through language. Although Insoo's notions certainly changed through time, a glimpse into her views on the construction of reality through language is possible from publications she authored as well as presentations she made. For Insoo, language did not reflect reality, it actively created it. She believed that "people develop their sense of what is real through conversation with and observation of others…as people interact with and observe one another, their perceptions and definitions of what is real frequently shift, sometimes dramatically" (Berg and De Jong 1996, p. 376). This aligns most closely with assumptions of social constructionist theory (Gergen 1999) and fits with her views of interpersonal influence and change. For Insoo, problems were experienced personally and could be influenced through conversation. Although problem description often infers permanence, solution-building language is "more positive, hopeful, and future-focused, and suggests the transience of problems" (de Shazer, Dolan, Korman, Trepper, McCollum, and Berg 2007, p. 3).

The postmodern emphasis on language within Insoo's clinical work extends into the supervision realm. She felt that a "conversational style" of language was more conducive to learning and change than exchanges dominated by professional or clinical jargon. Her guiding image is, "Imagine sitting in the kitchen of your home, having a conversation with someone" (Berg n.d., SFBTA Archive #10128-0064).

> Since language is the only tool we have in working with people, it is essential that as managers and supervisors, we are thoughtful about the use of language in our daily lives. It is not just what we say or not say it but HOW we say it that matters and shapes the relationship. This question immediately levels the relationship and puts us in a "not-knowing" posture and that of a person curious about the complex thoughts behind the staff members not showing up for work on time, not completing the paperwork on time, and a multitude of other problems that become issues in managing and supervising a staff. This new posture reduces the defensiveness of those being managed or supervised, thus, staff members rise to the challenge and start to think for themselves and take actions based on (this) sense of competence, rather than always defending his/her position. Not allowing supervisees, staff members, client, or even one's own children or partners to lower themselves to a defensive position is the most respectful, empowering, and yet demanding posture we can take. (Berg n.d., Hot Tips III, p. 2)

As with SF therapists, supervisors should use tentative language when the context allows it (Berg 2003). There are times supervisors must speak in the imperative form, including directives regarding policy violations or licensure requirements. However, Insoo believed that exploratory language that maintains curiosity invites discussion and respectful feedback as well as promoting therapist learning. This practice of "hedging" (Rudes et al. 1997), described in more detail in Sects. 3.13.7 and 4.4, is a cornerstone concept in her supervision practice.

3.11 Therapists' Perspectives in Supervision

Cooperative SF supervision relationships require an open space for expressing one's perspectives and the valuing of each person's views. For such honesty to come forth, it is the supervisor's responsibility to invite disclosure and create the safety that must accompany it. One way to influence therapists is to embrace their perspectives, attempting whenever possible to perceive clients and cases as therapists view them. Like SF therapy, which emphasizes a not-knowing perspective (De Jong and Berg 2012), Insoo believed supervisors should accept the therapists' *experiences* and invest themselves in viewing the session, case, or concept through the therapists' eyes. "Many supervisors make the mistake of thinking therapists don't know anything. And so we keep telling (rather than asking). But just as I (believe) about clients, I absolutely believe that all therapists have lots of abilities. And my job is to bring it out" (Berg n.d., SFBTA Archive #10128-0064).

3.12 Clients' Perspectives in Supervision

"The flow of conversation in sessions of solution-building supervision is organized around inviting workers to see clients through clients' eyes rather than their own .... It is the task of supervision, then, to continually teach workers to listen to the client's

3.12 Clients' Perspectives in Supervision

view of how useful the service is to the client" (De Jong and Berg 2012, p. 281). Seeking clients' perspectives in the supervision process was extremely important to Insoo. She developed clear questions for supervisors to ask therapists when seeking client views and emphasized their value to supervisors in her publications and presentations. They include:

What parts of the interview would the client say were most useful?

What was it about those parts that the client would say made a difference for her/him?

What would the client say about how you and the agency could be most helpful to the children and the family? (De Jong et al. 2012, p. 11)

....

What do you suppose she appreciated most about what you did?

How could you find out what the client wants? Anything else?

What would the children say would be most helpful for them?

What would her best friend (partner, mother, etc.) say she needs right now?

How would you make sure you listen to her idea of how to ensure the safety of her children? (Berg 1999a)

Ahead of her time, Insoo elicited first- and secondhand views from clients during supervision. Described in more detail below, this orientation is more than a practice technique; it shows her dedication to several important ideas in SF supervision. First, supervisors have no direct access to therapists' experiences—therapists must express their views in conversation. Given her belief that therapists' perspectives are valuable in the supervision process, it is important that supervisors elicit therapists' ideas about the clients' experiences and the therapist/client relationship.

Second, Insoo placed a strong commitment to promoting the clients' voices in the supervision process whenever possible. Since live supervision and team consultation were a prominent part of training at the Brief Family Therapy Center of Milwaukee, accessing client experiences and views of supervision was a natural progression in this tradition. She used several means to bring forth client viewpoints. Insoo might send the therapist into the therapy room after a mid-session consult to ask the client questions about session process, therapy goals, or therapist performance (always framing questions to draw forth helpful responses). She often entered the room herself, seeking the client's ideas to improve both therapy and supervision.

Finally, I see Insoo's systems orientation in her active solicitation of client (and therapist) viewpoints in the supervisory process. This was most prominent in her use of relationship questions in this practice (Berg 2003). Illustrated below, relationship questions are the most common examples of how systems ideas permeated her supervision approach. But her systems orientation was also revealed in her recursive view of learning: "I as a supervisor learn from supervision. I take away something from this interaction as well as the supervisee...so we both contribute and we both learn..." (Berg n.d., SFBTA Archive #10128-0064). Supervision is a constructed process, unscripted and improvisational. This made supervision fertile soil for Insoo's own personal growth as a practitioner, supervisor, teacher, and colleague.

3.13 Practices

3.13.1 Highlighting Successes and Exceptions

From the very beginning of the supervisory relationship, Insoo focused attention on what therapists had done well.

> When I interview potential supervisees, I would ask, "Tell me about your success cases. So in what way have you, did you, have you been successful in what kind of cases? And what have you done to be successful with those cases?" (Those) would be my first questions. (Berg et al. 1991)

Noting and learning from success was the action research method Insoo used to develop her supervision and mentoring manual for child welfare services (Berg 2003), an extension of the SF tenet of focused curiosity. Highlighting "what works" was perhaps the most prominent supervision method Insoo put into practice, as it exemplified the SF approach and its direct commitment to solution building more than most other techniques. Locating and drawing attention to therapists' constructive contributions to client change places emphasis on positive outcomes, the data SF supervisors use most often to motivate therapists toward goal attainment. This also creates a context that is isomorphic to therapy built on SF principles.

To illustrate, this segment of a transcription is among the first questions Insoo asks in Sect. 5.2 in this book:

IKB: Okay, so in the two sessions you have met with them, what would…the mother say you have done that has been helpful?

This beginning, asking the therapist to articulate possible success experiences within the therapy sessions via a relationship question, sets the stage for the consult's focus on success and change. Many additional examples of this practice are found and noted in Chapter 5, "A Tap on the Shoulder."

3.13.2 Scaling

A powerful tool for assessing change, scaling permeates SF work. Creating a scale draws a distinction and invites one to consider differences. SF approaches emphasize the creation of goals and evaluating progress toward them, which makes scale creation indispensable and monitoring of progress possible. This practice was commonplace in Insoo's supervision work and promoted as a supervisory practice (Berg n.d., SFBTA Archive #10128-0064; Berg 2003; De Jong and Berg 2012).

3.13.3 Complimenting

As in SF therapy, complimenting the therapist "is among the simplest, easiest, and most useful" ways to begin the SF supervision process, and "(c)omplimenting begets gratitude and reciprocal complimenting" (Berg and De Jong 2005, pp. 51–55). Insoo's methods included direct, indirect, and self-complimenting (see Sect. 4.5 for an extended description of these methods), and she encouraged shadowing (Berg and De Jong 2005; De Jong et al. 2012) as a means to this end. Shadowing—accompanying therapists on client home visits—provided multiple opportunities for compliments at the end of the client sessions as well as when conducting follow-up. Writing the agency management and including compliments regarding the therapist's planning, positive interactions with clients, documentation, and cooperation in the shadowing process is one common example of follow-up complimenting.

Insoo's supervision agenda was larger than case consultation. She believed in the importance of acknowledging others' contributions to client and workplace contexts. An important approach that included compliments and acknowledgement has been called sharing credit by Furman and Ahola (1992): "The best way to build team spirit and increase a positive working atmosphere is the liberal use of compliments and of giving credit to workers, both in the presence of other workers and in private" (Berg 2003, p. 57).

3.13.4 Being Indirect

Although she denied it, even to some of her closest colleagues, I believe Insoo's connections to the Mental Research Institute (MRI) model and the genius of Milton H. Erickson revealed themselves in her practices. A deliberate technique with Ericksonian origins was her consistent commitment to indirect communication. One cannot be sure of the influences involved in this indirectness; family background and culture probably played a part in how she participated in relationships, as did her training with John Weakland and others at MRI. However, what *is* clear is that when Insoo chose to be indirect, it was deliberate. She had a phenomenal range of interpersonal skills, from blunt to subtle, and no one who knew her would say she lacked assertiveness. Therefore, I assume Insoo cultivated this communication skill and applied it thoughtfully to bring about the best results and foster the supervisory relationship.

An example of this planned use of indirect communication comes from a supervision conversation with a California therapist. A spontaneous conversation on postmodernism and supervision, this portion of the exchange is particularly revealing of Insoo's intentionality (Berg 1997, SFBTA Archive #10149-0074):

Colleague:	It's interesting that you say that you find students very curious—
IKB:	—yes—
C:	—it reminds me about how we co-create, or at least systemically, that your curiosity brings out the curiosity—
IKB:	—their curiosity—
C:	—of others. And the way that you present things—
IKB:	—right—
C:	—and you listen. It's very much like (pause) I think the word for that is a co-created or socially created phenomenon.

IKB:	Right, right. And you know sometimes, we (a supervision team, including therapists she supervises) sit behind a mirror and I say, "Wow, that's fascinating that she said that!" And they look at you like "oh, it is?"
C:	—laughing—
IKB:	"I guess it is."
C:	Yeah, right. Right—
IKB:	—Don't you see that?—
C:	—(laughing) yeah, right—
IKB:	And they look at you sort of like, "Oh, I guess it *is* fascinating—
C:	—yeah, yeah—
IKB:	—Yeah, I guess it is."
C:	Without ever saying, "You should be interested in this."
IKB:	Oh, no no no! "Oh, fascinating—I never thought of it that way."
C:	…It is fascinating, this whole concept of (creating) interest.

Although some may see this approach as manipulative, I view it as an example of indirect communication within the overall context of Insoo's supervisory oeuvre. Her commitment was to cooperative relationships; at times, this meant that she would exert influence. While some supervisory styles favor confrontation or directness, Insoo's range allowed her to playfully pique others' curiosity simply by introducing meaningful randomness through distraction into the context (Bateson 1972; Keeney 1983). The resulting shift of attention was (more than likely) a positive adjustment in the supervisory moment. Other supervision transcription examples of her indirectness can be found in Chap. 5.

3.13.5 Asking Questions that Consult the Client/ Relationship

This practice, discussed further in Sects. 3.12 and 4.1.4, was but one way Insoo invited the clients' voices into the supervision process:

Direct Client Information: When using a one-way mirror, after the session is finished "the supervisor goes in, and asks the client right after the session, 'What did this therapist do that was helpful for you?'" (Berg n.d., SFBTA Archive #10128-0064). Many cases within the Archive feature Insoo providing supervision using this approach. In this way, clients were introduced to the therapists' supervisor while at the same time they were consulted on progress and therapist performance (see Todd, Joanning, Enders, Mutchler, and Thomas 1990). Various methods for soliciting client feedback are included in Sects. 3.12 and 4.1.4.

Indirect Client Views: Using relationship questions in supervision, Insoo would request therapists' views on client experiences. This indirect technique requested speculation by therapists, but it also reinforced therapist successes while indirectly including very important perspectives in the supervision. Here are a few examples from Insoo's Japan presentation on SF supervision (see Appendix E):

> You can ask, "What would the client say you could do to be more helpful to the client?"
>
> A supervisee talks about a case, and then I would say, "On a scale of 1 to 10, if I were to ask your client, what would he say how much you were helpful to him?"
>
> On a scale of 1 to 10, how much progress would your client say he has made since he has started therapy with you? (Berg n.d., SFBTA Archive #10128-0064)

3.13.6 Using Silence

"As a supervisor, you need to master the effective use of silence and train yourself to be comfortable with silence in order to generate the worker's solutions" (Berg 2003, p. 46). Sitting patiently with a therapist is required when one asks difficult questions. Thoughtful silence allows one the time to ponder questions and seriously consider possible responses (Korman and Söderquist 1999). This method is especially useful in SF supervision because so many of the questions supervisors ask are met with "I don't know" as a first response. Silence can also create conversational pressure, but respectful anticipation that becomes a supervisory practice creates safety for therapists to think aloud, giving voice to ideas they might not consider without the accepting posture of the supervisor. Waiting expectantly for 5–7 seconds (Berg 2003) allows for the second right answer to emerge (and often the third and more, depending on how often you ask, "What else?") (Iveson 2005).

3.13.7 Hedging

Another example of indirect communication practices has been called hedging (Rudes et al. 1997):

> Male therapist "Well, I talk a lot during the session because, because the client wasn't saying anything!"
>
> Supervisor/IKB: OK, so talking a lot is one way. I may ask then, "So, what else can you do next time when the client doesn't talk?"

Insoo doesn't *actually* ask a question here—she says she "may ask." This invites the therapist to generate his own ideas of "what else can I do?" if he chooses to do so instead of responding to a direct question.

The notion of tentativeness is discussed in Sect. 1.2.2 of this book. Based in postmodern thinking, staying tentative is a more encompassing posture capturing indirect communication, hedging, not-knowing, and other practices important to this supervision approach.

Insoo called hedging "using tentative language":

> Getting in the habit of using tentative language helps to facilitate collaboration and negotiation. So, what is tentative language? Phrases such as, "It seems like…," "Could it be …?" "It sounds like…," "Perhaps…," "I am not sure…," or "I wonder…," and many other questions that are put forth with a tentative tone of voice facilitates collaboration. (Berg 2003, p. 48f)

Further exploration of this concept is found in Sects. 3.13.7 and 4.4 of this chapter, and multiple examples can be examined in Chap. 5 transcriptions of and commentary on Insoo's supervision.

3.13.8 Using "Suppose…"

Although one could consider this technique a form of hedging, using the word "suppose" was Insoo's way of assisting the process of imagination with supervisees (Berg and Szabó 2005, p. 38). This practice usually involves placing your mind into the future, assuming the premise embedded in the question (examples (a) through (c) below). It could also involve a simple reflection and drawing tentative conclusions, thinking aloud without stating facts (see example (d) below—if you "suppose" a client appreciated a particular action, which is different from stating what she actually appreciated). Her work is replete with examples relating this concept to supervision, including:

(a) "Suppose the client were to think your usefulness to her or him had improved 1 point. What might she or he notice you are doing differently?" (De Jong and Berg 2012, p. 281)
(b) "Suppose I were to ask your workers to rate you on a scale of 1 to 10, where 10 stands for the best supervisor they have ever had, and 1 stands for the worst supervisor they have ever met, or 'a supervisor from hell.' What number would they give you?" (Berg 2003, p. 34)
(c) "Just suppose…all these worked out right somehow. It may sound strange, but somehow it worked out like magic, that all this is behind you right now. What would you be doing then that you are not doing right now?" (Berg 2003, p. 50)
(d) "What do you suppose she appreciated most about what you did?" (Berg 1999a)

3.13.9 Using "You Must Have Good Reasons to…"

Rather than attributing behaviors to malingering, noncompliance, or character flaws, Insoo assumed people had good intentions whatever the outcome. Although this may appear naïve, it is an extension of the stance of nonpathology discussed earlier in Sect. 1.2.3. One must start somewhere, and SF approaches (and Insoo) begin by giving people the benefit of the doubt instead of assuming the worst (Berg n.d., Hot Tips III; Korman and Söderquist 1999):

> "So, it occurs to me that perhaps I may not have looked at this problem from your perspective and it is very likely that you must have a very good reason to … (pause) not be able to meet the deadline again with your paperwork. Perhaps I have been insensitive to your circumstances. Can you tell me what are some good reasons you have for this difficulty? I wonder if there is something I can do to be helpful?"…If the worker cannot come up with a "good reason," then you might suggest that you end the conversation with an understanding that you will get together again soon and in the meantime the worker can give some thought to this. If the worker has an alternative idea of how to solve the problem, then you can proceed with discussion for the purpose of finding a solution, not to make the worker feel guilty or responsible for the problem. You want the worker to be responsible for solutions. It is important not to be sarcastic or cynical, but to speak with genuine curiosity and sincerity and to listen to the solution offered. (Berg 2003, p. 46ff)

3.14 Concluding Thoughts About Insoo's Approach

> People need to hear the spirit part of (the SF approach). It's not just a technique but it's a willingness to learn from clients, as they are the driving force of this, and some sense of humility, of modesty. It's not about us, it's about the clients, and it's about their life and how to make their life better. I think that's a very important part of it. I would say that's what people need to keep remembering. (Berg and Wheeler 2006, p. 6)

Insoo assumed the presuppositions and methods of solution building were the same in SF therapy and SF supervision (De Jong and Berg 2012). What people often do not realize is that she also taught ideas and demonstrated skills that were unique to supervision, covering topics such as administration, ethics, co-learning, client feedback, evaluation, and education. Many of Insoo's ideas and practices are developed throughout this book, so it is important to give credit to Insoo Kim Berg, Supervisor Extraordinaire, for what she contributed.

Chapter 4
SF Supervision Practices

Volumes of theory have been written about supervision, with substantial emphasis on supervisor development and little research evidence to support its significance in relation to either supervisor effectiveness or client outcome. Rudes, Shilts, and Berg (1997) speak about the supervisor's "conduct" (p. 204) and the dearth of literature about what supervisors actually *do* in supervision. Supervisory practices have not been studied using deductive methods because of what may be a common understanding: *that* supervisors stimulate change is unchallenged, but the techniques supervisors use to bring about change are as unique as snowflakes. My ambition for this section of the book is to articulate practices that originate with SF pioneers such as Insoo Kim Berg as well as methods from my own work and those of close associates. The result is not intended to be scientific or generalizable; instead, I hope to invigorate and inspire the supervisor toward experimentation. After all, SF approaches are built on "what works," and what works in general may not translate to your context. As Bateson said (1979, p. 43), "the generic we can know, but the specific eludes us."

SF approaches have long been accused of being nothing more than a collection of techniques. Because there is no theory that unifies the practice or directs research, people often have difficulty understanding the "why" of the SF approach. "Why does it work?" is the wrong question in SF circles; "What works?" is the continuing question. This SF position is in keeping with Gregory Bateson's proposition that

> explanation contains no new information different from what was present in the description. Indeed, a great deal of the information that was present in the description is commonly thrown away, and only a rather small part of what was to be explained is, in fact, explained. But explanation is certainly of enormous importance and certainly *seems* to give a bonus of insight over and above what was contained in description…for some reason, human beings enormously value this combining of ways of organizing information or material (into explanation). (Bateson 1979, p. 86f, emphasis in original)

The SF approach has been working *inductively* for most of its history (De Jong and Berg 2012). While most therapeutic models are developed deductively, with ideas guiding theory development, research, and practice, experiences of success in clinical contexts have guided much of SF's elaboration over the years.

When something seemed useful, the procedure was examined carefully by the BFTC team, fine-tuned through frequent application (when appropriate to the context), and continued as a SF practice if it fit with existing techniques and minimal assumptions. Generating premises wasn't a goal in this process, but acceptance of practices that work has always been restricted by commonly held SF ideas. For example, even if a technique brought about change, generally it was not included in SF practice if it did not fit with the idea of collaboration (i.e., if it was forced by the therapist). When the assumption that clients are the experts on their lived experiences became commonly accepted in SF circles, practices imposing expert knowledge (e.g., correcting faulty thinking, a common practice in cognitive approaches to psychotherapy) were rejected even if they "worked." And when the SF approach shifted from a model defined by systems thinking into a more language-based practice, categories of practice became even more widely accepted.

In this chapter, I will outline what I consider to be the most common SF supervision practices as well as add others that I consider useful in SF supervision. Each practice category in this outline will include basic SF assumptions that define and challenge their inclusion. Because there is no unanimity about what is and is not a SF practice, I predict disagreements will ensue among SF supervision practitioners. Passions run deep in the SF community, and I welcome continuing conversations regarding assumptions and practices.

4.1 Goal Setting: Active, Responsive Goal Creation and Assessment

No wind favours a ship without a destination.

~ Montaigne

This section includes the active process of setting goals. Here I will discuss the feedback structure that makes goal setting responsive and alive, supervisor agendas and therapist/supervisee goals fitting together in the process, competencies required by law, ethics, and professional and personal goals of both supervisor and therapist. Forms I have created will be introduced here to assist the reader's understanding of the process.

I see goal setting as a flexible, organic process. Differing from traditional goal setting that may establish fixed endpoints, goal setting and evaluation in this book denotes a less static process and implies a continuous negotiation of both ends and means. Goal setting is interactive, involving both the therapist and supervisor prior to a (tentatively) final outcome.

I liken this practice of goal setting to partners learning how to ballroom dance. The unique abilities, experiences, and limitations of each partner play into the decision-making process involving multiple goals as they learn to dance together. If the partners are young, fit, and inexperienced, then the pace and expectations are quite different from

4.1 Goal Setting: Active, Responsive Goal Creation and Assessment

a partnership made up of two older, veteran dancers with physical limitations. There are moves each must master, but they must also be synchronized. In addition, the male may have personal goals that differ from the female's, but they must be complementary for both to work toward individual achievements in a context requiring partnering. And as they improve as individuals and as a couple, goals continuously transform—what they could not imagine doing when they began the journey is now habit, and achievement of preliminary goals leads to bigger and bigger dreams. Finally, if a mutual goal of the partnership is enjoyment, then each must openly communicate their experiences with the other so adjustments in means and goals can be made on a continuous basis. Supervision parallels dance in many ways, and although the dance metaphor may not fit every decision made in supervision, it sketches some of the basic ideas of a good partnership. Both individual and partnership goals must be clearly communicated, and review is recurring. Novice therapists can only imagine how they will think, perceive, and participate as therapists, but as their performance becomes more expert and requires less effort, their goals should adapt as well. The life experience more mature therapists bring to the supervisory relationship, no matter how many hours of clinical practice they have, may alter goal-setting processes designed for younger professionals. Plus, I do believe enjoyment is a relational goal—cooperation and satisfaction improve learning.

The goal-setting process can be understood and partitioned into many different subjects of focus. Since SF approaches avoid commitments to theories of change, there are no prescribed or proscribed ways to think about therapist development; therefore, if one finds conceptual maps useful to organize supervision, it is more a reflection on the supervisor's desire for conceptual organization than on SF approaches themselves. What seems common is that supervisors know there are qualitative differences between novice and expert therapists and accommodate for these differences in supervision. Whether one adopts a theory of therapist development such as Stoltenberg and McNeill (2010), borrows from expertise development literature and research (Benner 1984; Skovholt 2001), or simply adjusts to individual learning and practice differences on a therapist-by-therapist basis, good supervisors adapt to fit with the needs and goals of therapists.

I have developed a goal-setting schema that incorporates distinctions from Benner's (1984) research on the development of expertise in nursing—perceptual, conceptual, and participatory—and adds two unique to psychotherapy supervision: case management and therapeutic relationship skills (see Appendix C for descriptions of each). These features regarding the qualitative development of expertise (from novice to expert) as well as the different dimensions of expertise (Benner's perceptual, conceptual, and participatory abilities) dovetail with the work of others on expert performance (Dreyfus and Dreyfus 2005; Ericsson, Krampe, and Tesch-Römer 1993; Etringer and Hillerbrand 1995; Kahneman and Klein 2009; Skovholt 2001; Skovholt, Rønnestad, and Jennings 1997; see Thomas 2012b, 2008, 2000). Table 4.1 summarizes these ideas on the development of expertise as conceptualized by Benner (1984) and Skovholt (2001).

The number of "stages" of change within a concept (or even thinking of change as stages) is less important than the progression itself. *That* experts think, see, and perform differently when compared to beginners is rarely disputed. Whether one has to have a

Table 4.1 Expertise development

Concept	Expertise development (Benner 1984)	Professional development (Skovholt 2001)
Perception	Facts determined without experience; parts; details; all parts equally relevant → Recognition of similarity after experiencing several examples → Perspective chosen by the therapist, picks out items salient to the situation → Perspective "presents itself"; patterns; wholes; attend only to the most relevant parts/patterns	Dependence on external → Reliance on internal "Impersonal data" → "Interpersonal encounter" (p. 32)
Conception	Therapists' reliance on abstract principles, context-free methods to solve problems → Recognition of more subtle features of situation → Sees actions tied to goals, conscious awareness, efficient → context-free "rules" begin to frustrate, theory is a useless trapping → Pattern development from experience, guided by past examples, creates a larger repertoire	Detached, theory-driven → Shedding less useful, incongruent ways of thinking → Adding new schemas → Increased congruence with person-of-therapist; Theories are simply "models for approximate experience" (p. 30) Continuous focus on power of therapist to change others → Focus on taking a therapeutic position; increased patience, seeing therapist's (small) part in change process Judgmental of clients' choices, frailties; categorizing others → "Heightened tolerance and acceptance of human variability" (p. 35)
Participation	Performance is inflexible, laborious, detached observation → Situational factors improve performance → Performance is guided by nuances of the situation → Involved performer, full participant, involves self in understanding the situation	Received knowledge → Constructed knowledge Professors as teachers → Clients as teachers Imitator → Performer Prescribed → Professional, personal Voice others' ideas → Gain one's own voice

certain level of expertise to be effective is debatable. So the emphasis here is on seeing difference and does not require one to adopt a particular theory of change.

Beginning with Benner's (1984) distinctions, therapists' *perceptual skills* change as they expand expertise. While beginners focus on minutia, with everything equally relevant, therapists with greater expertise have an easier time choosing the salient from the irrelevant. Expert therapists sometimes have difficulty articulating *how* they perceive; they describe the perceptual process as emergent rather than thoughtful. Skovholt's (2001) descriptions fit this perceptual skill distinction as well when he talks about perception moving from external to internal and from facts to relationship (interpersonal) as therapists develop expertise.

Change in what Benner (1984) calls *conceptual skills* moves from abstract theory with little experience from which to draw to a more goal-directed thinking and finally to a more pattern-emergent thinking informed by experience. Thinking for novice therapists starts with books and rules; conceptualizations by experts are context-specific and more inclusive. Skovholt (2001) talks about therapist conceptualizations as moving from detached and theory driven toward a more congruent way of viewing and making sense of therapy tied to the person of the therapist. Again, conceptualization moves from sorting and categorizing with novices to wholism and emergence for experts.

Finally, how one performs and interacts also changes with the development of expertise. What Benner (1984) categorizes as *participatory skills* has been called executive skills in family therapy supervision literature for over 30 years (Tomm and Wright 1982). Most therapists begin their careers either mimicking experts or inflexibly applying techniques. Later, according to Benner, performance is guided by situational nuances, with each moment calling for a different performance. Expert participation is characterized by even greater immersing of oneself in the role and relationships. Skovholt (2001) notes significant shifts in participation as well. He sees the shift as moving from imitator to performer and from scripted activities to improvisational and responsive actions.

Based on years of supervisor and therapist feedback, I added case management and therapeutic relationship skill development to my goal-setting process. Although these differ qualitatively from Benner's (1984) distinctions within expertise development, goal setting in these two areas is vital to therapist success and positive client outcome. Therapists must be integrated into the psychotherapy community, and part of this process is learning the activities of the culture. *Case management skills* can take many forms and is sensitive to therapists' work contexts, but learning how to document what one does as a therapist to meet best-practice standards is important to one's survival in the profession. Documenting client contact, appropriately acquiring and maintaining informed consent, communicating with professional peers and superiors, and recording information for reimbursement purposes are best learned in vivo, not in the classroom. Efficiency and effectiveness are usually gained through experience under the tutelage of seasoned peers and supervisors, making this a crucial area of goal setting for most therapists. In addition, practicing and improving one's *therapeutic relationship skills* is an important goal-setting activity, especially for early career therapists. Since the therapist–client relationship accounts for a significant amount of the therapeutic change process no matter what model is used, supervisors should assume attention to this area of therapist development that is important despite claims of superior, evidence-based effectiveness by certain approaches. Without a clearly supportive therapeutic relationship, even models with significant research support will fall short (Wampold 2001).

Extensive research across many disciplines supports the assumption that the development of expertise takes time, and it is unlikely that changes or development resulting in expert therapist performance can be hurried (Thomas 2008). Skovholt and his associates say this: "Our own view is that expertise occurs when the practitioner has evolved to an internalized style after thousands of hours of practice and an average of 15 years of professional experience" (Skovholt et al. 1997, p. 364). I doubt that the process to expert SF work is any different. I have witnessed demonstrations by SF practitioners that solidify my views in this area: expert practitioners' applications of the SF approach differ significantly from novices', and the differences cannot be taught in a university course, workshop, or short-term training program. I have written elsewhere that "we owe ourselves the patience that qualitative shifts toward expertise require, and perhaps the first step in this process would be to instill a sense of wonder and responsibility in the lives of students and inexperienced therapy practitioners" (Thomas 2008, p. 35).

To guide this supervision goal-setting practice, I have reproduced my goal-setting form in Appendix C as well as included therapists' completed goal setting and evaluation documents (printed with permission). I have been using and revising this form for over 12 years, keeping it simple while making it useful for therapist and supervisor alike. The five areas of goal setting are case management, therapeutic relationship, perceptual competencies, conceptual competencies, and participatory competencies. The case management goal area focuses on the nuts and bolts of agency practice. This encompasses learning agency policies and procedures, attaining skills in case note writing and documentation, and context sensitivity (including what on-site supervisors commonly call "compliance with policies"). This goal-setting area is partially prescriptive; together with their on-site supervisors, therapists create goals that fit the expectations of the on-site supervisor and the agency where they work.

In addition to goal setting, I ask therapists entering supervision for other information including their ideas about success, learning styles, and strengths related to therapy and supervision contexts. One of the most fruitful areas of inquiry involves therapists' relational style preferences: *How can I (and peers) best help you meet your goals?* Therapists usually have clear ideas on how they learn best, and some of these supportive practices may seem less than SF. Many therapists know that they learn from mistakes; others say they want criticism and suggestions on how to improve. Few request SF approaches such as exception-finding and deconstructing questions when answering this question. "Point out where I went wrong," "demonstrate a technique so I can see it," and "offer alternatives I can choose from" are very common replies to this question. Most responses are tied to therapists' learning styles. Since most people are visual learners, it should come as no surprise than many therapists seek out video examples and savor demonstrations by peers and supervisors alike. In addition, even though the SF approach highly values successes and exceptions, there is an educational component to becoming a therapist that may not parallel therapy (Wetchler 1990). Therefore, listening to therapists' ideas and requests and responding in helpful ways is an important aspect of the goal-setting process.

Goal setting and evaluation of progress in SF supervision should be *responsive, interactive, challenging to the therapist,* and *responsive to client and other systems*. I will discuss both therapist and supervisory goal setting (focusing on the therapist/supervisor relationship, not on the supervisor) where appropriate.

4.1 Goal Setting: Active, Responsive Goal Creation and Assessment

4.1.1 Responsive with Supervision

Goal setting is *responsive* when it influences and is influenced by the process and experience of supervision. This responsiveness maintains a future focus but includes sensitivity to a goal's current fit within the therapy context and supervisory relationship. For example, therapist Jason begins part of his goal-setting process with a desire to create open options for clients rather than limiting choices. While this is laudable in general, such an orientation is at times impractical or even inappropriate in certain therapeutic contexts. A significant number of Jason's initial sessions involve clients in crisis, including people who have experienced intimate partner violence (IPV). Best practices in cases involving IPV would begin with a restriction of choices in several areas and the delay of some long-term decisions. The best first-session practice usually limits conversation to immediate safety concerns for self, minor children, pets, and other vulnerable persons and foregoes discussion of items like, "Should I divorce my partner?" Through supervisory discussions, Jason began revising this goal to include contextual sensitivity:

> Jason's Initial Broad Goal (Conceptual): *to create more options and choices for clients*
>
> Revision #1: *to develop greater sensitivity to client needs, both immediate and long term, regarding the creation or limitation of choices. I will notice and appropriately respond to clients' limited choices 90% of the time I hear them in-session.*

4.1.2 Interactive

While therapy clients do set their own goals, it is an interactive process, as therapists have legal, ethical, and personal limits on how they participate in the setting and attaining of client goals. If a client's goal were "to find ways to hide illegal income from his wife and the IRS," a therapist would probably have limits in all three areas that would inform her cooperation with this client's objective. Although rare, inappropriate therapist goals can be proposed as well, to which supervisors must respond. Often conversations initiated by supervisors regarding limitations and expectations around goal setting are clarifying, with reduced embarrassment.

The therapist and supervisor continuously review therapist and supervisory goals to optimize awareness around revisioning. In addition to interactions around therapist-initiated aspirations, supervisors create goals in particular areas and introduce the process whether therapists do or not. These topics may be required by regulatory boards, the clinical practice site, or the university program, for example. So even though therapists do not set goals for clients (even mandated ones), supervisors may have demands placed on them by overlapping systems. In addition, supervisors might require certain activities or actions. While clients can choose whether or not to return for additional sessions, therapists are not usually given this choice in supervision.

Supervision contracts often require certain actions by therapists, including the submission of weekly risk/change charts (see Appendix D) or similar reporting mechanisms, which are not negotiable. *That* certain goals will be set may not be negotiable, so *how* these prescribed goal-setting processes come about is the interactive challenge for supervision.

4.1.3 Challenging to the Therapist

Change happens; it's unavoidable. Some may take this premise a step further, believing that the simple passage of time is all that's required for one to grow and develop as a therapist. Several years ago, I passed the 1,000,000-mile marker as an automobile driver. Because I have commuted long distances to the workplace and driven thousands and thousands of miles on vacations (including many miles driving on the left side of the road!), I have accumulated enough driving time to total more miles than 40 trips around the equator. However, I know I am not an expert driver simply because I have accumulated miles. Watching the skills demonstrated by young drivers on the NASCAR circuit or X-Games RallyCross racers reinforces the fact that I don't have their driving proficiency and probably never will. What one must also keep in mind is that once one factors out alcohol, most automobile deaths among young men in the US are the result of driver error, with excessive speed and poor judgment as the major factors. Simple confidence or even innate ability will not make up for lack of experience and purposeful skill development. I believe the analogy fits when discussing the development of therapist expertise...and supervisor expertise (to be discussed later in the book).

As with clients, therapists' goals should require significant attention and effort. De Jong and Berg (2012, p. 90) explain this aspect of goal setting when working with clients: "By reminding clients about the necessity of hard work, the practitioner is able to place responsibility for change and solutions on the client, without directly saying so." Similarly, in some contexts, therapists may become passive, expecting supervisors to teach them and be responsible for therapist progress. When supervision is mandated in an agency or by licensing boards, the goals can often be minimal. If an agency requires ongoing supervision with no contract or time limitation, clear goal setting will not happen without supervisor insistence. Sometimes, the only goal therapists have in the licensing process is reaching the minimum number of clinical and supervisory hours, and supervision is merely a weekly meeting that allows them to continue the accumulation of hours. The literature is quite clear that expertise does not simply happen because of the passage of time—careful practice plus attention to feedback to correct or refine skills is necessary if one is to become proficient (Dreyfus and Dreyfus 2005; Skovholt 2001).

This attitude can be especially prominent in university settings where student therapists are often just beginning their training. Educational contexts have to accept much of the blame if students view themselves as submissive recipients of knowledge and act accordingly. Often, students have lived this passive-learning reality for more than 15 years before they enter master's programs. To counter this, clinical program faculty must require student initiative from the beginning of the program through final examinations and theses. If the *program* constantly and consistently requires initiative from students and holds high expectations regarding the expectation that they must instigate change, goal-setting processes in supervision are simply more of the same.

4.1.4 Responsive to Client and Other Systems: Creating a Supervisor/Therapist/Client Feedback Process

In the SF approach, a common expectation is that therapists learn to see the world through their clients' eyes, becoming sensitive to clients' frames of reference (De Jong and Berg 2012). In supervision, this involves the development of therapist empathy (Berg 2003), and this viewpoint must be incorporated into the focus on goals to ensure optimal service delivery. After all, therapist skill development is not just about individual growth; the touchstone must always be avoiding exploitation and promoting client safety and benefit. This section will focus on client systems, but the principles and practices outlined here are applicable to other systems encountered by therapists.

"Although client outcome is considered the acid test of supervision efficacy…, to date we do not have clear, methodologically sound data on client outcome and its relationship to supervision" (Falender and Shafranske 2004, p. 202). Although research and SF supervision will be addressed in Chap. 6, this quote is relevant in this section because of the important link that must be made between supervision and client outcome. I am in full agreement with Worthen and Lambert (2007) when they write:

> We argue…that it is time for therapists and supervisors to incorporate outcome monitoring and brief client assessments into ongoing counseling supervision… Clinical supervision has two primary aims: (1) the facilitation of competency as a counselor and professional (i.e., developing theoretical coherence, case conceptualization skills, basic attending skills, understanding and adherence to ethical guidelines, developing multicultural competence, etc.), and (2) the monitoring of client welfare and progress towards beneficial outcomes. (p. 48)

If our only purpose as SF supervisors is to create competent, knowledgeable practitioners, we fail; SF supervision also should aim to impact client outcome and satisfaction. One of the ways to incorporate more direct client responses into supervision is to create what Duncan and his colleagues call a "feedback culture" (Duncan, Miller, and Sparks 2004, p. 97) in which therapists directly seek client's views and integrate these data into supervision. To complete the feedback loop, information discussed in supervision should be responsive to client input, with therapists returning to consequent sessions with ideas and practices directly linked to client feedback. Since therapists are often reluctant to initiate and formally acquire client responses, it falls to the supervisor to introduce the concepts and measures and monitor therapist progress.

Guiding Ideas. Client feedback in supervision has the potential of making significant contributions to therapist development. First, it provides unique information to supervision. Live supervision and case consultation privilege supervisor and therapist viewpoints; the clients' experience of the therapy and therapist has to be inferred. First-hand client data can confirm the positive direction of therapy, but they can also provide information regarding unknown problems, disillusionment, and inadequate client–therapist alliances. Second, client feedback can be corrective, as therapists tend "toward overly optimistic appraisals of (their) clients' progress" (Worthen and Lambert 2007, p. 52; see Norcross 2003). Next, supervisors can also get caught up in Pollyanna thinking (Thomas 2007a), focusing only on strengths and successes and turning a blind eye to deficits and mistakes.

It is important that client feedback *not* become a part of therapists' formal assessment and that this decision is clearly communicated to therapists (Sparks, Kisler, Adams, and Blumen 2011). The goal is to create a feedback process that takes advantage of all client responses, from positive to less than positive. If formal evaluation is part of this process, therapists may become reluctant to secure all sources of client feedback, cherry picking only (what they assume will be) positive client reports and biasing the information from which they can learn.

Practices. One of many ways to promote sensitivity to client and other systems is to require therapists to get client feedback on their therapeutic services. The goal-setting template in Appendix C requires it:

> Decide and outline how you will gain client feedback on your cases plus other ways you will use to acquire a better sense of clients' perspectives. I expect you to seek direct client responses to your work and also take advantage of third-party (i.e., peer and on-site supervisor) feedback and review of video recordings, starting immediately.

Therapists are often reluctant to elicit clients' views of their work together. Whether novice or experienced, therapists can feel threatened and insecure if they have never engaged in such activities; after all, requesting feedback may invite criticism. Therefore, I often offer a range of options for those who have never sought out client feedback, from less-direct methods involving minimal exposure to live client evaluation of therapy (Barnard and Kuehl 1995).

Less-direct methods usually encourage client feedback that protects their anonymity. Performance metrics or rating scales can be completed by clients as they leave the therapy room or mailed in between sessions. Some like the Outcome Rating Scale (ORS) or Session Rating Scale (SRS) (Miller 2012) are simple and short, requiring only a few minutes of thought from the client and are adapted for individual adults, children, and groups. Client feedback utilizing these scales can establish a baseline of effectiveness, and they are free for the individual practitioner to use. Therapists can download the ORS and SRS forms and use them immediately.[1] For agencies or universities wishing to commit to client feedback and research and

---

[1] See Miller (2012) for the internet link (URL).

at the same time aid therapist development, Miller's (2012) scales or the OQ®-45 (OQ Measures 2012) are excellent investments. At least for beginning therapists, use of the ORS and SRS may improve client outcomes, which of course is one of the quintessential goals of supervision (Reese, Usher, Bowman, Norsworthy, Halstead, Rowlands, and Chisholm 2009).

An intermediate step in accessing client experiences of therapy (and therapists) is based on the *ethnographic research protocol* developed by Todd and his associates (Todd, Joanning, Enders, Mutchler, and Thomas 1990). This method, which obtains information during the therapy process rather than posttreatment, involves some logistical coordination between therapists, but the results can be rewarding both for the therapist as well as clients. The key is for the process to be experienced as something *other than* therapy so the interview is not confusing to the clients. The best procedure is for two therapists to coordinate, interviewing each other's clients (after securing client permission, of course). The process is described at intake, and the clients are allowed to opt in or out of the interviews. The goal for the interviews is stated openly: the therapist wants your feedback, and sometimes it is easier to share your views with an intermediary. The pragmatics are outlined: another therapist will come into the room for the last 5 minutes of every other session, she or he will ask for your feedback on the therapy, the interviewer will take handwritten notes of your responses and not comment or engage in discussion, and she or he will relay your responses to the therapist within the next few days (no secrets will be kept). For example, every few sessions, Juan would switch rooms and ask some standard questions of Tiffany's clients while Tiffany does the same with Juan's. Each interview would only take a few minutes' time at the end of a session, and the questions asked by the interviewer are crafted by the therapist to coordinate with his/her goal-setting process and the client's context. A family therapy case with small children, a highly conflicted couple, and a single individual would each require different time considerations and careful attention to questions so they fit each context. This methodology allows therapists to craft questions and get direct feedback from clients without having to actually listen to their responses, which at times can be uncomfortable.

The most direct methods to obtain client viewpoints are face-to-face. These can be as simple as asking some preplanned questions of all clients in a certain time period (cross-sectional) or deliberate and unscripted across an entire single case (ongoing or longitudinal) (Barnard and Kuehl 1995). *Preplanned questions* work well when therapists are working on particular skills and wish to know clients' experiences of changes in these goal areas. I call these debriefing questions and utilize them with beginning master's level student therapists to seasoned professionals. Some sample questions include, *What fit well for you? Tell me about a moment in this session when you felt affirmed. Tell me about a moment in this session when you felt hope. What did I do well?*[2] In the best SF tradition, I ask therapists to follow each item with the question, *What (or when) else?* This allows clients to offer more than

---

[2] Some of these are not questions, they are imperatives. Changing between the two linguistic forms is a way to minimize the possibility that the person being interviewed feels cross-examined (interrogatory [questioning] and interrogation have the same root).

one positive moment in each category: appropriateness, affirmation, creating hope, and positive therapist performance. The risk of negative responses is quite low, and most therapists' experiences move from initial awkwardness to honest enjoyment.

Direct Methods. SF supervision has a long history of involving client feedback in the supervision process, and most of the video examples in the SFBTA Archive involve direct conversations with clients and are consistent with the SF approach itself. Insoo (Berg n.d., SFBTA Archive #10128-0064) had a practice she called "client-driven supervision" when using a one-way mirror during live supervision. After the session is finished, "the supervisor goes in, and asks the client right after the session, 'What did this therapist do that was helpful for you?'" She would follow this with, "what else?" to elicit other responses from the client. Insoo used this approach with the therapist in the room and as a post-session interview. For supervision teams fortunate enough to have live supervision, this can be accomplished with or without a one-way mirror. As outlined in Lane and Thomas (Contribution 7.5 in this book), the supervisor can be situated in the therapy room if the communication structure is clearly outlined for everyone. In this structure, the supervisor sits to the side during the therapy session, only interrupting with permission from the therapist to have a supervision consult (with the client present) and limiting conversation to therapist–supervisor or therapist–client to minimize confusion. At the end of the session, the supervisor can request to speak directly to the client and ask Insoo-like questions, momentarily changing the structure to benefit the entire system.

Other direct methods of drawing out client feedback involve the therapist without the supervisor present. Therapists should start this practice with, "what was helpful today?" using "what else?" types of questions. Once therapists get used to soliciting positive responses, I like to introduce them to *"ongoing evaluation"* (Barnard and Kuehl 1995). These authors focus on therapeutic relationship ("working alliance," p. 161) in this process, but other lines of questioning could be created to assist in therapist goal setting. They did a wonderful job creating this evaluation context that can be adapted so therapists can find out what clients are experiencing:

> Each episode of questioning should be prefaced by something such as the following: "I'd like to stop what we're doing for just a few minutes to talk about how and what we're doing. Please answer as honestly as you can, because if there are any difficulties, I'd like to address them before we get any further into the counseling. Please don't be afraid of hurting my feelings. Rest assured that I can take whatever you have to offer. I have found this to be a very valuable way of getting more accomplished more quickly than what otherwise occurs." (Barnard and Kuehl 1995, p. 168)

The frame, which emphasizes client benefit, is honest; a parallel benefit is that therapists hear clients' viewpoints of therapy which informs their change process. The authors break questions into three categories to coincide with the beginning, middle, and termination of therapy. Questions in the beginning of the case are about logistics, expectations, and general therapist performance: *Do you have any concerns about the therapy? Are we doing what you thought we would be doing? Does it seem like I am "getting it?"* Middle-stage questions open things up as they request information about clients' comfort and confusion: *Are we taking a good direction? Do the goals we've set make sense, and are they still relevant? Do you have suggestions on how we could move forward to make this work even better for you?* Finally, questions near the end of the therapy case are more evaluative of the experience and the therapist: *How satisfied are you with our work together? With the outcome? What was most helpful to you? On the other side, what did I do that maybe wasn't that helpful? What suggestions do you have for me if I had another person/couple/family with a problem/situation similar to yours?* Barnard and Kuehl (1995, p. 170) have found that clients are very responsive when asked questions relevant to their experiences, and their enthusiasm is marked when asked to "'give back' something to the therapist." Although ongoing evaluation can be the most threatening, it can also reap the most rewards for therapists adventurous enough to engage in the process.

4.1.5 Initial Goals

The supervisor needs to prepare for initial goal setting in an early meeting (if not the initial meeting) with the therapist. The goal-setting template in Appendix C has some examples of goals to which therapists can refer, but examples can limit as well as expand imagination. Sometimes, beginning therapists simply adopt the examples as their initial goals, which makes sense because the examples are drawn from novice therapists' forms over the years. After discussion about the various categories and how they relate to supervision, therapists need to put some reflective thought into creating a draft for the next supervisory meeting. My introduction of the goal-setting process is quite simple: aim high but stay realistic, make it personal, keep it relevant, and remember the goals are beginnings in a lifelong process of learning.

If supervisors are part of a system that requires evaluation, I would suggest separating most of the goal-setting process from performance evaluation. Some agencies base salary increases or bonuses on performance, and university practicum courses may require grades based on demonstrations of competence. The difficulty that results if achievement forms the basis for reward is that therapists aim low; under these circumstances, therapists often avoid the possibility of failure by taking fewer risks, as small success and reward can be more enticing than risking more and failing. If supervisors have a voice in the compensation process, they should try to influence the decision-making practice toward other aspects of therapists' performance if possible. In the university setting, grades can be based on content mastery regarding ethics, application, assessment, and other clinically relevant topics, leaving supervisory goals out of the equation.

4.1.6 Practice: Revisioning and Recalibrating One's Goals

SF practices are simply ways of working—they aren't magic, and they don't work better cumulatively so you don't have to try to cram them all into a supervision session. Below is a fictional supervision example involving therapist-revisioning goals. This recalibrating practice helps create the best chance of successful goal setting and offers an opportunity for supervisors to assist in the activity. In this example, Chris is a newly licensed counselor who has committed to learning SFBT at the agency where Ricki supervises. Chris's experience is limited, but the passion to learn comes through in the goal-setting process and case management meetings:

Supervisor Ricki: Hey Chris—how'd the work on revising your goals go for you?

Therapist Chris: Well, it wasn't difficult to find holes I need to fill, that's for sure! There's just *so* much to work on…maybe I bit off more than I can chew…

R: Let's start where we always start—where did you make the most progress? *(starting off with success talk, a good way to set a positive, hopeful tone)*

C: I think it was in my conceptual competency goal.

R: Well, tell me about the progress have you made on that one since our last review.

C: My conceptual goal was to apply EARS (*SFBT practice: Elicit, Amplify, Reflect/Reinforce, and Start over*) with 90% of my clients after I heard an exception in the session. That's gone really well! Finding ways to document this in the client case notes has been a challenge at times, you know, but I was able to keep track of it pretty well.

R: How did you do that, keep track of it? *(question about agency, assuming Chris made a choice here rather than attributing success to chance)*

C: Mostly I made notes at the end of the session, then recalled times I *didn't* use EARS during that session, and just tallied them up in a little notebook…works for me!

R: Is this notebook process something you've used before? *(searching for exceptions)*

C: Not in this job.

R: So you've used it before in some other place, some other part of your life? *(eliciting exception talk, amplifying success)*

C: Yeah. I use it all the time to keep track of my eating. I'm trying to maintain my weight where it is, which is pretty tough sometimes! But I met my goal on losing weight a year ago, and part of that was tracking vegetables and fruits—you know, how many portions per meal, that kind of thing. I would recall what I ate each day—I eat four small meals a day—and use a notebook to track veggie/fruit portions *and* when I didn't have any with a meal. That way I can see holes that I need to fill…you know, with more veggies and such.

R: "Holes you need to fill"—that's the second time you've used that phrase. I thought it was about deficit, but there seems to be more here than talk about what you're *not* doing.

C: Yeah, it's just pretty simple, something I'm used to.

4.1 Goal Setting: Active, Responsive Goal Creation and Assessment

R: A plan you've transferred from your personal life to work—Nice! I like it! *(compliment)* I'd like to come back to this process you've figured out sometime soon, if not later in our time today—I think you're onto something here that might tell me more about how you learn and change, which could really help me in our supervision.
C: Cool…hadn't thought that it might help *you*, but I can do that.
R: So, how are you on the "90%" part of this goal?
C: Actually…I think I'm there. I've got a way to track that I can keep up if I need to, but as far as this goal and learning SFBT, I don't see how I could reset this goal, you know? I really don't have to spend that much time thinking about this goal anymore because it's sort of natural…
R: Yeah, sounds right. So, what's next with this goal? If it's coming naturally, is there anything we need to do to maintain this? *(assumes supervision could play a supportive role in maintaining this practice)*
C: No…I think I'm good. Knowing I'd be asked about it here in supervision has helped me focus on it, make a lot of progress.
R: Glad to help! OK, let me know if I can help with this one in the future. What else is better with your goal setting? *(assumes multiple points of progress)*
C: I'm still working on getting client feedback.
R: What's working for you so far? *(eliciting success and exception talk)*
C: I ask clients what they thought about the session at the end, and that's really been interesting…
R: And what was the goal you set for yourself in this area?
C: Oh, yeah—I was going to ask clients for feedback 25% of the time. I started out using SF-type questions, like "What went well in this session?" and "What was most helpful today?" Now I've added more, well, risk on my part! I'm using some of the Barnard and Kuehl (1995) types of questions…
R: Give me a few examples.
C: I asked one client something like, "Is there anything I've said today that was confusing to you?" He really thought about that one, and then he said, "Well, we talked about that one time today I wasn't sure what you wanted, and we cleared it up."
R: Did you know you'd get a favorable response from this client?
C: No, not really. I remembered that moment when he was puzzled in-session, but I didn't know he would say it was positive. I thought it might be a negative.
R: So…where would you say you are on that goal of 25%?

C:	I think I've gone past that…I'm learning from asking them, but I'm also enjoying it!
R:	Time to rethink that goal?
C:	Yeah, past time. I need to go for, say, maybe…75%.
R:	75% of clients or 75% of sessions you have? (*seeking specifics*)
C:	75% of sessions. I need to get feedback from all my clients, but I don't want to wear them out, you know?
R:	Yeah, makes sense. OK, write that up on your continuous goal-setting form for the next time we meet so we can keep track of it…but don't wait until then to get more client feedback. Don't let *me* hold you back! (*laughter*)

Establishing and evaluating goals is a major tool in SF supervision. While aspects of goal setting can be cumbersome, most therapists appreciate both the experience of change and the collaboration with supervisors as they track success. When possible, goals should concentrate on obtainable results within the grasp of therapists, require hard work, and be reviewed and adjusted on a regular basis. Just like the athlete who puts a note on the mirror that says, "finish a mini-triathlon by August," goals serve a teleological function: they pull us into the future, creating possible futures we could not imagine before we started imagining.

4.2 Highlighting Exceptions and Successes

"Wait—do you realize what you just accomplished?!" Whether it's your son's first success at tying shoelaces or your daughter's graduation from college, this question coming from a parent can make a major difference in a child's life. Reviewing a success and reflecting on its meaning in one's life can bring about ramifying changes. Part of this impact comes from the success itself, but the effect can be heightened by reflection and relationship.

We are always looking around to see if anyone else notices what we do. I recently took a tumble crossing a street—I tripped on a crack in the asphalt and did a complete forward roll, ending up flat on my back. Unhurt, the first thing I did was look around to see if anyone had witnessed my misfortune. After getting off the street and onto the sidewalk, I realized I was not embarrassed…but I felt I would have been if someone had seen me take the fall. And the context mattered. We take scores of falls every week as we practice aikido, a martial art related to judo that requires controlled falls while practicing with partners. Someone witnesses *every* fall I take at the dojo, but I've never been embarrassed smacking onto the mats there. I have praised others' falls many times. So "taking a fall" requires context to be understood, and witnesses can alter the experience.

While at the shooting range recently, I shot every round—a group of 15—in the center or "10 ring," something I'd never done before at that distance. I set my handgun down and clicked the toggle switch that motored the target from downrange to my shooting position, letting it hang in front of me for a few seconds. Enjoying the moment, I didn't notice the range master standing behind me (since everyone wears ear protection, it's easy for him to walk around unnoticed). He tapped me on the shoulder, raised his thumb, and mouthed, "nice shooting!" before walking on. My pride swelled—he's an expert, and he liked my performance! The holes in the target were the same, but the significance changed.

I believe one of the most important things I can do as a SF supervisor is to notice success and positive difference in therapists and their clinical work. This is a long-standing practice in SF supervision (O'Connell and Jones 2001; Selekman and Todd 1995; Thomas 1996; Wheeler, J. 2007), and for good reason: it matters. But while simple noticing may be positive, reflecting on these moments with therapists compounds success.

Identifying exceptions requires purposeful attention. Whether supervision involves reviewing files with therapists, case consultation (McCollum and Wetchler 1995), video review, or live supervision, SF supervisors must make a concerted effort to locate and highlight these differences. Since SF approaches hold firmly to the assumption that exceptions exist, this presupposition biases the supervisor's observing of therapists' clinical work. Supervisors already hold a different position in relation to the therapist/client system, so their views will differ from other participants' experiences; bringing a bias toward exception finding magnifies this differences and increases the likelihood that positive change is noted.

Not all exceptions are of equal importance (Nyland and Corsiglia 1994). Differences related to therapists' goals should float to the top as one takes notes, and this requires reviewing their goal information prior to supervision meetings. Just as most therapists review their session notes to refresh their memories regarding shifts, significant information, and tasks assigned in the last therapy session, supervisors should get in the habit of preparing for supervision by taking a moment to reread materials related to each therapist's aspirations.

When participating in live therapy as an observer, SF supervisors should note specific differences, changes, and exceptions, especially those related to current goals. Generating a list on a notepad creates a record of success and allows returning to these moments when the therapist and supervisory sit down to discuss the session. Reviewing video recordings with therapists is a supervision practice with a long history. The impact is delayed; conversations related to recordings will not have the real-time impact that supervisory interventions have during live supervision. But there is an added value: reviewing allows for reflection on a particular moment when the video is paused, and supervisor and therapist can take time to reflect on a segment and build significance that cannot be done in real time. What often sets live and video observation apart from case consultation is detail. There is greater value in noting specific moments or behaviors than generalities that result from summaries. When two people observe an event, the result is stereoscopic (Bateson 1979)—depth is created from double description. Case consultation is one person's account of an incident, and detail is usually lost. Consider this: Let's say a client had a conversation with a helpful friend, wrote a summary of that conversation, and brought the summary to his therapy session. Instead of having a personal discussion about the client's current experience, the summary becomes the focus of the encounter: the therapist asks questions about the client–friend discussion and the client recalls and reveals details that were not included in the written summary. The only person in the room with a first-hand experience is the client; the therapist is interviewing a witness to the event and is not a part of the event itself. Although this could be interesting, few would say it is equivalent to the therapist–client experience of therapy. Being one step removed loses detail.

So in video review supervision, inquiry about exceptions usually focuses on client experiences and therapist/client interaction. The following questions illustrate ways the supervisor might enter the conversational space:

"Dave, could I ask you a question? (*Therapist gives his approval*) You noticed and called attention to Ashley's changes this week, times she was feeling 'hope.' How might these changes affect your work together?"

"This change that Ashley experienced…Was this unexpected for you?"
"Has Ashley had other changes like this during your therapy together?"

"Ashley just paid you a compliment! What does this mean to you?"

Video reviewing in supervision can have delayed impact on clients' lives and therapist/client interaction, but it also allows for candid conversations about therapists' exceptions and successes. Using this method, the supervisor can pause the video and draw attention to a specific exchange, focusing more on the therapist's actions and meanings:

"OK, so Ashley is talking about a pretty significant change here, and you attend to it by asking for her to reflect a bit on it. How did you decide to do that?"

"You noticed something pretty subtle here. How is it that you saw this? I don't know if many therapists would have…"

"Ashley gives you partial credit for the changes she's made, and you responded with, 'Thank you.' That's quite different than other times I've seen you receive a compliment – you used to reject them. What do you think this says about you?"

"Was it easy or difficult for you to make this recent shift?"

"How were you able to make this change?"

"If Ashley were here and I asked her, 'What other ways has Dave had a positive impact in therapy with you?', what do you think she'd say?"

Finally, case consultation and case file review allow for broader perspectives on therapist change, a potentially valuable time of reflection on success across time and cases (McCollum and Wetchler 1995). Connecting successes to goals is an important task for supervisors working in a SF way. The questions asked are often presuppositional. Assumptions are "embedded in the question," and "any answer to a question affirms the presupposition embedded in the question, even in those cases where the presupposition may not be true" (McGee, Del Vento, and Bavelas 2005). Noticing exceptions that may be important based on the therapist's goals and your own views on the person's change process leads to reflective questions that assume both change and significance:

"You've been consistently seeking client feedback these past few weeks, which is quite a change from the first months we've been meeting together. What changed for you? How are you making this happen?"

"When clients notice exceptions in their lives, you are really quick to call attention to them by asking for detail. This seems in line with your perceptual goal in this area. How easy is it for you to notice? What do you think this says about you, that you've been able to make this adjustment?"

"You're closing cases pretty quickly—your average number of sessions has dropped from 20 to nine over the past year we've been meeting, and at the same time your client satisfaction reports are improving. How did you get this to happen? What do you think it says about you? Your therapy? Your relationships with clients?"

Highlighting therapist exceptions, success, and progress is a feel-good experience. Although some therapists remain uncomfortable with this practice, most adjust to supervisory praise within the questions and respond reflectively.[3] Also, evaluation of therapist performance is affected—supervisors can note positive changes without ignoring prominent therapist shortcomings and areas that need improvement.

4.3 Scaling

Scaling is a public phenomenon. Marketing and social researchers use scales on a regular basis to assess consumer opinions and rate particular services or products. Medical professionals (e.g., APGAR scales for newborns) and even people evaluating attractiveness ("She's a '10'") use scaling to evaluate and gauge progress. And because this is both ordinary and useful, scaling is among the most commonly used SF techniques (Berg 1994; Berg and de Shazer 1993; de Shazer 1988). Insoo made scaling a high priority when supervising and when teaching supervisors (Berg 1999a). She and collaborator Peter De Jong wrote:

> We encourage supervisors to make extensive use of scaling questions and relationship questions to monitor the progress their clients are making. These questions are useful in discovering and getting details about practitioner successes and also serve as a gentle tap on the shoulder to invite them to wonder about what they may have missed about the client's frame of reference and what else might be done to make their interactions with clients even more solution focused. (De Jong and Berg 2012, p. 281)

Multiple contributors to this volume endorse and illustrate its value in supervision.

"Scales are used to 'measure' the client's own perception, to motivate and encourage, and to elucidate the goals and anything else that is important" (Berg and de Shazer 1993, p. 9). This practice assesses progress and motivates people toward change (De Jong and Berg 2012; Lloyd and Dallos 2008; Macdonald 2007a; O'Connell and Jones 2001; Wheeler, J. 2007). In its simplest form as an assessment tool, SF scales are generally constructed with the client and range from zero (or one) to ten, with higher numbers indicating better outcome or higher value. Creating

---

[3] See Hsu and Kuo (Sect. 7.4, this volume) for less-direct complimenting methods adjusted for cultural differences.

space for differences to be noticed, scaling moves experience from artificial dichotomies toward ranges of experience. Although there are some dichotomies in life (e.g., being pregnant or not), most dichotomies are simply epistemological habits. We say, "I have/don't have the problem," but these are personal constructions confined to a particular time period. "I have/don't have a weight problem" is not measurable or observable by another person, and change cannot be externally verified. Its resolution cannot be described by anyone except that person defining the problem, who is informed by social, medical, and other factors regarding ideal weight, body size and shape, body fat percentages, and so on. One can use a bathroom scale to assess change, but the goal and significance of progress regarding a "weight problem" are not dictated by the scale itself—it simply informs.

Scales related to change can also be used as motivational tools. Noting difference does not indicate significance, as significance is assigned. But eliciting information about change using scaling calls attention to difference, and further exploration of these differences often creates meaningful points of incentive, building excitement around the change process and taking advantage of the snowball effect described in Sect. 2.1— change begets change. These SF scales are anchored in the client's experience; that is, they have been found to be valid portrayals and, when used consistently, they are *reliable* measures of difference (Franklin, Corcoran, Streeter, and Nowicki 1997; Thomas and Nelson 2007). If I say my satisfaction regarding the service I received at the auto repair shop was a "7," I had some internal or external comparator that guided me to assign that number to my encounter. And if the survey research company asked me, "What would need to change so you could give us a '10'?" I would probably be able to generate ideas about specific changes or additions that, if met, would enhance my *experience* and my resulting *rating* of the service. These distinctions are important in supervision for several reasons. First, the goal-setting process itself creates an expectation of change—therapists presume establishing goals is an exercise of progress and/or achievement, and scaling is a vital aspect of evaluating these. Also, multiple exceptions or successes across different clinical sessions or cases can be tied to scales. "So considering these exceptions together, how would you rate your ability to notice positive changes in your clients now compared to when you started?" is an example of a question that crosses several contexts but relates to specific therapist knowledge. In addition, positive change builds confidence and activates motivation. Finally, being able to discern a desirable change that results from one's own efforts creates a sense of hope in one's clinical development. Attending to specific skill acquisition and improvement is much more powerful than general statements that could fit any person or situation, and specificity expands possibilities and feeds the desire for new heights. Snyder (2002, p. 251) refers to this belief in one's ability to affect change as agency. "Agency thought—the perceived capacity to use one's pathways to reach desired goals—is the motivational component in hope theory…we have found that high-hope people embrace such self-talk agency phrases as, 'I can do this,' and 'I am not going to be stopped.'" Goal setting, noticing exceptions, highlighting success, and scaling progress all contribute to therapist agency.

The major topics to keep in mind regarding SF scale construction include simplicity, self-anchoring, ease of use, and aiming toward the presence of what is desired. First, therapists must grasp the point of the scale without a great deal of meaning negotiation—that's the point of a numerical scale. Discussion should focus on the number assigned by the therapist and differences experienced. Scales should simplify the process, not create greater complexity. Further, scales should be anchored in the therapist's experience. Each scale should be unique to the therapist and supervisor; although there may be commonalities across therapists' desires and successes, canned scales will not fit the context as well because of differences between therapists' goals and the specific language used in each supervisory relationship. Next, supervision scales need to be easily constructed and accessed. Zero (low) to ten (high, desired) are easy to construct and remember across supervision meetings. If the scale is anchored by a therapist's description of problem/solution or lack of/presence of success toward a goal, then using "0-to-10" talk is quite easy. Finally, improvements on the scale (toward higher numbers) should indicate more of what the therapist wants. Goals need to be stated as the presence of what is desired rather than the absence of a problem (De Jong and Berg 2012); scales function similarly.

Many therapists, like clients, tire of constant scaling or scaling that sounds preplanned. Scaling around motivation and confidence is best applied at particular junctions in supervision, such as times of initial goal setting and reviews. Once therapist and supervisor have a sense of where the therapist is on the scale and the direction of change (as setbacks happen as well as successes), conversation should center on influences that assist progress.

Scaling questions can have several intentions, but the categories found by Strong et al. (2009) in their research of SF scaling questions used in therapy clarify three common purposes that fit well with the supervisory context:

1. "To quantify the (person's) subjective experience of a concern…or confidence in attaining an articulated goal" (p. 175). An example of the former scaling question might be: "On a scale from zero to ten, with 'zero' being 'overwhelmed' and 'ten' being 'calm,' where were you at when the client said she was suicidal?" A question that attempts to ascertain confidence would be similar to this: "OK, you say we've talked this through enough and you feel confident you'd be calmer with the next suicidal client. How confident are you, 0-to-10, with '10' being 'completely confident'?"
2. "To 'scaffold' solutions or find…exceptions from a previously scaled concern or goal" (e.g., "what will help you get from a '6' to a '7' in achieving your goal?") (Strong et al. 2009, p. 175).
3. "To reevaluate a prior scaled rating of a concern or goal" (e.g., "if you were at a '5' in terms of confidence at the start of your session, where are you now on that scale?") (Strong et al. 2009, p. 175).

My supervision mentoring has provided me with many opportunities to observe supervisors learning the craft of scaling…it is simple, but not easy to perfect. Practicing scale construction with an understanding therapist who tolerates "mulligans" (or a do-over) is an excellent way to improve one's aim and simplify the scale. The most common supervisor mistakes include trying to scale too much experience in a single scale, neglecting therapist language, failing to secure the scale to therapist goals, and overusing scales to the point of annoyance. In closing: "Suppose this therapist you are supervising were to think your helpfulness to her had improved one point on the useless-helpful scale you've created here in supervision-of-supervision. What might she notice you are doing differently? How would you find that out?" (Adapted from De Jong and Berg 2012, p. 281).

4.4 Hedging

Hedging (Berg 2003; Rudes et al. 1997) is a way of communicating information as well as stating that there are multiple, equally valid views that could be constructed in a situation. Semantically, hedging can have effects on group membership (by using "inside jokes" or terms), views of truth (e.g., "the original texts are not preserved, but our best guess is…"), or what Varttala (2001, p. 34) calls "illocutionary force" (such as, "do you really want to do that?") (Lakoff 1973). Viewed pragmatically, hedging is used widely, from everyday speech practice to academic discourse and physician-to-physician communication. Parents hedge frequently to create latitude in decisions:

Child: Can we go to the park?
Parent: *Maybe* later today, but tomorrow *looks even better*—we have to pick up your aunt in a few minutes.

Scientists strategically use hedging to construct arguments without full commitment, liberally using words like "probably," "possibly," and "potentially" in written discourse (Varttala 2001). Similarly, physicians approximate a great deal of the time when diagnoses or options are unclear, using words and phrases like "about," "I think," and "probably" to portray uncertainty or incomplete commitment (Prince, Frader, and Bosk 1982). An example:

Physician 1: What's the diagnosis?
Physician 2: I'm *almost* certain it's Crohn's disease—she's a smoker and has a family history of that. *I think* we'll *have a better idea* after the culture and blood test results come back to *possibly rule out* celiac disease or ulcerative colitis. (*Notice that Physician 2's position is to "rule out" other diagnoses, a common hedging practice that does not arrive at a specific diagnosis but eliminates some alternative explanations.*)

Hyland (1996, p. 437) went so far as to call hedging "polypragmatic," a very ordinary practice used both innocently and intentionally in written and oral communication.

In SF supervision, this technique involves being tentative in one's responses, rejecting a privileged position of knowledge and recognizing and welcoming multiple views. Although it appears unilateral, hedging is actually used to generate a responsive process of co-construction in conversation. This is a prominent aspect of Insoo's supervision style, emerging from the "not-knowing" stance she incorporated into her SF practices in the 1990s (De Jong and Berg 2012). "From the constructivist position that (Insoo) values, she is letting the trainees know, through hedging (…'I think that probably') that her responses are her construction and that she does not have a privileged position of knowledge" (Rudes et al. 1997, p. 209).

4.4 Hedging

When hedging, the supervisor leaves room for questioning and dialogue after making a statement or raising a question. Phrases like "I wonder if," "Maybe it's," or "Is it possible that" are not conclusive or directive; they invite conversation. Hedging allows space for difference and requests alternatives and even disagreement ("or, maybe it means..."). Berg and her colleagues (Rudes et al. 1997) saw these exchanges as a recursive process, with hedging influencing supervision and supervision influencing hedging. Since this practice invites additional opinions, supervisor and therapist have a greater variety of possibilities to consider prior to agreement (or even moving forward without a clear conclusion). Here are examples of hedging from Rudes' (1992) transcription of a supervision session led by Insoo[4]:

Therapist:	One of the things that struck me was her admission and realization or statement, I should say, that she doesn't play with him like she used to. And he has asked her to do that and she has said that "you're too [big]."
Insoo Kim Berg:	Too big for that.
Th:	She can't fool around with him anymore because he is too big for that and I think then she can turn around and say if things are going well I could probably do that.
IKB:	Yes—right.
Th:	"If he would do these things I'd probably give him what he wants."
IKB:	And also *maybe if* he is too big I could give to him in a different way, not pinching him. *Like* she was talking about pinching him a lot but instead of pinching him *maybe* there are other things she can do. *Maybe* more age appropriate so potential solutions will come out of her head.
Th:	Yeah.
	...
IKB:	Right—it's her kid's problem so she is coming in telling us about this serious problem that her son has so—*I think* we should accept that, *at this point*.
Th:	Right, I do too.
Team member:	And I still have the question by pursuing the miracle so far I want to know what she got or what you think she got.
IKB:	OK, *I think that probably* what she got was she *probably* saw these things from her perspective. We got her to see these things from a different person's perspective, what the husband would say—you notice difference?
Th:	Uh-huh. (Rudes 1992)

---

[4] A more complete case transcription is included, with annotation, in Chapter 5 in this book. Used with permission from Jim Rudes.

I believe these examples of hedging resulted from Insoo's mental commitment to not-knowing, a "getting into the habit of using tentative language" (Berg 2003, p. 42). I doubt she was being strategic, thinking about how to phrase her questions or responses for a desired effect; she simply spoke what she was thinking in less-than-certain ways that allowed the therapist and team members to consider her view as one possibility out of many. Insoo was cognizant of her position as a supervisor consultant on the case and very aware of her position power, and hedging had the effect of increased openness to ideas from everyone in the discussion and building a collaborative, respectful team discussion that did not require deferring to the guest supervisor's ideas.

A supervisor working from a more certain, modernist stance might take more instructional positions in supervision or assume a directive stance sooner than a SF supervisor. A less collaborative approach might lead a supervisor to say, "What needs to be challenged is the client's…" or "This is the next step you need to take with this client…."[5] A SF supervisor working from a not-knowing position maintains flexibility as long as possible to flatten hierarchy and create options for the therapist. Hedging is not a gimmick; it is both a technique and a mindset. As one begins the intentional use of hedges, it may not feel authentic; however, I have found that using it transparently is a productive approach[6] that often leads to a comfortable habit and (potentially) to an attitude so one hedges naturally. I openly discuss with therapists how my "default mode" of supervision may be experienced as indirect, even when they ask for answers and direction. Then I work to be responsive, adjusting to the therapist's learning style and experience level whenever possible. I do not capitulate and abandon my not-knowing stance or hedging practice simply because a therapist requests it, as we both have ideas and limitations on what we believe is helpful and appropriate. So when therapist Phil feels my supervision has been too indirect, we process our experience:

Phil: I just want some answers, some direction here…
Frank: …and what you're asking for is *the* answer. Do you think I've got the answer and am withholding it?
P: No…maybe…I don't know! It's just frustrating sometimes when I want to be told what to do and you won't tell me.
F: So part of this is my style, being indirect, and part of it might be my refusing to tell you what to do.
P: You just did it—"might be"!

---

[5] Note the use of "might" in these last two sentences, used to hedge against disagreement, as I am not including *all* non-SF supervisors or *all* modernist supervisors. It also creates leeway for SF supervisors to educate and direct therapists when supervisors believe the context requires such action.

[6] See the discussion on "metaphor, semaphore, two-by-four" later in this chapter; see Sects. 3.13.4, 4.5.2, and 4.7 plus Lane and Thomas (Sect. 7.5) for more on indirectness in supervision.

F: Yeah, it's a habit, sorry about that…but right now, it really is how I see things connecting (*transparency*). You ask me to tell you what to do with this client after we've generated three options together. All these options look good to me, and I can't predict the future so I don't know which might work best—that's why they're called "options." And there's no danger in the options—any of these seem safe to both of us. And the client is real clear that there's no danger in his situation. So we're back to risk versus danger—this is about you taking the risk in a fairly safe way, with little danger to the client. And I'm not going to make that decision—you are.

P: Yeah, I get it…sometimes it would be nice if you just told me what to do.

F: How would that be helpful?

P: I wouldn't fret as much…my anxiety would go down.

F: So part of this is related to anxiety…about what?

P: I like to plan, and I want his therapy to go well…

F: So part of the question is about when this would be helpful—when anxiety is high.

P: Yeah.

F: OK…well, I'm still leaving the decision up to you here—I don't think getting into a habit of me choosing among your options when the therapy is going well is a good way to supervise. So, could we talk about reducing anxiety instead of me making decisions for you? Can we start there?

P: OK…maybe the real problem is getting a better grip on my anxiety.

F: Now *you're* hedging! (*laughter from both*) That might be a good place to start…I know you learn from success and from struggle. Let's scale anxiety. If you have less anxiety, you have more what?

P: Hmmm, gotta think about that one. (*The discussion moves on, including talk about goals related to in-session anxiety, creating a scale on anxiety/"calm" [the 10 on his anxiety scale], exceptions/differences in-session and in other related areas of life around "calm," and his agency around these experiences.*)

Hedging is a common conversational experience that can be utilized as a tool to create collaboration and space for difference of opinion. For multiple examples of Insoo's use of hedging in supervision, see Chap. 5.

4.5 Complimenting

Insoo insisted that SF therapists "compliment whenever possible" (Berg 2000, "20 minutes interview"; cf. Berg n.d., SFBTA Archive #10128-0064). She clearly carried this commitment forward into supervision. Complimenting has been a basic element in SF practice since early in its evolution (Berg and Miller 1992; de Shazer 1979; de Shazer and Berg 1997; Korman and Söderquist 1999; Rudes 1992; Thomas and Nelson 2007). It remains essential in defining SF in some circles (Beyebach

2000), and it is certainly common in practice, training, and supervision today (Berg and De Jong 2005; De Jong and Berg 2012; Ratner, George, and Iveson 2012). Some questions have been raised regarding the possible contradiction between this practice of complimenting and maintaining a not-knowing position. As Iveson (2005, p. 5) wrote:

> This most extreme version of the many ways solution-focused brief therapists try not to know puts into question the necessity of both tasks and compliments. Solution-focused tasks require, in their indirectness, a significant amount of thought in which information about the client is processed. … The fact that it is not a "problem focused knowing" makes it no less "knowing." Compliments, too, require a form of knowing that does not sit easily with the principle of "not-knowing." They are, after all, the product of an assessment. We only have to give a bad compliment (e.g., one which celebrates a positive quality within our own culture which is regarded differently within the client's culture) to know how flimsy and provisional these assessments can be.

For me, speaking from my experience moves away from these contradictions. "I like that" expresses my opinion, which fits within the not-knowing stance. Complimenting can take many forms, including direct, indirect, and self-complimenting (Berg and De Jong 2005). Within each of these three frames one can offer compliments that are opinions supported by facts, opinions that are drawn from therapist's expressions and experiences, and group deductions or conclusions. I agree with Iveson that all assessment/opinions are "provisional," but I don't believe not-knowing is equivalent to know-nothing—I know my own experiences, and if my conjectures do not fit with another's views of the same set of facts, that simply supports the postmodern nature of this approach. I don't abandon all hope of holding or expressing an opinion; I simply offer compliments as opinions and "watch (people's) reactions to the affirmations," as "their reactions will give you important clues about whether the compliments make sense to them…if they do not, you can reevaluate your thinking" (De Jong and Berg 2012, p. 124). This works across therapeutic and supervisory contexts—the compliment, kindly and tentatively offered, is assigned meaning by the other, which should recursively inform my views and future actions.

Therefore, I believe offering compliments can be an important practice in supervision. It can take many roles in the supervisory relationship, from prevention to intervention. But I see the primary role of supervisory compliments as a way to engage, contributing to therapists' confidence, sharing credit for change, and encouraging therapist reflection (Berg 2003; Berg and De Jong 2005; Furman and Ahola 1992; Thomas 2012b).

Descriptions of different types of complimenting common to SF practices is in order. The distinctions among direct, indirect, and self-compliments were clearly outlined in Berg and De Jong's (2005) article, "Engagement Through Complimenting," giving us a touchstone to which we can compare and contrast different types of complimenting.

4.5.1 Direct Compliments

A direct compliment is a statement made by the supervisor about the therapist or the therapist's work, often coming across as factual. "You are less anxious with this client" would be an example of a direct compliment. One important point to keep in mind is direct compliments can easily be dismissed by the other because (1) they are stated as facts, which often cannot be verified, or (2) they assume factual knowledge of something that is not factual or cannot be directly known. In this case, the supervisor's compliment assumes knowledge of the therapist's inner state, which cannot be known by another. (Even self-disclosure does not directly portray inner states, so one cannot have direct, unambiguous knowledge of another's experience.) A SF supervision approach seeks to avoid either/or distinctions whenever possible because such distinctions are so easily dismissed and lack collaboration ("You are relaxed"; "No, I'm not"). But the primary reason for avoiding such declarative compliments is that telling people what they are or what their experiences mean violates the principle SF assumption that therapists are the experts on their experiences. A better place to begin on this declarative–suggestive complimenting continuum is basing one's compliment on and limiting it to observable behaviors:

Sadie (Supervisor): I see you sitting forward when she was discussing her marital separation.
Ted (Therapist): Yeah, I've been working on that.
S: Let's see, here's your goal-setting form…One of your goals is to "vary my nonverbals in ways that show increased attention when clients are distressed." Is that the one you're talking about?
T: Uh-huh, that's the one. That was on my mind right when she started talking about the separation because she teared up, which cued me to engage even more and use my body to do that. I usually just sit back all the time, so this was an experiment.
S: Well, I noticed your posture changed during that exchange, and I liked that—seems like you do, too.
T: Yeah, that's what I see as well—glad you noticed!

In this illustration, Sadie moved toward complimenting in several steps, paying attention to Ted's responses as she eased into it. The therapist's feedback informed Sadie that she was on the right track, and tying her compliment process to Ted's goal made a connection of significance within the supervision rather than just complimenting something she liked about the therapy session. This exchange only took 45 seconds, but the effect was compounded because Ted found it meaningful. In addition, Sadie hedges her statements, which supports this complimenting technique—"seems like you do, too" allows for therapist disagreement or modification.

If a different supervisor (Nathan) had declared, "You're attending to your client better than in the past" at the same point in the supervision, the resulting discussion would probably take longer, and Ted would be put in the position of teasing out the reasons for the supervisor's conclusions:

Nathan: You're attending to your client better than in the past.
Ted: What do you mean?
N: Well, you're leaning forward at the point she teared up.

T: How is that better? I mean, I think it is, but I'm wondering what you're thinking.
N: That forward lean is what you need to do to let the client know you're present and listening.
T: I was listening before I leaned in…but I leaned in because I'm trying to use my body more to communicate with clients.
N: Why?
T: Well, one of my goals is to …. let me get my goal sheet out…here it is, one of my goals is to "vary my nonverbals in ways that show increased attention when clients are distressed." I've read that body lean shows interest, so I've been trying to keep this in mind in my sessions so I lean in more when the intensity is raised because of something the client does, like a different expression of emotion or something…
N: Oh, I see…so you did this on purpose?
T: Yeah.
N: OK…good. Good job.
T: Thanks (wondering, "for what?").

In the second scenario, supervisor Nathan starts at the end, and therapist Ted is forced to prove his intent, the purpose behind his change (his goal), and his reasoning. Nathan's attempt to compliment at the start of the conversation—"You're attending…better"—ends with, "Good job." Nathan starts with a declarative and ends with another. It's difficult to discern Ted's views in the second scenario, and there is little in Ted's responses that lead me to believe he agrees with Nathan's assessment—one could question whether or not Ted thought he did a "good job" from this exchange.

In conclusion, it's easy to see that I'm not a fan of direct compliments. They are too easily dismissed and can be culturally inappropriate. Direct compliments can also be insensitive to feedback (except for rejection) and open the door to disagreement. By being less direct and focusing on behaviors and context including therapist goals, supervisors can still utilize compliments as part of their repertoire while maintaining a respectful, not-knowing position.

4.5.2 Indirect Compliments

> This type of complimenting is not about being less direct or suggestive. Instead, indirect compliments are elicited from clients by asking them questions from the points of view of those familiar to clients. By formulating questions this way, we are asking clients to view situations through the lenses of those who know them better than we do and those often more credible. (Berg and De Jong 2005, p. 52)

Brought into the supervision context, indirect compliments should be tied to specific relationships relevant to therapists' goals. While clients can draw from every possible relationship regarding successes, exceptions, or perspectives (including relationships they have with casual observers, pets, or even the deceased), supervision compliments of this type are most effective when connected to the therapists'

4.5 Complimenting

clinical and supervision contexts. Rather than pulling from spousal, sibling, or stranger perspectives less related to therapists' goals, I find indirect compliments drawn from therapy or peer contexts are most likely to be appropriate. With clients, I ask questions about change and request that they create indirect compliments that might include the person on the street ("If some guy on the train saw you today after this big change, what would he see?") or nonhuman observers ("So Fido's your best pal, someone who knows your every mood. If she could talk, what would she say was different about you today after you moved from a '5' to a '7' on this 'moodiness' scale?"). I have even included deceased loved ones in my requests for indirect compliments with clients: "When you came in, you said you felt like you had betrayed Grandpa because you weren't moving on with your life. He always urged you to 'live your bliss,' if I remember right. What would he say about these past few weeks when you've been back 'on track' and enjoying yourself?". However, therapists are quick to notice when questions are too far afield, when supervisors go on fishing expeditions to locate significant change or perspectives. Their goals are coupled to two specific contexts: therapy and supervision. Our realm of curiosity is more limited because our contract is more specific. Therefore, indirect compliments are best solicited from therapists relating to their therapeutic and peer relationships: "If your client Will noticed this new confidence you have, what might he say was different about you?" "You do a lot of team therapy with Pei-Fen; if she witnessed this new boldness in setting boundaries, what might she say about this change in your work?"

Asking for clients' perspectives of differences when interacting with therapists is very appropriate when discussing a specific case or reviewing a video. It is immediate, having chronological significance, and relevant because clients are often the only witnesses to therapist change. These indirect compliments involving clients can range from specific to general, as illustrated below:

Therapist Peter:	I've really been working on validating clients' viewpoints.
Supervisor Gwen:	How so?
P:	Well, the one that comes to mind this week is with Cathy. In the past when she would tell me about the pain she was in, I was rushing to get to exceptions. This week I said, "That must've been difficult for you," even though she was repeating something she'd told me the week before about losing her job.
G:	Do you think she noticed?
P:	I don't know, really.
G:	Suppose she noticed that you affirmed how difficult losing her job was, and that this was a new response from you. And let's say I was to ask her, "What do you think this change says about Peter?" What might she say?
P:	Hmm…well, maybe something like, "I think he cares more."
G:	"Cares more?"
P:	Yeah—I mean, before I would just nod and then ask her about when things were better for her. This time, now that I think about it, she smiled when I validated her.
G:	Ah! That sounds nice.
P:	Yeah!

G:	What else might Cathy say about you, if she noticed the change you made?
	... (*late in the supervision hour, after reviewing several of Peter's cases*):
Gwen:	OK...you feel like you've taken some steps forward on these goals: validating clients more, listening more closely, and noticing exceptions.
Peter:	Yeah, I think I have.
G:	I think we're in agreement here—I like the changes you've made, too. (*Gwen then scales the changes with Peter, anchoring this difference in his goal-setting experience over these three areas.*) Now...what do you think your clients would say is different about you this week from the last time you met with them? You know, generally?
P:	Well...I guess maybe that I've slowed things down a bit.
G:	They'd say, "Peter's changed the pace, slowed things down."
P:	Yeah.
G:	And might they say that's a good change?
P:	Yeah...except for Kevin—he likes things to go as fast as he can talk, which is pretty fast!
G:	(laughing) OK. What else might your clients say is different about you this week, based on these changes you've noted here with me today?
P:	They'd probably say, "You're listening better."...and maybe, "You're more positive."
G:	Who would say, "Peter's more positive?"
P:	Probably Kevin. He said at the end of the session that he liked the compliments I gave him, and they *were* pretty positive this week.
G:	Nice! Now, which of your clients might say, "Peter's listening better this week?"
P:	Oh, Tom and Andy—they would.
G:	And what would they say?
P:	Tom would say, "You're getting us this week." I think they both would say I've got a clearer understanding of their situation.
G:	So what would Andy say?
P:	Probably something like, "You talked less; you let me talk, and you got Tom to talk—Nice job!"
G:	No hesitation there—sounds like you're pretty confident they'd noticed the changes you've made, too?

4.5.3 Self-Compliments

This type of complimenting is created by encouraging reflection on therapists' experiences and the meanings of those experiences. Asking questions that probe their change processes, progress toward goals, and moments of pride allows reflection on events that can all too often be passed by without a second thought. This process allows therapists to assign significance, examining the impact of the moment on them as well as their impact on the moment.

As a photographer, I try to capture a perspective that is not obvious. This can happen by changing a point of focus, increasing background blur (bokeh) or simply shifting elevation or distance. I don't want a photo when I can create a visual story. What begins as a tourist's snapshot—say, a smiling friend in front of the Eiffel Tower—can be shifted significantly if I change the camera's perspective. By backing away, adding distance, and directing him to stretch his arm out to the side with palm up, my friend now appears to be holding the Tower in his hand; by laying on the ground and focusing on his face as he looks away from the camera and up toward the top of the tower, he appears to be enthralled by the height. Similarly, self-complimenting is a process of perspective brought about by supervisor questions. I ask therapists to pause, reflect, and research the event as well as what the event means. An example:

Supervisor Sadie:	So, you redirected the mother to speak directly to her daughter instead of talking to you.
Therapist Ted:	Yeah, I've been working on that with other families but not with these two…for some reason, this was harder for me.
S:	How did you know it was the right time to do this in this case?
T:	I'm not sure…Maybe I'm finally confident enough to try redirecting their conversation…
S:	That might be true as well, but what I'm curious about is, how did you know you should try it *now*? (*Ted's comment was about an inner ability; Sadie's question was about judgment; so she redirected the question*)
T:	Oh, well…the topic wasn't as negative, so there was less of a chance they would say something nasty to each other.
S:	So you noticed the difference in their conversation and used that opportunity to redirect.
T:	Yeah, I think that's right.
S:	OK…and it went well?
T:	Yeah—they were able to talk pretty openly for a while. I kept my eyes on the floor and nodded as they talked.
S:	A good skill, one you've been working on. What do you think it says about your progress here, in this area?
T:	Hmmm…maybe I'm catching on to those moments when clients are ready to do something different in the session.
S:	I like that. And what do you think your catching on easier says about you?

T: I'd like to think it says I'm gaining confidence, that I'm ready to take more risks … be more assertive.
S: And these are all good things, for you?
T: Oh yeah—I get run over by clients too often because I hesitate and let them just talk without giving them some structure, you know, things that can maybe help them talk differently with each other in the session.
S: So, this change sounds more significant than when we started talking about it.
T: It is…talking about it makes me think more about what I did, what it means to my growth as well as what it did in the session.

Complimenting is an art. Subtle differences can result in overstatement (insincere flattery) or understatement (unnoticed difference). The SF approach offers multiple means toward complimenting, but it is important to keep in mind that the supervision relationship can have a significant influence on the results.

4.6 Future Focus

> *Sooner or later, a person has to look at things real hard and decide that fixin' tomorrows beats fixin' yesterdays.*
>
> ~ Bill Branon, *Devil's Hole* (1995)

One of the defining characteristics of the SF approach is a focus on the present and future rather than a focus on the past (de Shazer, Dolan, Korman, Trepper, McCollum, and Berg 2007; Durrant 2012). Techniques such as the Miracle Question (De Jong and Berg 2012; de Shazer 1988; see Sect. 5.1) and presuppositional questions ("*When* [not if] things are better, what *will* [not might] you notice that is different?") (McGee et al. 2005) concentrate attention on possibilities. Imagining a future different from the present or past creates a "pull" toward change that is important within this approach.

Future focus in SFBT is largely envisioning a positive change or difference, a future in which one's problem or reason for seeking therapy is resolved, dissolved, or replaced. This future orientation has been called one's miracle, goal, preferred future, and "best hopes" (Ratner et al. 2012, p. 63), but the concept is consistent: conversation centers on the yet to come and the client's desires.

Future-focused practices in the SF approach emphasize detail and personalization. However, SF supervision differs from SFBT in some ways because supervision is much less concerned with specific problems. Resolution of a single complaint does not mean supervision is completed (although it may mark significant success), and many therapist goals are not connected to complaints but focused on skill development and education. Solution building in SF supervision takes place on multiple fronts, attending to personal, clinical, administrative, professional, and other goals simultaneously. Therefore, a supervisor's future orientation must show flexibility and sensitivity to therapists' goals and desires.

4.6.1 Future-Focused Question Examples

Questions that connect possible therapist resources to the situation, goal, or context are the keys to maintaining this focus (Thomas, Wheeler, Lowe, Durrant, Fleckney, and Greaves 2002). What follows are examples of future-focused questions, coupled with topics relevant to supervision:

- Stuck cases: *When this situation has improved, how will you know? What will be the first thing you notice that will tell you, "I'm not as stuck as I was"? And then what will you notice? What have you done in the past that helped you when you were stuck with similar situations (or different situations)? How did you do it? What will you take from your past success into this stuck case situation?*
- Skill development around a goal of "participating more authentically": *Let's say two weeks from now you come to supervision and you are excited to report a change—you are "more authentic." What will you tell me? How will you prepare to notice these differences in the next two weeks so you have the best chance of reporting a change?*
- Goal setting with clients: *You've set goals with me for supervision, and we've discussed how you formed them. What will you take from our discussion about your goals today and apply to this goal-setting situation with your client? Of the things you've just told me, which are happening in some small way already? How did you get that to happen? How will you keep that going with that client? With other clients?*
- Anxiety with higher-risk client complaints: *From zero to ten, with zero representing "high anxiety" and ten being "relaxed" (therapist's term), you said you're at a "four" in these situations. When you're at a "five," what's the first thing you'll notice about your experience? What will you notice you are doing differently? What would your client notice, if anything? What about the session will be different when you're more relaxed?*
- Procrastinating about a case management deadline: *What's the smallest thing that you can think of that will tell you, "I'm making progress on this"? When you are procrastinating less, what will you be doing more? What will I be seeing from you when this procrastinating thing isn't interfering?*
- Skill development in complimenting: *What will your team members notice about your cases when you are complimenting your clients in a way that's more satisfying to you? What will your clients notice when your complimenting improves?*

4.6.2 Categories of Future-Focused Questions

A few categories of future-focused questions emerge from these examples:

- Questions that center on imagining a future that is different and the process of noticing difference—*When this changes, what will you notice?*
- Questions that assume a preferred future—*When you've made "significant progress" in this area, what will be different for you and your clients?*
- Relational questions—*What will your client/team member notice about you that is different, once these changes happen?*

- Questions that include a chronology, which creates the possibility of continuous change—*What will happen first? And then what will result from that first event?*
- Scaling questions that create space for incremental future changes—*Zero to ten, where will you be after you take this action compared to the number you just gave me?*
- Resource-focused questions that acknowledge current abilities or access other assets and bring them to bear on the situation—*When this happens, how will you have done it? Who may be helpful in this process?*

The techniques used to create and sustain a future focus in SF supervision may vary, but the commitment to the concept is vital. Although it may seem artificial, rehearsal and repeated use of future-oriented questions is a time-tested means to developing this skill. Using language that presupposes difference does not feel as natural as questions regarding the past (e.g., accessing details about problem development) or the present (checking in with someone's current experience of a conversation, such as, "How do you feel right now?"); therefore, like most skills, the path to improvement is focused practice and reliable feedback (Dreyfus and Dreyfus 2005; Ericsson et al. 1993). I close with a question: *What will be the first thing you will do to improve your future-focused questioning?*

4.7 Utilizing the Indirect–Direct Communication Spectrum: Metaphor, Semaphore, and "Two-by-Four"

One of the first workshops I ever offered on SF supervision included an intense exchange during the question-and-answer period with a seasoned family therapy supervisor regarding therapists who "won't do what they're told to do." While some of the points he made were clearly outside the scope of a "SF" supervision workshop (and other attendees confronted him during the question-and-answer period, making my arguments for me), he and I did agree on one crucial thing: there are times supervisors must be very direct with therapists. So rather than attempting to take an indefensible position that SF supervisors don't speak in the declarative form, I offered this spectrum: metaphor, semaphore, and two-by-four.

There will always be occasions when SF supervisors must intervene directly, but as a practice, the supervisor must develop a range of communication styles in order to fit with SF assumptions as well as differences among therapists and contextual demands (such as moments of emergency) (see J. Wheeler's work, Contribution 7.11, in this book). Since maintaining a not-knowing position and being tentative are central tenets of SF supervision, one starts by being less direct whenever possible. Similar to the options regarding complimenting discussed earlier in this chapter, SF supervisors should practice a range of directness, from vague to emphatic, to promote collaboration in supervision as well as therapist and client welfare (Thomas 2010b; see Pichot, Contribution 7.6, in this volume).

Supervisors can always become more direct, decreasing ambiguity and increasing confrontation. Initial offerings of ideas, suggestions, alternatives, and information should start off tangential and increase in candor when less-direct approaches fail. This technique is addressing our supervisory delivery and relationship, not content. Supervisors do not maintain a philosophical position to the neglect of regulations, policies, or ethics requirements; there are standards of practice that must be upheld. But to begin with a heavy hand demands (and usually results in) compliance, stifling collaboration and cutting off therapists' own attempts to correct errors, learn through self-discovery, and maintain motivation. So, whenever possible, I supervise by starting with indirect stories and ideas (metaphor), moving to suggestive messages (semaphore) when vagueness does not result in change, and resorting to directives as my last option ("two-by-four," a type of building lumber that can be wielded as a club).

4.7.1 Metaphor

Metaphor refers to "relating stories that create space for interpretation and choice by the therapist. Well-crafted stories and metaphorical examples are more ambiguous than the semaphore messages because possible directives are...less obvious to the therapist" (Thomas 2010b, p. 221). This end of the indirect–direct spectrum would also include presuppositional questions, requests for indirect and self-complimenting, and other less-than-direct methods in SF supervision. Therapists who have clinical experience and appropriate confidence fitting their level of expertise seem to prefer indirect methods and discussion over instruction, as it supports collaboration and portrays faith in therapists' abilities. Supervision exchanges tied to metaphor may look like this:

Therapist:	I'm not sure what else I can do in this situation.
Supervisor:	I'm not either...I heard a story once about a therapist who...*(short story about taking action even when one isn't certain)*
T:	So, you're telling me to—
S:	– No, it's just a story that came to mind. I thought it might fit our discussion somehow, but I wasn't sure how...*(honest statement by supervisor, as there were multiple points of convergence with the therapist's experience and no clear "moral" to the story)*
T:	Well, I see myself in that.
S:	How so?
	....
S:	How were you able to end your session on time, since you said that's difficult for you? *(indirect, presumptive – assumes intentionality and agency on the therapist's part)*
T:	Well, I think it's because...(talks about a recent class discussion on the importance of boundaries with clients)
S:	And as you continue setting these limits, how do you relate this to ethics in other areas? *(moving the conversation toward general awareness of ethics code requirements and ethical practice)*

4.7.2 Semaphore

Semaphore is a signaling system used by navies throughout the world. Through positioning flags in various arm positions, the signaler spells out words to a person within sight. My father was a signalman in the US Navy, so I grew up hearing stories about successful and less-successful (and sometimes humorous) signaling between ships at sea.[7] Therapists with little experience may prefer semaphore-type communication over metaphor because directness can quell anxiety that often accompanies novice performance (Benner 1984; Dreyfus and Dreyfus 2005; see Pichot, Contribution 7.6 of this volume). This type of communication is very common in all types of supervision: supervisors send messages often hedged and qualified, and therapists communicate "message received" (even though what was received might not correspond directly to what was sent). Semaphore is less direct than an instruction because it is a method, not a message. "Please pay attention to what I am saying" is the method, which differs from a message within the method. For example:

Supervisor Becky: OK, so you're wondering how to talk about violence with this couple, and you have your suspicions about possible violence here…Is it possible that an intimate partner violence (IPV) questionnaire might give opportunities for people to communicate their risks?
Therapist Tom: I'm sure it would. But I thought SFBT didn't use assessment tools?
B: Where did you get that idea?
T: I'm not sure…
B: Would it surprise you to know that there's some pretty convincing research on this, combining SF approaches and systems ideas in working with couples experiencing IPV? (see Stith, McCollum, Rosen, Locke, and Goldberg 2005)
T: I didn't know anything about it…
B: Yeah, it's covered in a course I don't think you've taken yet—how about I send you the reference and you check the book out from the library this week? It's just one chapter…
T: That would be helpful, thanks.
B: And next time we meet, I wonder if you and I could talk about this and other ways to create space for people to disclose information besides answering your questions in therapy… there may be more than you imagine!

It's likely that Tom will read this professional book chapter this week and return to the next supervision session with new ideas, information, and curiosity regarding not just SF approaches to IPV but also the possible place for assessment tools in SF

---

[7] Current smartphone users have similar stories due to auto-correct blunders when texting.

work with clients. Since Tom's options are likely to increase in a short period of time, many positive outcomes are likely—clients will benefit, Tom will engage in the learning process and stay motivated to locate new sources of information, and the communication between Becky and Tom will remain open. Tom has a suspicion that may or may not be true in this couple's relationship, but what is certain is that more options for disclosure will open up from Tom's reading and their supervisory discussions in the very near future. Becky could have been heavy-handed, lecturing Tom on the seriousness of IPV and pointing out his lack of resourcefulness, but the results would probably have been limited—Tom would have complied in his work with this couple but not necessarily engaged in the self-supervision practice of continually informing his practice through research or challenged his assumptions regarding SF approaches and assessment.

4.7.3 Two-by-Four

To achieve compliance and instant results, supervisors can *always* resort to the "whack on the side of the head" approach and require specific therapist actions. There are times the supervisor is the expert; some situations require immediate, definitive acts to correct therapists when what they are doing is misinformed, dangerous, unethical, or illegal. No matter how innocent the motive or pure the model application, supervisors must, at times, step in to correct or prevent major offenses (see J. Wheeler, Contribution 7.11 in this volume). Although occasionally necessary, SF supervisors resort to this only when the clinical context demands immediate action or when other less-direct methods have not been effective.

Supervisor Becky: So, catch me up on the report you made to Child Protective Services on this case. It has to be done within 48 hours, and 24 hours have gone by since you met with them.

Therapist Victoria: I didn't report it…I've given this a lot of thought, and I think I can work with the family better if I don't report it.

B: Here's the deal, Victoria: You have to report this. The law here in Texas[8] gives you 48 hours to make the call, and it is clearly a case of abuse. I'm in complete agreement with the agency's policy on this, which doesn't give you a choice in the matter.

---

[8] Time limits differ from jurisdiction to jurisdiction. It is clear in the Texas Family Code, §261.101 (2012): "If a professional (this term includes mental health professionals, medical personnel, teachers, day-care employees, and many other licensed and certified people) has cause to believe that a child has been abused or neglected or may be abused or neglected, or that a child is a victim of an offense … the professional shall make a report not later than the 48th hour after the hour the professional first suspects that the child has been or may be abused or neglected or is a victim of an offense…"

V: Well, *you* can make the call—
B: – No. The law states that you can't delegate this to someone else. *You* have to call and report this. Here are the choices you have: You can call right now—I'll put this on speakerphone, and when the state case worker answers, you'll respond to the questions—or you can take an hour to collect your thoughts and come back so we can call the hotline together then.
V: OK…I'm pretty upset right now…let's do it in an hour.

No supervisor can allow children to be put at risk once abuse or neglect has been identified as actual or imminent. In addition, supervisors cannot condone therapists' violating the law or agency policies, especially when the responsibilities and required actions are clear. At times, we must be direct and act accordingly. Even in postmodern practices, "not everything is relative all at once" (Stewart and Amundson 1995), and supervisor obligations to wider systems exist (Fine and Turner 1997).

One of the power differences between supervisors and therapists is that supervisors have greater latitude with regard to the ways they communicate with therapists. It is usually inappropriate for therapists to be obtuse, and allegorical stories originating from the therapist would be out of place in most supervisory relationships. Therapists have opportunities to practice along this same indirect–direct spectrum with clients, and they should, but this freedom is typically limited to supervisors within supervision. On the other hand, SF supervisors should practice this latitude mindfully, as liberty is not license. Simply because supervisors *can* be indirect does not mean they *must* be, and directness in SF supervision should be exercised when the context requires it.

4.8 Dilemma Talk

Whenever possible, I collaborate on decisions with therapists in supervision. When a challenge is created that affects either the therapist's future choices or our relationship, my first guiding thought is, "How can we work together on reaching a solution to this?" One supervisory practice I use quite often in these situations is posing dilemmas. By presenting my views in the form of an impasse concerning the features of a decision that must be made, I maintain neutrality as much as possible and invite wondering aloud together as the next step in the quandary. This allows choices to be as open as possible, encouraging co-construction of alternatives and direction (Sluzki 1990; Thomas 2007c).

Dilemma talk can be general or specific depending on the topic. A common experience in supervision relates to whether or not therapists share supervisors' opinions:

> "Here's how I see my predicament: I know what I would do, but that may not be what you would do. What are your thoughts on this?"

> "I feel like I've got a dilemma here. I could tell you what I think, or we could wait and see what happens. Which would be better for you, both short and long term?"

4.8 Dilemma Talk

But proposing conversation is also useful when moral dilemmas involving the supervision relationship arise. Moral questions are not merely intellectual problems to be solved, as strong emotional responses also come into play (Jordan and Meara 2008).

A clinical example may help clarify the value of dilemma talk. In our supervision together, therapist Lorraine revealed that a couple she has been seeing for marital therapy was really struggling. Crystal and Jermaine were prompted to see her after Crystal admitted to her husband that she had engaged in a short-lived affair. Jermaine's reaction was both expected and surprising: he alternated between yelling and crying over the course of a week, taking time off work because he was too upset to be productive. Lorraine had seen them three times as a couple, carefully assessing past violence (none) and current risk of violence (which according to all parties was low) and then setting couple goals regarding trustworthiness and respect. In the fourth session, they revealed information regarding recent encounters with a local psychologist whom Crystal had seen for psychological testing required as a condition of employment. Crystal reported in the couple therapy with Lorraine that the psychologist told her, "You need to divorce him—he's bipolar, he's violent, and he will never change." The psychologist said this to Crystal based only on her responses to his questions that preceded the testing; the psychologist had not met her husband nor had he completed assessments with him. Later, at the psychologist's insistence, Crystal and Jermaine met together with him for separate sessions. In her second session, the psychologist scolded Crystal: "Your affair was wrong and you know that, don't you?" In a separate individual session with Jermaine, he reported that the psychologist said, "I could not do what you have done (stay with someone who had an affair)." Lorraine related to me that both clients were very upset by their meeting with the psychologist, who was insisting they return for additional individual sessions.

Many ethical questions regarding how to act arise from this scenario regarding the psychologist's behaviors, but there are moral questions that influence the supervision discussion as well. How much of my opinion about the other professional and his actions do I disclose to Lorraine? How much does Lorraine reveal her opinions to the couple regarding the psychologist and his views? Does Lorraine have an obligation (with clients' permission) to contact the psychologist and discuss this case? If so, for what reasons? (Reasons could include coordinating treatment, investigating a possible violation of the psychologist's code of ethics, personal desire to know more and to assist her own therapy with the couple, find out the terms of testing for Crystal, and others.) How does Lorraine engage this couple around infidelity and violence fairly, given the other professional's opinions/intrusion? These questions and many more come forth as I think through Lorraine's description of events. As I ponder Lorraine's predicament, a few dilemma proposals come to mind for my supervisory discussion with her:

> "I have ideas and strong feelings about the psychologist's views and actions, but I feel caught. Sharing these views with you may bias your actions, and these folks are *your* clients. On the other hand, I may have ideas beyond what you have thought of so far that might be helpful in sorting this out. Where should we start?"

"You said you have a desire to contact the psychologist. There are aspects of this we can easily discuss—what releases you would need from the clients, familiarizing yourself with his code of ethics, and others. There are other motivations for contacting the psychologist that I've thought of, but telling you about them might prejudice your views. And because I'm your supervisor, you might even hear my thoughts as suggestions or directives. So I'm a bit apprehensive as we talk about possible contact with the psychologist. What do you think about what I've just described?"

"You have clear goals with this couple; the psychologist has muddled things for them, and this muddle has spilled over to your couple therapy. You may have already sorted out how you will proceed with them. But I have some views on this, too. My views may help you professionally in the long run—you know, your professional development—but they might make things even more muddled in your current work with Crystal and Jermaine. So we have several options: talk now, talk later, or maybe talk only as you bring things up in supervision that relate to my views. What do you think?"

This section has simple and complex dilemma proposals, and I use both quite often. I think of this as a conversational invitation resulting from my desire to be as transparent as possible as long as it benefits therapists and clients. I see dilemma talk as bridging the gap between what the therapist already knows and educating; that is, there are times when therapists lack knowledge or experience with clinical and ethical decisions, but providing information or opinions in a critical moment may remove the tension required to learn from the decision-making process. This is a prelude to self-supervision. Therapists need to learn when to act, when to restrain action, when to consult with peers, and how to think through difficult situations without depending on an authoritative source to provide "the" answer. Dilemma talk can assist in this process.

4.9 Promoting Self-Supervision: Ideas on the Self-Sustaining Therapist

The aim of supervision of clinical work ought to be supervision of the therapist's own self-supervision. As Confucius said, "Give a man a fish and you feed him for a day; teach him to fish and you feed him for a hundred years. (O'Hanlon and Wilk 1987, p. 264)

Simply educating a novice on the mechanical features of an automobile and teaching this beginner driving skills falls short of appropriate mentoring—*learning how to learn how to drive* promotes a level of responsibility every driver should embrace to ensure a lifetime of safe driving. For example, everyone has heard the phrase, "Drive defensively." However, simply advising someone to heed this warning does not teach the skills of defensive driving, nor does it advocate self-learning when contexts (international destinations, complex city interchanges, the race track) or conditions (snow, ice, personal reaction time) change. One must learn how to learn how to drive in order to act defensively and safely across a lifetime.

Similarly, one of the vital practices of SF supervision is to work myself out of a job by equipping therapists to supervise themselves. Although some may endorse

4.9 Promoting Self-Supervision: Ideas on the Self-Sustaining Therapist

merely training people in techniques when teaching a SF approach, most care enough to address the importance of context, ethics, and professional development as well. Psychotherapy is an art, not a trade or job, and the nuances of practice are not simply pragmatic. To continue practicing the art across a career, one must learn to self-supervise (Thomas 2007a). In fact, practices supporting self-supervision should undergird and frame all other SF supervision practices—if therapists leave supervision without the skills to self-supervise, I have fallen short of my goal.

The concept of self-supervision is used broadly in psychotherapy literature with no common definition. But authors agree that the ability to self-reflect is necessary. Some include perceptual and conceptual skills in their definition: "Self-supervision includes mindfulness; awareness, attentiveness to assumptions; sensitivity; and attention to potential sources of bias, judgments, and discomfort" (Vargas and Wilson 2011). Others, like Pond (1997, p. 167), mention goals around confidence and participatory skills vital for self-supervision: "As supervisors we can commit ourselves to… helping to produce therapists who may be described as self-confident, able to generate appropriate custom-made interventions, and who know when to ask for help and how to get help." What seems clear is that the abilities necessary to self-supervise may not simply result from ordinary supervision practice. Therefore, SF supervisors must create goals with therapists around becoming self-sustaining and practice toward those ends.

The SF approach is a postmodern approach; few question this conclusion. Postmodern approaches in general hold that the "self" in self-supervision should be understood moment-to-moment in context rather than locating "it" within the person of the supervisor. Self-supervision then moves from developmental ("I am better") to self-reflexive ("How am I 'better,' with whom, and in what ways?"). This self-reflexivity acknowledges the importance of reviewing with sensitivity to context and invites the influence of supervisors, consultants, and peers in this ongoing routine.

Roger Lowe, a respected scholar in SF and other social constructionist forms of supervision, advocates for self-supervision (Lowe 2000; Lowe and Guy 2002; Philp, Guy, and Lowe 2007). Upon review of the scarce literature on this topic, he supports the use of the term "self-sustaining therapist" and invites attention to the benefits of such practices (Lowe 2000, p. 511). Self-supervision, according to Lowe, creates therapists who take responsibility for their own supervisory needs and are aware when they need additional consultation. Like Todd (1997a), Lowe believes self-supervision is more than an intermediate position inferior to ongoing conventional supervision; supporting therapists toward becoming self-sustaining should be a goal of supervision because it is indispensable.

Monk and Sinclair (2002) also offer an excellent review of the self-supervision literature. They found most authors centered on development of an internal self and were quite humanistic in their assumptions. Monk and Sinclair's own postmodern, social constructionist ideas contrast greatly with traditional self-supervision notions, and some of these ideas fit nicely with SF supervision. Specifically, their attention to "multiplicity, contextuality, and active construction of meaning" (p. 116) in self-supervision dovetails nicely with SF supervision tenets.

Notions unique to self-supervision and practices supporting it are outlined below. General SF supervision ideas blend well with these concepts and activities as one continues to maintain a SF stance while incorporating them into self-supervision.

4.9.1 Embed Self-Supervision in Supervision

Lowe (2000, p. 516) situates recurring self-supervision in the supervisory timeline.

> This sequence will typically involve the following steps: therapy session → self-supervision → case consultation (with supervisor) → self-supervision → next therapy session. Thus, the actual case consultation occurs between the two sessions of self-supervision. It arises from and builds on the therapist's prior reflections, and its immediate contribution is to the ensuing self-supervision session, rather than directly to the therapy itself.

This contextualizes self-supervision as a practice related to a particular case, which corresponds with Monk and Sinclair's (2002) practices.

4.9.2 Challenge Isolation and (Resulting) Insularity

In addition to SF assumptions previously outlined that can be applied here, we need to remember that self-supervision can simply become self-verification: without outside consultation, one's self-supervision can easily justify what one has always done. Isolation brings increased risks for harm to clients and possible resulting ethics violations (Curtin 1996; Cooper 2009; Zur 2005), so encouraging lifelong case consultation as a part of self-supervision is a vital service component of supervision.

4.9.3 Be Transparent

Todd (1997b) has said, "ideally, the goal of supervision is 'learning how to learn' (Bateson 1972)" (p. 23). He proposes several practices that coincide with the SF approach, including adjustment to the therapists' learning styles and emphasizing "well-formed goals and questions" (p. 21). But perhaps the most important stance related to SF supervision is "be transparent" (p. 23). Todd urges supervisors to be open about what they do *as supervisors* so therapists can learn their methods and apply them in self-supervision in the present and future (see Sect. 2.2.2.1 on mimetic isomorphism).

4.9.4 Set Goals Around Self-Supervision

In addition to creating goals on therapist expertise, SF supervision should involve establishing self-supervision goals (Lowe 2000; Todd 1997b). Much like required goal setting around case management, it is very unlikely that therapists would generate self-supervision goals without clear expectations stated by the supervisor. While some might believe self-supervision goal setting is an activity near the end of therapists' training, the clinical aspects of many education and training programs may be so brief that the processes must parallel one another. A case in point: school counselors in Texas are only required to complete one semester of practicum, involving a minimum of 80 client contact hours. Upon graduation with the master's degree and successfully qualifying for the school counselor certification (which requires a written examination but no personal interview or clinical demonstration), there is no further supervision requirement. Thus, the only clinical supervision these professionals receive may be in that single semester of practicum—there may be no "later" in their supervision history beyond this 5-month period in their careers.

4.10 Promoting Self-Supervision: Practices

Here are some ways to embed self-supervision in the supervision process. I have adapted several of the practices below from Lowe (2000), Todd (1997b), and Monk and Sinclair (2002), and I am indebted to their work in this area.

4.10.1 Goal Setting

The process of fashioning self-supervision goals can be interlaced with other goal-related projects. Setting up the expectation by articulating one's expectations for therapist self-supervision prior to and after supervision (see above) and reviewing goal progress on a regular basis makes this seamless. Distinctions must be drawn and negotiated to distinguish self-supervision from supervision itself.

Goal-setting questions:

- *How can our time together here complement your personal reflections on this case?*
- *OK, how can you take this case consultation into your own self-reflection before you meet with these clients again?*

4.10.2 Highlighting Competence

As with therapist successes in supervision, self-supervision requires one to notice and reflect on achievement and challenges. Learning how to initiate self-complimenting (described earlier in the book) is a part of this learning process. In addition, Lowe (2000, p. 517) notes that "it is important to focus on prior self-supervision as well as prior therapy sessions," which broadens the context and information to be considered when underscoring competence.

Competence questions:

- *What have you accomplished with this case that you can reflect on in self-supervision?*
- *"If you had been confronted with the same situation a year ago, how would you have gone about working through this case on your own? How would you describe the difference?"* (Lowe 2000, p. 517)

4.10.3 Identifying Challenges and Resources

The complement to highlighting competence is to recognize challenges and resources that can be brought to bear on these challenges (Lowe 2000, p. 517). Honest assessment of one's limitations and current resources when working in a particular case as well as ongoing assessment of personal challenges that continue to surface for the therapist are crucial activities.

Challenges/resources questions:

- *How did you make the decision that this case needed further review? What did you bring into supervision today from your self-reflection since the last session? How do you use this to cue you into times when you might need to seek consultation in the future?*
- *Are there challenges you recognize all the way through this process—from therapy session to self-supervision to meeting with me? When supervision isn't scheduled in the future and you are self-supervising, how do you plan to fit all the parts in?*

4.10.4 Deconstructing

Monk and Sinclair (2002, p. 117) state that deconstruction is "the practice of exploring the taken-for-granted assumptions." Although more closely associated with narrative therapy (White 1994), practices within SF approaches may be viewed as either constructive or deconstructive (Strong 2007).

Deconstructing questions:

- *What are you assuming about this client? About what you're doing in this session? What maybe needs to be examined before moving forward?*
- *What did you ignore in this session that you should reconsider, both now and when you self-reflect prior to the next session?*

4.10.5 Being Temporarily Certain

Similar to Stewart's (2003) notion, "this stance allows therapists to hold their professional knowledge lightly and through the encounters with their clients be prepared to revise" (p. 122). Assisting therapists in this process of acting in the moment as well as reassessing the value of temporary knowing is a valuable skill in self-supervision.

Temporary certainty questions:

- *What assumptions are you making in this situation? How can this be useful to the client as a resource while you remain tentative yourself? (Follow up): Now, how do you remind yourself to "hold lightly" to something you've assumed or temporarily concluded?*
- *Are there things that I "know" or the client "knows" generally about this type of problem that might be utilized here? (Follow up): How can I practice this so I don't become permanently certain and generalize knowledge to other cases inappropriately?*

4.10.6 Contributing Without Imposing

I firmly believe the general practice of supervision should be no "imposition without permission" (Thomas 2007a, p. 398). If creating goals around self-supervision is compulsory, then creating freedom for dissimilarity in the self-supervision learning process is the supervisors' responsibility. To do this, questions should be posed that presume change in this process is inevitable, self-supervision is an understood goal, and difference is welcomed.

Contributing questions:

- *"When you reflect on our sessions, how have you learned when to act on my suggestions and when to ignore them? What helps you decide?" (Lowe 2000, p. 519).*
- *I don't want to impose in this relationship, but I also want to be responsive. What are the best ways for me to speak to questions you have now to prepare you for a future when we're not meeting regularly?*

4.10.7 Keeping a Future Focus

Supervision should look at short- and long-term self-supervision goals. Helping therapists evaluate what they know and what they still need to learn in supervision are elements leading to self-sustaining practices. Keeping a future focus involves forming clear goals, but it also includes reflective conversations.

Future-focused questions:

- *How "ready" are you to self-supervise? How do you know?*
- *What will tell you that you need to consult on a case in the future when supervision isn't a part of your normal routine?*

- *OK, now I've offered some resources that are important in this case. In the future when you are not in an ongoing supervision relationship, how will you know when to seek out resources? How will you practice reflection that includes the question, "Do I have all the information I need here, and how do I learn more if I'm not sure?"*

4.10.8 Teaching Therapists to Fish: Skills of Self-Education

One aspect of self-supervision that is often overlooked is the ability to locate resources and create a plan for lifelong learning. Many therapists I have trained and supervised used to call me for print resources in areas of clinical work, supervision, research, ethics, and theory…until I refocused my efforts toward self-sustaining continuing education. Now I work to focus therapists' curiosity toward both immediate (case consultation) and long-term (self-education) practices. With the geometric expansion of the internet, access to resources is more a matter of motivation than availability.

Self-education questions:

- *Now that we've talked through some resources and how I found them, what have you learned that might assist your future self-education?*
- *Most people are pretty passive learners in their required continuing education. How will you sustain your desire to learn and set aside the time to educate yourself so you carry on this tradition of self-education you've started?*

Although methods may vary, nearly everyone who considers the concept of self-supervision sees its value. Case consultation is still encouraged, and ongoing supervision is of course highly recommended. But the realities of practice—limited time, case management, continuing education, to name a few—often leave little space for professional supervision unless required by the government or institution. So it is only right—both "appropriate" and "morally correct"—to support the creation of self-sustaining therapists who can reflect and adjust plus seek consultation appropriately. Hopefully the notions and practices outlined here provide guidance in what may be a novel undertaking for the SF supervisor.

4.11 Inviting Supervision Feedback from Therapists

No description of supervision practices would be complete without a discussion of therapist feedback. Client feedback to therapists and the supervisory system is vital to creating and maintaining clinical relevance; supervisor-to-therapist responses provide input and direction to therapists' goal-setting and evaluation processes along with educational and administrative information and correction. But in spite of extensive research on therapist/supervisee views of supervision, supervisors may neglect this crucial aspect of relationship health and responsiveness.

Hierarchy must be considered when inviting therapists to comment on supervisors' performances and the supervision context. Ungar (2006), Fine and Turner (1997), Gardner, Bobele, and Biever (1997), and Monk and Sinclair (2002) have thoroughly addressed the importance of attending to power disparities in supervision, and these documents should be required reading for supervisors—whatever their model or theoretical orientation—to sensitize them to power differences and prompt supervisor actions that may reduce those differences.

In addition to "minding the power" (Fine and Turner 1997, p. 229), supervisors need to draw out therapists' feedback, as overt responses may never come about without it. Fashioning feedback prompts that fit the therapist, the relationship between therapist and supervisor, and the supervisor's own sense of security requires planning and reflection, but one can assume that developing expertise as a supervisor will be hindered without it (Dreyfus and Dreyfus 2005; Skovholt et al. 1997).

4.11.1   Formal Methods of Therapist Feedback[9]

Two well-crafted methods stand out as potentially useful in this process. Wainwright's (2010) Leeds Alliance in Supervision Scale, or LASS, is an excellent session feedback form. Following the configuration of Miller's (2012) Session Rating Scale (SRS) used for client feedback, Wainwright's three-question LASS allows for quick assessment that most supervisors and therapists would find relevant. (It can be downloaded and used without charge by sole supervisors—see Miller 2012 [URL link can be found in Appendix A, footnote 8, and in the Reference List].)

Lehrman-Waterman and Ladany (2001) have created the Evaluation Process Within Supervision Inventory (EPSI), a robust research questionnaire and potentially useful supervision feedback tool. This self-report document can be completed by sole therapists, group supervision members, and university practicum course members, providing rich data for the supervisor to consider. It was "developed...to assess the degree to which trainees thought their supervision was characterized by effective goal setting and feedback" (Lehrman-Waterman and Ladany 2001, p. 171), so the relevance to SF supervision is obvious. The items are included in this article, but the measure itself must be secured from the authors.

4.11.2   Less Formals Ways to Invite Feedback from Therapists

No matter how one fine-tunes a measure or questionnaire, most are biased toward the aggregate; that is, the purpose of most supervision measures is to gather information from groups of therapists, not from a single therapist in a specific supervision

---

[9] Any form or questionnaire should be used only with appropriate permissions.

context. Here are techniques for eliciting feedback that accesses the individual therapist's supervision experience and provides corrective feedback for the supervisor that are less formal but potentially more useful.

4.11.2.1 Making Use of the Therapist's Goal-Setting Form Responses

Appendix C offers questions to which the therapist responds in the initial phases of supervision. These responses can be used by the supervisor at the end of a session or periodically during a contract period to access the therapist's ideas on what is working and what can be improved. Questions such as the following, formed from the Appendix C items, may jump-start the process:

- *You told me in your goal-setting form that one of the ways I can best help you meet your goals is to _____. Am I on target? On a scale of zero to ten, with zero being "not helpful at all" and ten being "couldn't be more helpful," where would you put my use of this method?*
- *How am I making use of your interpersonal strengths in our supervision? Are there strengths you've told me about that you think I need to pay more attention to?*
- *If you were to rate the "success" of our session/time together, using the now-familiar zero-to-ten scale (with ten as complete success), where would you rate it at this point? What could I do to move that number up one on the scale?*
- *You told me on your goal-setting form that you best learn by _____. I think I've been taking advantage of this, but I'm not sure if I'm getting it to your satisfaction. What have I done that fits with your learning style, and what more could I do to fit better?*

4.11.2.2 Research-Informed Inquiry

Many ideas on prompting therapist feedback can evolve from the research literature. Even if a supervisor does not wish to use a formal feedback form or questionnaire, one can lift relevant and timely concepts from formal research and create conversational questions or topics specific to the therapist and her/his experiences in supervision. A few examples:

- *Scaling how focused we were today, from zero (not focused) to ten (very focused), where would you rate our session?* (based on the Leeds Alliance in Supervision Scale [LASS], from Wainwright 2010; cf. Miller 2012)
- *If you would scale how helpful this session was for you today on that same zero-to-ten scale (ten being very helpful), how was it? What might make our next session together at least one point higher on that scale?* (based on the LASS, from Wainwright 2010; cf. Miller 2012)
- *Regarding your goal setting, do you think this one, "_____," is easy to measure and assess? Why (not)?* (based on the Evaluation Process Within Supervision Inventory [EPSI], from Lehrman-Waterman and Ladany 2001)

- *We're partway through our contract and I want to know: Are you getting enough feedback from me regarding how you're doing as a counselor? (If yes) What have I been doing that you've found beneficial in this area? (If no) What has been missing, and how can we set this back on track?* (based on the EPSI, from Lehrman-Waterman and Ladany 2001)
- *You say you learn when I note those things you're doing well and when I comment on things you could improve. How's the balance? What can I do to keep it balanced for you?* (EPSI, from Lehrman-Waterman and Ladany 2001)

4.11.2.3 Inquiry Guided by the SF Supervision Stance[10]

A favorite method I use is to fashion questions and create dialogue around my stance as a SF supervisor. As outlined in Sect. 1.2, any of these values—pragmatism, tentativeness, nonpathology, curiosity, or respect—can inform the creation of a feedback structure with a therapist that is meaningful to both parties. A few questions that may illustrate the concepts, all of which can be scaled (zero to ten) to assess status and future change, include:

- *Has our time in supervision together today been practical enough for you? Did you get clear ideas or tools that you needed?* (pragmatism)
- *Is my curiosity headed in a good direction today? Am I missing something that I need to know more about so you can get what you need?* (curiosity)
- *When do you feel respected in our supervision time together?* (respect)
- *Was there a time when your view of your therapy or competence as a therapist was more negative than mine? Did my view make sense to you, or can I try to clarify it?* (nonpathology)
- *In our session today, when did you feel I privileged your view of a situation over my own? Did you expect it, or did it take you by surprise?* (tentativeness)

4.12 Parting Thoughts on Practices

We all know that what we look for we see (often called selective perception) (von Glasersfeld 1995). SF supervisors are not immune to such effects; asking about positive client change and therapists' roles in these changes biases our views of therapists' abilities and gains. In addition, anticipating particular outcomes often affects performance ("When errors of observation do occur, they tend to give results

---

[10] One of my favorite sources is Barnard and Kuehl's (1995) method of ongoing evaluation. Their questions are easily adapted to supervision, and their stance of increasing honesty through feedback, though not necessarily a primary SF stance, continues to inspire my personal quest to create transparent supervision relationships.

more in the direction of the investigator's hypothesis" [Rosenthal 2002, p. 3]). Our expectations of therapists' success may influence their actual performance in a positive way. In addition, supervisors should remember that noting therapist progress can affect us as well. There is no objective place from which to assess, nor should there be—evaluation is interactional, and we are affecting and being affected by the process.

From astronomers observing galaxies to physicists detecting subatomic particles, what we look for we see and we affect what and who we observe. A difference that makes a difference within SF supervision may be the stance from which we practice. We are looking for, noting, and encouraging positive change; what we seek, we often find.

Chapter 5
A Tap on the Shoulder: Supervision with Insoo Kim Berg

Of the many ways one can learn about supervision, few are better in printed form than transcriptions. The SF community places great value on research methods that examine actual therapy (Bavelas 2012; McGee, del Vento, and Bavelas 2005; Tomori and Bavelas 2007), including research grants and awards for microanalysis of psychotherapy sessions. Some of the best-selling SF books in the marketplace include extended transcription segments of psychotherapy to illustrate the approach (De Jong and Berg 2012; de Shazer, Dolan, Korman, Trepper, McCollum, and Berg 2007). However, most of the leading texts on general psychotherapy supervision only offer vignettes and little primary data from which readers can learn (Bernard and Goodyear 2009; Stoltenberg and McNeill 2010). Perhaps the major difference between SF approaches and other supervision texts falls along the inductive/deductive continuum. SFBT historically began with observation and moved toward generalizable practices. Solution-building approaches were and continue to be developed inductively, focusing on the pragmatics of success as it unfolds in practice. With little emphasis on theory, SF practices fall on the inductive end of the continuum. This is in stark contrast to most approaches in the field of psychotherapy, as theory and practice are usually developed through hypothesis testing and logic, applying scientific methods to understand the nature and predictability of change. While inductive and deductive methods have their values and limitations, ground-up induction is often much closer to the raw data.

In keeping with SF traditions, this chapter offers a unique window into the supervision practice of Insoo Kim Berg. Two complete transcripts are included here. The first transcript involves a team supervision session including Insoo, the therapist, and three team members who focused on a psychotherapy session viewed by Insoo and the team the previous night. The second transcription involves a one-time consult between Insoo and a therapist who has sought her supervision on a particularly troubling case. Though quite different because of geographic diversity and the number of people involved in each session, these were both single supervision consults.

Since both of these examples are one-time supervisory consults, several features of ongoing SF supervision are not present. This fits with Insoo's claim that her supervisory, consulting, and training styles differed in several ways (Berg n.d., SFBTA Archive #10128-0064). As single consults, there are no attempts at formal goal setting, and Insoo does not attempt to generalize her comments to other cases. But goals are still relevant and evident, especially in the second case example. Also absent are formal discussions of the therapist's clinical approach, which would be common in most ongoing SF supervision to connect therapist skills to model assumptions.

Throughout the transcribed text, I will mark and annotate SF supervision practices Insoo is using, being careful to use terminology already articulated earlier in the book. Annotations are my views, not Insoo's, and are certainly open to alternative understandings. In addition, a discussion of general ideas follows the end of each transcription, with commentary on supervision principles such as education, therapist agency, goal setting, and other concepts and methods that recur in each session.

5.1 Supervision Session 1: "Pain in the Butt"

This 48-minute supervision meeting[1] was conducted by Insoo in a Midwestern United States family therapy clinic in the early 1990s. The therapist was a veteran practitioner who had never experienced a face-to-face supervision session with Insoo, although she had previously viewed the therapist's work via video recording and conducted supervision long-distance. This supervision experience included the use of a one-way mirror as Insoo and the team witnessed the therapist's first attempt to utilize the SFBT approach. The team members were also new to supervision with Insoo, but all had some previous experience practicing SFBT.

The therapy session was the therapist's initial consult with a 40-old mother whose chief complaint was the behavior of her 14-year-old son. The woman and the child's father were married and lived in the same household, but only the woman was involved in the therapy session. The mother reported that her son, the only child of this marriage, was getting into trouble at school, including confrontations with school staff as well as peers. But the client was most disturbed by her son's persistent back talk, as they would have heated arguments in which the son would insist on having the final word.

Per a normal SFBT structure, the therapist attentively listened to the mother's concerns before shifting to a SF format. He then asked her the Miracle Question,[2]

---

[1] Heartfelt thanks to Jim Rudes, Ph.D., who has given his permission to print this complete session transcription. This team supervision consultation was the basis of Dr. Rudes' (1992) dissertation and has never been published in its entirety.

[2] "Now, I want to ask you a strange question. Suppose that while you are sleeping tonight and the entire house is quiet, a miracle happens. The *miracle* is that *the problem which brought you here is solved*. However, because you are sleeping, you don't know that the *miracle has happened*. So, when you wake up tomorrow morning, *what will be different* that will tell you that a miracle has happened and the problem which brought you here is solved?" (De Jong and Berg 2012, p. 91 [emphasis in original]; see de Shazer 1988):

5.1 Supervision Session 1: "Pain in the Butt"

and the client was quite responsive, offering several differences she would experience with her son if a miracle happened in her household. Relationship questions were then proposed by the therapist with input from the team, asking the mother who else would notice these differences she had articulated. After a break near the end of the session, the therapist returned from meeting with Insoo and her team members and gave this message to the client:

> It sounds like your son can be a real pain in the butt, but we felt that he is a good kid because we think you have done a good job with him because he has shown you that he can do it when he wants to. That's a good start. The next step for him is to behave when he doesn't want to. It will take hard work for you to get him to do what you know he can do, to use what he knows how to do. Between now and next time we get together, we'd like you to pay close attention to any indication that lets you know he is using what he knows he can do. And act like you are not watching him so it is as natural as possible. (Rudes 1992, p. 80)

The entire consultation is transcribed and included here, using line numbering to make referencing easier. Edits were only made to maintain client confidentiality or clarify dialogue when the recording was inaudible. Throughout the transcription, I will note SF supervision assumptions that are in play as well as SF practices described earlier in this book, using *italics* to highlight the concept or method. I do not call attention to many responses such as active/responsive listening, showing empathy, and other common supervisory activities although they are important to the supervision context; I limit my notations to skills and ideas that are specific to Insoo's SF supervision approach.

Transcription key

IKB	Insoo Kim Berg, supervisor
Th	Therapist
TM	Team member
(pause)	Notes a particularly significant pause of two or more seconds
..	Brief pause (less than 2 seconds)
word	Underlining is used to show vocal emphasis
–	Indicates a cutoff in the dialogue, an interruption, or cross talk
[bracket]	Entry that was not part of the conversation, added for clarification
(comment)	Comment regarding a noteworthy nonverbal or extraverbal event <u>or</u> an edit created to ensure confidentiality
(*Comment*)	*Editorial comments* from this author regarding SF supervision

5.1.1 Supervision Transcription 1 and Commentary

001 IKB: (to the therapist) Are you thinking back to last night?
002 Th: Yeah—uh-huh.
003 IKB: OK, sometimes I think it takes a while to be reminded…we haven't had time to debrief from last night's session, we just walked out of here. What was your overall feeling, your reaction to the session? The way it was done?

(Inviting participation: *"Your" in this segment is plural, since she led into this with "we just walked out of here" just prior to the questions. This opens space for everyone to voice their reactions with little guidance. Insoo did not ask for positive or negative "reactions"; she asked for people's "overall feeling" to the session and to "the way it was done," which could be very different.*)

004	Th:	Well, I had a very strong reaction.
005	IKB:	Yeah.
006	Th:	A couple of things. When I was doing the miracle (question)?
007	IKB:	Yeah.
008	Th:	I was beginning to feel like I was pushing her too far.
009	IKB:	Oh.
010	Th:	And I guess that's just me. And (team member 1) called (on a telephone in the therapy room), you called, and (TM2) called in and kept asking for more "What else – What else," so I was glad that happened because I think I back off from those questions sooner than most people would.
011	TM:	Oh, I don't know about sooner than most. I would have backed off.
012	Th:	Well maybe that's why I'm here because it's part of the training process. Because..
013	TM:	That's why I'm here, I felt oooh—more. (laughter)
014	Th:	That was my reaction when they called in, I thought, "You're kidding me – you want me to do more of this?" This woman is going to hit me with her purse or something.
015	TM:	She's already saying, "Fine asshole – fine."
016	Th:	I was just beginning to feel like, "Oh no!" but I did it.
017	IKB:	Yeah.
018	Th:	Because you know that's what I'm here for.
019	IKB:	Yeah.

(Complimenting: *Without the visual, it is difficult to ascertain Insoo's nonverbal cues, but she affirms both statements by the therapist—"I did it" and "that's what I'm here for"—resulting in group laughter, so my sense is that her agreements were experienced as compliments.*)

020	Th:	(everyone laughing) People are watching. I had to do it. I couldn't say no but I did it and uh, what I could have done, I could have blamed it on (TM2). I could have said, "I feel like I'm pushing you too far, but (TM2) still wants to know. So I could have done that but I didn't 'cause I felt I needed that. To do it. It was a good thing that I did it. It was a good experience for me—I think it's one of the things I have to work at, at my practice is you know to push this further to get a lot, to milk it for more.
021	TM:	Oh, me too.
022	Th:	There's a lot more to be gotten out of it. Now the question I had—I wanted to go on to some scaling, and obviously the team didn't want me to and then I started thinking, "Well, why are we doing all this training?"

5.1 Supervision Session 1: "Pain in the Butt"

023 IKB: Yeah, (laughing) right.
024 Th: You're not going to scale if you're not going to find out where she is.
025 IKB: OK.
026 Th: It gets a little unwieldy to me because now, let's say, what happens when the kid comes back—do we do the same thing? With the two of them together, with him separate, what do we do? And I was just wondering why in retrospect, why push so hard for the Miracle Question and then say to her, "We agree this kid must be a pain in the neck...the butt," so I was just trying to put that all together last night—I don't have it together in my own mind.
027 IKB: OK.
028 Th: I liked the intervention that we did... that we supported her.
029 IKB: Yeah.
030 Th: And then we gave, planted some seeds for things she could start looking for. That he's already doing. I just didn't know how the miracle answer could—
031 TM: —the miracle usually to me is having them paint a picture of how it will be afterwards, in very behavioral terms—I will serve strawberries for breakfast, I will get up with a smile, I will get up earlier.
032 IKB: Yeah.
033 TM: Hers was more, the locus of control was external.
034 IKB: Yeah, the child will do this—the child will do that and he will do this and he will do that. So what's wrong with that? What was your question about that? (Curiosity: *Insoo redirects this discussion from a statement of certainty ["the locus of control was external," line 033] back to a place of curiosity ["What was your question about that?"].*)
035 TM: I don't know how that helped her—I don't know what that helped her to see.
036 IKB: Um.
037 TM: I thought that was very useful for her to say, "Oh yes, he does do that but only when he wants something."
038 IKB: Right, OK.
039 TM: But still... you pointed out well, that he can do that.
040 IKB: Right.
041 Th: It also helps us to see that she's probably a visitor or a complainant not a customer at this point.
042 TM: She doesn't have a problem
043 Th: It's not her problem—she's not a customer.[3]
044 IKB: Right—it's her kid's problem, so she is coming in telling us about this serious problem that her son has so.. I think we should accept that, at this point.

---

[3] For explanation of visitor, complainant, and customer relationships, see De Jong and Berg 2012.

		(Hedging: *Insoo's use of "I think" and "at this point" qualifies the acceptance of the client's view of the situation, allowing space for team members to comment as well as changing her mind in the future.*)

045 Th: Right, I do too.

046 TM: And I still have the question by pursuing the miracle so far, I want to know what she got or what you think she got.

047 IKB: OK, I think that probably what she got was, she probably saw these things from her perspective. We got her to see these things from a different person's perspective, what the husband would say—you notice difference?

(Hedging, education: *Insoo's use of "probably" [twice] hedges her response to the team member who said, "I want to know what she got or what you think she got." Since there is no way to know the former ["what she got"] and second requires speculation ["what you think she got"], Insoo speculates but remains tentative. Then she states her view of what she believed the therapist and team were able to accomplish: getting the client to consider different perspectives. Her last question, "You notice difference?," invites conversation around her speculation and views on change in the client's experience.*)

048 Th: Uh-huh.

049 IKB: So help her to get outside of herself and what husband would say that is going on between me and my kid. You know. So someone else's perspective on this.

050 TM: That's a very good point.

051 IKB: And the girl's perspective. "What would the girl see different with me?"

(Education, relationship questions: *Lines 047, 049, and 051 are examples of relationship questions, which ask someone to take another's view of a situation. I see this as a moment in which Insoo attempts to indirectly educate the group. She is reinforcing the use of relationship questions in the therapy (an important SF technique) while pointing out the additional perspectives that may have been created for the client.*)

052 Th: One of the things that struck me was her admission and realization or statement, I should say, that she doesn't play with him like she used to. And he has asked her to do that and she has said that you're too [big].

053 IKB: Too big for that.

054 Th: She can't fool around with him anymore because he is too big for that and I think then she can turn around and say, if things are going well, I could probably do that.

055 IKB: Yes—right.

056 Th: "If he would do these things I'd probably give him what he wants."

5.1 Supervision Session 1: "Pain in the Butt" 133

057 IKB: And also maybe if he is too big I could give to him in a different way, not pinching him. Like she was talking about pinching him a lot but instead of pinching him maybe there are other things she can do. Maybe more age appropriate so potential solutions will come out of her head.
(Hedging: *Insoo's use of "like" and "maybe [if]" [three times] allows for differences of opinion within the discussion. The therapist states that the child "is too big" [line 054], but Insoo's statement encourages other possibilities rather than agreeing with the therapist's conclusion.*)
058 Th: Yeah.
059 IKB: You see that?
060 Th/TM: Yeah.
061 IKB: So any further thoughts about the session?
(Collaboration: *Insoo asks a very open-ended question of the group, seeking to create another direction of inquiry rather than restrict conversation to what had become fairly specific.*)
062 Th: Very early in the session I felt I had a picture about the problem. I knew what the problem was.
063 IKB: You did?
(Being tentative: *Insoo's comment is a challenge to the therapist's statement, "I knew what the problem was." Since being tentative in one's conclusions is a key aspect of both SF therapy and supervision, Insoo's questioning of the therapist's stance of certainty results in a move toward intervention ["I need to get her into solution talk," line 067].*)
064 Th: I felt I did.
065 IKB: OK...
066 TM: Big deal, honey. (everyone laughs)
067 Th: Yeah, big deal. I know it's a big deal and so it was a good experience for me because I kept saying to myself, that doesn't make any difference, I need to get her into solution talk.
068 IKB: That's right.
(Complimenting: *Insoo affirms this statement, which leads to further team discussion of the solution direction and some self-complimenting by the therapist.*)
069 Th: If you don't have a solution... you know what the problem is but that's no help, you need the solution here. I kept finding myself at least initially wanting to go back to the problem. I was feeling like an idiot, I was going so far with the miracle. I felt she would say, "Is that all you know how to do? Aren't you trained to do anything else?" (much laughter, all voices)
070 Th: I wanted her to know I knew I would rather do other things too, but I couldn't tell her (jokingly). She found me out! Actually I have a greater repertoire, I'm just using one tonight. (much laughter)

071 TM: (Speaking for the Th:) "They're making me do this, it's not my problem."
072 Th: That was a real good experience for me. I've never gone that far, I've never gone that far with it, I've never pushed that far and I think when I'm alone with somebody there are lots of other things I can fall back on when I become uncomfortable pushing the miracle that far.
073 TM: Yeah, when I feel I'm irritating them—when they give me that look.
074 IKB: Now why do you think she didn't turn around and hit you with her purse? Why do you think she didn't do that?
075 Th: Well, she probably wasn't irritated by it as much as I thought she was.
076 IKB: Right—Obviously that was not good manners for her. She is a good-mannered person.
077 TM: She wasn't raised that way.
078 IKB: Wasn't raised that way.
(Complimenting: *Insoo's statement that the client is a "good-mannered person" and her agreement with the team member by echoing "wasn't raised that way" exemplify her assumptions about the client: the mother is doing the best she can. The previous discussion about the client's rough play with her son [pinching from line 057 and "smack" in line 079] could define the mother, but Insoo offers a compliment that serves as a counterargument and creates doubt about what kind of woman the mother is.*)
079 Th: She did say she smacks her son.
080 IKB: You're right, she did say that. She wasn't about to do that with you. I think beyond that, beyond that, when you take a real curious posture, curiosity—you don't know what she is going to say. (long pause) So you are really curious about what she will say next. When you take that posture, I think you can push as far as you want and client will still cooperate with you.
081 Th: As long as you're really curious.
082 IKB: Yes, curious. You're asking out of curiosity, you're not asking her to tell you about the miracle picture in order for her to get an insight. That's not your purpose. Your purpose is to really find out what she [thinks].
(Education: *Insoo is teaching the group about the Miracle Question and the stance of curiosity. There is a bit of hedging here ["I think" is used twice] but that is addressing clients' responses to being insistent in follow-up with the Miracle Question. The other statements are quite emphatic as she educates the group on how one persists in a SF approach using a stance of curiosity.*)
083 Th: I recently had a bad experience with a colleague of mine who did push somebody too far. (to IKB:) I think you did hit the nail on the head. He's not very good at, he didn't maintain eye contact. He turned his back to her and kept pushing as if there were some right answer that she wasn't coming up with.

5.1 Supervision Session 1: "Pain in the Butt"

084 IKB: Right, that she wasn't coming up with.
085 Th: She burst into tears since she had a history of being intimidated by men. And I was appalled by that. But he's another extreme, I would never go that far. But also this attitude of curiosity—that you really care and you're curious—
086 IKB: —you're curious.
087 Th: Not that there is some answer that you're looking for and you have been too dumb to come up with.
088 IKB: No, no, no. That's not the posture you take. The posture you take is out of absolute curiosity. I have no idea what the solution might be, I have no idea. When I ask those questions I have, I am, an absolute blank about what might help her. And I think that once you take that position, clients sense that and know that.
(Not-knowing: *A clearer statement could not be made—"I am an absolute blank about what might help her." Insoo's stance of not-knowing leads her to seek responses from the client—"absolute curiosity"—rather than appealing to theory, reasoning, or understanding.*)
089 Th: So it's really like [brainstorming].
090 IKB: Yeah. It's pretty much like trying to put myself in clients' shoes and look at things from their point of view rather than my point of view. I think clients know that so that's why I think I can push them about miracle for whole hour and still clients don't get offended by that.
(Education: *Continuing the theme she began in line 082, Insoo consistently uses "I think" in lines 088 and 090 when she is referring to clients' responses to the Miracle Question and speaks emphatically when discussing the importance of therapist curiosity ["That's not the posture you take. The posture you take is out of absolute curiosity."].*)
091 Th: I learned the same thing yesterday with (TM2) in second session where she said she does that for at least 20 to 30 minutes. I do it for 5 or 10 minutes and then I have to get on with the rest of it. I think I need those two things that I think are gaps in my competence or repertoire that I just don't know what to do at that point.
092 TM: Well that was real important for me, too. I would have asked the Miracle Question a lot sooner. Would you?
093 IKB: Depends.
(Hedging: *... a clearer example would be difficult to locate!*)
094 Th: Well, I was a little confused about that. I was tempted to move into the Miracle Question right away but also I wasn't still quite sure what the problem was. I didn't know if this was something new with this kid. Or (something) he just started doing? Or is it something that has gone on all his life? I kind of had a feel for some exceptions or something with this kid just because I didn't want to assume, right off the bat, that this is a kid who just blows up all the time and is irritable.

095 TM: Was that OK that he asked that question, how long this is going on?
096 IKB: Sure. I think it's all right.
(*Hedging, affirmation: Insoo's response both agrees that was "OK" and hedges ["I think it's all right."]. This saves face for the therapist without a firm commitment from Insoo.*)
097 Th: I wondered whether I should, but somehow I needed to know. Not that I wanted to do any analysis of the problem, but I wanted to know what I was looking at. I mean this is a lifelong situation.
098 IKB: Right, right.
099 TM: There's nothing that says he's adopted.
100 Th: Well that's an assumption. I don't know.
101 TM: I'm just saying.
102 IKB: Yeah, I don't know, we haven't gotten into it. So we don't know what the mother's picture of that is. Is it because she thinks, "It is because he is adopted" or (because she thinks) she could have done a better job?
(*"Leading from one step behind": This is an example of Insoo pointing out a deficit in the available information. By raising questions about what the group does not know and speculating aloud, she encourages conversation on the topic.*)
103 Th: That's one thing I never did, I never asked her and maybe I should have asked her. What do you think it is? What do you think is causing this? (to IKB:) Would that have been helpful?
104 IKB: I think better phrasing would be, "How do you explain this to yourself?"
(*Hedging, education: Insoo offers an alternative way of asking the question with a hedge, moving inquiry away from asking people [clients and team members] to speculate on causes toward clients' experiences of making sense of their lives. This is more in line with SF assumptions regarding meaning.*)
105 Th: OK.
106 IKB: You are a family, how do you explain to yourself his poor manners?
107 TM: Would you want to hear her answer if she says he's adopted?
108 IKB: OK—that gives you some information about how she thinks. How she explains the problem. So we will know for sure instead of guessing.
109 TM: OK.
110 IKB: Instead of guessing that she thinks it is because this kid is adopted.
111 TM: But is any of that relevant to a solution?
112 IKB: Not to solution per se but I think that maybe to the way we talk about the rationale. We suggest because he is adopted, because he comes from different genetic background, we might put it that way. Again it is not because we believe it.
113 TM: But it might be helpful.

5.1 Supervision Session 1: "Pain in the Butt"

114 IKB: To use that later. We use it as a way of framing, because he is adopted. You know some parents will say he never bonded so if he never bonded, if this mother says that. Because the next task for him is to bond with you. Then this is what we suggest as a bonding process if that's how they frame it.

115 Th: I think we need to know something about her reality, about her world. And if her view includes the adoption, I should ask that.

116 IKB: Right, how do you explain this? To give you enough information without going into detail. What is her frame? What would she say her husband thinks about son? Do you follow?

(Education: *Insoo directs the team toward thinking about using information rather than simply knowing client perspectives or explanations. She moves the discussion from deciding on a fact ["it is not because we believe it," line 112] or simply knowing the client's perspective, to* utilizing *the responses ["framing," line 114] as a possible intervention ["we might put it that way," line 112]. Then she contributes ideas on the methods that might be used: "How do you explain this?" and "What would she say her husband thinks about (their) son?" Here, Insoo is clearly teaching the group about how to use information to intervene.*)

117 Th: Yes, right.

118 IKB: Any other thoughts about the overall session?

(Collaboration: *Since she has been teaching for the last set of exchanges, Insoo opens up the conversation once again to additional team ideas about the entire session.*)

119 Th: No, the only thing I might assume, if he comes back with her, I'm not sure now if logistically in my mind, do I treat her as a second session and him as a first session, or him as a second session? I don't know where to go with that. Somehow it seems, it might make sense to see him alone and treat him as a first session.

120 IKB: Sure, I understand with an open agenda acknowledging that his mother was here. You might start out with what you (the boy), "Suppose your mother thinks is the reason, why she thinks she needs to drag you here." I mean those kind of things might be opening gambit, so acknowledging that it is not his idea he has to be here. I can't imagine him calling you up and telling you he has bad manners and wants to see you.

(Expert knowledge: *Insoo offers several ideas in direct response to the therapist's uncertainty, with some hedging ["you might start out with..."]. Although there are many directions a supervisor could take, Insoo offers ideas that guide but don't dictate—"you might start out with" and "might be an opening gambit" allow for therapist comments and alterations.*)

121 Th: (as if the boy was saying) "I get these bouts of rudeness." (the team laughs) And then I suppose the intervention may or may not involve both of them. I'll have to wait and see.

122	IKB:	Right. So if you were to do that and see the boy alone for the next session and that probably means you will see the mother alone for a while as well because we gave her some suggestions to do. Not just bringing the kid, because we gave her some suggestions. What I might do in that situation after I see the boy alone and then have him go into the waiting room, and then see the mother again. I might say to the mother, "He's a nice kid, a nice kid, isn't he?" Just opening with something like that. That sometimes gets the mother to be in a more positive mood and somehow give the impression that you talked about something positive about mother. His positive feelings towards mother. Sometimes I try highlight, you see that's the building of a relationship and expectation and then she will more likely react in a positive way. So you are building a bridge, so any chance you get for her to consider – for her to think about son in a positive way. (IKB: as mother) "He is—what?" (Expert knowledge: *Again, Insoo is working to get a concept across to the team—how to create the possibility for a positive client response—by drawing examples from the situation of introducing another person into therapy. She hedges, using "probably," "I might" [twice], and "sometimes" to discourage the possibility that the therapist would take what she has said verbatim and apply it in the next session.*)
123	Th:	In this first session, there was no reference to the husband not being here, I never asked her and she never explained. When I talked about her son coming in, I deliberately didn't say, "Bring your husband, too." Traditionally, I would have. I didn't, I'm not sure why I didn't. Do you think I should have looked into that?
124	IKB:	OK. How would you have done that? How would you have looked into that during the session to give you more information? (Hedging: *By now, it is quite clear that there are many ways to introduce words and phrases that hedge one's statements—"might," "suppose," "perhaps," and so on. Here, Insoo simply does not answer the therapist's question, "Do you think I should have looked into that?" She hedges her response as to whether or not she "should have looked into that" and simply asks her to generate alternatives if she had "looked into that." So instead of offering expert opinion, which was requested, Insoo creates a learning moment.*)
125	Th:	I could have asked her why she decided to come in without her husband. That has the implication that he wants to come in.
126	IKB:	And that she should have.
127	Th:	I'm not saying that she should have, but she made that decision. There may have been a good reason for it.
128	TM:	But it implies that his coming with would have been the ideal. Because "why" is implicit. … explain why it's not better.
129	IKB:	OK—There are much better and much more sophisticated ways of asking that. That is in the miracle picture, there is much more

5.1 Supervision Session 1: "Pain in the Butt"

information about what the husband will notice that goes on between the mother and the son. Sometimes that gives you very rich information. (Education: *Again, Insoo directs the group to consider a SF practice—the Miracle Question—that can help the therapist acquire the perspectives she seeks rather than continuing a discussion that was searching for the "right" question to ask the client in order to get similar information.*)

130 Th: You would ask even more.

131 IKB: More about what father would notice, that goes on between mother and son.

132 Th: I don't have a lot of responses here (referring to the session).

133 TM: You know I think if we were to view this we would see that you could ask more, you could have varied the first word of the question more so that you would not have felt you were doing the same thing over and over.

134 IKB: Yes, yes.

135 Th: What else?

136 TM: Well you did a lot of "what else," a lot of "how," instead of "who, what, where." And I think that would have given a lot of richness, the variety so you wouldn't feel so much (repetition).

137 IKB: Also, client's perception would change as well. "Where will he see you do this, what part of the house, where?" And getting that information would give you some idea about how much father is involved. "Will you find out?" "He's never home and he never sees what goes on between me and my kid."
(Education: *As the team begins to discuss Miracle Question possibilities to gain information, Insoo once again points out additional changes that could take place while being curious about the client's miracle. Here, these include potential changes in client perceptions using relationship questions ["where will he see you do this..."] and additional information about the father's involvement.*)

138 Th: Uh huh!

139 IKB: That will give you some ideas. Or sometimes she might say, "He thinks it's my job to raise the boy." In saying that, I think she gives you information. So instead of asking outright, "Have you thought about bringing your husband?" or, "Has your husband (come) along?" or, "Has your husband thought about coming along?" We have different ways of getting at this information.
(Education: *Insoo teaches the group more about the use of the SF approach ["We have different ways of getting at this information"], pointing out differences between SF methods and other, more direct lines of questioning.*)

140 Th: The one thing I did notice but that I didn't do anything about it, it seems like father's major mode of dealing with the kid was to spend time on Saturdays after work. They did something together, the two of them, that was real important. Kind of unusual for a 14-year-old—

141	IKB:	—for a 14-year-old to spend—
142	Th:	—a Saturday with Dad.
143	IKB:	So I think that is important information to go after. What do you suppose son would say he likes about spending time with dad on Saturday afternoons? What do you suppose he would find helpful? This could give you a rich feel about what goes on in their relationship. (Hedging, education: *While hedging ("I think," "suppose," "could"), Insoo offers her opinion on a potentially fruitful direction in the inquiry. At the same time, her ideas are based on the SF tenet of curiosity, not on gathering facts but on illustrating how the SF approach would inform this line of questioning.*)
144		(long pause)
145	TM:	How did she receive your compliment and task about how she has done with her son?
146	Th:	Well, she liked the compliment or the statement about the kid being a pain in the butt. She reacted very strongly to that. She was physically moved by that. Those were raised eyebrows and everything. That was really noticeable. I think she took in the rest. That was my assumption. And I think she will actively look for times the miracle is already happening. I think she is the kind of woman who will do it. Also I got the impression that she would believe there was something positive to look for. I don't know about keeping it a secret (I liked that part of intervention), but that doesn't make any difference, whether she does or doesn't.
147	IKB:	Right.
148	TM:	I thought saying, "Obviously the kid is a pain in the butt" was brilliant, and clearly it was. I had this picture of her subconscious with a smile ready to receive whatever comes next. A triple yes—all in one.
149	Th:	Yeah, that was really good. I wouldn't have thought of that. I would have said something much more [tame]. That really validated her. (about mother) "You know what you're doing. You know what you're talking about. You're coming here for a good reason."
150	TM:	"I understand you. I heard you."
151	Th:	Anyone of us with the same problem would be suffering, too. There's nothing you want to hear, there's nothing worse than going to see someone complaining about a problem with your son and have them say, "So what's the big deal, what's wrong with your kid?" That would be unproductive.
152	IKB:	I agree, that would be very insulting to the person.
153	TM:	And very authoritarian.
154	Th:	Well, we wanted to communicate as many positive things as we could to her about this kid. But at the same time he's terrible.
155	TM:	But we didn't say he's terrible.
156	Th:	We said he's a pain in the butt.

5.1 Supervision Session 1: "Pain in the Butt" 141

157	IKB:	That's right, he's a 14-year-old boy. We conveyed to her how difficult a child he can be.
158	TM:	Sometimes my 29-year-old can be a pain in my butt.

(Collaboration: *Note how Insoo has simply been participating as a group member from line 145 to 158. Twice she agrees with other team members' observations but does not direct the flow of the conversation.*)

159	IKB:	I guess we have been talking about both of your reactions in front of and behind the mirror, in this session. Any other thoughts you have aside from what we discussed so far?

(Collaboration: *As supervisor, Insoo takes responsibility for redirecting the conversation toward general ideas and reflections once again, again hedging ["I guess"] rather than stating a fact about the previous conversation.*)

160	TM:	It was wonderful having her do it. Having her out there and me behind the mirror. I saw myself out there and I could be as critical of you as I am of me, which is very critical. As opposed to having one of you (clinic staff therapists) out there, you do it so perfectly, it's like seeing a gymnast who doesn't fall.
161	IKB:	(laughingly) You should see us fall.
162	TM:	So I was back there, going, "Ask how, ask when, ask where" or, "Do the miracle, do the miracle." I felt discomfort in my gut because I was in there with you so completely and it helped me see where my blinders are.
163	IKB:	Ahh!

(Empathy, affirmation: *Insoo attends to the team member's experience in her inimitable way: a minimalist "Ahh!"*)

164	TM:	And the lack of range of questions and where I get stuck and when you kept saying, "Ask her another way" because I'm so used to clients saying, "Well, I don't know." "What if you did know?" I had one client, who when I said, "That's wonderful – how did you do that?, she'd go, she'd say, "Oh, you're such an actress" (much laughter). And I wasn't any more that way than any of us are here, I was totally appropriate, but she was so unused to having that kind of validation and that made me self-conscious and so I said to her, "I mean it, how did you do that?" and she'd come back with the same thing and I kept pushing and finally she'd say [inaudible]. And I have a very sophisticated—
165	IKB:	—How did you stay with that line of questioning? That's good.

(Exceptions, indirect complimenting: *This question and "that's good" both imply Insoo approved of the therapist's behavior in the case description.*)

166	TM:	I didn't, I didn't think about it, I just did it.
167	IKB:	You didn't—
168	TM:	—No.
169	IKB:	You must have figured out that was good.

170 TM: Just trial and error.
171 IKB: Is that so. That's good. So you have this open mind about wanting to try different things.
(Complimenting: *Although it is unclear whether the team member hears Insoo's statement "That's good" [twice—lines 165 and 171] as compliments, they were clearly stated as opinions about the team member's persistence. What follows is a two-level discussion of how a client experimented and how the team member/therapist can utilize this client's experimentation to "make a difference to the client" [line 179].*)
172 TM: Umh! Now that's really good. So you really summarize what the client does.
173 IKB: Summarize. What client does—she just grab for this straw. Sometimes client will say, "That I just grab for the straw, I didn't know what I was doing." That's good. How did you know that straw to grab? For that straw, not for some other straw?
174 TM: "Well I grabbed for other straws too, but this is the one I'm telling you about. The other straws didn't work."
175 IKB: Ok.
176 TM: But then you said, "Oh, a person who experiments!"
177 IKB: Experiments.
178 TM: Because she truly is. She is a 45-year-old and the man she has lived with for 20 years has Alzheimer's. She's trying everything to make it better, and she is this high-power (professional) and she has to juggle.
179 IKB: OK, then use that. Whatever the client gives you, you can use. It is something to build on, to make a difference to the client.
(Education: *Insoo speaks in the imperative form ["then use that"] and urges the team member/therapist to "build on" this client's success "to make a difference." She is clearly encouraging the team member/therapist to take action in such circumstances rather than simply consider the possibility of utilizing the information.*)
183 Th: I didn't want to do it, but I'm glad I did it. The thing about that is it was like a first interview in many respects.
184 IKB: Yeah.
185 Th: Because I couldn't fall back on other things.
186 IKB: That's true.
187 Th: And I was thinking, "Why is this bothering me? I've done a million of these interviews. You can do this with your eyes closed, with your hands tied behind your back."
188 IKB: That's right.
(Indirect compliment)
189 Th: But not with a solution approach. I wouldn't allow myself to fall back under the circumstances 'cause it's real easy to get uncomfortable and do something else and that was a real good experience for me. I think everybody should do that. It was like the first interview I ever had.

5.1 Supervision Session 1: "Pain in the Butt" 143

190	IKB:	Yeah. It was in many ways. It was because you have never been taped before. You never had this group of people watching you. Many people watching.
191	TM:	To me that's the ultimate horror.
192	IKB:	What?
193	TM:	It's being judged by all of these people.
194	IKB:	But you look at it as being judged, you can also look at it as being supported. (Reframing: *Insoo offers a possible reframe to the team member, an equally viable alternative to the seemingly factual statement, "It's being judged by all of these people." Reframing is an integral part of the MRI model within which Insoo trained before the founding of the SF approach.*)
195	TM:	Oh I know, but there's a part of me that goes, "OK, I need to be perfect because I'm being watched and I'm being taped."
196	IKB:	But I think it's an opportunity, an opportunity. (Hedging, reframing: *"I think" allows Insoo to state her opinion about what "being watched" could mean without negating the team member's experience of feeling judged.*)
197	TM:	Very much so, I would like to do that as an opportunity.
198	Th:	I think we should do more live supervision and the comfort factor will increase for both of us.
199	TM:	I would love to do the work I did with (another supervisor who uses a different model) with someone from here (clinic). The problem that I brought to him, because he solved it by doing, by saying, "When, where did that originate?" and doing some "What does the child feel?" It was about certain people that I give up my power (to). I just get, I want to disappear, and one of—
200	IKB:	—OK, do you want to do that?
201	TM:	Yeah.
202	IKB:	OK, and we can go with some different ways to handle that. *(Lines 203–209 are removed to preserve team member confidentiality)*
210	IKB:	Keep up the good work. (Therapist), is there any other questions you had about the session? (Collaboration: *After a discussion centered on a team member's experiences of being judged and struggling with power differences, Insoo returns the focus of the supervision time to the therapist and the session the team all observed.*)
211	Th:	Well, why didn't you want me to scale that last night with the mother where she was at? I think you were the one who called in and said, "Why don't you ask her what parts of it are happening now?"
212	IKB:	Yes, yes. Because I don't think where she was at, the way she was looking at him, would have been in a positive scale.
213	Th:	You think it would have been negative?
214	IKB:	Pretty negative. I think then they would be locked into that.

(Hedging: *Using "I don't think" [line 212] and "I think" [line 214] are responsive to the therapist's request for a direct answer ["why didn't you?" line 211]. Insoo also hedged when asked, "you think...?" [line 213] by responding, "Pretty negative" and "I think..." [line 214]. She offered her opinions without closing off other possible understandings of "where she was at" or results of that line of inquiry.*)

215 Th: OK.
216 TM: But going for exceptions and hearing "miracle, miracle," all that she wants to happen. Then at the very end you said, "When does a little bit of that happen now?"
217 Th: "Cause I asked her for exceptions and she said, 'Very, very seldom.' "Could you kind of give me a little piece of when he does?" and she was able to give me something.
218 IKB: The one about when he wants something.
219 Th: Right. That's where she came up with that.
220 IKB: Right.
221 Th: And he won't talk back to you if he wants to [inaudible]. That was productive because that let us and her know that he has this gift. He knows how to do it. He may turn it off and on and he may not turn it on very often but the skill is there.
222 (Long pause)
223 TM: You kept saying the day after the miracle. My mind is so literal that I had to go through a little thinking, instead of just acting the miracle. It gives me much more freedom to not be just the day after.
224 Th: I've noticed the way I've changed that over time. I'm not completely sure how I want to do it but I've noticed that you people are very specific about how you ask that question. In terms of it's not, "What will be different after the miracle?" but, "Assuming this miracle takes place tonight without your knowing, what will –
225 IKB: – TELL you!!! that miracle happened?"
(Education: *Insoo emphatically corrects the therapist's rendition of the Miracle Question. She used the phrase, "what will [tell you that the miracle happened]," and Insoo amends it for the entire team, making it clear that there is a better or preferred way to ask this SF question.*)
226 Th: "What will you notice that will let you know?" I think that phrasing is important.
227 IKB: Yeah.
228 Th: I'm not sure of all the subtleties in that.
229 IKB: The other thing that I wanted to add to that about the Miracle Question was how to make a smooth transition into what (TM3) would say is getting them into trance. Thinking about miracle picture. A smooth transition is like connecting up with today's session. You're not doing it directly but implied it, that—"After we meet

5.1 Supervision Session 1: "Pain in the Butt"   145

today, you go home, you go to bed,..." and so there is some sequence to this and there is a progression to this. "And while you are sleeping... OK, so after today's meeting you and I talk, you go home, you go to bed and while you are sleeping, ..." You pace them and you lead them into thinking about miracle. In a gradual fashion, so I think it is much smoother. Client will respond this way. Sort of get them into revelry, rather than "Oh no, this is not going to happen." Rather than bring it out abruptly, the client is willing. "Let's pretend... Who me?—I'm not that kind of person." So you entice them.

(Education: *This didactic monologue is a response to line 228, "I'm not sure of all the subtleties in that." Insoo takes the opportunity to teach the group about the "subtleties" involved in asking the Miracle Question, including some team member understandings of the Miracle Question as a form of trance induction. There can be no doubt that she is providing education on the delivery of this iconic SF intervention.*)

230 TM: "And a miracle happened and you wake up in the morning, what will tell you that miracle happened?"
231 Th: "How will you know?"
232 IKB: "How will you know?" or, "What will be different that would tell YOU 'umm, something is different (with surprise),' maybe a miracle happened last night?" That gets them to look for really small changes. Not this fantastic miracle.
233 TM: Yeah, "What's different?"
234 IKB: Or nothing will be different. Difference is what we are concerned with.

End of Transcription

5.1.2 *Observations on Supervision Session 1, "Pain in the Butt"*

Collaboration. Collaboration is a supervisory stance exemplified by Insoo's attempts to create space for new questions and ideas throughout this team meeting. On four different occasions (lines 061, 118, 159, and 210), she invites new beginnings in the conversation—"Are there other questions?"—and invariably, these lead to new inquiries. She also shows deference to team discussion (lines 145 to 158), allowing the team members' conversation to flow without interruption or attempts to direct.

Complimenting. Insoo compliments the therapist, team members, and even the client throughout this supervision session. Many of her compliments are indirect. At times she simply affirms a team member's statement (line 068), which acts as a prompt for the person to continue speaking and (often) self-complimenting. Other times she compliments the client, who is not present (line 076), and that introduces new ideas and shifts team talk toward a strength focus. Even when the effect is uncertain (lines 165 and 171), Insoo attempts to validate therapists' efforts and direction.

Curiosity. Curiosity is a stance and an educational theme in this supervision meeting. Insoo seeks additional team views several times by asking if they have other ideas or questions about the therapy session. She also emphasizes the SF stance or "posture" (line 088) of curiosity, especially when one is asking and following up on the Miracle Question (lines 080 and following).

Hedging. The linguistic practice of hedging is prominent in this transcription, with too many examples to discuss in detail. I see Insoo's hedging practice coming from positions of being tentative and collaboration. Believing her view is simply one of many that could emerge from the data or conversation, Insoo's hedges result in openings for others' experiences and evading hard conclusions. In addition, hedging allows Insoo to introduce ideas to the team members indirectly (e.g., lines 104, 120), creating learning moments without taking an expert position.

Education. Education is front and center in this team session, in contrast to the second supervision case below. There are several possible reasons for this, including the fact that session one is a group team context at a training center while session two is a one-time consult with a sole therapist. However, what is central is the conspicuousness of education in this example of Insoo's supervision. Working both indirectly (lines 047 to 051) and very directly (lines 082 to 090), Insoo weaves teaching into this supervision by taking advantage of conversational opportunities. When the use of the Miracle Question in the therapy session is raised, Insoo intervenes with information, corrections, and directives (e.g., lines 088 and 129). In addition, she models the SF therapy approach while teaching, giving examples of questions that could be asked of clients to get at useful information (such as the relationship questions examples in lines 051, 137, and 143). So at times her educational approach is didactic, while other times it is indirect.

Balancing Being Expert and Being Tentative. Insoo artfully demonstrates how one can have expert knowledge and be tentative in the same conversation. Experts know things, and expert knowledge has a place in supervision. When team members asked her direct questions, at times she offered direct responses (line 088: "No, no, no. That's not the posture you take. The posture you take is out of absolute curiosity."). Other times she hedges, but her responses still contain valuable information from her years of experience with opening conversations (line 122) and use of the Miracle Question (line 129). Finally, Insoo maintains the SF tenet of being tentative when she evades the request for expert knowledge (line 124), becomes cautious in her responses (line 047), or challenges statements of certainty (line 063).

Using SF Supervision Techniques. Finally, Insoo incorporates SF techniques into her supervision. In addition to the relationship questions and the Miracle Question examples above, she uses reframing in reference to the therapy case the team witnessed (lines 114 and 116) as well as with a team member in supervision (lines 194 and 196).

5.2 Supervision Session 2: "One-Off Consultation on a Sad Little Girl"

A female therapist in her forties asked Insoo for supervision time. Insoo thought it was going to be a role-play demonstration for a video, but as you will see, the therapist immediately asked for supervision, and Insoo agreed to it. As a one-time (or as my British friends say, "one-off") supervision meeting, some may be surprised that Insoo does not ask for a great deal of background information. But Insoo stays with her supervision philosophy: "Instead of (an) emphasis on what, pay attention to how. Anybody can get concrete information. That's not hard. What's difficult is how to use the 'what,' the information you have" (Berg n.d., SFBTA Archive #10128-0064). The identity of the therapist is unknown, as there is no date or location indicated on the original video recording. Insoo died before this video came to the attention of the Archive, so I could not consult her for context or her views on this supervision session.

As with the first example, the entire consultation is transcribed here (Berg n.d., SFBTA Archive #10173-0092). Edits were minimal and usually made to protect confidentiality. Throughout the transcription, I will point out examples of SF supervision assumptions and practices described throughout the book. And as in the first case transcription, I restrain myself from pointing out other important supervisory responses to note skills specific to Insoo's SF supervision approach.

Transcription key

IKB	Insoo Kim Berg, Supervisor
Th	Therapist
(pause)	Notes a particularly significant pause of two or more seconds
..	Brief pause (less than 2 seconds)
Word	Underlining is used to show vocal emphasis
–	Indicates a cutoff in the dialogue, an interruption, or cross talk
[bracket]	Entry that was not part of the conversation, added for clarification
(*comment*)	*Comment* regarding a noteworthy nonverbal or extraverbal event or an edit created to ensure confidentiality
(Comment)	Editorial comments from the author regarding SF supervision

Transcription Begins

5.2.1 Supervision Transcription 2 and Commentary

001 IKB: Okay, we are going to pretend that I am your supervisor.
002 Th: I actually have a real case. If you are comfortable with it um it (my case) is a mother and a four-year-old child.
003 IKB: Okay, sure. No problem. Um (pause) Let's see. How many times have you seen them?
004 Th: Twice.

148   5 A Tap on the Shoulder: Supervision with Insoo Kim Berg

005 IKB: Twice. Oh, that's good.
006 Th: Yeah.
007 IKB: Okay, so in the two sessions you have met with them, what would they say…what would the mother say…obviously the child isn't going to say anything…what would the mother say you have done that has been helpful? (Relationship question: *Insoo immediately brings an additional perspective to the session that she as supervisor cannot provide or access. Although speculative, it has a significant effect: it redirects the therapist's presentation of case material.*)
(Indirect complimenting: *By asking what the client would say has been helpful, Insoo creates an opportunity for the therapist to compliment herself.*)
(Focus on the positive/success: *This is an initial attempt to focus the supervision on success. Although the therapist had not begun with a problem focus, a supervisor of Insoo's experience would probably assume the therapist's bias toward filling the supervisor in on all supposedly relevant information.*)
008 Th: I don't know that she would… I don't know that she would say that I have been helpful but she would say that the child is doing better. She had gotten a little better before she came and she has gotten better still since she has come two times.
(Self-complimenting: *The therapist does not self-compliment, but she pauses and considers the possibility that she had done something that the mother might say was helpful as she responds to Insoo's question.*)
009 IKB: Okay, okay. So…she would say that she is happy about that part.
010 Th: Umm…
011 IKB: That the child is doing better.
012 Th: Umm, I don't know if she would say that she is happy but she is less worried about her daughter. She was very, very, very worried.
013 IKB: Wow…Oh boy. Okay, so…So from what you are saying, you were able to recognize some changes between the mom and child in the first meeting. Is that what happened?
(Presuppositional statement: *Insoo's assertion, "you were able to recognize some changes…" assumes the therapist's activity in this information. Although the therapist did not self-compliment or take any credit for the changes, she does accept credit for recognizing the changes. A supervisor could just as easily have said, "So the mother told you about the changes…" and not include the therapist in the recognition of change.*)
(Perceptual skill building: *This is the type of question that calls attention to the therapist's SF abilities to notice difference, especially difference related to positive change.*)
014 Th: Yeah, yeah.
015 IKB: Okay, great. (Complimenting)

5.2 Supervision Session 2: "One-Off Consultation on a Sad Little Girl" 149

016   (Long pause, therapist thinking)
017 Th: The reason why I bring that case up is that I am stuck on it. I don't really know. I am not sure what to do with the case. I am worried about the little girl. I am worried about her, not so much her safety, but her welfare (pause) because she is so very, very, very sad.
018 IKB: Oh! At four years?
019 Th: At four. Usually as a therapist, I am usually really good about going home and leaving cases but this particular case has been hard to leave because she is so young.
020 IKB: Yeah.
021 Th: I have had to really work to not take it home with me every night emotionally because um she uh sucks her fingers all the time, all of her fingers in her mouth at once, and she told me in the first session that she was not happy.
022 IKB: Noo…really? She said that?
023 Th: She said, "I am not happy." Her parents separated and she is very, very sad about that. I have a feeling but I don't really know, I know that mother tells me that every time her father calls her she cries profusely. I'm not sure what that is about. Whether dad says something or whether she just misses dad but whenever dad calls she really cries a lot sometimes for as much as 2 h—
024 IKB: —Ahh wow—
025 Th: —after dad calls her.
026 IKB: Ohh.
027 Th: "Dad won't come to see me. I asked dad to and he refused to come in, and …uhh—
028 IKB: —So there's a contact between the father and the child.
(Exception—*tentatively probing for* positives: *In the midst of a description of problem behavior, Insoo notices a potential positive: father's involvement with the child. In spite of the report that the child is very sad, cries a great deal, and sucks her fingers, plus the difficulties the therapist is experiencing around this case, Insoo moves toward exceptions.*)
029 Th: Right, right. The father calls. They're only separated, but *(edited for confidentiality)* the father calls her (pause) they don't keep a schedule of any kind, kind of just once a week, whenever dad has a day off he calls and gets the kid and spends the day with her. But it's not on any sort of schedule or any sort of routine. It's just once a week he comes over and gets her and that's pretty much the only contact they have. Occasionally there is a phone call but the little girl is crying all the time, she is sad, she refuses to eat.
030 IKB: Oh my gosh.
031 Th: She has lost weight… She has lost probably 30% of her body weight.
032 IKB: *(gasps)* Wow. That's a lot at that age.
033 Th: Yeah, so you see why I am bringing up this case. I am really worried about her.

034 IKB: *(forward lean)* Yeah.
035 Th: You know, my experience with solution-focused therapy is I kind of just sit in my chair and be a therapist and stay in my role and they get better and I don't know how but it works, and it's amazing. And it's happening in this case as well, because she is getting better but I just kinda wanted to bounce it by you to see…if you can say if there is anything I am missing in terms of my questions or the way I am working.
036 IKB: Ah.
(Goal setting in supervision session: *Since this is a one-time consultation, there are no long-term therapist goals discussed. Here, the therapist asks Insoo to tell her "if there is anything I am missing." Her proposed goal is also very broad—from specific ("in terms of my questions") to general ("or the way I am working"). Insoo does not agree to these goals or to therapist problem talk (017, "stuck"); she simply acknowledges the therapist's previous contribution to the dialogue with "Ah." This speech act encourages the therapist to continue speaking without agreeing to what was requested. Insoo later addresses the therapist's experience of being "stuck" but does not make problem talk the focus of this section of the supervision consult.*)
037 Th: To try to help her family.
038 IKB: Would the mother say, does the mother say the child is doing better?
(Exception talk: *This is a return to the theme Insoo suggested right at the beginning of the consult [008]. It is a break from the therapist's last several statements that focused on problems (weight, weight loss) and session goals. Insoo chooses not to attend to either the therapist's request or problem talk; she creates the structure of the consult around exceptions and success.*)
039 Th: Oh definitely.
040 IKB: And you agree with her?
041 Th: Uh huh (yes). Yeah, she looks better. She is starting to eat again a little bit. Since she has been coming, she has started to eat. Um, she, as far as I know, she rarely sucks her fingers since she has been coming to counseling.
042 IKB: Oh my gosh.
043 Th: Um, but she was doing that until they would bleed, literally.
044 IKB: So, okay. What else is better?
(Exception talk: *Again, Insoo returns to exceptions and successes when the therapist offers additional problem information.*)
045 Th: *(sighs)* I think, I am speculating, but I think I have a sense from mother that she finds comfort in coming to me, having somebody else to hold it besides her. I think, I think she feels my support. Especially in the session, she acts really relieved.
046 IKB: Uh huh! *(yes)*
(Exception talk: *Even though it is a simple "Uh huh," the affirmation of the therapist's positive influence is clear.*)

5.2 Supervision Session 2: "One-Off Consultation on a Sad Little Girl" 151

047 Th: To be there, to come. She has had to cancel a few times and she really, really, really doesn't like cancelling, she likes to come in. Her life is pretty chaotic anyway, the rest of her life. I have the sense that she really, really likes the counseling and feels the support but I am speculating, she hasn't really told me that in her words.

048 IKB: So (pause) the child looks better, you are saying she is eating more, not sucking her fingers. Does mother also look better?
(Exception talk: *Continuing the consultation theme, Insoo includes all persons in the client system in the exception talk.*)

049 Th: Oh yeah. She also wakes up at night, just about every night (pause) used to wake up every night with a nightmare. That used to be, before they came to counseling, but now it has been reduced down to about two nights a week.

050 IKB: Oh wow! That's a lot. That's a big change.
(Highlighting exceptions/success)

051 Th: So, I haven't asked that question again to see if, there are so many problems that, when they come in, it's kinda (pause)

052 IKB: Yeah, okay.

053 Th: Like one of my challenges is not wanting to focus on the problems and yet needing to. I sorta want to know if she is safe and uh..

054 IKB: You mentioned the safety..also anything you are aware of, that (pause)
(Attending to safety: *See comment below, line 064*)

055 Th: Just to make sure that she is eating enough, and not hurting, I guess the weight loss would make it a safety issue directly, but also the, I did ask her to take her to her family doctor to have him check cause I want to make sure that she hadn't lost enough weight to where it is dangerous for her.

056 IKB: Yeah, yeah.

057 Th: 'Cause she lost quite a bit of weight.

058 IKB: How did she look to you?

059 Th: Um, well apparently, before this all happened, she was a little bit overweight and now she uh, she looks like a normal weight child.

060 IKB: Ohhh.

061 Th: So she hasn't lost enough weight (pause)

062 IKB: So she doesn't look emaciated..

063 Th: No, not yet. Hopefully, hopefully we can stop that, I hope.

064 IKB: Okay. All right. So there is no obvious reason for you to be worried about her safety or health.
(Attending to safety: *This summary addresses the therapist's concerns and repeated statements about safety. Insoo seems satisfied that the therapist is attending to safety concerns. Keep in mind that this is a one-time consult and Insoo has no ongoing supervisory relationship, so safety ultimately falls to the therapist who has competently assessed the risks and attempted to involve appropriate medical professionals in the case.*)

065 Th: No. Not if I based it on what I saw in the session. The things they were concerned about when they first made the appointment seemed to have stopped.
066 IKB: Yeah.
067 Th: And it seemed to be headed in another direction now.
068 IKB: Good, that's good. So how did the child relate to you in the session? (Participatory skill-building questions) Was she alert? Was she able to—
069 Th: —Yeah, oh yeah. She is very, she is not a real verbal child. She has limited language and she sticks to one or two word sentences. Most of her language is like naming things. She doesn't sit and have a conversation too much.
070 IKB: No..
071 Th: Which is also another challenge. Usually in a child that young, you see her with her mother because she doesn't have enough language to do much else.
072 IKB: What was the interaction between mother and child? What was your observation?
(Perceptual skill-building question)
073 Th: Very connected to her mom. She is affectionate. She loves her. In the session when she first came, she seemed almost frightened. I think she was worried for her daughter.
074 IKB: Okay.
075 Th: Scared.
076 IKB: Yeah. So she knew whatever was going on wasn't right for her daughter.
077 Th: Um hum.
078 IKB: She was concerned enough to do something about it.
079 Th: Yeah.
080 IKB: Yeah. Okay, so she knows—
081 Th: – Um hum—
082 IKB: – What a good parenting or a good standard of how she should be behaving.
083 Th: Yeah I think so.
084 IKB: That she shouldn't be having nightmares, or crying all the time, or that kind of stuff.
(Highlighting client competence: *In this exchange, Insoo summarizes, specifically noting the Mom's competence.*)
085 Th: Right, right. She was worried about that.
086 IKB: So you are not concerned about parenting issues.
(Therapist temporary certainty and competence: *Immediately after drawing attention to Mom's abilities as a parent, Insoo moves to elicit the therapist's assessment of both parents' competence.*)
087 Th: Umm…the only thing I am still concerned about and I have no real way of getting to the information, if I worry about why she cries still when dad calls. And I can speculate but mom doesn't know what dad

5.2 Supervision Session 2: "One-Off Consultation on a Sad Little Girl" 153

		says either and the child isn't verbal so we don't know whether she is just upset because she's not, because she misses dad because when she does go with him she seems to enjoy it and she says she misses dad.
088	IKB:	Yeah…
089	Th:	But then she cries so much when dad calls… like 2 h of crying.
090	IKB:	Sooo just the telephone call makes her cry? Or…
091	Th:	Telephone calls.
092	IKB:	Just the telephone call… So when he drops her off, does she cry?
093	Th:	She's grumpy, so, you know, all kids do that when their parents switch for half a day or a day but not outside of what other kids do. Just the crying, and I kind of wonder what it is.
094	IKB:	But you have no way of knowing that.
095	Th:	Yeah, short of telling Mom to listen in on the phone call, but—
096	IKB:	– Oh no, you can't do that. No.

(Direct communication: *Although this is not the normal way Insoo communicates in supervision, it is an example of very direct communication on a range from indirect to direct. She was not opposed to such direct talk, but it was not her preferred method in supervision.*)

097	Th:	No, so…
098	IKB:	Okay, okay. All right. Sooo, what. I want to come back to this. You are not concerned about her parenting.
099	Th:	No.
100	IKB:	Or father's parenting.
101	Th:	Mmm-mmm (no) (head shake)
102	IKB:	Aside from the fact that they are separated.
103	Th:	Mmm-mmm (*no*). I don't know about the father because he wouldn't, I'd call and ask him to come to, come to meet with me and his daughter and he wouldn't come. So I really don't know…
104	IKB:	So Mom doesn't complain about him and his parenting?
105	Th:	No, no, and she doesn't say that he ever hit her or was abusive to her or her daughter, so she wouldn't lie about that. Or even verbally violent. But she says she doesn't have any concerns about dad being verbally abusive.
106	IKB:	So she's okay with the father taking the child.
107	Th:	Uh huh (*yes*).
108	IKB:	That's good.

(Attending to safety: *Once again, Insoo has checked with the therapist about safety, this time surreptitiously by asking about Mom's view of Dad's parenting.*)

109	Th:	Yeah, she feels like he is safe. She, I think, she wishes that the um father would be more involved. He only comes like once a week and I think she would like him to be more involved and come see her more often and he doesn't.
110	IKB:	Uh huh (*yes*).
111	Th:	It's very evident from her words that the father is very angry with her for leaving him.
112	IKB:	Oh, she left him?

113	Th:	Yeah. She chose, I guess, my understanding is that he was in (*particular industry*) and I guess mom just felt like she tried to get him to take a chance at something else and move on in his life and finally she got tired of it and left him and now he is employed at a really good job. (*laughing*)
114	IKB:	(*laughing*)
115	Th:	He is still very, very angry with her for choosing to leave him.
116	IKB:	Of course, of course.
117	Th:	She just moved back with her sister as far as I know.
118	IKB:	Ohhh okay, okay. So when he takes the child he goes to (his relatives' house)?
119	Th:	He lives with friends, I believe, in another city, about an hour away, so he takes her to (another city), actually.
120	IKB:	Ohh.
121	Th:	And um, he goes there.
122	IKB:	So, what makes you feel so stuck? What part makes you stuck? (Goal setting: *Approximately half way through this consult, Insoo returns to the therapist's request to talk about her stuckness, which was obviously a part of the therapist's agenda for this consult.*)
123	Th:	That's a good question. Uhh, two things: Maybe more than two, but I'll start with two. (pause) Why she cries so much when dad calls, and if there is something there that I don't know about that I can't know that would be helpful to know but I can't know. That dilemma kind of bothers me.
124	IKB:	Yeah.
125	Th:	(pause) and then the other thing I think is just that uh, just to see a child so very young so very depressed that, that is hard for me to even take that in. That a child that young could be so depressed. That's just sort of um sobering, I guess. Sobering to have that kind of a case. I have worked with a lot of kids (pause) I um, but I have never seen one that little.
126	IKB:	Yeah, you are right. That's a very young age.. that kind of serious reaction to separation.
127	Th:	Yeah, it's real interesting because I ended up with um, with their insurance case and I wound up speaking to one of their (insurance company's) clinical supervisors and I ran it by them and I knew, their reaction was, "hold on a minute, let me get my supervisor" and her supervisor came on the line and I, I think it ultimately made it bigger than it was because everyone is like, ohhhh!
128	IKB:	Yeah.
129	Th:	You know. 'Cause you know, the little girl, she is so depressed. Um.. The thing I felt bad about too is, I don't know if you know this, but in (this state) we have a law called parity where all insurances are required for certain diagnoses of the DSM to provide coverage only if the person has serious depression, schizophrenia, or bi-polar. Anything else insurance doesn't have to cover, and that depends on how good their insurance is, but those three diagnoses <u>all</u> insurances have to cover that.

5.2 Supervision Session 2: "One-Off Consultation on a Sad Little Girl" 155

130 IKB: Okay.
131 Th: So I was in the position with this little girl of having to decide whether to go ahead and put that label on her, which for me was a very difficult—
132 IKB: —difficult—
133 Th: —thing to have to say that a four-year-old had major depression. It's such a weight to put that label on a child. I explained to the (insurance company's) clinician when I did it that you know, if this were any other insurance, I would call this adjustment disorder, but in this case, had I done that, I would not have been able to treat the family.
134 IKB: Yeah.
135 Th: And because of the seriousness of her symptoms, I didn't really feel good just, um, you know, list a referral on another sheet, so that was a little bit of an ethical dilemma for me, and then I, it wasn't as though I made up the diagnosis, because I actually went to the DSM and added up all of the symptoms and she clearly matches the criteria.
136 IKB: Yeah, it sounds like she did.
(Hedging: *This is a clear hedge. Since this is a very complicated situation in a one-time consult, Insoo's supervisory response is to encourage the therapist to move forward in the conversation. She does not engage in discussion about the accuracy or necessity of a diagnosis, the ethics of attaching a diagnosis to a four-year-old that may have long-term insurance implications, or the ethical conflict around diagnosis in order to receive payment for therapeutic services. All of these are worthy topics of discussion in ongoing supervisory relationships, but it was inappropriate here.*)
137 Th: But I, uh, felt bad about it. I felt bad about it. It is bad enough to have to put a label on a four-year-old but I ended up discussing it with Mom a little bit in detail, just talking to her about it, that in order for us to do this, I have to get a label and call this something. But that was a dilemma, too.
138 IKB: So let me come back to this… Sort of, so what did mother say made her start eating better, stop sucking her fingers, and the less frequency of nightmares? What would she say is different? She is doing different? Something different? That the child is doing different?
(Exception talk: *This return to questions about the mother's views and actions around the child's problems is an obvious move away from continued problem talk regarding being "stuck," redirecting the conversation to previous exception talk.*)
139 Th: I don't know. I don't think she would identify anything. You know, maybe, I don't think, it might not be true about this case, but I don't think that she, because it was starting to get better before she came in to see me.
140 IKB: Ahh.
141 Th: I don't think she would identify anything other than just something magical that she just got better. Yeah.

142 IKB: So (pause) okay. She would not be able to explain to you why, what's different about the life.
143 Th: So I could explore that the next session more, cause, I am fairly sure that she is continuing to get a little bit better.
144 IKB: Right.
145 Th: My guess is there are things she is doing that are helping her get better, but—
146 IKB: —That would be my guess too. But we don't know for sure.
(Hedging: *In this hedge, Insoo encourages the therapist's search for things the mother is doing that help her child "get better." By hedging, Insoo actually fuels this urge to know; "...but we don't know for sure" feeds the therapist's curiosity to learn more.*)
147 Th: Yeah. What it is that might be different? or What she might think is different?
148 IKB: Right. Something is different. Something is better.
149 Th: Yeah, she's better.
150 IKB: That's a good sign.
(Supporting therapist language and competence: *The therapist decides, without prompting, to "explore that (exceptions) in the next session more." In this exchange, Insoo reinforces the direction the therapist has decided to take. She does this by using the therapist's language ["different," "better"] and encouraging the direction the therapist has already decided to take. It is the therapist's decision to ask more about this in subsequent sessions, but Insoo posited the seed for this through her questions in line 138.*)
151 Th: Yeah, talking with you about it and kind of reiterating everything that's different is helping me to kind of get my focus off of everything that I am worried about.
152 IKB: Oh, okay.
153 Th: Not to, 'cause when I came in, I think I was focused on, oh, she is going to start sucking her fingers again, she might stop eating again, she might lose more weight, and I was going through all of that list and I'm starting to look at that and inventory, "Now wait a minute, it's been three weeks now and she hasn't sucked her fingers as far as I know of. I will see her when I get back."
154 IKB: Yeah.
155 Th: And uh, she hasn't lost any more weight, and she is now beginning to eat a little bit, but she is still very sad.
156 IKB: Yeah. Of course.
157 Th: But we have already dropped three of the five things we were worried about.
158 IKB: Yeah—
159 Th: —So, that's good—
160 IKB: —That's good, okay, all right (pause). So what would… what needs to happen with this case for you to feel like, ahh, "I'm not, I'm over the

feeling stuck and I feel like we are, we are moving forward, I don't have to be so concerned about the, about the child?"
(Goal setting, future focus: *Insoo returns to "feeling stuck" but moves it from a discussion of what or why to one focused on the future.*)
(Hedging: *Note that Insoo starts with the eradication of the stuckness ["for you to feel like, ahh, '… I'm over the feeling stuck'"] but then moderates the statement through hedging ["..I feel like we are, we are moving forward, I don't have to be so concerned about the, about the child."]. Though the usual grammar of hedging is not present, the resulting statement is clearly addressing both continuous concern about serious problems and therapist change.*)

161 Th: Okay. (pause) What needs to happen here? Or in the case?
162 IKB: In the case. We are talking about the case.
163 Th: I guess just a few more weeks of her continuing to get better.
164 IKB: Okay.
165 Th: I had predicted at the beginning that it wouldn't take very long. To myself I had predicted, I hadn't told the mother this. I predicted it to myself and the insurance and I don't know quite why I believed that but I think because she is so young, I had some confidence that we can stabilize this and get her, get her back on track, and that's happening.
166 IKB: Yeah, that sounds like it, that sounds like it's happening. And really quickly, too.
(Highlighting exceptions and success: *Insoo agrees with the therapist's view that some of what needed to be "stabilize[d]" is currently materializing.*)
(Hedging: *While agreeing with the therapist's views that some positive changes are happening, Insoo also hedges by using the phrase "sounds like." Since all of the information being considered in this consult has come from the therapist, we can assume Insoo recognized that the database was limited—Insoo had no direct contact with the clients or therapy, and the clients' views were presented second hand throughout the discussion. Supervisors should hedge at this point to encourage the conversation to move forward, as making statements about the limited viewpoints present in the conclusions would disrupt the conversation's direction toward "what needs to happen."*)

167 Th: Yeah. So I guess just a few more weeks of her being a little better. What I would really like is that, I would really love it if dad would meet with me, but I don't think that that's going to happen.
168 IKB: Of course, of course. Will you be able to talk to him on the telephone?
169 Th: I'll try!
170 IKB: You know, you might be able to, um, be stopped by this, or feel like you're not getting anywhere. Just, would he be willing to talk to you on the telephone and give you some ideas about his daughter?
(Indirect communication: *Embedded in this series of questions is Insoo's suggestion that the therapist talk with the father on the telephone.*)

171	Th:	Yeah.
172	IKB:	I'm sure he is worried about his daughter as well.
173	Th:	I don't think he is, that's the thing, but I don't know that—
174	IKB:	—Well, you don't want to say that—
175	Th:	—assume that he might be—
176	IKB:	—Of course, you want to assume this.
177	Th:	Yeah, that's a good point, OK.
178	IKB:	And that might also give you some chance to assess, what, how is this man, (*unintelligible*) different, so different or, (*unintelligible*). We may never find out, but also it might give you some ideas about an opportunity to find out for yourself. Is the dad different or, you know? Or if he absolutely refuses to even help you out, for his daughter's sake. (pause) (Indirect ←→ direct communication: *Insoo alters between suggestions and directives in this exchange [172 to 178]. More discussion on this exchange follows below in the commentary.*)
179	Th:	Right. Yeah.
180	IKB:	That's different information again, isn't it? That's a whole different information.
181	Th:	Yeah, if he wouldn't talk to me.
182	IKB:	Right. I can understand someone who doesn't want to come in, but, um (unintelligible). Just take some 10–15 minutes to talk to you on the phone.
183	Th:	Okay. I'll do that. I'm pretty sure that—
184	IKB:	—It will be helpful for you to do that. (Direct communication: *When the therapist hedges ["I'm pretty sure…"] after making a clear commitment, Insoo becomes more direct. She also appeals to the therapist's desire to be helpful to everyone involved.*)
185	Th:	Yeah! 'Cause it's like I'm working in the dark.
186	IKB:	Right.
187	Th:	So if I can find some way to not have that be a mystery, that will help.
188	IKB:	All right. Okay.
189	Th:	Okay.
190	IKB:	Got it?
191	Th:	I got it. We're done! Thanks!
192	IKB:	(*laughter*)

End of Transcription

5.2.2 Observations on Supervision Session 2, "A Sad Little Girl"

Emotionally Engaged and SF. Insoo is fully engaged in the therapist's emotional responses and confusion. This exchange hopefully communicates her professional commitment to the therapist and her predicament:

5.2 Supervision Session 2: "One-Off Consultation on a Sad Little Girl" 159

031 Th: She has lost weight…She has lost probably 30% of her body weight.
032 IKB: *(gasps)* Wow. That's a *lot* at that age.
033 Th: Yeah, so you see why I am bringing up this case. I am really worried about her.
034 IKB: *(forward lean)* Yeah.

Even though she is absorbed in the moment, Insoo stays with her SF supervision approach. Instead of processing the therapist's emotions or reasoning, she seeks to return to solution building. After a longer statement by the therapist regarding her own solution orientation, Insoo follows with this focus on possibility:

038 IKB: Would the mother say, does the mother say the child is doing better?
039 Th: Oh definitely.
040 IKB: And you agree with her?
041 Th: Uh huh *(yes)*. Yeah, she looks better.

Exceptions. While symptoms may draw attention and must be addressed when safety is a concern, SF and related approaches are:

> not impressed with symptoms or troublesome behavior. We accept that people will behave badly or in a bizarre fashion at times. Within this model this is not even considered very interesting. What is fascinating is how well people do under adverse and seemingly impossible circumstances. (Skott-Myhre 1994, p. 5)

Insoo attends to the seriousness of the client's situation, including the risks in the child's condition and behaviors. But after assessing the therapist's view on risk (and, I believe, choosing to trust the therapist's professionalism regarding risk of harm), she presses on toward exception talk (lines 038, 044, and 048).

Goal Setting. In line 017, the therapist says she is "stuck." Insoo only comments on this appraisal near the end of the consult (line 122), as being stuck is a problem that may not even inform the goal for the supervision session. The goals for the session revolve around lines 35 through 37. Part of being a SF supervisor is creating a guiding structure that emphasizes success and resources, and part of a supervisor's expertise is knowing how to optimally configure a conversational exchange, which is isomorphic to the therapist's expertise when counseling. Therapists are experts on *what* they are experiencing, including what they believe they need from the supervision consult; supervisors are experts on *how* to attend to therapists' requests, including the timing of discussions within the consult hour.

"So let me come back to this…" (line 138). Stated in the imperative form, it would be difficult for the therapist to continue on with her talk about diagnosis and stuckness (line 137). Insoo used this type of statement often in her therapy and supervision. "We will get back to that" and "Let's get back to that" sound similar, but they have different functions. "We will get back to that" (and all similar phrases) is a technique Insoo used to put off a particular topic or exchange until later in the session or case (Berg 1995). It is unclear if this was simply a way to delay discussion on a theme or if it was her way of politely rejecting its relevance in the session, as she did not always revisit these topics she pushed to the side. "Let's get back to that" is an

imperative that connects to a theme she had brought up previously and resulted in a return to talking about exceptions already noted (lines 028, 038, 044, and 048).

Therapist Feedback. The therapist reviews the changes she has experienced during this supervision consult in lines 151 to 160. Unprompted, the therapist states that conversation about "what's different" helped: "Talking with you about it and kind of reiterating everything that's different is helping me kind of get my focus off of everything that I am worried about" (line 151, with more detail on what she was focused on in line 153). She states that she experienced a change from problem focus to possible solution building (line 153), seeing exceptions and positive change while not losing track of the significant problems the child and mother have experienced. The therapist "dropped three of the five things we were worried about" (line 157), but Insoo does not ask what three were dropped and what two worries remain. Insoo simply takes advantage of the therapist's success in this consult and returns to goals they have been working toward: "I'm over…feeling stuck," "moving forward," and "I don't have to be so concerned…about the child" (line 160).

Therapist Agency. The therapist's statement, "but I don't think that that's going to happen" (line 167) is passive; Insoo challenges this conclusion and other statements quite directly several times in this supervision consultation, especially in the final few minutes. I believe part of her directness is connected to the consult time limit, as this supervision time ends about 90 seconds after line 167 and they both quickly leave the room. Insoo's directives—"Well, you don't want to say that" and "Of course, you want to assume this"—are in direct response to the therapist's stated desire to involve the father in the therapeutic system and her pessimism about this possibility found in line 167. This push from behind is not Insoo's usual style, but sometimes "leading from one step behind" means you have a different view of possibilities that the therapist may not have considered, and one-time consults leave very little time for hints about options and therapist choices.

Chapter 6
Research and SF Supervision

Steve de Shazer and Insoo Kim Berg (1997) said, "Ever since I (de Shazer) began practicing brief therapy in the early 1970s, my 'research' question was 'What do therapists do that is useful?' In the 1980s, we changed this to 'What do clients and therapists do together that is useful?'" I believe this type of question is very informative when discussing research and SF supervision, but the questions become more complicated because of the additional therapist/client interactional system. Freitas (2002, p. 364) summed up this convolution well when he wrote:

> When one thinks of the complexity involved in studying supervisor-supervisee-client triads, it is little wonder that the studies in this area are susceptible to criticism...Given the complexity inherent in studying simply therapy outcome...it may be some time before we arrive at a clear understanding of the impact of specific types of supervision on therapy outcome.

In an attempt to honor both the importance of research and the intricacy of the questions, this chapter will cover three areas related to supervision. The initial section will briefly summarize the state of psychotherapy supervision research in general, pointing out the difficulties as well as the expectations. The second segment takes a look at the existing research on SF supervision, with a special emphasis on the prominence that has been placed on investigating supervisee[1] and client voices in the process. Finally, in keeping with the importance of investigating supervisees' experiences of supervision, I will review literature relevant to the SF supervision stance discussed in this book and offer some "best practice" recommendations for professionals working at becoming the best possible SF supervisors.

---

[1]"Supervisee" is the most common term used in the literature, in contrast to my use of "therapist" throughout this book. Some confusion results from using supervisee, a generic term which does not discriminate between students, beginning therapists, and seasoned mental health professionals. Throughout this chapter, I will use "supervisee" (to align with the research literature) and "therapist" (in keeping with this volume's commitment to decreasing the hierarchy in the supervision relationship) interchangeably.

6.1 Psychotherapy Supervision Research

Usually, scientific advancement moves from descriptive studies (often qualitative research conducted with small numbers of informants) to research that tests clearly defined variables with valid and reliable instruments paralleled by the development of hypotheses from emerging theories. Process research requires a major investment of time but offers great promise in understanding supervisor–supervisee experiences and measures relating to supervision alliance and relationship continue to be created and tested (Bernard and Goodyear 2009). However, most supervision literature remains theoretical in nature, not research based (Inman and Ladany 2008). And while there has been a continual increase in research publications on psychotherapy supervision, most of the investigations still involve small samples and/or are qualitative in nature. So it appears the field is still searching for relevant variables, suitable research designs, and appropriate statistical methods (Ellis, D'Iuso, and Ladany 2008; Freitas 2002). To me, this means that supervision is recognized as critical to the field of psychotherapy but lacks a clear direction. Inman and Ladany's review of the supervision literature "highlight(ed) the disconnect that exists in theory, research, and practice" (2008, p. 511). So, those assessing research to understand the field of supervision (and SF supervision in particular) will have to rely on inference rather than a convincing body of knowledge to inform their beliefs and practices.

Since the issues still seem to outnumber the answers, I will review studies in several areas of supervision research that I believe have relevance to the de Shazer and Berg research approach mentioned earlier. The question I begin with is this: *what do therapists and supervisors do together that is useful?* This question guides the areas of inquiry and the research publications reviewed here, and its importance to supervision is supported by a significant number of investigations (Crocket, Pentecost, Cresswell, Paice, Tollestrup, De Vries, and Wolfe 2009; Milne, Pilkington, Gracie, and James 2003; Reese, Usher, Bowman, Norsworthy, Halstead, Rowlands, and Chisholm 2009; Wheeler and Richards 2007).

6.1.1 *Supervision Alliance and Interaction ("What Do Therapists and Supervisors Do Together that Is Useful for Therapists?")*

In their review of the research, Stoltenberg and McNeill (2010) concluded that *the single most important factor in successful supervision was the supervisory relationship or alliance*. Therapist confidence, "refined professional identity" (p. 141), improved intervention skills, and positive conceptual capabilities are often credited to a supervisory alliance that supports the therapist in struggles and successes. Inman and Ladany's (2008) review of supervision research concluded that "supervisory alliances (are) at the heart of effective supervision" (p. 502). Much like therapeutic alliance is a major component of positive client outcomes, the supervision alliance is the scaffold that supports other supervision activities. Bordin's (1983) model is among the most commonly used to conceptualize this supervision alliance. Even though it has been criticized, its three areas—agreement on goals, agreement on tasks, and an emotional bond—are touchstones in the ongoing study of this relationship. *Agreement on goals* in Bordin's model refers to the objectives created with and for the supervisee plus the methods to be used in achieving these objectives. *Agreement on tasks* "is the understanding of the responsibility that the goals would impose on the supervisor and supervisee" (Wainwright 2010, p. 18). Finally, the *emotional bond* addresses safety, trust, and enjoyment of the other. In other words, the supervision alliance involves clear goal setting, respectful reflection, and commitment to relationship. These vital components of successful supervision bolster Insoo's assertion that supervision, training, and consultation are very different activities (Berg n.d., SFBTA Archive #10128-0064)—success in supervision requires alliance. One distinction that can be drawn from the research literature is that without a trusting relationship and cooperative interaction, it is unlikely that supervision will be effective.

Since supervision alliance has been studied extensively, a fairly clear *set of factors that supervisors contribute* to creating this relationship, negative and positive, has been established. Supervisors who are less effective are more rigid and less tolerant of therapists' errors and progress. Their expectations lack clarity, resulting in therapists seeking out peers or other supervisors for ideas and support. Supervisors' exaggeration of their own competence as well as focusing on their own cases more than therapists' can have a negative effect on this relationship. Also, negative outcomes result from supervisors who show less support and fail to follow up on therapists' concerns. In addition, their lack of engagement is tied to providing less education and emphasizing negative aspects of therapists' performance.[2] On the other hand, supervisor behaviors that promote positive alliances are easily identified as well. Giving clear feedback regarding therapist mistakes as well as successes is important to building this bond. Supervisors who are sensitive (in both consultant and teacher roles) and show empathy contribute to positive partnerships. Supervisor self-disclosure can be constructive when it is moderate and not centered on the supervisor's personal struggles. Exhibiting a high ethical standard is also key to forming strong bonds, which includes respect for therapists' time (e.g., not allowing phone interruptions during supervision) as well as showing high regard for both client and therapist well-being (Bernard and Goodyear 2009; Inman and Ladany 2008; Kilminster and Jolly 2000; Ladany and Lehrman-Waterman 1999; Levenson 1984; Nelson and Friedlander 2001; Worthen and McNeill 1996).

One key idea related to isomorphism (see Sect. 2.2) is that the supervisor and therapist may not have to match on personal characteristics or theoretical orientation for therapists to feel satisfied with the supervision process or form a working alliance. Simply stated, *good working supervision relationships do not require that the therapist's treatment model and the supervisor's approach match* (Cheon, Blumer,

---

[2] For a thorough list titled, "How to Be a Lousy Supervisory: Lessons from the Research," see Bernard and Goodyear (2009).

Shih, Murphy, and Sato 2009). A one-to-one match between orientations is rare, and even if a therapist is a single-model practitioner, the supervisor herself may use an integrative approach. This can be especially encouraging for SF supervisors working with therapists who utilize a variety of clinical models or have created integrative approaches.

Another aspect of supervision that can have a significant effect on the alliance is *evaluation*. Anxiety is often heightened by evaluative processes, especially for novice therapists (Weatherford, O'Shaughnessy, Mori, and Kaduvettoor 2008). Although some have speculated that evaluation in any form is a negative that must be overcome or avoided, most research offers a different, data-informed view. "Goal setting and feedback strengthen the supervisory relationship…trainees seem to feel more connected to their supervisors when they (supervisors) provide clear and specific feedback regarding trainee strengths and deficits" (Lehrman-Waterman and Ladany 2001, p. 174). In addition, review of the research reveals a close connection between establishing goals, feedback activities, and supervision alliance: when therapists create goals and supervisors provide effective feedback (positive and negative) related to the therapists' aims, the alliance is stronger (Inman and Ladany 2008).

For many reasons, *open communication* is always a goal of supervision. This requires the creation of a safe environment for disclosure of information, discussion, and questions, and there is strong research evidence that establishing this transparency can be problematic. Ladany, Hill, Corbett, and Nutt (1996) found that up to 90% of therapists withhold information from supervisors. They concluded that most nondisclosures were connected to shame; that is, fear—of ridicule or "political suicide" (p. 10) based on past experiences with those in authority—was the basis for silence involving benign and potentially important information (Todd 1997a). Other reasons for nondisclosure include the fear of hurting the supervisors' feelings, anxiety regarding exposure to future supervisory criticism, or desire to avoid harming the therapist–supervisor relationship (Klinger, Ladany, and Kulp 2012; Reichelt, Gullestad, Hansen, Rønnestad, Torgersen, Jacobsen, Nielsen, and Skjerve 2009).

There seems to be some disagreement in the literature when comparing *administrative and clinical supervision*. While some have found a definite difference in supervisees' experience of these two distinct supervisor roles (O'Donoghue 2012; Triantafillou 1997), the survey research of Tromski-Klingshirn and Davis (2007) found no significant differences between the satisfaction of supervisees receiving only clinical supervision and those whose supervisor served both clinical and administrative roles. "Furthermore, the majority of supervisees receiving clinical and administrative supervision from the same person did not view this dual supervisory role as problematic (82% of n=70), and 72.5% reported specific benefits" (p. 294). Overall, the research tends to explain satisfaction as a product of supervisory alliance rather than the number or types of roles the supervisor plays.

Finally, *using a variety of methods or techniques* adds to a more effective supervisory alliance (Milne, Aylott, Fitzpatrick, and Ellis 2008). Even though skills training and supervisor feedback are the most common activities in supervision, Norcross and Halgin (1997) found that a broad variety of supervisory techniques is more effective in therapist development. These methods include "didactic presentations, reading assignments, open-ended discussions, personal modeling, experiential activities, video demonstrations, case examples, and mini-case conferences" (p. 209).

Despite limited publication on *the supervision alliance from a SF perspective*, it is evident from a review of the general supervision literature that relationship factors cannot be ignored. Some (including Wheeler and Greaves 2005) have openly discussed establishing and nurturing warm, trusting relationships as a vital part of the supervision process, but few SF supervision authors attend to it. The research is clear: supervision alliance is crucial to success, whatever the supervisor's model or approach. The SF supervision approach includes several factors that contribute to this alliance: well-defined goals and evaluation processes built on success and needed improvements, reducing hierarchy to create respectful collaboration, flexibility to meet therapist goals, and commitment to positive client impact. Encouraging the development of trust through support, safe communication, appropriate self-disclosure, encouraging supervisee feedback, and sensitivity to therapists' abilities and deficits is the responsibility of the supervisor.

6.1.2 Client Outcomes ("What Do Therapists and Supervisors Do that Is Useful to Clients?")

Of the little research, there is to support the impact of supervision on client change, most only addresses immediate impact on a single therapy session and not overall client outcome (Bernard and Goodyear 2009; Freitas 2002; Holloway and Neufeldt 1995; Sparks, Kisler, Adams, and Blumen 2011; Watkins 2011). However, there are a few exceptions to this. Callahan, Almstrom, Swift, Borja, and Heath (2009) reviewed archival data and concluded supervisors have "a moderate effect" on client outcomes (p. 72). The research of Bambling, King, Raue, Schweitzer, and Lambert (2006) is a rare find in that it has a strong design with randomized assignments and valid and reliable measures. They found significant supervision effects on client outcomes, but "the mechanisms by which supervision enhances alliance and treatment outcome are not clear" (p. 327). Reese and colleagues (2009) found promising client outcome results when student therapists received supervisory feedback, but they admitted that the complexity of the client–supervisee–supervisor relationship makes it very difficult to connect supervision with positive client outcomes. Freitas (2002) cited Triantafillou's (1997) research involving solution-focused clinical supervision as one of the best-designed studies on supervision from 1981 through 2001, and Triantafillou found positive supervision influences on client change. However, Inman and Ladany (2008) reported only approximately 18 studies attempting to ascertain connections between supervision and client outcome over the past 30 years, with mixed results. Wheeler and Richards (2007) have written an exceptional review of studies examining the supervisor–therapist–client impact, and their overall conclusion is that "the link to improve outcome for clients (through supervision) is tentative and no studies in this review offer substantial evidence to support improvement in client outcomes" (p. 63).

Lichtenberg (2006) has gone so far as to say if we cannot link positive effects from supervision to client outcome, then protecting clients—one of supervision's ethical purposes—needs to be reexamined. While the field clearly holds to the idea that supervision *should* have positive impact on clients, this does "not support the notion that a complete 1:1 transfer of actions from supervision to therapy necessarily makes for good therapy" (Milne et al. 2003, p. 200). In line with Bordin's (1983) theory, it is often the emotional support from supervision that keeps therapists focused on client needs by addressing therapist distractions and emotional responses, improving client outcome (Wheeler and Richards 2007). *That* psychotherapy outcome should be monitored for supervision effect *and* for informing the supervision process is gaining traction (Lambert and Hawkins 2001). Research evidence suggests therapists tend "towards overly optimistic appraisals of our clients' progress" (Worthen and Lambert 2007, p. 52), supporting the necessity for further research on supervision–therapy connections.

6.2 SF Supervision Research

6.2.1 General SF Supervision Research

Most of the literature pertaining to SF supervision is theoretical or anecdotal. Studies that have been published in peer-reviewed journals or presented at peer-reviewed conferences are scarce, and many are difficult to generalize because of their qualitative designs and limited subject or informant numbers. But several research investigations are worthy of examination to inform the development of a SF approach in this field.

Hsu (2007, 2009), (Hsu and Kuo, Contribution 7.4 of this volume; Hsu and Sun 2008; Hsu and Tsai 2008). Hsu and her colleagues have contributed greatly to the development of SF supervision by studying school counselors' experience with this approach. All of these studies involve qualitative methodologies with small samples, but their work stresses the importance of goal setting, feedback, education, and exceptions/successes in the SF supervision process. More than anyone in the world, Hsu and colleagues have committed to careful design and analysis of supervision meeting transcription, supervisee experiences, and model development. As a result, SF approaches are receiving national recognition in Taiwan. Multicultural understanding of SF therapy and supervision approaches has also been enhanced as a direct result of their research and Hsu's commitment to international publication and presentation.

Koob (1999, 2002). Koob hypothesized that a focus on (1) therapist successes, (2) therapist development, and (3) the notion that there are many right ways to conduct therapy (all SF supervision assumptions) would have significant positive impact on therapist self-efficacy. Fifty-five supervisor–supervisee dyads were studied, and the majority of supervisors subscribed to eclectic theories of change. Using standardized measures of therapist self-efficacy, Koob found that attending to therapist successes and development "demonstrate(s) an association with perceived self-efficacy" (2002, p. 175). He also found that a focus on therapist development (rather than a traditional focus on client development, also known as "therapy-once-removed" in which the supervisor treats the client indirectly through the therapist) was associated with greater therapist self-efficacy. Although limited in its conclusions because these data could only be understood as correlational, Koob provided a carefully designed and analyzed study of important factors intrinsic to SF supervision.

Rudes (1992) and Rudes, Shilts, and Berg (1997). Covered in Chap. 5, this careful analysis of supervision by Insoo Kim Berg brought early credibility to the study and development of the SF supervision approach. Rudes' research, using a recursive frame analysis method of inquiry (Chenail 1995), supported several tenets of SFBT including the creation of a cooperative relationship and attention to strengths and resources rather than errors or deficits. Additionally, Rudes and his colleagues noted that Insoo took a nonprivileged stance and sought to flatten the hierarchy inherent in supervisory relationships by using particular methods including hedging, collaborative dialogue that creates a more "facilitative role" for the supervisor (p. 213), and a coordinated effort on the part of supervisees and supervisor to utilize language in a redescription of therapy leading to more useful conceptualizations and actions.

Triantafillou (1997). This research was cited by Freitas (2002) as one of the best-designed studies on the effects of supervision on client outcome in the 20-year period from 1981 to 2001. Noting that nearly two-thirds of supervision in mental health settings was administrative, Triantafillou proposed a SF supervision approach involving four specific steps: (1) "establishing an atmosphere of competence" in which the therapists' strengths and successes are emphasized rather than mistakes and failures (Triantafillou 1997, p. 311); (2) supervisor and therapist focus on clients' conceptualizations and experiences over their own professional views; (3) clear feedback from supervisor to therapist, including compliments, focusing on therapist goals, and intrasession reflection; and (4) supervision follow-up sessions based on the SF structure of EARS (elicit, amplify, reinforce, and start again) (De Jong and Berg 2012) and connected closely to details of client progress. His research found this SF approach to supervising clinical cases resulted in greater job satisfaction for therapists and improved client outcome when compared to administrative supervision only. Therapists' responses also called attention to the increase in supervision productivity and an improvement in morale. Client outcomes in the primary context, a residential treatment setting, were also significantly impacted: incident reports of serious behavior problems decreased by two-thirds at the facility, and reliance on psychotropic medication use showed a considerable decrease (prescribing psychiatrists were blind to the supervision study). In addition, the experimental facilities reported 75% fewer client incidents than the control group facilities, which only had administrative supervision. Triantafillou's recommendations, including elements of SF supervision practice, are excellent starting points for building a research-informed SF supervision practice.

6.2.2 "What Do Researchers Say SF Supervision Does that Is Useful?"

Due to the limited number of formal research studies, I can only draw two general conclusions and one tentative idea from the existing research literature on SF supervision. Hopefully avoiding the creation of a stereotype or straw-man argument, the first conclusion is that *SF supervision appears to differ significantly from what might be called traditional supervision.* Koob's (2002) major conclusion was that "Solution-Focused Supervision is a viable construct, different from Traditional Supervision" (p. 177), and comparisons to the research variables and outcomes of other supervision approaches support this assumption. More traditional approaches to supervision from psychodynamic or developmental perspectives emphasize relationship dynamics such as parallel process (Koltz, Odegard, Feit, Provost, and Smith 2012), client development (Hess 1980), therapist personal problem resolution (including personal therapy) (Schröder and Davis 2004; Wheeler, S. 2007), and supervisor–supervisee conflict (Korinek and Kimball 2003; Nelson and Friedlander 2001), and research on the more traditional supervision models often concentrates on these factors. In contrast, research on SF supervision addresses competence (Triantafillou 1997), goal setting and feedback (Hsu 2009; Triantafillou 1997), flattened hierarchy (Thomas and Shappee 2001), and skill development (Cunanan and McCollum 2006). The focus on competence and solutions is prominent, with developmental theory playing little or no role in guiding the process (De Jong and Cronkright 2011). Assumptions about change are tied to skill building; that is, one's future actions and understandings are altered by experience, and insight is not necessarily a prerequisite for change (De Jong and Cronkright 2011; Thomas and Shappee 2001). Finally, a commitment to openness, collaboration, and curiosity is more important in the SF supervision stance than theories of role conflict or therapist development (Rudes et al. 1997). These contrasts in research emphases and outcomes support the idea that SF supervision is qualitatively different from most other traditional forms.

Second, *therapist self-efficacy* may be significantly impacted by SF supervision. Self-efficacy is defined as "the belief in one's ability to perform specific tasks" (Lehrman-Waterman and Ladany 2001, p. 169) and is commonly seen as a significant outcome factor in general supervision research. There is substantial research support for the idea that supervision positively impacts therapist self-efficacy (Wheeler and Richards 2007), and SF supervision research falls in line with this conclusion. Studies by Koob (1999, 2002), Barrera (2003, who utilized Koob's data), Hsu (2007), Hsu and Sun (2008), and Hsu and Tsai (2008) all report increased self-efficacy connected to key factors found within SF supervision. Although the number of studies is very small, examination of self-efficacy and SF supervision merits further study because of these research results.

Finally, one tentative idea from the research is that *SF supervision may have positive influences on client outcomes.* Triantafillou's (1997) study has clear credibility due to the careful design and intentional focus on client outcomes, but it is the only quantitative study that hypothesized positive client impact and used a controlled design. Trenhaile (2005) and Hsu and Tsai (2008) both noted positive client outcome connected to SF supervision, but the evidence is anecdotal. Because the evidence connecting supervision and client outcome is limited whatever the supervision model, evidence that some research connects SF supervision to positive client influence should provide impetus for future investigations and instill hope for SF researchers, supervisors, and therapists.

6.3 Researching Supervisees' Perspectives

6.3.1 Key Non-SF Research ("What Do Supervisees Say Supervision Does that Is Useful?")

There is some disagreement in the literature regarding the attention given to supervisees' perspectives in supervision. Here are two seemingly opposing views:

> Little academic attention is given to the development of supervisees' skills and to full understanding of the purpose and process of the supervision relationship from the perspective of the supervisee. (Barretta-Herman 2001, p. 7)

and

> Despite the recognition of the importance of the supervisor's role, a majority of the research has focused on the supervisee's experience…. (Inman and Ladany 2008)

I doubt the 7-year period between these quotations was overwhelmed with new research on this topic, so it is fair to say that researchers' perspectives differ on the significance assigned to research on supervisees' viewpoints. Of the peer-reviewed publications I could locate specifically researching supervisee experiences, the majority were published since 2004; the previous 30 years only produced approximately 23 articles and book chapters. Since SF supervision is committed to collaboration, understanding supervisees' perspectives on the process, content, deficits, and failures of supervision is important to our work. What follows is a summary of relevant general research regarding supervisees' experiences and views, with further research specific to SF supervision reviewed in the next section of this chapter.

Gazzola and Theriault (2007). For this study, a small ($n = 10$) sample of therapists gave semi-structured interviews regarding their experiences of supervision. Themes resulting from the data analysis that are particularly relevant here are tied to supervisory feedback. These supervisees stated that clear feedback created better learning experiences. Feedback that was ambiguous or too theory laden was not as helpful and, at times, even hindered therapist progress. "The most common complaint was that supervisors simply failed to provide enough positive feedback. In the absence of positive feedback, supervisees felt overly criticized and did not feel appreciation for what they may have done well" (p. 197). In other words, in the absence of compliments, self-criticism is often the default direction therapists take regarding their clinical work. This is in line with the research of Heath and Tharp (1991) articulated below and a common research theme regarding supervisees' experiences with supervisor feedback: affirmation benefits supervisee development and performance as well as the overall supervision alliance.

Gershenson and Cohen (1978). One of the earliest publications on supervisee perspectives was Gershenson and Cohen's (1978) review of live family therapy supervision and their own experiences of this modality. Still students at the time of publication, this was a refreshing if risky endeavor to notate their personal supervision experiences and conclusions. These student therapists articulated their development as moving along a continuum from beginning stage fright, to midstage "reduced verticality" or hierarchy (p. 228), and finally to making connections between supervision and the cases themselves. Gershenson and Cohen stated that "behavior preceded understanding" (p. 228); that is, they were performing differently (and more effectively) prior to actually conceptualizing or internalizing the changes they experienced. This fits well with the common SF assumption that it is not necessary for understanding to precede change (Ray and Nardone 2009; Thomas and Nelson 2007).

Heath and Tharp (1991). Though cited quite frequently in the SF supervision literature, I was actually present when this workshop was presented in 1991. The themes of their research continue to resonate because this was among the earliest research of therapists' views on supervision in the field of family therapy. A major tenet of SF supervision, Heath and Tharp emphasized respect for supervisees' experiences, views, and needs throughout their workshop. Respect is a recurrent theme in the non-SF supervision literature as well (Bernard and Goodyear 2009; Gazzola and Theriault 2007; Torti 1997). This supervisor–supervisee presentation team outlined seven research themes that emerged from their investigations. I have collapsed these seven themes into four areas (thus the odd numbering sequence) directly related to the literature on supervisee experiences in supervision:

1. "We want relationships based on mutual respect. We want mentors."
2. "You don't have to be a guru."
6. "Listen to us. Make supervision a human experience."

As one of the four major supervisory roles identified by Morgan and Sprenkle (2007), mentoring is a factor that distinguishes therapy from supervision no matter what the approach or model. While hierarchy may have to be maintained (the administrator role) and expertise (being a "guru") may be valuable (the coach and teacher roles), engaging in the mentoring role of the supervisor allows supervision to be more level and certainly more human (Morgan and Sprenkle 2007).

3. "Supervise us or evaluate us. Not both."

It is interesting to note that these supervisees did not request the cessation of evaluation; they simply asked for clarity in supervisor roles. Role ambiguity is a common complaint across the research, as supervisees struggle to recognize and respond to supervisors who are vague in their requirements and directives (Nelson and Friedlander 2001; Olk and Friedlander 1992).

4. "Assume that we are competent. We are hard enough on ourselves already."
5. "Tell us what we're doing right. Affirm us. Empower us."

These two statements are especially pertinent because they agree with themes in other research, including the belief in therapist competence (Triantafillou 1997) and the necessity for compliments (Gazzola and Theriault 2007; Thomas and Shappee 2001). Assuming therapists have skills and abilities—whatever their level of experience—is a major theme in research of supervisees' experiences. However, "assume that we are competent" can be understood several ways. For some supervisors, this may come across as misplaced confidence, the statement of someone who overextends or exaggerates.[3] Others may read this as a plea for praise: "because we don't believe in ourselves, please believe and tell us we are capable." What the research has found is that believing in the inherent competence of therapists as caring humans who do their best given their level of training and experience fuels therapist confidence and directs supervisors' attention to compliment-worthy thinking and behavior.

   7. "We want different things and sometimes what we want changes."

Responsiveness to therapist needs is part of the feedback structure that SF supervisors must develop in each relationship (see Sect. 2.1 for discussion on systems). And fitting with research on supervisee perspectives from Gershenson and Cohen (1978) to the present, qualitative changes take place no matter what theory (or lack of theory) supervisors hold regarding therapist development. This is not a statement of indecisiveness; it is simply true. Whenever possible, supervision should fit the therapist rather than the Procrustean bed of supervision ideals or templates (this includes supervisors who eschew developmental theories).

Lehrman-Waterman and Ladany (2001). These authors found that supervisees require and value goal setting and feedback in successful supervision. Goal setting had to be specific, with measureable and attainable outcomes. Feedback in this research meant clear, regular responsiveness about the supervisees' performance, "balanced between positive (praise, compliments) and negative (criticism, corrective)" (p. 168). Meeting these supervisee needs resulted in stronger working alliances, improved therapist self-efficacy, and increased satisfaction with the supervision process. Lehrman-Waterman and Ladany's work is important because they surveyed a significant number of supervisees ($n=274$) who were not homogenous. In the process, they developed the Evaluation Process Within Supervision Inventory, or EPSI, which has found support as a valid and reliable instrument used in further research.

O'Donoghue (2012). A carefully constructed qualitative study of 16 social work practitioners in Australia, O'Donoghue found several themes worth noting here. Fear as an initial response in supervision was a significant theme (echoing Gershenson and Cohen 1978), but definite qualitative changes were reported as these therapists (1) experienced greater safety within the supervision and (2) gained experience over time. The shift through time that was most noteworthy involved a movement from case consultation to more professional development activities. The author called this change a shift in personal meanings from "being supervised" to "my supervision" (p. 227). An additional finding of importance was that these supervisees were more satisfied with their supervision when they were able to exercise some choice in supervisors.

---

[3]Fictional psychologist and supervisor Dr. Alan Gregory said this to his inexperienced supervisee who was practicing beyond her competence: "The degree of difficulty you're considering for this dive may be well beyond your demonstrated ability" (White 2010, p. 225). Hubris, loosely translated as excessive confidence or arrogance, is certainly a problem with some therapists (and supervisors) and cannot be ignored.

Roffman (2007). This dissertation surveyed a large ($n=201$) population of master's and doctoral therapists-in-training. Roffman found that:

> Both (a) focus on strengths and constructive focus on deficits were important predictors of satisfaction with supervision. Focus on strengths, however, was a stronger predictor than constructive focus on deficits, accounting for almost three times as much unique variance (34% compared to 12%) in satisfaction with supervision. This result suggests that supervisors should focus more on strengths than on deficits. (pp. 142–143)

Roffman's careful national sampling and use of standardized measures allows for generalization among supervision approaches. Both affirmation *and* correction are important to supervisees, but the more important of the two is specific support and validation of competence and clinical success.

Thomas, Coffey, Scott, and Shappee (2000b). This research team approached supervisors and supervisees with questions regarding competence, and several themes emerging from supervisees' experiences can inform SF supervision approaches. In addition to valuing supportive relationships, the theme of compassion developed. Supervisees said warmth and understanding undergirded positive supervision, which is in line with Bordin's (1983) idea of the importance emotional bonds play in successful supervision. A "no-cloning" attitude emerged, which was tied to the importance of trusting supervisees' abilities and intentions. As other research has found, belief in supervisee competence is key to building therapist confidence and positive expectations. Finally, supervisees stated that supervisors' willingness to model skills played a vital role in successful supervision, a theme that recurs throughout SF and non-SF supervision research.

Torti (1997). Although Torti's research investigated supervisees' experiences of narrative supervision, two of his five themes are especially relevant to this discussion. Supervisees identified equality of participation and the supervisors' nonexpert stance as especially significant to their learning and growth. Encouraging participation of all persons with varied backgrounds on an equal basis was defined as "equality," and when the supervisee informants identified supervision being conducted with a minimum of hierarchy and expert positioning, it was classified as "nonexpert stance." However, the nonexpert stance had its limitations as well. Supervisees made it clear that when more directive supervision was requested, indirect methods were not helpful. If a supervisee asked for specific guidance and the supervisor said, "Well, what do you think you should do?" (or its equivalent), it was experienced not only as negative but also as irritating.

Worthen and McNeill (1996). This phenomenological study only examined "good" supervision events, sampling doctoral students across several settings. What these researchers found was that both the supervisory relationship and attention to skill development were involved in "good" supervision experiences. Relationships were characterized by "warmth, acceptance, respect, understanding, and trust" (p. 26). In addition, these relationships included appropriate supervisor self-disclosure, permitted mistakes, and encouraged experimentation. Skill development was adjusted to the supervisee's level, and there were some outcomes for more advanced therapists/supervisees that are of particular interest to this discussion. Advanced practitioners found the supervisory relationship empathic and validating. The adjustment to their developmental level allowed for the "reexamination of therapeutic and professional assumptions" and an "acquisition of metaperspective" that permitted clearer therapeutic patterns to emerge (p. 28). Of particular interest in this work is the supervisors' adjustment to the supervisees' level of expertise. Many studies only survey or interview novice student therapists with limited clinical experience. This research tapped into the advanced therapists' experiences and examined the value of supervision to "increase therapeutic perception" and "expanded (one's) ability to conceptualize and intervene" appropriately (p. 28).

6.3.2 SF-Related Research ("What Do Supervisees Say SF Supervision Does that Is Useful?")

Corcoran (2001). Corcoran looked at the role reflectivity plays in therapist development for therapists experiencing two supervision approaches, reflecting team (Andersen 1987) and SF. She conducted ethnographic interviews with nine doctoral students and found "for this diverse group of students, the combination of a reflecting team format and a solution-focused supervision model was effective in teaching students to engage in reflective process" (Corcoran 2001, p. iv). This outcome relates to the reality of supervision: most supervisors work from multiple viewpoints and are integrative in their approaches, so a SF supervision approach could be combined with other models with positive results.

Cunanan and McCollum (2006). Cunanan's (2003) thesis research resulted in this very informative article highlighting the isomorphic connections that exist between SFBT and SF supervision. Themes from the 15 informants' interviews included the significance of the nonexpert supervisor role, the focus on competence and therapist strengths, and modeling/demonstrating the SF therapy approach. These findings are also important because they fit with non-SF supervision factors as well. Most research examining effective supervision has found important links between successful supervision experiences and reduced hierarchy ("nonexpert"), supporting therapist strengths and competence and supervisor modeling. One outcome of note was that SF supervision of therapists learning SFBT did not necessarily result in a "purist" mentality or practice. "While a pure environment seemed to help participants learn SFBT, it doesn't appear that they necessarily implement the model in pure form once they have learned it" (p. 63). One idea that evolves from this conclusion is that SF supervision can support broader therapist development, not just SF skill building.

De Jong and Cronkright (2011). In this article, the authors summarize the development of a skill-building course with university social work students. By encouraging student therapist feedback, the course itself was changed to produce better results for those learning SFBT. De Jong and Cronkright classified several themes that can inform SF supervision thought and practice, two of which are particularly relevant here. First, they identified a theme they called "knowing is doing" (p. 29). This idea was based on the connection between course content and laboratory practice. Performing in the presence of a supervisor through role play was vital to learning a technique as well as personalizing it, and constructive feedback added value for the learner. Second, informants found observation of others very useful. Being able to witness peers practicing a skill in a safe environment assisted the observers' learning of the concept. This research calls attention to a facet of supervision that is difficult to replicate in therapy: observation of others. While many SF practitioners utilize role play with clients, observation of others successfully practicing a skill is usually dismissed as irrelevant since it is the client's own exceptions and successes that are repeated in SFBT, not another's. Observation as a supervisory technique sets it apart from the practice of therapy, and its importance for supervision cannot be underestimated.

Thomas and Shappee (2001). Two key questions were asked of more than 20 therapists who had experienced SF supervision. First, *what about the style, behavior and attitude of your SF supervisor(s) has proved to be helpful to you over time?* Four major themes emerged: the importance of the person of the supervisor, collegiality, focus on therapist strengths, and focus on solutions. The second question is, *do aspects of this SF supervision experience continue to influence the way in which you work with clients today? If so, how?* Again, four themes were identified: collaboration and sensitivity (including seeing possibilities), ongoing evaluation, a focus on goals, and a focus on client competence. Other valuable themes include continued SF skill development and the ability to self-supervise. All of these themes are supportive of a SF approach to supervision, but several stand out. First, collaboration in supervision continued for these therapists in their clinical work. Also, ongoing evaluation as a part of an overarching theme of self-supervision persisted for these therapists after supervision ended. Finally, it is worth noting the overlapping theme of competence—therapists who received support and strengths/solutions focus report carrying it over into their clinical work, focusing on client capabilities and believing in client expertise. These are hallmarks of the SF supervision approach, and this research endorses these tenets and practices.

Wheeler and Greaves (2005). This article was coauthored by a supervisor (Wheeler) and therapist (Greaves) who had worked together extensively. They trace early influences and experiences through to the termination of their supervisory relationship, calling attention to therapist experiences that informed their work and reflectively inform others' SF supervision. Wheeler carefully attended to the unique learning styles of Greaves (and all of his supervisees). They noted the sensitivity Wheeler showed to Greaves' insecurities in the beginning of the relationship, and the value of reflection and reflective dialogue was emphasized. Finally, Greaves' assumed competence was mentioned throughout the article. It is important to note the communication processes inherent in these experiences. Articulating his assumptions about Greaves' competence as a therapist led to an easing of anxiety and a clear experience of Wheeler's warmth, and their reflective discussions validated the underlying assumption of Greaves' competence. Sensitivity was experienced not only through openness but also through the adjustments Wheeler made to fit with Greaves' learning modes and personal goals.

Overall, this phenomenological piece stands out as exemplary supervision from both supervisee and supervisor perspectives.

6.4 Research-Related Guidance for SF Supervision

The guiding question for this chapter has been this: *what do therapists and supervisors do together that is useful?* Some may feel that each supervision relationship is unique, so general research is of little value. Though it is true that general knowledge does not predict a specific outcome, ignoring research as a source of information for supervision would be, in my view, shortsighted. Few hard conclusions can be drawn from the research literature, but here are a baker's dozen ideas and assumptions that give direction to the SF supervisor:

1. *Nurture a supervisory alliance.* Creating an alliance has to be a primary goal. This requires support and empathy, with an emphasis on mentoring over teacher, coach, or administrator roles. Commitment to decreasing hierarchy and reducing power differences can contribute to this alliance, and taking a nonexpert stance whenever possible builds collaboration toward this goal.
2. *Establish safety to promote open communication and appropriate disclosure.* Remember that most supervisees are anxious at the beginning of a supervisory relationship and may withhold information until they experience the environment as safe.
3. *Assume therapist competence AND evaluate.* Everyone has limitations, but showing confidence in the therapists' abilities and intentions, coupled with active goal setting and evaluation of progress, connects supposition to accomplishment.
4. *Provide clear feedback.* Be specific, basing your feedback on performance whenever possible. Theory has its place, but ambiguity often results when theory takes precedence over responses founded on direct observation.
5. *Set well-defined goals, provide clear feedback (positive and negative), and evaluate progress.* Goals and honest feedback are undoubtedly related to positive alliance and therapist improvement.
6. *Focus on strengths and success, but do not neglect honest assessment*, as both are important to most supervisees. Supervisees value praise as well as assistance with their struggles, deficits, and mistakes. The ratio of positive to critical comments should lean toward the positive, but more effective supervisors include compliments and critique.
7. *Adjust supervision to fit the supervisee.* Whether or not one holds to a developmental view of change, supervision must adjust to meet the differing needs of all supervisees *and* the differing needs of each supervisee over time.
8. *Use a variety of techniques in supervision.* In addition to discussion, include teaching, assigned readings, modeling, role play, video-recording review, and case examples. Discuss these techniques with the supervisee to fit with his or her learning styles and goals.

9. *Request and respond to therapist feedback.* Collaboration means creating something together that works for all involved. Safety is supported when supervisee requests for adjustment are honored.
10. *Communicate respect.* Hold therapists and clients in high regard, maintaining a supportive position for valuing all persons involved in the overlapping systems.
11. *Keep in mind that successful supervision does not depend on matching clinical and supervision approaches.* Rigidity exhausts a relationship, so insisting therapists conform to the supervisor's therapeutic model or approach will be less positive than a flexible response to the therapists' personal goals for learning.
12. *Intentionally and persistently include client voices in supervision.* There is great variety in how this can be accomplished, but connecting supervision with clinical impact and outcome should be a primary focus of SF supervision. If supervision isn't useful for the therapist *and* clients, supervisors should seek additional forms of feedback.
13. *Remember, doing often precedes understanding.* A quotation from the late Heinz von Foerster (1984, p. 308) comes to mind: "If you desire to see, learn how to act." Combining contextual sensitivity so adjustments are made for each supervisee with these ideas and assumptions makes for a research-informed *and* useful approach to SF supervision.

Chapter 7
Applications

7.1 Introduction

> *Standing on the shoulders of giants.*
>
> ~ quote written on the edge of the British two-pound coin,
> attributed to Sir Isaac Newton

When contemplating the possibility of writing this book, I could not imagine it without a section written by professionals from around the world who supervise from a SF perspective. I took my inspiration from De Jong and Berg's (2012) Applications chapter that has a format similar to this one, and I began contacting the best people I knew to solicit his/her participation. Every contributor to this chapter shared their knowledge and experience out of profound respect for Insoo Kim Berg, Steve de Shazer, and other founders of the SF approach. If I approached someone to write for this book, I was certain that person would freely credit those who blazed trails before him/her and write out of a sense of responsibility to our common SF heritage and community.

I have been fortunate to share experiences with these colleagues in many contexts, including universities, conferences, previous writing projects, and association committees. It has also been my honor to learn with three of them in supervision as we spent hours and hours together honing our skills, developing our approaches to therapy and supervision, and reflecting on the processes. Three others are or have been university colleagues of mine, so our interactions around supervision have been influenced by educational contexts that limit and inspire us. I have also had the privilege of presenting supervision workshops with two of these professionals, and I have been fortunate to attend international presentations given by several. Some have written on this topic in the past, but others composed their thoughts on SF supervision for the first time when they contributed to this volume.

Scattered around the world, these valued colleagues have experimented with SF supervision ideas and practices for years, so their experiences with this approach are unique, intimate, and invaluable. Contributors to this SF supervision book were educated and trained in other supervision approaches, but their dissatisfaction with the concepts, research, methods, and/or ethics of other models led them to create something different. They articulate some of their innovative thought and practices here, and I am grateful for their work because it adds depth and practicality to the topic. (A brief biographical sketch and contact information can be found in the introductory material in this volume.)

7.2 Integrating Spirit: Solution-Focused Supervision for Pastoral Counseling

Duane R. Bidwell

For many years, two attributes set pastoral counselors apart from other mental health practitioners: they were ordained ministers, and they were formally accountable to a (typically Christian) religious community. This is no longer the case. The practice of pastoral counseling has broadened to include a range of religious traditions, spiritualities, and mental health practitioners. Some pastoral counselors are clergy, but most clinicians at pastoral counseling centers today are social workers, counselors, marriage and family therapists, and psychologists—clinically trained and licensed, but not ordained or theologically educated. Many, in fact, do not participate in a formal faith tradition or spiritual community. Yet all engage in critically informed dialogue among counseling theories, counseling practices, and various spiritual, religious, and theological conversation partners (Townsend 2009).

This diversity signals a need for a more accurate (and less parochial) word than "pastoral" to describe the integration of spirituality, religion, and psychotherapy that has evolved from the historical practice of clinically trained ministers in the twentieth century. Thus, in my context, we use the phrase "spiritually integrative counseling" to signal the breadth and depth of the psychotherapeutic, spiritual, and theological training we provide to therapists from a variety of racial, ethnic, professional, and religious backgrounds.

Supervision for spiritually integrative counseling, as I have come to understand it, focuses as much on identity formation as on the development of clinical and professional skills. A solution-focused approach to this process emphasizes the resources and agency of the therapist in moving toward a preferred professional identity that integrates the clinician's theological and spiritual commitments in a responsible and holistic way. The solution-focused practices of "generating options" and "doing something different" can be particularly useful in this process.

I find that spiritually integrative counseling invites me as a supervisor to embody and model spiritual presence (in both knowing and being); attend to the formation of pastoral, spiritual, and professional identities; enhance abilities to address spiritual and theological issues in therapy; and oversee the use of psychotherapeutic theory and practice in the service of spiritual guidance (see Townsend 2009). At the same time, I must protect counselees from harm while seeking to sharpen therapists' clinical skills. And through it all, I ask: "What conditions would allow this therapist to be 'known-through' by Mystery, to move beyond 'spirituality as diversity' to participation in Being Itself?" (see Bidwell 2007). Approaching these invitations from a solution-focused stance adds yet another layer of complexity to the supervisory task. Finally, the ultimate goal of supervision is, for me, the formation of clinicians who are capable of self-supervision—especially the sort of self-reflexivity that alerts them to when they need to consult with colleagues.

This contribution offers a snapshot of how I adopt a solution-focused stance in the supervision of spiritually integrative counseling. It's an image from a certain angle in a certain slant of light, of course; it comes from a particular context, at a particular point in my own clinical development, and it cannot capture the complexity of a supervisory moment. It certainly isn't "the way" to do solution-focused supervision. Rather, my hope is that it can be generative for your own supervisory practices and understanding. I simply want to describe my five "best" and favorite practices and then illustrate my approach through a specific case.

7.2.1 My Supervisory Context

I provide group and individual supervision to therapists enrolled in a 2-year master's internship or doctoral residency at The Clinebell Institute for Pastoral Counseling and Psychotherapy in Claremont, California. The residency and internship are a part of the coursework for three degree programs: the M.A. and Ph.D. at Claremont Lincoln University (an interreligious graduate university with Jewish, Muslim, Christian, Jain, Buddhist, and other religious partners) and the Doctor of Ministry at Claremont School of Theology (a Christian seminary affiliated with the United Methodist Church that is a part of the Claremont Lincoln consortium). On a regular basis, I serve as training director for the clinical seminar that these therapists are required to take, and because clinical and academic work are integrated in our program, I often teach therapists as students in nonclinical classes as well. Two other faculty members share teaching and supervisory responsibilities in these programs; each of us also maintains a small clinical practice at The Clinebell Institute.

The majority of therapists I supervise are Ph.D. students in their second and third years of course work; a majority is also Korean or Korean-American women, typically from conserving Christian traditions that are hierarchical in nature. Although these therapists tend to be more progressive than the churches with which they are affiliated, they often have a high view of biblical authority, and they have grown up in a neo-Confucian culture that shapes gender roles, relationships to authority, understandings of polite and virtuous behavior, and values and expectations about learning and academic performance. Many are married to pastors and therefore have a regimented role in the life of their faith communities. Often, their denominations will not ordain women. Other therapists I have supervised include Anglo and African women and Korean and Latino men. At any given time, as many as a third of our trainees have been gay and lesbian; many are single, and many are not ordained.

The clinicians I work with in supervision learn a variety of therapeutic approaches: relational–cultural, narrative, cognitive–behavioral, multicultural, and solution-focused therapies. They primarily practice liberation, process, feminist, and postcolonial approaches to practical theological reflection. In cooperation with professional staff, they provide individual, couples, family, and group therapy to a variety of counselees from the community, especially those who cannot afford mental health services without a sliding fee scale. The therapists I supervise also work with counselees from three special populations: residents of a 6-month transitional program for women newly released from prison, including those who have been serving life sentences (about 17% of the total caseload in 2011); residents of a short-term homeless shelter for women, children, and families (about 14% of the total caseload in 2011); and at-risk adolescents (and their families) being mentored through a community agency (about 3% of the total caseload in 2011). Despite the acuity of some counselees, The Clinebell Institute does not offer crisis intervention, and there is no psychiatrist or social worker on staff; clinicians partner with appropriate community resources to address the extra-therapeutic needs of counselees.

7.2.2 "Greatest Hits": My Favorite (or Habitual) Supervisory Practices

Five practices adapted from solution-focused therapy are my "go to" interventions in the supervision of spiritually integrated counseling. They include focusing on the future, generating options, doing something different, repeating what works, and asking, "What else?" These practices are not specifically "spiritual" in nature, but facilitate the integration of spiritual and theological concerns, content, and formation into the supervisory process (as demonstrated in the case study below).

Focusing on the Future: Solution-focused therapy emphasizes the present and future; this is one reason it communicates a sense of hope and possibility to counselees and therapists alike (Bidwell 2000). I focus on the future in supervision by asking questions like, "Now that you see how this approach (or idea or assumption or intervention) worked in this case, how do you think it will shape your practice in the future?" or "Given what you've learned from this counselee, how do you want to be different in the future?" In my experience, this helps therapists generalize learning from a specific case to other situations; it also contributes to their personal, professional, and pastoral formation by intentionally developing their preferred identity of themselves as clinicians.

Generating Options: New therapists often come to supervision asking, "What should I do?" Likewise, seasoned therapists seek suggestions for intervention. Before I share my ideas in response to these requests, I almost always ask, "What options do you see?" After the therapist has answered, I offer two or three additional options that I can identify. Finally, I ask therapists which options seem like the best choices to them and why. Then we choose a strategy collaboratively. This practice helps decenter the supervisor (and therapist) as "expert"; it also emphasizes the solution-focused assumption that there are multiple pathways toward action when a therapist feels stuck (rather than one "right" way to do therapy). Developing an ability to generate multiple therapeutic options and spiritual, theological, and religious perspectives also seems important for clinicians who will supervise themselves in the future.

Doing Something Different: The adage "if it doesn't work, do something different" has been a longtime premise of solution-focused therapy. It's one of the first avenues I explore when a therapist feels stuck with a particular counselee or when I notice an unhelpful pattern in interventions or communication. It's also one of my first actions if I am feeling stuck in supervision. For example, if I ask two or three times about a therapist's use of authority, and she continues to tell me that what I see is not congruent with her stated values, but I do not see her behavior change, I am unlikely to ask about it again. Instead, I will do something different. I might adopt her style of authority in a supervisory session, for example, or suggest a role play that calls for the use of authority. This keeps me from being frustrated and provides the therapist an opportunity to experience herself differently, rather than just talking about what she does (which is the only intervention I have tried up to that point).

Repeating What Works: When therapists complain of being stuck or not knowing what to do with a counselee, I often remember the solution-focused adage, "if it works, do it again." It reminds me to (a) ask about practices that have been effective with that counselee in the past and (b) encourage the therapist to try those practices again. Likewise, I repeat supervisory approaches that succeed with particular therapists. For example, if a therapist tells me it was really helpful to see me model a re-goaling conversation, I am likely to model other techniques in the future. Likewise, I begin new supervisory relationships by asking what was helpful about prior supervisors; then, I try to include those helpful behaviors in my repertoire with that therapist. This helps build the therapeutic alliance and makes for more effective supervision, faster.

Asking, "What else?": I learned this strategy from Eve Lipchik (2002), who asks, "What else?" when a counselee finishes answering a solution-focused question. I use the question liberally in supervision; I find that it evokes detail, creativity, and germane information often missing from therapists' first responses to my supervisory questions. Asking "What else?" is especially helpful when reflecting on the spiritual, religious, and theological dynamics of a therapy session; it can invite a therapist to be still and attend contemplatively to images and ideas that arise from beyond the intellect that could be useful to understanding the counselee or making meaning of the situation.

7.2.3 What Therapists Say Is Helpful

It is easy for me to identify how solution-focused therapy shapes what I do in supervision. But what I do—the way I intervene—isn't always "the difference that makes a difference" to therapists who engage in supervision with me. So often, supervisors can be unaware of what therapists find helpful about supervisory conversations. Thus, I asked five clinicians who have been in supervision with me during the past 2 years to identify (a) what they found useful about our supervision together and (b) where they saw solution-focused thinking at work in my approach. Here are four practices that they identified in response:

Enhancing Agency: Some therapists say supervision enhances their sense of agency by allowing them to make choices about their work and by focusing on their competencies. My take: An enhanced sense of agency is one benefit of asking therapists to identify and repeat practices that have been successful in the past and of requiring therapists to generate their own options before the supervisor shares ideas. This outcome reflects the solution-focused emphasis on honoring and strengthening the counselee's agency.

Emphasizing Goals: At the beginning of each semester, I ask therapists in supervision with me to write two or three concrete learning goals. I check their sense of progress toward these goals throughout the semester; I also point out when something we do in supervision relates directly to their learning goals. Some therapists find this quite helpful to their development as clinicians; they say it keeps them focused and accountable. This practice is congruent with solution-focused therapy's emphasis on specific, time-limited, effective, and measurable goals as the starting point of an effective therapeutic process.

Giving Compliments: I try to make at least one authentic compliment during every supervisory session. Sometimes, the compliment is general—such as communicating the potential I see in a particular therapist; sometimes, it is specific—such as acknowledging a skilled intervention or growth in a particular skill. Some clinicians experience compliments as empowering; some even find them surprising. Compliments are especially valued, perhaps, by therapists who grew up in educational systems that used shame and criticism as primary pedagogical methods.

Modeling Authority: Therapists call my supervisory style egalitarian, collegial, vulnerable, playful, relational, and transparent—which are all values I consciously strive toward. Some say those values provide a model of receptive power and an alternative form of authority, especially an alternative form of pastoral authority. Female therapists who grew up in an overtly patriarchal culture, and those from religious traditions that emphasize rigid male authority and leadership, say it is helpful to experience this type of "nonnormative" power and authority, especially from a man. Modeling power and authority is not something I do explicitly in my supervisory relationships, but I am beginning to understand that my style provides a new experience of authority for some clinicians; therefore, it is an important dimension of the supervisory relationship. This aspect of the relationship reflects my chosen values about power and authority in psychotherapy, and it is strongly influenced by postmodern counseling theories, including solution-focused and narrative approaches.

7.2.4 *"Not Doing Enough": An Example of My Supervisory Approach*

Haneul,[1] a Korean woman in her mid-thirties, is halfway through the first year of her residency in spiritually integrative counseling. A decade ago, in Korea, she completed a master's degree and was ordained as a Christian pastor before coming to the United States for doctoral study. She converted to Christianity as an adolescent in Korea, where she belonged to an evangelical Korean church, while the rest of her family remained Buddhist. Her father was a fisherman, and as a child, Haneul experienced poverty and what she now identifies as mental illness and alcohol addiction in her extended family. Advocacy and action for social justice are central to her pastoral identity.

During several months of her doctoral training, Haneul counseled a woman living at the shelter for the homeless. After leaving the shelter, the woman stopped taking antidepressants, failed to attend or appropriately cancel counseling appointments, and began having hallucinations and suicidal thoughts. Every few weeks, she calls Haneul during a hallucination or a 72-hour psychiatric hold; the calls are for support and to make a counseling appointment, which she invariably does not attend because of transportation difficulties or some other circumstance. One of these phone calls occurred the morning of a regularly scheduled supervisory appointment, and Haneul told me during the meeting about her frustration with the counselee.

DUANE: It does sound frustrating. But from what you've said, she's safe, and she's not thinking about harming herself....

HANEUL: No. I just wish I could do more. All I can do is listen when she calls! (*I immediately wonder whose goal is being frustrated—the counselee's or Haneul's—and decide to clarify for myself.*)

DUANE: Does she ask you to do more?

HANEUL: No. (*Silence.*)

DUANE: Does she find your conversations helpful?

HANEUL: I think so. She always thanks me and tells me that she loves me. She says it gives her comfort to know she can always call me, and I will call her back. (*Silence.*)

DUANE: Well . . . if she doesn't ask for more, and she finds your conversations helpful, and she doesn't keep her appointments, do you think it's possible that she's getting what she needs from you right now? (*I am thinking, "If it works, do more of it!"*)

HANEUL: But I am not a good counselor; I am not doing enough. (*Haneul makes an interpretive statement about her identity as a spiritually integrative*

---

[1] The therapist's name and identifying details have been changed to protect her identity. She gave permission to use her story for this contribution; she also reviewed and commented on the case study prior to publication.

	counselor: She is not sufficient; she is not "good" at what she is doing. I make a mental note of this; it might be a source of her distress.) I should do more! I should help her! It is not enough just to talk to her on the phone two or three times a month. That doesn't give her a place to live or food to eat or medications!
DUANE:	You're right; it doesn't. (*Pause.*) You can't give her those things.
HANEUL:	No. (*Silence. She shakes her head slowly.*) I feel helpless.
DUANE:	That really bothers you. (*Haneul nods her head.*)

At this point, I am confident that Haneul's expectation that she "ought to do more" has not been communicated to her by the training program or the therapeutic model. I am curious, then, about the source of this idea. There might be a lack of congruence between Haneul's embedded identity as a spiritually integrative counselor and the realities of the case. (It seems to me that the counselee needs a case manager rather than a mental health counselor.) But I am leery of becoming mired in "problem talk" in supervision. I decide to shift the conversation.

DUANE:	I wonder . . . what could be going on here theologically? (*I invite Haneul to reflect on the situation from a different perspective; this indicates my choice to "do something different" rather than continue talking about the problem—Haneul's distress and frustration. Haneul looks away, thinking intently.*)
HANEUL:	Scripture says, "I was hungry and you fed me, I was naked and you clothed me, I was in prison and you visited me." That is the foundation of my ministry. Good pastors—good Christians—do those things. I am not doing those things for [the counselee].

Like many evangelical Christians, Haneul holds a high view of scripture; Jesus, as portrayed in the Bible, is her primary reference for how Christians are to act in the world. Responding to my question, she references a parable in Matthew 25, a gospel passage in the Christian New Testament that can be interpreted as an instruction to feed, clothe, and visit the needy. In the passage, Jesus says to his followers, "Truly I tell you, just as you did not do it to one of the least of these, you did not do it to me." Those who fail to do these things, he says, will "go away into eternal punishment" (Matthew 25: 45–47, New Revised Standard Version). Haneul feels she is not doing enough for the counselee because she is not living into the vision of Christian discipleship described in this passage—a passage that she makes central to her identity and practice as a minister. She now describes herself as feeling guilty for not doing more.

DUANE:	Ahh . . . your embedded theology tells you that you should do more for [the counselee], but she doesn't want more from you. And your therapeutic model tells you that you should honor what the counselee wants. But if you do what the counselee wants, you are not being a good minister, a good Christian?
HANEUL:	Yes! Exactly. I am not being faithful.
DUANE:	You feel helpless and unfaithful.
HANEUL:	Yes. And I don't like it.

DUANE:	I wonder ... how helpful is your embedded theology in this situation? (*I move toward "doing something different," because Haneul's "viewing" of the situation creates distress and prevents her from being as effective as she could be.*)
HANEUL:	Not very helpful. (*She makes a sad face, then laughs.*)
DUANE:	Can you think of other theological perspectives that might be useful? Something in the tradition that might affirm what [the counselee] finds helpful—and see what you are providing as good, faithful ministry?
HANEUL:	Like what?
DUANE:	Well, I have some ideas. But why don't you try to come up with some first? Just two or three. Then I'll share mine. (*Here I use "generating options" as a way to help Haneul identify her own pathways toward action.*)

We begin by reflecting on what the counselee finds helpful: access to the counselor through telephone calls and text messages, which we interpret as the consistent presence of a trusted person who knows her story. From this premise, after several "What else?" questions from me, Haneul identifies two possible alternative theological frameworks: God's presence with the counselee as Emmanuel (literally, "God-with-us"), mediated through Haneul's presence as therapist, and Martin Buber's concept of the I–Thou relationship, in which the divine is experienced in the presence of the Other. I suggest one other possibility: "standing in solidarity with" those oppressed by systemic forces as a contemporary approach to the classical pastoral care function of "sustaining" those whose suffering cannot be alleviated. We explore these ideas a little as they relate to Haneul's work with the counselee. We also identify a community organization that can provide shelter and medication to the counselee during the upcoming weekend, followed by psychiatric assessment in the coming week. Then we continue our conversation.

DUANE:	So what seems possible now, after identifying those other options, that didn't seem possible at the beginning of our time?
HANEUL:	I need to keep reflecting. It's hard to accept that there's nothing I can do, myself, to improve her situation. But it is helpful to remember that presence is important—that it can be sufficient, that ministry is not just solving problems, but being present with people wherever they are. I really like the idea of standing in solidarity with [the counselee], of seeing her as more than someone with mental illness, more than a suicidal person, more than a homeless woman, no matter what she experiences from other people.
DUANE:	How do you think that will affect your practice as a pastoral counselor in the future? (*Here I "focus on the future" as a way of solidifying learning and inviting Haneul to be intentional about shaping her personal, professional, and pastoral identities.*)
HANEUL:	I don't know. Maybe I will not feel so helpless when there is nothing I can do materially for a client? Because being present, listening, has value, even when I forget that. God works through me, even when I can't do anything.

Many weeks later, in a phone call, the counselee told Haneul that one reason she continues to call is that Haneul always listens—she doesn't try to *do* anything or make anything better, like other professionals the counselee meets, but just *hears* the counselee when she needs to know that someone cares about her as more than a problem to be solved. Haneul's ability to receive and celebrate this important feedback authentically—and to generalize it to other appropriate therapeutic situations—depended in part, I think, on the alternative theological understandings she first identified in supervision and then worked to appropriate and integrate into her own understandings of spiritually integrated counseling in the following weeks.

7.2.5 Contextual Challenges for Solution-Focused Supervision

I have written elsewhere (Bidwell 2000) about some limitations of solution-focused theory for the practice of spiritually integrated counseling. Two limitations create particular challenges in my supervisory context. First, SFT lacks a coherent theory of humanity. Second, SFT pays insufficient attention to larger systemic and contextual issues. These areas of concern have a profound influence on counselees and therapists in my context, but remain under-theorized by solution-focused thinkers. My task as supervisor is to straddle these theoretical gaps in ways that are congruent with a solution-focused approach.

The first challenge, SFT's lack of a coherent theory of humanity, is particularly important. In the absence of a cogent, solution-focused understanding of the person, spiritually integrative therapists often rely on personality theories to understand their interactions with counselees. The literature of pastoral counseling, the forebear of spiritually integrated counseling, relies primarily on psychodynamic understandings of the person; the therapists with whom I engage in supervision are often especially influenced by object relations theory. These theories of humanity are often deficit based and problem oriented. Each religious and theological tradition also has a theory of the human person (often called "theological anthropology" in the Christian traditions), which shapes a therapist's understanding of human development, behavior, motivation, and health in relation to ultimate reality. Sometimes, these religiously normative understandings of the person—especially when they are pre-reflective or nondeliberative—are not a good fit with solution-focused assumptions.

In the midst of competing claims about the nature of human beings, and thus of what is necessary to help troubled people, I find it helpful to draw from narrative theory, narrative theology, and narrative psychotherapy to encourage therapists to hold lightly their "knowledge" of human beings. Deconstructive questioning, identification of subjugated stories, discourse analysis, and other techniques, applied to clinician stories about their counselees or about human beings more broadly, can help "open space" for other possible understandings of the person in front of them. It also creates an opportunity for me to encourage therapists to privilege the counselee's own understandings of what is happening, why, what will help, and so forth. I understand this as focusing on the "viewing" dimension of counselee experience, which SFT often ignores in favor of the "doing" dimension. These supervisory practices help me stay solution-focused in spirit, if not in technique.

The second challenge, SFT's insufficient attention to systemic and contextual issues, becomes important because of the number of counselees in my context who face barriers to solutions because of rigid and often-invisible issues that they cannot influence. What can a woman newly released from prison do, for example, when she has earned the appropriate degree and credential but encounters legal employment discrimination against a person convicted of a felony? One task of spiritually integrative counselors is to help people identify and resist the deforming effects of such situations—to refuse to believe dominant accounts of who they are and to hold larger systems accountable for the violence perpetrated against them. As a supervisor, then, my task is to help therapists find ways to practice "appropriate knowing" (see Gorsuch 2001) so that they can help counselees see and understand the political, socioeconomic, market, religious, and other forces that create larger contexts and systems that oppress them. This often requires me to encourage therapists to broaden the lenses with which they examine a counselee's situation—to "do something different" than focus simply on the counselee's immediate experience and to "generate options" for making sense of why the counselee is suffering.

7.2.6 Conclusion

The creative work of supervising the integration of spirituality and psychotherapy can be enhanced by solution-focused ideas and practices. A solution-focused approach to supervising spiritually integrative counseling allows supervisors and clinicians to embody spiritual presence, attend to multiple facets of identity formation, enhance abilities to address spiritual and theological issues in therapy, and become facile at using psychotherapeutic theory and practice in the service of spiritual guidance. The practices of "doing something different," "doing more of what works," generating options, asking "What else?" and focusing on the future are particularly helpful to these processes.

7.3 On Being Solution-Focused in Adversarial Places: Supervising Parenting Evaluations for Family Court[2]

Jeff Chang

Conducting parenting evaluations for family courts is a professional activity from which most mental health practitioners run and hide. Most therapists do not wish to be subjected to adversarial legal processes, particularly cross-examination.

---

[2] Thanks to Tracy Mitchell, M.Ed., R. Psych., and David Nylund, Ph.D., LCSW, for their support in the preparation of this contribution. Thanks to all the family intervention practitioners who have helped me develop the ideas presented in this contribution, in particular the supervisee who agreed to my using part of her supervision. Concerns over client confidentiality meant that the supervisee could not be named, but she knows who she is.

Solution-focused (SF) therapists are likely to eschew the mantle of "expert witness," which seems contradictory to a not-knowing position (Anderson and Gehart 2006) or leading from one step behind (Cantwell and Holmes 1994). To top it all off, parenting evaluations draw a disproportionate number of regulatory complaints, as the clients in these matters may use a complaint as a litigation strategy to disqualify the expert opinion or to express their sense of being aggrieved.

This contribution describes how I have operationalized SF ideas when supervising novice parenting evaluators.[3] First, I describe theoretical ideas within and outside of solution-focused brief therapy (SFBT) that inform my thinking about parenting evaluation and describe the personal and practice context in which I started to apply SF ideas to this area of practice. Next, I discuss the competencies required. I then describe some SF-informed supervision practices I use with novice parenting evaluators. Finally, I comment on the limitations of the SF approach to supervision in this context.

7.3.1 Interpretation, Social Construction, and Context

Experts in psychological evaluation assert that they practice an objective and scientifically based activity (Erford 2012; Harwood, Beutler, and Groth-Marnat 2011). Examined on its own terms, it is. However, examined from a distance, psychological evaluation is embedded in culture, discourse, and social context. It is an interpretive process, in the sense that Gadamer (1989) conveys. Multiple interpretations of the same "data" from different perspectives are possible. For Gadamer (1989), "knowledge" (in this instance, "expert opinion" about parenting capacity) is not an objective reality awaiting discovery but the product of an intersubjective interpretive process between an interpreting subject (the evaluator) and "another" (the client).

My early career training in SF and narrative therapies taught me to listen for what clients do to build solutions. I found a coherent home for my hybrid therapeutic approach (Chang 1998) in social constructionist thinking (Shotter 1993), in which language does not simply represent an internal reality, but constitutes or "makes up" our reality. Psychological evaluation is a socially constructed and socially constructing process that constitutes a reality in a specific context.

Working in children's mental health agencies in Calgary, Alberta, Canada, I developed strong relationships with child protection workers. Once I entered private

---

[3] It is important to note the distinction between parenting capacity assessments, conducted at the request of child protection authorities, and child custody evaluations, undertaken to decide postdivorce parenting arrangements. In the former, the parents' capacity to care for children is questioned. In the latter, by and large, the competence of individual parents is not at issue (Pearce and Pezzot-Pearce 2004). For the purposes of this contribution, I refer to them collectively as "parenting evaluations."

practice, they asked me to provide them with parenting evaluations. My solution orientation helped me to engage parents, who were usually court directed and suspicious of my role as an evaluator. Asking them what they were doing well, I sought to understand their lived experience, motivations, and desires as parents. SFBT taught me to listen carefully to what parents were willing and able to do—what is doable and practical—and for how I could conceptualize parents as customers for change. I would listen carefully for solution behavior that I could compliment. I attempted to reflect all this in the written report that would be placed in evidence, and when necessary, in my testimony. I brought a similar sensibility to my work when I started doing custody evaluations with divorcing families. When I opened my own office, I was able to refer child protection evaluations to my junior associates and supervised them when necessary. Over the years, our practice evolved into a local training site for parenting evaluators. Accordingly, the approach I describe here arose in a private practice in which bureaucratic constraints were few, and I had the discretion to decide how to do things.

7.3.2 Family Court Processes as Language Game

De Shazer (1991, 1994; de Shazer, Dolan, Korman, Trepper, McCollum, and Berg 2007) operationalized Wittgenstein's (1953) idea of "language games." The meaning of words is derived from how they are used, rather than having inherent meaning, and our use of language follows certain rules. These rules are usually implicit and can vary starkly from language game to language game. For example, the word "game" has a huge variety of meanings, from "peakaboo," to tag, chess, basketball, poker, political campaigns (Heilemann and Halperin 2010), and family interactions (Berne 1964; Selvini-Palazzoli, Boscolo, Cecchin, and Prata 1978). Confusion typically arises when participants interpret utterances from one language game according to the rules of another. Developing a parenting evaluation for potential use in court is a very different language game than therapy, although it may look quite similar at times—a family resemblance, as Wittgenstein says. The conventions, processes, and terminology of family court define meaning in this context.

7.3.3 Competence in Parenting Evaluation

Competence is a primary ethical imperative and entails "knowledge, skills, judgment, and diligence" (College of Alberta Psychologists [CAP] 2005). In this section, I specifically focus on knowledge and skills. Supporting the development of judgment and diligence is a function of the relationship with the supervisor and the supervisor's example.

7.3.3.1 Knowledge of Relevant Ethical Standards and Best Practice Guidelines

It should go without saying that parenting evaluators must know and abide by the ethical codes, standards of practice, and best practice guidelines for their discipline and jurisdiction. In addition to general standards and ethical principles, there may also be specific guidelines for parenting evaluation (e.g., American Psychological Association 2010; Association of Family and Conciliation Courts 2006; CAP 2006a, b), which parenting evaluators must follow.

7.3.3.2 Knowledge of Legal System and Court Procedures

Parenting evaluators must understand the legislation and case law governing legal matters in which they provide expert opinion. For example, in a child protection situation, they must know the different legal statuses described in the legislation, or the maximum duration that a child can be in the care of the child protection authority, to make appropriate recommendations. In divorce matters, parenting evaluators must know the limits of the court's discretion to order parents to do particular things or the weight that the court may give to past conduct. In all cases, it is necessary to know the nature of the application before the court: who is asking the court to do what?

Parenting evaluators must also understand court procedures. For example, it is essential to understand the parameters of expert evidence, the process of being qualified as an expert in court, the requirement that each party in litigation disclose the evidence that they intend to rely upon (which could affect report deadlines), and the process of cross-examination. Novice parenting evaluators may not be accustomed to adversarial questioning and should understand that this is the *modus operandi* of most family lawyers. Finally, it is important to remember that the trier of fact (in most cases, a judge) is the ultimate decision-maker. Accordingly, a parenting evaluator does not decide the question before the court but offers a position based on multiple perspectives.

7.3.3.3 Background Information

Parenting evaluators must have the background knowledge to connect the client's current and historical functioning to present-day parenting. This would include, but not be limited to: static and dynamic risk factors for specific problems (e.g., physical or sexual abuse, substance abuse, and particular mental health problems), an understanding of attachment and child development,[4] and the psychological science on parenting (Dishion and Stormshak 2007). While taking a critical stance toward the discourses that are embedded in this knowledge base, it is important to understand

---

[4] The discourse on "attachment," while widely accepted in North American family courts, is subject to much critique, discussion of which is outside the scope of this contribution. For one example, see Ross (2011).

that courts rely on these ideas a great deal. Accordingly, it is necessary to be fluent in these ideas while standing back from them to view them critically.

7.3.3.4 Interviewing: Getting the Information

Supervisees usually have adequate basic interviewing skills but require observation, practice, and feedback to acquire a fluid interview style that both elicits the necessary background information and is experienced by the clients as collaborative, not interrogative. Some of my supervisees have been trained in SFBT and therefore have developed a curious, not-knowing questioning style. In this regard, there is no contradiction between collaborating with clients and evaluating their parenting. Skillfully developing a description of *what the client wants* increases the likelihood that parents will be more forthcoming about their shortcomings than if they felt interrogated. A strong working alliance is particularly important with involuntary clients (Mee-Lee, McLellan, and Miller 2010).

As Anderson and Gehart (2006) state, not-knowing is not a strategy. It should not be confused with taking a "one down" position (Watzlawick, Weakland, and Fisch 1974) to induce clients to accept the evaluator's perspective, offer information, or get the client to "spill the beans." Enacting a not-knowing position by attending to multiple voices is more of an investigative interview style to support an interactional pattern that invites client participation.

7.3.3.5 Psychological Testing

Parenting evaluators must be competent in administering and interpreting relevant psychological tests. This includes understanding their limitations and the discursive critique of practices that quantify human experience (Parker 2004). It may be *de rigeur* in one's jurisdiction to administer comprehensive personality inventories, like the Minnesota Multiphasic Personality Inventory, 2nd edition (MMPI-2; Butcher, Dahlstrom, Graham, Tellegen, and Kaemmer 1989) or the Millon Multiaxial Clinical Inventory, 3rd edition (Millon, Davis, and Grossman 1994) to screen for psychopathology. Tests like the Beck Depression Inventory, 2nd edition (Beck, Steer, and Brown 1996), and the Beck Anxiety Inventory (Beck 1993) sample specific problems. The Parent Child Relationship Inventory (Gerard 2005) and the Parenting Stress Index, 4th edition (Abidin 2012), for example, assess clients' perceptions of their parenting. Supervised practice interpreting these tests is required. Courts value standardized testing highly. While this may seem at odds with SF ideas, in my view, it is necessary to enter into the language game of the context in which we work.

7.3.3.6 Report Writing and Work Flow

Because they are writing documents that could be evidence in civil trials, family court evaluators' reports must clearly detail the data on which their clinical opinion is based, integrate the data into a defensible case conceptualization, and write in an even, noninflammatory tone. In many cases, parents' behavior is egregious, which may invite even the most collaborative practitioner to be biased or judgmental.

Because practitioners often are doing several assessments concurrently, it is also necessary to plan and maintain work flow well. I suggest that my supervisees write sections of the report as they conduct the interview that provides the data for that section.

7.3.3.7 Case Conceptualization

Case conceptualization is a "… method and process of summarizing seemingly diverse case information into a brief, coherent statement or 'map' that elucidates the client's basic pattern of behavior…. a clinician's 'theory' of a particular case" (Sperry 2005, p. 354). In parenting evaluations, it is necessary to be direct about vulnerabilities and potential barriers to progress and give prognostic statements. My SF perspective taught me to embed compliments in my case conceptualizations. This can help to smooth the rough edges off the necessary discussion of clients' difficulties and allow them to see a path toward change. I aim to support supervisees to develop case conceptualizations that are as empowering as possible, to incorporate multiple perspectives, and to state their views with integrity. A collaborative document that invites cooperation and is clear about a parent's vulnerabilities may assist the parties to settle, as opposed to inflaming adversarial passions.

7.3.3.8 Testifying in Court: Being a "Not-Knowing Expert"

A former clinical director once told me with a wry smile, "An expert is just someone who is asked questions about something." While this characterization was tongue-in-cheek, it accurately reflects the interactional nature of expertise, which is situated in a hierarchical relationship between the expert and the receiver of the expert's knowledge. SF practitioners are encouraged to hold a not-knowing perspective, to understand the multiple stories that are circulating about the client, and to refrain from "filling in the blanks." In parenting evaluations, this means making space for stories that adversaries (e.g., child protection worker and parent, or two parents) have about one another, without accepting the perspective of either *a priori*. While the language game of civil litigation seeks to embed expertise in a hierarchy, I suggest that parenting evaluators take up a more interactional, less hierarchical view of expertise.

7.3.4 Process: Being a Solution-Focused Supervisor

My supervision is geared toward supporting novice parenting evaluators to acquire the competencies I have just described. Supervision occurs in a variety of

7.3 On Being Solution-Focused in Adversarial Places... 193

formats: observing interviews, modeling interviews and court testimony, discussing psychological test interpretation and case conceptualizations (with groups and individuals), writing detailed feedback on reports, and conducting mock run-throughs of testimony with a group.

In my practice as a parenting evaluator and a clinical supervisor, I distinguish between solution-focused techniques and solution-focused presence. Solution-focused techniques like the Miracle Question, exception questions, relationship questions, scaling questions, and compliments are easily identifiable and, in my view, more easily learned than solution-focused presence. Solution-focused presence is an abiding belief that the supervisee is already doing a great deal of what he/she would like to do, carefully noticing openings to ask about what the supervisee is doing that is consistent with his/her stated goal and thinking about how one can invite supervisees to notice and do more of what works. While my supervision encompasses techniques from outside of SFBT, I strive to maintain solution-focused presence. What follows is a description of my supervision approach.

7.3.4.1 Hypothetical Solutions: Recognizing Good Practice

SFBT begins with a description of what the client wants—hypothetical solutions, often in response to the Miracle Question. When I ask the Miracle Question of supervisees as an initial step in goal development, they may speak of mastering certain psychological tests, writing professional reports, gaining confidence as an expert witness, or developing a lucrative private practice. When asked to imagine how they might accomplish this, they describe attending workshops, reading, receiving and incorporating supervisory feedback, or networking with family lawyers. However, because this is a new professional activity that they have not yet actually done, their frame of reference for imagining hypothetical solutions is limited compared to therapy clients who describe scenes of family harmony, satisfying work, or upbeat mood. I provide supervisees with further grist for the mill of hypothetical solutions in several ways.

I offer supervisees a variety of exemplary reports, written with different organizational structures and in different styles. This gives them several specimens to use as a departure point to develop a report writing style that fits for them and that integrates the necessary background information. In supervision, I ask them to comment on the reports they have reviewed, their strengths and weaknesses, and how different styles may or may not fit for them. I ask how they might move in their preferred direction and what will be different when they do.

With clients' consent, I invite supervisees to observe me interviewing clients. As I interview for social and family history, past and present parenting practices, and risk factors, I am also attending to coping, previous exceptions and solution behaviors, and resilience factors. I ask the supervisee to track the intent and effect of my interviewing, my coverage of the required content, and my interview style. When debriefing, I invite the supervisee to incorporate his/her observations into a description of future practice.

In Alberta, courtrooms are open unless otherwise ordered by the presiding judge. Whenever possible, I have supervisees attend court to watch me testify, especially if they have never participated in a court proceeding before. I ask supervisees to track the tone and content of my direct examination. When I am being cross-examined, I ask supervisees to observe my responses and evaluate how well I have maintained the narrative to which I wish to orient the judge. During cross-examination, I attempt to maintain a calm demeanor while responding to the substantive questions and ask supervisees to note this for future discussion.

Exemplars of competent practice can help supervisees flesh out their miracle picture. As a supervisor, I can then utilize a supervisee's hypothetical solutions, originating from the modeling of others, to cocreate the vision of what the supervisee wants.

7.3.4.2 Crystallizing and Amplifying Solutions

Once supervisees are actively practicing, I help them identify and amplify real-life solutions through live supervision, case consultation, review of written reports, and mock testimony.

Live Supervision: In our practice, live supervision occurs with the supervisor in the interview room, typically entailing a pre-session, the interview, and a post-session. After eliciting a description of the clients and the issue, hypothetically, the pre-session might go something like this:

Supervisor: So, Terry, what are your best hopes for your session with Hank?
Supervisee: Well, I think our engagement is OK. He seemed pretty open about how he slipped up and lost his temper with his son. So that's OK, I think. But I want to make sure that I am not missing anything, you know. Also, I feel kind of pulled between the need to get all the information I need and not sounding like I'm grilling him, you know?
Supervisor: So you'd like to strike a good balance between being task-oriented enough to be thorough, while not sounding like an investigator. Without worrying for the time being about how you would get there, tell me what would be happening when you are able to do that.
Supervisee: Well, I would feel clear and focused. I would be able to track how he is reacting to my questions, feel like he is on board, and maintain a good pace that feels somewhat like a natural conversation.
After eliciting more details…
Supervisor: So let's both be on the lookout for the times when you are able to keep that balance, and we can chat about it when we wrap up.

The post-session might include further specifics and compliments:

Supervisor: So, Terry, what went in the right direction in this interview?
Supervisee: Well, I was quite pleased. I did better at the balancing, getting all the information with just taking my time and looking for strengths.
Supervisor: I noticed that, too. How do you account for that? How did you do it?

Supervisee: Well, I think it is easier for me now that I have done a couple of these, for me to be calm about making sure I get all the details. I feel more confident. Also, I am able to tell myself, "It's no big deal if I miss something. I can go back and pick it up later."
Supervisor: So how does being able to remind yourself of this help?
Supervisee: It just helps me calm down. And when I calmed down, I could listen for Hank's perspective without being worried about my agenda.
Supervisor: How do you think Hank experiences you when you calm down?
Supervisee: I'm guessing, I would hope anyway, that he would see me as accepting of him and maybe even supportive.
Supervisor: What else went right for you in this session?
The post-session continues with further elaborations of solutions the supervisee enacted.

Case Consultation: While there is no substitute for live supervision, most of the time supervision takes the form of group or individual case consultation. This provides ample opportunity to review the developments of the previous week or two. I typically use the EARS approach (De Jong and Berg 2012) to *elicit* recent steps in the right direction, *amplify* them by obtaining a detailed account, *reinforce* by asking about the effects of the solution on the supervisee and others, and then *starting over*, when warranted. In group supervision, other supervisees contribute to solution development.

We typically spend significant time discussing psychological test interpretation. This domain typically requires me to do some teaching and lead a Socratic-style discussion about the limitations of particular tests and the minutia of scales and profile configurations. I later review test interpretations when I read supervisees' final reports.

Reviewing Reports: I review supervisees' reports before they are released. In the first handful of reports by any given supervisee, the learning curve is steep, and most supervisees require a good bit of direct, corrective feedback which I provide via "track changes." However, they have invariably done a great deal of work that is worthy of compliments. I compliment the supervisee's engagement in the evaluation process (e.g., "I can see that you worked the steps in your MMPI-2 interpretation in a systematic way."), product (e.g., "You did a great job integrating the clinical interviews, collateral contacts, and testing."), and work flow management ("I really appreciate that you got this to me for review 2 weeks before the report needs to be filed in court."). Sometimes more work is needed, requiring me to give corrective feedback (e.g., "I know the father's behavior was pretty egregious and you don't want to soft-pedal it, but I think a more evenhanded, descriptive tone is needed. Here are some ideas...."). As much as possible, however, I give "keep doing what you are doing" suggestions (e.g., "It seems like you have settled into a routine for report writing that works well for you—keep doing it.").

Preparing for and Debriefing Testimony: When litigation does not settle and the parties are bound for trial, I work with the supervisee to prepare his/her testimony. It's my practice to invite other supervisees, which has the dual benefit of contributing to the learning of others and providing multiple perspectives. For first-time witnesses, this may include a basic orientation to courtroom layout and procedures. For example, in contrast to US courtroom dramas, witnesses in Canadian courts stand in the witness box unless permitted by the judge to sit. And, lawyers do not approach witnesses and "get in their face," but rather question witnesses from behind a podium. Since we often give evidence that is uncomplimentary to one or both parties, how does one deal with potential awkwardness of meeting clients in the courtroom? (My advice: Greet them, shake their hands, and sit by yourself.) Where can one get a glass of water in the courtroom?

We work together to walk the supervisee through his/her direct examination. Then, based on the potential limitations of the report and likely cross-examination strategies (Brodsky, Hendricson, and Scott 1991), we prepare for cross-examination, although it can be hard to predict the direction some lawyers will take. Finally, we debrief after court with a heavy dose of exception-finding questions (e.g., "How did you maintain focus on the story that you wanted to bring out?" "What worked to help you control your anxiety?").

7.3.5 *Limitations of a Solution-Focused Approach*

Parenting evaluation and clinical supervision are not therapy. In therapy, the practitioner's purpose is fully facilitative and supportive of change. On the other hand, both parenting evaluation and clinical supervision combine evaluation and support. In parenting evaluation, evaluation dominates, while in clinical supervision, evaluation and support are more or less equally weighted. Because SF approaches are largely silent on the issue of evaluation, and because some teaching and direct feedback are required in this work, I have gone outside of SF techniques to develop a viable way of working. I have attempted to strike a pragmatic balance while striving to maintain solution-focused presence through it all. If one defines SF approaches by technique, I could not accomplish what I need to within the SF box. But the SF model, in the form of solution-focused presence, has sustained and supported me to develop the approach I have described here.

7.3.6 *Conclusion*

In this contribution, I have described how SF ideas can be applied to the supervision of practitioners doing parenting evaluation. I reviewed some key theoretical ideas within and outside of SFBT. I describe theoretical ideas supporting my practice, review the necessary competencies for parenting evaluators, describe specific supervisory practices, and articulate the limitations of SFBT. In my view, SF ideas, in direct practice and in clinical supervision, have the potential to greatly enhance practice in this challenging arena for mental health practitioners.

7.4 Solution-Focused Supervision with School Counselors in Taiwan

Wei-Su Hsu and Ben C.H. Kuo

7.4.1 The Context

In 2006, several high school guidance teachers in the Tau Yuan District in Taiwan recognized the need for a group model of supervision. I (Wei-Su) am known as an active advocate for implementing solution-focused (SF) supervision in training school counselors in the Taiwanese high school system and was privileged to be invited to act as their supervisor to facilitate such a supervision process. Having taught in middle and senior high schools in Taiwan, I firmly believe that the fundamental philosophy of solution-focused brief therapy (SFBT) blends well with Chinese cultural values and is thus a suitable counseling and helping approach to be used in the schools in Chinese society. Consequently, this group of guidance teachers began receiving supervision grounded in solution-focused principles and subsequently came to acquire counseling training and skills in SFBT. This supervision approach was well received and supported by the participants as an effective and fitting model to help aid their professional development. The supervision program is ongoing and moving into its seventh year of existence.

The supervision group meets 3 hours monthly (except during winter and summer vacations), for a total of eight supervision sessions over a 1-year period. Originally, individual participants would only attend occasionally, but over time, it became a more consistent group of 12–15 regulars. The group includes 3–5 directors from the offices of guidance counseling in the schools involved, each director having 4–10 years' counseling experience. As a result of having a consistent and cohesive group grounded in the principles of SF supervision, members became close and provided mutual support to one another even outside their professional lives. As a case in point, in 2009, this group of guidance teachers independently founded The Solution-Focused Brief Therapy Center of Taiwan, housed in the basement of the Chung-Li Senior High School. The center serves as a critical resource for other school guidance teachers within the same district.

In this contribution, we will share the key strategies that evolved out of this group supervision process and also shed light on why this SF supervision model works in the Taiwanese societal and cultural context.

7.4.2 Implementation of SF Supervision: Process and Outcome

The current SF supervision approach endeavors to work with the supervision format that is most familiar to the participants. Each session focuses on an individual guidance teacher who presents a selected client from her/his current caseload. These cases usually involve difficult, involuntary clients or clients who are in crisis. Incorporating SF supervision principles with feedback from members of the group, I facilitate and maintain the group process in the following manner:

- Ask the counselor to briefly describe the client's background, interventions that the supervisee has tried, and the difficulties the supervisee faces, then identify the supervisory goals of the supervisee and the supervisor (10–15 minutes).
- Clarify the presented information and solicit additional information about the case (10–15 minutes).
- Lead open discussion among all participants, using SFBT skills, to explore more about the goals, strengths, exceptions, and improvement of the client; the successful interventions and strengths of the supervisee; and brainstorm possible interventions for future sessions with this client about targeted objectives and exceptions (30 minutes).
- Present final positive feedback and direct suggestions (in a SF manner) from the supervisor (20 minutes).
- Reach final conclusions, discuss, and wrap up (10 minutes).

In a qualitative study that interviewed supervisees after completing this model of supervision, participants identified three levels of benefit from SF supervision (Hsu and Tsai 2008, 2011). The participants noted that the model (a) enhanced their ability and professional efficacy to provide counseling to their difficult involuntary clients and clients in crisis by applying SFBT more fluidly, (b) enhanced their sense of self-efficacy in promoting school counseling and in-crisis management more broadly at the larger school system by utilizing available resources and facilitating the cooperation and communication among diverse parties involved in a particular case and operational unit, and (c) improved their sense of personal and positive development and growth, including becoming more in tune with their own emotions and well-being and acquiring a more positive attitude about life in general and about their interpersonal relationships.

More specifically, based on the study, the SF supervision model impacted the participants' guidance counseling in several different ways. For example:

1. This supervision model increased the degree to which participants recognize and identify with the positive philosophy and the postmodern perspective associated with SFBT. Consequently, this helps reduce the participants' doubts about SFBT.
2. This model minimizes the tendency for clients to view the role of a counselor as the "expert." Instead, it allows the clients to believe they are the experts on solutions to whatever problems they face. By so doing, this further prevents the clients from being unknowingly affected by the subjectivity of their counselors.
3. Through this supervision approach, the participants become familiar with the implementation of SFBT techniques. This can include participants becoming more confident in the usefulness of SFBT, understanding SFBT as a relatively easy and accessible counseling approach, engaging in the modification and adjustment of their own counseling orientations, and experiencing some breakthroughs in the mastery of SFBT.

4. The supervision increases the participants' sense of self-efficacy and confidence in utilizing the professional knowledge and skills grounded in SFBT directly with their clients.
5. The approach further underscores the appropriateness of applying SFBT with counseling adolescents. This is attributable to the emphasis on viewing clients from a positive psychology perspective which, in turn, allows the clients to establish a favorable working relationship and alliance with the counselors in a relatively short time.
6. This approach also enhances the counselor's effectiveness in crisis management. It increases the counselor's sensitivity and ability to discern warning signs or symptoms associated with high-risk clients as well as their own vulnerability and limitations in working with clients in crisis.

Secondly, while the focus of the supervision is on the client being presented, the study participants also noticed an impact on their ability to operate within their school system and to promote school guidance within the larger school system. In this regard, they became more effective in utilizing available resources and in problem solving when encountering difficulties in their counseling work. The participants also found improvement in their ability to facilitate cooperation and communication among diverse parties involved in a particular case and operational units within the school system. This often led to a better relationship among the client, his or her parents, and the client's teacher.

Thirdly, this supervision experience resulted in serendipitous gains for the participants at the individual, personal level. The participants grew from this model of supervision by gaining a more positive view of themselves, by experiencing an increased sense of self-efficacy and confidence, and by becoming more in tune with their own emotions and well-being. They acquired a more positive attitude about life in general and about their interpersonal relationships, becoming more accepting and respectful of individual differences and cultural diversity.

7.4.3 Supervision Review of the Video Recorded Role-Play Session in SF Group Supervision

After nearly 3 years of running this SF supervision group, I offered an additional 48 hours of basic SFBT training to these guidance counselors. At that point, they decided to form a study group to study and discuss SFBT-related books and materials. In these study group meetings, I addressed questions raised by the participants. Following these developments, the format of the group supervision was modified to align more closely with the structure of SFBT and to address the learning needs of the participants. The group supervision evolved from being primarily case presentation to including mock role plays of the counseling interaction and observations and analysis of the microprocess of the counseling sessions.

7.4.3.1 Process, Part I: The Mock Role Play

Each supervision meeting involved one school counselor role-playing the client and another playing the counselor, and the two engaged in a 30-minutes counseling session. This counseling role-play session was video recorded, while the members of this supervision group watched the entire session via TV monitor in a conference room. These observers constituted "the supervisory team" to offer peer supervision to the target counselor.

Following the role-play session, the target counselor entered the conference room to receive feedback from his/her peers that lasted for about 10 minutes. Then, the target counselor returned to the counseling session and the role-play "client." The counselor provided feedback to the client based on the principles of SFBT and his/her team discussion.

7.4.3.2 Process, Part II: Supervision Review of the Videotaped Role-Play Session

The client and the counselor in this role-play exercise returned to the conference room to rejoin their peers and me, the primary supervisor. The peer supervisors offered affirming feedback and constructive suggestions to the target counselor. Focus was placed on the strengths of the counselor.

This was followed by viewing of the recorded session. The video was stopped for discussion whenever anyone had questions or comments. The process provided a forum for participants to exchange ideas and opinions. The supervision process ended with group sharing among the participants about what they had learned.

Building on the approaches described above, a study with six counselors was conducted for the purpose of identifying the helpful aspects of the SF supervision-based supervisory model (Hsu 2009). A total of 24 counseling sessions were transcribed and analyzed based on the qualitative method. Seven critical elements associated with the SF-based supervisory process emerged: (a) positive opening and problem description, which established a favorable start to the supervisory relationship and focused on the interactions between supervisees and their self-identified difficulties; (b) identifying the concrete and constructive supervisory goals; (c) exploring the exceptions for supervisees and clients; (d) exploring possible alternative explanations, perspectives, and solutions to a problem; (e) receiving clear feedback and timely teaching from the supervisor; (f) conceptualizing counseling progresses and successes in small steps; and (g) evaluating and identifying supervisees' growth and changes over time.

On the basis of these findings, I organized additional training accordingly.

At the initial point, the school counselor trainees were taught the fundamental principles and the concepts of SFBT. Then these guidance counselor trainees were divided into a group of three or four: one individual took the role of the supervisee, one played the supervisor, and one (or two) took the role of the observer. The training was then broken down into segments that corresponded to the seven critical elements of SF supervision described above. In the small training groups, members of the group practiced the specific skills associated with each of these elements of SF supervision and subsequently processed their experiences with each other. Following each practice session, I identified and introduced the key elements of the session based on the structure/principles of SF supervision and provided concrete examples as illustration. Subsequently, the person role-playing the supervisee identified difficulty with his/her counseling work with the "supervisor." The latter adapted the principles of SF supervision to offer guidance to the former. This process took place, while the observer or observers recorded their observations. At the end of this process, the groups collectively shared and processed what they learned and experienced. The entire process concluded with my facilitating a final discussion, offering feedback, and addressing questions of the participants.

The participants were also encouraged to apply this model of counseling training and their learned experiences as a supervisor grounded in the SF supervision approach to their work with parents and teachers and to the management of three-way relationships (student–teacher–counselor or student–parent–counselor). The participants noted that this training enabled them to reframe situations and circumstances in terms of strengths and to offer constructive feedback. In turn, these participants found themselves becoming more accustomed to providing positive and constructive feedback to parents or teachers who sought their assistance. Punitive and disapproving responses to parents, for example, diminished as a result of this new personal development. The skill to offer constructive and timely opinions to others (e.g., parents) is paramount for a counselor in the Taiwanese context. This is because help-seeking parents in Taiwan often view the guidance counselor as an expert or an authority figure. Hence, the ability to offer clear and concrete suggestions or recommendations for parents in distress and the ability to provide appropriate psychoeducation to them in a timely manner are viewed as highly valuable assets.

7.4.4 Team Case Conference as a Peer Supervision Approach

The group of school counselors described above was introduced to the team case conference approach (i.e., a model similar to the solution-focused reflection teams first described by Norman 2003) through training from Lance Taylor (2010). This approach was appealing due to the straightforward nature of the model and its effectiveness. The participants responded to this model of supervision extremely well because it is grounded in a peer supervision framework and can easily be adapted and implemented in the participants' respective schools with other colleagues working within the school's guidance office. They found that the approach creates a collaborative climate and environment that reduces competition among colleagues. It allows counselors of SFBT orientation and non-SFBT-oriented counselors to work together when discussing clients, despite coming from different theoretical backgrounds. It is as if the team case conference afforded them a shared language to work as a collective body and enhanced a sense of team unity and cooperation among colleagues. Based on these observations, I consulted with Lance and received further guidance and input. I then identified and summarized the principle elements of a successful team case conference with Taiwanese guidance counselors into the following six points:

(a) Preparation

A team is formed with one director, one supervisee (the case presenter), and four to five other team members. The director plays a critical role, as he or she must monitor the team process and keep it on track with SF principles at every stage of this supervision process. The director must manage the group dynamic effectively and ensure that group process conforms to the spirit, the values, and the techniques of the SF approach. This segment is typically 40–60-minutes long.

(b) Presentation

The target case presenter briefly describes information related to the client and the client's response to the counseling interventions. The presenter then identifies his or her expectations from the team conference and the group. Finally, the director verifies the goals of this conference with the presenter before proceeding. This segment lasts about 10 minutes.

(c) Clarification

For the next 15 minutes, members of the team conference take turns posing questions to the presenter with the aim of gaining further information about the client's background and the quality of the client–counselor interaction in the counseling relationship. Each member is allowed to ask only one question per round, in a random order. The questions posed must be in line with the SFBT approach; that is, the director informs the members to focus their questions on soliciting factual information about the client as opposed to offering one's subjective opinions. The emphasis is placed on being inquisitive as opposed to being evaluative, opinionated, or judgmental when posing the questions. This process of posing questions is repeated for three to four rounds.

(d) Affirmation

For about 4–10 minutes, team members are asked to take turns offering affirming feedback to the case presenter. This might include highlighting the presenter's good efforts, unique strengths, or positive counseling outcomes. Interestingly, through trial and error, we discovered that this affirmation process worked best when the case presenter was asked to sit outside the group circle but in close proximity so he or she could still hear the praise offered by the peers. When a presenter simply cannot receive direct verbal praises from others, the team members can still convey their comments by indirectly expressing their appreciation, admiration, respect or honor to the presenter by speaking among themselves as she/he sits outside the group circle and listens. From a cultural standpoint, having others lavish praise on an individual is both awkward and unfamiliar for the recipient in the traditional Chinese society because of the supreme emphasis and value placed on humility and modesty. Receiving compliments from peers in this indirect manner has proven especially effective for participants in a team case conference.

(e) Reflection

Following affirmation, the team engages in the process of reflection for the next 14–20 minutes. Every member in the case conference is asked to engage in critical self-reflection by asking himself or herself, "If I were the client under the given circumstance, what would I have liked to see happen next (e.g., the next small step)?" The director encourages members to take the presenter's feelings and reactions into consideration and to resist giving critical and evaluative feedback to the presenter. Tentative expressions using phrases such as "perhaps," "maybe," or "it seems that…" are recommended. The presenter is purposely asked not to respond to these comments but instead to simply listen and take in the discussions offered by the team. The process of reflection sharing is also repeated for three or four rounds.

(f) Integration

For the last 5 minutes of the case conference, the case presenter is invited back into the team circle and asked to offer a summary or synthesis of what he or she has received from individual peers and the overall team. The presenter identifies and comments on helpful insights, ideas, and strategies that emerged from the previous processes. No additional comments or discussions are invited from the team members at this point, rendering the focus entirely on the presenter and the presenter's gains.

The emphasis here is to give utmost respect to the case presenter's thinking and learning processes and to allow him/her to fully integrate the learning experiences that emerged from the case conference. Other matters are addressed only at the conclusion of this segment.

7.4.5 *Promotion of Team Case Conference*

The group of school counselors that I trained were convinced that promoting and implementing the team case conference approach in the middle school would be profitable. They believed it was a highly valuable and workable model to be used with supervising and training school counselors within the same school. Based on these beliefs, this group of counselors began to challenge themselves and boldly took on the role of supervisors for other middle school counselors working in the same or nearby district. After careful experimentation, discussion, and examination of the best ways to increase effectiveness and resolve problems associated with introducing this team case conference approach, we arrived at some insights. In essence, a successful team case conference can be led and introduced by two to three new supervisors but should adhere to the following three steps/guidelines:

- At the outset of supervision, the leaders/supervisors clearly inform and instruct the middle school counselors on the fundamental principles of SFBT and SF supervision as well as the procedures of team case conferences within the first 20 minutes. This is necessary to ensure that all participants are open to and possess the basic knowledge about these concepts and methods.
- The leaders/supervisors must run the team case conference directly. One of the middle school counselors should act as the case presenter, while other school counselors in the same school act as the peer members of this team in this process.

- For the next 20 minutes after finishing the stages of the team case conference, the participating middle school counselors can raise questions concerning the case presenter's client, if necessary. At this juncture, the leaders/supervisors can offer supervisory feedback drawing from SFBT and SF supervision, reminding the presenter of potential ethical issues related to the case and highlighting effective ways to mobilize resources within the school systems.

Over time, we discovered that those middle school counselors who had prior knowledge and understanding of SFBT were able to advance very quickly. In some cases, they even skipped some steps in the process. Additionally, these individuals were able to offer concise and relevant questions/comments during the clarification and reflection segments of the team case conference. On the other hand, middle school counselors who encountered SFBT and SF supervision for the first time during these conferences tended to expect more direction from the supervisor. They needed a greater top-down approach to supervision and wanted more directives and information from the supervisor to satisfy their learning and practice needs. Such a desire for guidance from authority by novice counselors is especially salient in Chinese society.

7.4.6 Conclusion

The opportunity to work and learn with this group of guidance counselors in Taiwan as we advanced in our SF journey has been extremely valuable and rewarding over the years. The experiences of the supervision approaches described in this contribution are a culmination of many years of learning and adaptation of SF principles through many humbling trials and errors and continuous dialogue with these counselor supervisees. Owing to their generous feedback and our persistent effort to adjust and refine the supervision and training strategies, SFBT and SF supervision have finally taken root and begun to flourish in the soil of Taiwan. This has contributed to a rise in popularity of SFBT across the school campuses in Taiwan as well as the recognition that the SF approach is the most effective counseling model to promote the professional development and competency of guidance counselors in that country. On this hopeful note, we continue to work diligently, dreaming of and aspiring to a brighter and fruitful future for SFBT and SF supervision in Taiwan for decades to come.

7.5 Live Supervision-of-Supervision: Lessons Learned the Hard Way

Donald Lane and Frank N. Thomas

Experience is often the best teacher, whether the lesson is positive or not. I (Donald) think of my contribution to this book as a reflection on my "greatest hits" (or what might be better referred to as learning from my "worst hits") during live supervision-of-supervision (SOS). Live supervision-of-supervision, also known as supervision mentoring, offers a unique way of practicing a collaborative model of supervision using SF principles. Using this strength-based approach to supervision allows for the supervisor-in-training (SIT, my position in this contribution) and therapist to be comfortable in demonstrating their skills in the presence of the supervision mentor (Frank). Even when confrontation becomes necessary in the supervision process, it is done from a collaborative stance and encourages further discussion.

7.5.1 *Roles and Rules in SOS*

Maintaining a postmodern social constructionist approach to supervision-of-supervision, the structure of this SF approach makes use of Tom Andersen's (1991) reflecting team ideas. As Constantine et al. (1984) indicated, it is important to maintain clear and workable role expectations for the SIT and supervision mentor. Failure to do so can result in blurring of boundaries among the roles of the therapist, SIT, and supervision mentor and the agreed-upon rules that govern their interaction. The result of this could lead to ineffective training of both the therapist and SIT. This unique live supervision-of-supervision structure is established at the beginning of the relationship: the SIT provides supervision to the therapist utilizing a video recording of one of the therapist's therapy sessions, and the supervision mentor observes the process. If at any time the supervision mentor has any comments or reflections to share, he/she can interrupt the process and ask permission of the SIT to dialogue with the SIT. The supervision mentor speaks directly with the SIT and rarely converses with the therapist. The reasoning for this: the supervision mentor does not want to diminish the importance or authority of the SIT in the therapist–SIT relationship. Seeking permission to speak with the SIT and restricting conversation to dyads help keep lines of authority clear and reduces the risk of diminishing the SIT's role in the supervision process for the therapist.

There are some who might view this structure as rigid; however, every relational context has rules, with some rules more covert than overt. Consider the following rules of the therapeutic context:

- A context of "collaboration" assigns a responsibility to the client as well as the therapist, although the client may not have been consulted on this.
- Therapists do not bring other professionals into the case without client consent; likewise, clients cannot show up with additional family members or friends without consulting the therapist beforehand and reaching an agreement.
- The time and place for each session are delimited, and the therapist is restricted by ethical guidelines to appropriate self-disclosure.
- Seating is often rule governed, with an obvious "therapist's chair" and appointed "client seating."

These structured aspects of the therapeutic relationship are part of the context, whether said (via informed consent forms, open negotiation, or professional ethics codes) or unsaid. This live supervision-of-supervision structure is simply overt, even prescribed, because it works well for me (Frank) and most of the SITs and therapists with whom I've worked over the years.

Prior to the end of the therapist–SIT supervision time, there is a reflecting dialogue between the supervision mentor and SIT in the presence of the therapist concerning the *supervision* aspects of the session. This allows the therapist to be a part of what Andersen (1991) referred to as an observing system and gain a different perspective than she/he would as an active participant in a dialogue (see Tomm and Wright 1982). Many times, the therapist finds it difficult to maintain the observer role rather than actively joining in the SIT–supervision mentor reflection exchange. It is important for the SIT and supervision mentor to demonstrate the ability to maintain the agreed-upon system rule in this conversation. Reminders to all parties should be very respectful, acknowledging the therapist's desire to speak by indicating that all three parties will talk later in the supervision time (a technique used frequently by Insoo Kim Berg). It is sometimes helpful early in the process when everyone is learning the structure together not to attend to the therapist's attempts to enter the conversation. A gesture signifying "Not now, please" (such as a raised index finger, a well-known cultural signal for "Please wait one moment") can be worked out prior to beginning the process. Having to wait to enter the conversation often leads to some anxiety for therapists, but they usually report that this method of exclusion helps them realize the importance of listening to the SIT–supervision mentor discussion. This technique is especially beneficial for therapists who reveal that their thinking of what to say in the therapeutic context gets in the way of their listening to clients. This was confirmed by Donald and Frank, as we sometimes perceived a lack of listening skills on the video recordings used in the supervision-of-supervision sessions.

At the end of this SIT–supervisor mentor dialogue, the SIT asks the therapist what was helpful about observing this process of supervision reflection. The SIT will often ask a scaling question in order to determine how helpful the overall session has been toward meeting the therapist's goals for their supervision time together. A follow-up question, "What would be more helpful to you in the next supervision meeting?" is then asked, with the SIT taking notes on the therapist's responses for discussion and reflection.

7.5.2 Example 1: Building Collaboration with "Susan"

The following examples of live supervision-of-supervision demonstrate the process of using the SF approach in supervision-of-supervision. How the supervision mentor (Frank) was able to build collaboration with the SIT (Donald) is illustrated as well as some of the ways Donald was able to build cooperation with the therapist, "Susan.[5]" Throughout this supervision-of-supervision process, I (Donald) demonstrated

---

[5] Of course, identities are blurred to protect the privacy of the therapist and the confidentiality of clients throughout this contribution.

different skills and techniques of SF supervision including using scaling, exploring exceptions, staying tentative, maintaining curiosity, seeking permission (collaborating), and moving along an indirect talk—direct talk continuum. These skills were also discussed in a post-supervision meeting between Frank and me as they related to my own supervisory goals, which included building collaboration skills, relating SF ideas isomorphically to supervision and therapist–client relationships, complimenting, maintaining a not-knowing position, and listening carefully for therapist goals and change.

This first example involved a student therapist (Susan), Donald (SIT), and supervision mentor Frank about halfway through their semester-long contract, meeting biweekly for 4 months. At the very beginning of the session, I was frustrated because Susan was late for the supervision time and unprepared for our work together. She did not have any specific questions for me that she wanted to explore during supervision, an agreed-upon activity that was clear in our supervision agreement. I expected Susan to produce at least two very specific questions that she would like to explore while watching a video recording of a therapy session she had chosen to present that week. This allowed Susan to be collaboratively involved in the process and respected her as the expert on what she needed from our time together.

When asked about the part of the recording that we would be viewing, the therapist started by saying that this was a session with "the disabled couple." I began asking questions about the couple's goals and progress. Frank politely interrupted the exchange between me and Susan, addressing me: "I have a thought that might be important to discuss right now—it may frame some of what happens from here on today. Can you and I have a short discussion on this?" A dialogue between Frank and I occurred, wondering aloud together if this was how the couple referred to themselves. The two of us further explored the idea that how we refer to our clients often affects how we relate to our clients. I then turned away from Frank and asked Susan if this was how the couple referred to themselves. "They think about themselves as functional," was her reply (to Frank rather than to me; Frank continued to take notes, not looking up). She further responded, saying, "That is how I thought you referred to them, Dr. Lane." I felt set up by this response and I was a bit upset. I didn't think of or refer to the clients as a "disabled couple" in past supervision—of this I was certain. In addition, Susan directly addressed Frank instead of me, violating (or at least challenging) our agreement on conversational rules. Although Frank didn't make eye contact with Susan as she spoke or respond to what she said, he also let the boundary violation go by without comment about the process we had agreed to.[6]

This exchange had a significant influence on the way I worked with Susan during the remainder of this session. I was feeling frustrated that our time had been cut short by Susan's tardiness, her lack of preparation, and (what felt like) her blaming

---

[6] Later, Frank and I discussed this—I felt he should have commented, but he felt he was keeping with our conversational rules by not engaging Susan. This fruitful exchange led to my taking responsibility to address therapists' attempts to engage Frank in this context, which worked out well for me and for my supervisory relationship with Susan.

me for referring to the clients as the "disabled couple." I was also annoyed that another focus of mine had been diverted: I had established a goal to be more active in this session than I had previously been, but I had hoped to be more collaborative and less directive. I wanted to stop the video more frequently in order to give compliments throughout the session rather than just at the end of the supervision time.

As Susan played the video, I found myself getting more irritated because I was not finding things I could compliment about Susan's work as the therapist. When I did pause the video and asked Susan a question, I felt she did not give responses that were sufficient or might be helpful for the couple. So I started giving suggestions; I even began talking about how I would have worked with the couple. Rather than working within the SF approach that I normally work from, I took an expert role and neglected to maintain a collaborative and strength-based approach in the supervision. In addition, we all had an agreement to end the time with Susan after an hour, and even after Frank had reminded me that the hour was over ("Dr. Lane, it's ten o'clock—just reminding you, as you asked me to"), I allowed the session to go 10 minutes longer than the agreed-upon stopping time. This resulted in a shortening of the time that Frank and I had to discuss the previous supervision hour.

The following dialogue is between Frank (F) and Donald (D) that took place after Susan left, and it demonstrates the isomorphic relationship between SF supervision-of-supervision and supervision using the SF approach. Although Frank was very direct with Donald, it is important to see how Frank worked to maintain a stance of collaboration. From Donald's point of view, Frank's suggestions were offered in a tentative manner and not from a position of authority. Frank started this part of the supervision-of-supervision session by asking Donald how best to proceed as well as seeking permission prior to providing feedback (unlike Donald, who gave advice to Susan and told her how he would have conducted the therapy session differently). Our comments are (*parenthetical, in italics*):

Frank: How would you like to proceed with our time together?
Donald: I don't know…maybe just ask me some questions to start with?
F: You sure?
D: Not really. (laughing)
F: OK…Would you like me to ask you questions, or would you like for me to just provide you my feedback as well?
D: Due to how limited our time is, I'd like for you to just provide me your feedback – be straightforward.
F: First, I thought that you were going to stop at ten o'clock. I am also surprised with how different you were today (than in previous supervision sessions with Susan). You were not as collaborative or inquisitive as you usually are. You did not ask questions of curiosity like you usually do. This doesn't match up with what you have written in your Philosophy of Supervision paper or the goals you've set for our meeting together…You did not stop the video frequently like you said you were going to so you could provide compliments. You were very directive, giving suggestions rather than asking questions. What do you think was going on today?

D: I am not sure. I was feeling a lot of frustration. I was trying to be more active during the supervision with Susan.

F: *(Frank pointed out the difference he saw between being collaborative in supervision-of-supervision and simply telling the supervisor how to act in the future.)* If it is all right with you, I would like to share some ideas on what you might do in the future. *(An example of his seeking permission.)*

D: Please!

F: OK…You might *(suggestive, being tentative)* want to write these words and phrases the top of the page on your supervision clipboard: "Compliment," "Question," "Would it be more helpful for me to offer a suggestion?" *(seeking permission)*, and "Reflection." During your future supervision session with Susan, you can put a check mark under each category when you do one of these. Doing this gives you a way to track how collaborative you are being during supervision. Using scaling questions to determine progress that has been made in the supervision process could also be helpful.

D: That's a great idea. I will do this the next time that I meet with her.

F: I hope that I have not been too hard on you. *(This highlights a difference from previous sessions in which Frank was less directive and gives Donald an opportunity to express his thoughts about the time that they had spent together.)*

D: No! Thanks for the helpful feedback. *(Donald then talks a bit about how he thinks these ideas might be helpful in future supervision with Susan and other therapists in supervision, prompted by Frank's repeated questions of "What else was helpful?" and "How might that be useful to you?")*

7.5.3 *Donald's Reflections on Susan's SOS and Our Debriefing*

On the 45-minute drive back to my therapy office, I (Donald) processed what occurred during this session. Initially I was confused with how direct Frank had been. Then I remembered that he had first asked how I wanted to use the time we had together and that I had asked for direct feedback. I got upset with myself that I had allowed my frustration to get in the way of providing the supervision experience that I believed was most respectful and useful to Susan. I started processing the feedback and suggestions that had been provided and how I might put them into effect during my next meeting with the Susan in order to create greater collaboration (and change my non-collaborative behavior).

Reflecting back over this supervision-of-supervision session, I believe it was a necessary session for me so I could find the balance between being fairly nondirective (and sometimes passive) and being overly directive, a step toward becoming the more collaborative and solution-focused supervisor I believe I am. As difficult as it was to hear the feedback, I realized that it was a major turning point in the supervision-of-supervision process for me, pushing me in a good direction toward meeting my goals of being a more skilled collaborative SF supervisor.

This isomorphic process allowed me to go back to the next supervisory meeting with Susan (without Frank present) and implement this supervision style. For me, Frank modeled a way of implementing process talk into my supervision of Susan and my other therapist-supervisees. During the next supervision session with Susan, I applied the techniques suggested by Frank. I was able to mark four times I offered compliments, one time when I asked permission before making suggestions, nine times that I asked SF-type questions (including scaling and curiosity questions), and four times that I reflected back to the therapist in collaborative ways.

7.5.4 Our Next SOS Session with Susan

During the next supervision-of-supervision session, I was able to continue the process talk and ask questions of Susan rather than being directive. Even when Susan brought up an issue where I could have taken an expert role, I was able to maintain a collaborative SF stance due in part to the feedback that Frank had provided. At the beginning of the dialogue between Frank and me after Susan had left the room, Frank started the conversation by asking, "How were you able to be so different from the last time we met?" The difference came in being able to stay focused on the process of maintaining a stance of curiosity by checking with the ideas I had written on the top of my supervision clipboard, as Frank had suggested. I added another word to the list which I have found to be extremely helpful: "Curiosity." This is an excellent example of how the SF model of live supervision-of-supervision opens up multiple possibilities and different ways of working with SITs and therapists in supervision.

I suggested this same technique to Susan during a subsequent supervision-of-supervision session. At the beginning of this session, Susan talked about one of her goals involving the process of supervision. She wanted more attention and time spent on the "macro level" of her therapy practice and less on the "micro level" of the one specific case being shown in the video. The following example helps to demonstrate how I was able to move from the micro level of a single case session video to the macro level of process talk that could be generalized to other cases.

After watching a clip of the video that Susan had brought in which the client had shared a partial success toward her goal, she made the comment that she should have complimented the client on this success and asked more questions around how the client was able to accomplish this partial success. The discussion between Susan and me turned toward how she would like to be able to process what was going on in the session as it was happening in real time. She made the comment that she would like to be able to "get out of her head" so she could recognize these opportunities during the session, not afterward.

The following conversation from this session demonstrates how the reflection process in live supervision-of-supervision can be beneficial to the therapist-in-training *and* to the SIT in accomplishing their individual goals. It starts with Susan and me talking about ways to be less focused on the thoughts in her head (her "agenda," as she called it) in order to be more open to recognizing the therapeutic process as it unfolds. Frank was sitting just outside our conversational space, taking notes and

7.5 Live Supervision-of-Supervision: Lessons Learned the Hard Way

keeping his eyes focused away from us. Our supervision discussion started by addressing how Susan could begin generalizing this change in her participation within the therapeutic process across all cases rather than just applying it to the specific case being observed on video during the supervision session.

Susan: I am not very good at processing what just happened in the session as it's happening. (*She continued to talk about ideas she had for the next session with this client, building on the success discussed in this session.*)

Donald: How were you able to come up with that idea after you sat back and processed it?

S: I don't know...Why couldn't I have accomplished that in the session? If I watch the video, I catch these things.

D: Well, I'm not sure ... How might you take this thought back into not only this session with her but to most of your cases, working with clients to take a successful experience and assisting them in generalizing change into other areas of their lives?

S: (*Susan talks about how she feels the need to strategize and develop a treatment plan for each case in advance because it forces her to think like this.*)

D: My thoughts? (*seeking permission*)

S: Sure!

D: I'm not sure you could think like this *prior to* this session. You can't necessarily plan for what will happen.

S: Right...I wouldn't have known that she would have opened up with this scenario.

D: I agree...I was just wondering what you might could[7] write on the top of your notes page as you go into a session (*curiosity, being tentative*). Something that would remind you, "I am going to look for how I can generalize this success over to other areas in the client's life." That way you start practicing how you can process this in the session, in real time.

S: For me to try to do this in "real time," to accomplish that, I would need to plan better.

D: What I am hearing you say is, "This is where I want to go. I want to be able to do this in the session, when it is pertinent, in that moment." Right? (*Susan nods.*) That way you can generalize it so that you are not just focusing on that thought (agenda in her head), so it is not the *only* thought in your head. Sometimes, when you feel like you have to remember everything you want to do, it might be difficult to listen intently to what the client is saying because your own agenda might start to get in the way of listening to what the client is actually saying. (*Susan nods again.*) Rather than just focusing on the opportunity to give a compliment during the session, maybe you could just write, "Generalize Success" (or whatever your agenda for the session might be), on the top of a piece of paper and put it next to you so you can just glance at it occasionally during the session to remind you, "This is what I have found to be helpful for me in the past."

---

[7] "Might could" is Texan for "could" (or "might"), a common phrase in this part of the USA.

That way you don't get so focused on what you want to do that you neglect what is going on at the moment.

F: (addressing Donald) So, Dr. Lane: May I jump in for a moment? (*Frank asks for Donald's permission to speak with him rather than just taking over, as per their communication agreement for this process. He pulls his chair into closer proximity to Donald without excluding Susan from the circle. The dialogue here is only between Donald and Frank while Susan listens in, making sure not to blur the boundaries between the therapist-in-training and the SIT.*)

D: Sure!

F: What you just said is right along the lines of what I was thinking. (*An indirect compliment, which reassures Donald that he is doing a good job. It also demonstrates the isomorphic process between supervision-of-supervision and supervision of the therapist-in-training, as the therapist is also working toward a goal of offering more compliments during her sessions.*) For me, the idea that Susan (*including her but referring to her in third person to mark the difference in this dialogue from previous therapist–SIT conversation*) is talking about is strategizing. I think that may preload her head regarding what she is supposed to keep track of. When one does that, I don't think *anyone* is going to listen in the same way. I am wondering (*staying tentative*) if there could be some experiment that she could do, like "I'm not going to do any preplanning for this one case this week." She might preplan other cases but not this one case. She can tell herself, "I am going to do my best to be present and listen without a strategy or plan." (*Therapist attempts to jump in and talk to Donald, but he and Frank ignore her for the moment.*) That way she can see if those process moments come up more frequently or not, while she is in the middle of the session and saying to her client, "Do you realize that you just did something there? You just described something that you might be able to take other places." If that were to happen, it might indicate Susan was listening carefully and thinking less about her own agenda. Rather than thinking, "This is where we have to get to; this is what we need to do in this session," she might think, "My gosh, that's a good example." More immediate processing might come for her *and* for her client.

D: OK…I like this. It fits what Susan wants to be able to do…Is it OK with you if Susan and I talk for a bit?

F: (*Thomas nods, looks down at his notes, pushes his chair back from the circle*)

D: (*turning to Susan*) What do you think about finding a case and going in with no preplanning?

S: (*With hesitation, Susan begins thinking about a case that might work for her. She starts to talk about what she has been doing, but then she ends with the following comments.*) I think it's starting to be less about me preparing and predicting what I am going to do and more about keeping the client's goals in the forefront…this will probably help me practice my listening skills. Listening to this dialogue here brought a new level of appreciation for these skills, and now I have more confidence that I can practice these skills.

D: I really like what you said. It sounds like you might be shifting in a couple different ways...(*Donald then talks about Susan's shift to listening and her greater attention to client goals, promoting those over her own agenda and strategies*). Now, could we talk about the moment when you tried to get into the conversation Dr. Thomas and I were having?

S: Oh, yes – I'm sorry! I even reviewed the reflecting team guidelines (cf. Andersen 1991) we agreed to for these sessions, but I just forgot... (*smiles*)

D: What was it like when we didn't allow you to join us in the conversation?

S: For a moment I was frustrated. I thought, "How rude!" But then I caught myself...

D: Yeah, most people would think we were being rude. What happened to change your experience?

S: I just remembered our agreement. I mean, Dr. Thomas doesn't interrupt the two of *us* when we're talking, and you always ask *my* permission before turning to him and asking him something...so,...I guess I just remembered our agreement and pulled back.

D: Yeah, I have caught myself "breaking the rules" at times when I first started doing this with Dr. Thomas. It's just a habit I needed to get going to keep this working the best it can.

S: Habit...(smiling)...Yeah, I'm needing to work on a lot of new habits!

7.5.5 Donald's Reflection on SOS #2

As one can see, the reflection process allowed Susan the opportunity to listen in a different way, opening up new possibilities of how she could work differently with clients in the future. Also resulting from this session, Susan gained more confidence in her ability to practice the therapeutic skills that had been discussed in *all* her cases. It also left me (Donald) more assured of my ability to effectively supervise. Frank's compliment triggered a realization that everyone's processes—Susan's, Frank's, and my own—were similar. We were all working collaboratively to improve our skills in the roles each of us had in the supervision-of-supervision process. This SIT–supervision mentor dialogue above also demonstrates the continuous progress toward the goal of a shared learning relationship between the SIT and supervision mentor that is important in the supervision-of-supervision process (Storm, Todd, McDowell, and Sutherland 1997). Although Frank entered the SIT–therapist conversation, he only did so because I allowed it—it did not become symmetrical or competitive (Storm et al. 1997).

7.5.6 Final Note from Frank

What the reader does not know is that Donald denied many of my requests to break into the conversation across our relationship because he wanted to continue his dialogue with the therapist. Donald and I openly discussed this freedom for Donald to ignore me in our supervisor-only times together, and we had come to a clear agreement. Also, even though Donald asked me to be "straightforward" in his feedback in the first example, there were many times in our relationship when I remained tentative throughout our exchanges, both in the presence of the therapist and in our supervisor-only time together. Asking questions from a position of curiosity was my normal *modus operandi*, with Frank-ness (please pardon the pun) usually taking a secondary role in our exchanges.

I've had many relationships in which I was the supervision mentor over the past 25 years. In addition to mentoring family therapists in their journey to achieve status with the American Association for Marriage and Family Therapy (AAMFT 2007), I have also mentored supervisors in pastoral counseling, counseling, social work, and psychology and taught several doctoral courses on supervision. Donald is one of the most consistent supervisors I have ever encountered when it comes to setting goals and working within his supervision model or approach. Don't let the title of this contribution or his humble introductory comments fool you—he's an outstanding supervisor.

I agree with Donald's observation (below) that there are times when direct and indirect discussions are valuable. I believe we created space for both, but moving along this indirect–direct scale should always be negotiable.

7.5.7 Final Note from Donald

What I found most useful about live supervision-of-supervision from a SF approach was this complementary, collaborative relationship that formed between Frank and me. This relationship led me to feel comfortable in trying new things, knowing I would be supported. A possible weakness of this form of supervision-of-supervision could be the supervision mentors' lack of directness, although one previous example in this contribution demonstrated how the supervision mentor could be direct while maintaining collaboration and working from a SF approach. The compliments that I received throughout this supervision-of-supervision process allowed me continue my practice of supervision with much more confidence than if the supervision mentor's model had been one that just tried to correct my faults and educate (read: tell) me how to be a supervisor.

Not only did this SF approach to live supervision-of-supervision fit me well, but the feedback that I have received from those I had the privilege of supervising reinforces my belief that SF supervision has similar effects on therapists-in-training. The best example of this came from a therapist-in-training I had been supervising who was receiving supervision from another supervisor in a different discipline during the same time period. I will never forget her statement: "The day that I hear a compliment from (that supervisor) will be a good day." This strengthens my belief that giving compliments in supervision opens up the process for multiple change possibilities to occur in all systems involved—for the therapist–client relationship, the therapist–SIT dyad, and the SIT–supervision mentor partnership.

7.6 Leading a Team from a Solution-Focused Perspective

Teri Pichot

I remember a professor stressing the importance of taking management courses during my graduate work. Her reasoning was that good clinicians get promoted. She went on to state one will not necessarily be a good manager just because one is good with clients. This made sense given that what I was primarily taught in graduate school was problem-focused theories and tools. One cannot be a good manager if the framework used is that of diagnosis, pathology, and deficits. I followed this professor's advice and took the suggested management courses. True to her prediction, I did find myself in a management position within 5 years of graduation. However, in those 5 years, I had discovered a completely different way of working with my clients: Solution-Focused Brief Therapy, or SFBT.

My new job was clinical supervisor of a county-based outpatient substance abuse treatment program; later the administrative supervision duties fell to me as well. Our clients were quite challenging. Because we were county based, we could not turn anyone away due to inability to pay. That meant anyone who could not afford services elsewhere, or anyone who was discharged from higher levels of care due to inappropriate behavior, "resistance," or other reasons, came to our program. Our clients were primarily externally motivated. They were referred by child welfare, probation, and other community agencies due to significant negative consequences related to their substance misuse. Despite this, the majority of our clients did not believe they had a substance abuse problem. Conversely, they believed they had a caseworker, judge, or other externally based problem. Add to that, our field doesn't pay well, so our agency attracted less experienced therapists who were seeking hours for licensure before moving on to private practice or other more lucrative work. It was a challenging job to say the least and my natural tendencies were to fall back to my solution-focused training rather than my management training. "People are people," I reasoned, "and what motivates and creates change for clients will do the same for staff members." Despite my former professor's words of caution, this decision to use a clinical way of thinking as a supervisor was one I have never regretted. When using this approach with my staff, I not only discovered an empowering way to manage professionals, I also effectively role modeled and taught my staff how to believe in and use this way of working with their clients. In this contribution, I will discuss some of the key elements that made this a success.

7.6.1 Systems Thinking and Acting in SF Supervision

Over the years, I have had the privilege of being a part of many professional SF work groups and worked with many SF supervisors. One of the most common factors that I have seen is the desire to take the not-knowing stance (described in Sect. 1.2.4.1) into the realm of supervision and work group facilitation. Well-intentioned professionals find the idea of trusting those they lead and believing that their employees hold their own solutions as refreshing concepts. And they are. However, there is a very important component of the systems perspective that changes when applied to supervision; left unrecognized, well-intentioned leaders leave their teams with poor direction and create emotionally unsafe work environments.

When applying SFBT to a work environment, it is crucial to remember supervisors are ultimately responsible for the work quality of the employees or the work group. The supervisor's reputation, employment, and future professional opportunities are directly impacted by the outcome produced by those within the agency system. It is the supervisor's job to set and enforce standards, to evaluate the quality of the employee's work, and to ensure the agreed-upon tasks are done efficiently and correctly. Supervisors cannot completely adopt this not-knowing stance and effectively fulfill their role. Instead, supervisors must at times adopt an administrative position. In this position, the supervisor does have an opinion and does ultimately make the decisions in certain areas. This fact is clearly communicated to the staff members so that there is no uncertainty about roles and rules. At the same time, the SF supervisor truly values the opinions of others and forms useful relationship questions that help employees explore what others within the system will see in them and as a team, so the desired work product is completed. The SF supervisor most often withholds his or her opinion until systems exploration has been completed, and the supervisor's final decision frequently encompasses these perspectives. It is the SF supervisor's role to provide the team with a clear definition of the desired outcome. This results in the supervisees taking a significant role in helping to design the process while trusting the supervisor to make the goal clear at the onset. Here is an example of what this process might look like:

Supervisor (S): I just received word that the state is going to be paying special attention to clients with dependent children during the upcoming audit. They most likely are going to be targeting client charts and paying special attention to ensure policies and procedures in this area are being followed. [*This is a fact the supervisor knows. It results from the overlapping nature of systems – see* Sect. 2.1 *in this volume.*]

Team members (TM): Ohhhh. We don't have time! There is already so much that we have to do! Great! More paperwork! When are they going to let us just get our work done with our clients?! [*These comments stem from the therapists' focusing on the clients and good client care to the exclusion of the viewpoint of the auditors. While this client focus is ultimately the work product the supervisor wants, the therapists are*

7.6 Leading a Team from a Solution-Focused Perspective

thinking too narrowly, only seeing the client/therapist system to the exclusion of systems overlap from the agency and state.]

S: I know. It is frustrating. Of course client care comes first. But remember, if the auditors reviewing the files don't see that we are providing good client care, we won't get the credit we deserve. We need them to see this in order to stay open, so we can help our clients. So…I want us to imagine that it is the day of the audit, and the auditors are packing up their bags to leave. They have seen all they need to see in the files, and they are convinced that clients with dependent children at this agency are receiving the best care that they could ever hope for! What will they have seen in the files that convinced them? [*By asking this question from the point of view of the auditors, the supervisor invites the therapists to begin thinking about their work from a different perspective. By defining the outcome as, "the auditors are convinced that clients with dependent children at this agency are receiving the best care that they could ever hope for," the supervisor is sending the message that this is the expected outcome. This outcome is not up for discussion . . . only how the therapists will have achieved this outcome. This clearly defined outcome provides the distinct expectation the team needs. It keeps the team focused and directs their attention to the expected goal while providing the supportive and understanding undertones to inspire collaboration.*]

TM: Well, I guess they would see that we were asking about the clients' children, and this was clearly noted in the family section of the file. They would see that we were giving referrals for bus passes and other items as needed… [*Once invited to think from the auditor's perspective, the therapists quickly buy into the need for clear evidence of their work within the clients' files.*]

S: Great! So how would we have found the time to ensure that each chart was clear and to make sure that nothing was missing? [*This question invites the team members to explore how they are going to bring this concept to life. It again sends the clear expectation that it needs to happen while inviting the team members to create the needed steps.*]

TM: I don't know! We just don't have time!

S: I know. There is so much to do. Suppose we did find a way? How would we have done it? [*The supervisor is gently asserting the expectation that this needs to happen. This is followed up with an invitation to explore from a future perspective in which the team was successful.*]

TM: Well, maybe we would have taken some time during team meetings...Maybe 30 minutes each week to make sure things are in order. I can also look through my files during the week and catch what I can. [*This question invites staff members to operationalize the outcome they previously discussed. Again, the supervisor sets the clear expectation that the auditors will be convinced the team is doing excellent work with this population. The supervisor then sets the stage for the therapists to create a plan to achieve this goal.*]

7.6.2 Application of SF Supervision with Those Within the Rest of the Work System

Working as a SF supervisor within a problem-focused agency has often been described as a frustrating experience. While SF supervisors have the ability to significantly influence those they supervise, influencing colleagues on the same management level or above can be a challenge. It has been my experience that those in management often shy away from conflict. While dealing with conflict is never enjoyable, being direct in a compassionate and respectful way is a necessary part of successful management. The solution-focused management stance of setting clear expectations and goals while using system-oriented questions to elicit practical answers as to how these goals will have been achieved is often different from the traditional management style. This different stance requires that SF supervisors clearly state expectations while simultaneously stepping back and being curious as to how the staff will achieve these in a way that satisfies everyone in the system. I have yet to discover a work environment in which upper management openly invites a SF supervisor to teach them this different way of managing. However, there are subtle ways that a SF supervisor can positively influence upper levels of management.

7.6.2.1 Solution-Focused Versus Solution-Forced (Nyland and Corsiglia 1994)

How human it is when one finds something that is effective to become overly critical of those who appear to be using something that is not working. I have found that working with the most difficult client is at times far easier for me than working with upper management within my own system. I expect clients to be difficult and to act in unacceptable ways. I have come to discover over the years that I have different expectations than my boss and those in upper management or in positions of regulatory authority. On some level, it is easy to fall into the assumption that they should have it together and address issues effectively. Unfortunately, this is not always the case. I have found myself in such moments wanting to explain that they should use

SFBT in their management style and to further tell them why their way is not working. It is in these moments that it is most important for me to take a step back and remember to use the very same principles that I would so easily apply when working with a frustrating client. I need to shift from thinking that I know and move to a place of curiosity. First, I need to hear their goal. *What is it that this person wants or the system requires? How would they know that the problem was resolved? Who are they? What do they value? What would let them know that they did a great job and were making a difference?* Second, I need to get a detailed description of this goal. *What would they see from each of the other systems if the problem was resolved? What would they see from middle management, from the programs and teams, and from the therapists? What would they hear (or not hear) from the community, the clients, and the regulatory systems? What difference would these things make for upper management?* It is in these moments that I have to remember that certainty and curiosity are incompatible, so at the very moment I think I know the answers to my questions, I need to step back into this place of curiosity and ask. The more I ask, the more genuine the curiosity comes…and the more I truly hear.

Next comes scaling, a practice to help me view where they see us as an agency in relationship to their goal. With ten being "everyone in the system agrees we are meeting the goal with flying colors" and one being "we are failing miserably," where would each team member place us on the scale? (When forming a scale, I purposefully use playful and somewhat exaggerated terms to ground the scale at each end. For example, I might say, "Ten is that the auditors are packing their bags and thinking we are the best agency in Colorado, and one is they shut us down immediately." I use these humorous extremes to ensure that each team member sees us solidly on the scale as well as to ensure the process is more enjoyable.) Once they have identified a number, I explore what lets them know we are at that specific number and not lower on the scale. It is human nature to focus on why we are not higher on the scale. By insisting that my staff explore why we are as high as we are, they are encouraged to shift their thinking to identify successes, resources, and team competence. *What are they seeing in the system that lets them know we are so high? What is working? Suppose we were just a little higher on this scale. What would let them know? Who would have done what? What would have bettered the odds that those employees would have done that?* As I listen to their responses to these questions, I need to set aside my opinions and do my best to just listen. I am a part of this system. I supervise some of the very people about whom they are speaking. I need to be in a place in which I can truly hear and understand what is working and what will be working better when we are higher on the scale. I have to remember that perception is often more important than reality. If my team is not getting credit for the quality work they are doing, then I need to listen to hear what the management thinks we could do differently in the future in order to get the credit we deserve. I need to then help my team understand this concept and explore what we can do, so upper management will give them credit. It is an incredibly important political lesson: to do good work *and* to work to ensure we get credit and are perceived how we want to be perceived rather than fighting to prove we are right.

7.6.2.2 Using Their Language

Once I move back into the place of curiosity, I am reminded that the reason for my questions is for me to understand, not for management to change and think like me. How easy it is for me to work with my clients from such a SF stance! I don't expect my clients to become solution-focused as a result of my questions. I ask questions to help me understand them and to help us both discover how they would have discovered their solutions. My goal in asking such questions of management needs to be similar. I ask questions to help me understand them, what matters, and what they need to see from us. I need to incorporate their language, meanings, and ways of viewing the world in order to hear, value, and respect their solutions.

I can ask more questions in some settings than in others. It commonly takes meeting in multiple settings to gather a sense of upper management's goals, to get a clear description of what they want, to arrive at an understanding of where we are in relationship to those goals, and to discover what next steps should be taken. It is a multilayered process. As we know from SF work with clients, "by going slow, we go fast" (Steve de Shazer, personal communication, October 19, 2002). The biggest struggle by far for most SF supervisors is to truly be curious during the process, continuously believing that upper management and those within that system generally want the best outcome possible for clients. By keeping these positive assumptions, we are more likely to become and remain curious. Supervisors can then bring this information back to the team and continue the important work of helping those we supervise to think from a broader perspective.

7.6.3 Matching Supervision Style

One of the supervision lessons from those early graduate-level courses was about the traditionally taught four styles of supervision. They are reviewed in most supervision classes and workshops and vary slightly from source to source. In summary they are:

1. Authoritarian—The idea that people need continuous attention/direction
2. Laissez-faire—The belief that one should hire good people and get out of their way
3. Companionable—A style that is based on a friendship-like relationship
4. Synergistic—The belief that joint effort is better than the individual effort

In talking with supervisors who regularly attend my classes on solution-focused supervision and management, I have found that most SF supervisors believe the correct style for a SF supervisor is synergistic. This is also the most comfortable style for most supervisors who are hoping to learn and adopt a SF stance. They are frequently surprised when I tell them that I don't believe this to be the case. I have discovered that each of the four styles has an important role in effective SF supervision. The key

7.6 Leading a Team from a Solution-Focused Perspective

is to match the style of supervision with the needs of the individual supervisee and to his/her level of experience, personality, and level of accountability. Newer, less experienced therapists frequently need a more authoritarian style as they learn the expectations, time frames, and priorities. As therapists become more experienced, confidence can be nurtured by adopting a more laissez-faire stance as long as it is interspersed with other management styles that respectfully give the expectation of accountability. Once the expectation of goals is set, a synergistic style to empower the team or individual team members to create the process needed to accomplish the goals can be helpful. This is best done through a supervisor's supportive presence and purposefully designed questions that assist team members in thinking from the perspective of all rings of the system. It is important to note that the use of a synergistic style without this gentle authoritarian explanation of the expected goals can result in role confusion, wasted time, and frustration as team members work toward goals that are not in line with the larger system. This fluid form of supervision style is key to effective supervision, and it encompasses the individualized nature that is so central to SFBT when used with clients. In working with SF supervisors, I encourage them to identify which of the four styles they are most uncomfortable in and challenge them to be more aware of and purposeful regarding the style from which they are operating at any given moment. This increased level of awareness and gentle challenge to have an explanation as to why they believe this is the best fit at any given moment help to ensure that they are working from the supervisee's needs rather than their own comfort level.

7.6.4 *Favorite Solution-Focused Supervision Tools*

7.6.4.1 Creating and Maintaining Safety

It might seem odd to classify creating and maintaining safety as a SF supervision tool; however, I have found that supervisors frequently overlook the idea of creating emotional safety on the team. In turn, it becomes one of the most well-intentioned yet neglected tools in use in professional settings. Supervisors readily recognize overt threats to safety such as physical or verbal threats or inappropriate behaviors. However, there are very subtle threats to emotional safety that result from peer caretaking, unclear boundaries, conflict avoidance, and lack of supervisory direction, purpose, or limit setting. These can be equally as damaging to a team as the more overt threats, and covert threats are even more likely to be undetected in SF settings due to our high value on collaboration and focusing on the positive. Unfortunately, in our efforts to be inclusive and respectful of all employees' thoughts, feelings, and opinions, we can inadvertently overlook unhelpful behavior and allow the creation of an environment which permits discussions that are unproductive and even harmful. These include holding discussions in team settings that are best done with individuals or ignoring things that a SF supervisor would be wise to gently and respectfully interrupt or redirect. Disagreements and differences of opinion happen, and without a strong focus on goals and clear expectations of desired team behavior, employees and work group members are not always mindful of the potentially negative impact they have on others and/or the work process. In my role as a SF supervisor, I frequently find myself needing to gently interrupt group conversations, insist that we table various conversations to more private settings, ask staff members to trust that I would be handling various concerns at a later time, request that they speak with me privately about various matters, and follow up with people individually. As the old adage goes, you cannot unring a bell. Therefore, it is the SF supervisor's role to ensure that the environment is safe for all to speak while ensuring that employees receive the necessary guidance to think from the entire system's point of view before saying something that does potential damage and that can't later be unsaid. Purposeful structure is not just helpful; it is necessary.

7.6.4.2 Team Miracle

Similar to SF work with clients, goal formation questions are at the heart of solution-focused supervision. The most well-known goal formation question is the Miracle Question (De Jong and Berg 2012). The Miracle Question can be quite effective when the goal is to help team members shift their focus to imagining how they would like their work environment to be. Key components of success when using the Miracle Question in the workplace are to clearly define the miracle and to stress that outside factors such as budgetary, facilities, and regulatory constraints remain in place. Here is how the miracle might be phrased when working with a team:

> So I want you to imagine that today you go home and do whatever you would normally do. And when you go to bed tonight, a miracle happens. The miracle is that despite all the regulations, financial constraints, etc., this is the most amazing place to work. . . even though these outside factors remain the same. . . working here is the best you could possibility imagine despite that! Now because you were asleep, you have no idea that this miracle happened. When you come to work tomorrow . . . and you first open the door to come into the building . . . what are some of the first things you will notice that let you know this miracle has happened?

Wording the miracle in this way helps to shift the team members' focus toward things that are within their control and away from the normal gripes of low pay, too much work, and so on. While employees will typically joke about wishing they could include such changes, they tend to quickly shift their thinking and discover very useful changes. Here are a few examples that a group of nurses gave when I asked this question of their team:

Staff #1: "Hmmm. I would have energy and be excited to start my day."
Staff #2: "I would be able to focus on preparing for my home visits. I would be able to quickly find what I need and wouldn't need to rush around."
Staff #3: "I would have a clear routine when I came in that allowed me to transition from home to work. I would even be on time to work!"

In between each person's statement, I asked additional questions to explore what they did to better the odds of this happening. For example, the following exchange occurred in response to Staff #1's statement above:

Staff #1: "Hmmm. I would have energy and be excited to start my day."
TP: Wow! More energy? Where did this energy come from?
Staff #1: Well, I would have been able to leave work at work, so I enjoyed my evening off and had a good night's sleep.
TP: How were you able to leave work at work, so you were able to enjoy being at home?
Staff #1: Well, I knew I had done my best the night before, and I just focused on letting go of things that I can't control.
TP: Have you always been good at letting things go?
Staff #1: [Laughing] No!
TP: Then how did you do it on that night?
Staff #1: I think just continuing to remind myself when the thoughts crept in.

Other goal formation questions such as the Fast-Forward question (Pichot and Dolan 2003) or the Suppose question (Berg and Szabó 2005, p. 38) can also be useful tools in team and individual settings to assist staff members' exploration of how they would like things to be and identification of things they could do differently. With a Fast-Forward question, the supervisor would pick a time (either specific or vague) in the future when the problem is resolved. The supervisor would then ask the supervisees to explore how they resolved the problem in a way that was satisfactory to the entire system (themselves included). With a Suppose question, the supervisor uses the word "suppose" to turn a complaint into a possibility for future change. For example, when a staff member says something is not possible, the supervisor can invite the idea of possibility by responding, "OK... Suppose it was possible..." This type of question has a powerful way of helping employees suspend their disbelief and move into a stance of possibility and exploration.

7.6.5 *Summary*

The mainstream thinking in administrative supervision is that one must rely heavily on traditional management training in order to be a successful supervisor and that the tools one uses in the therapy room are quite different from those used in supervision. When the therapeutic approach one is using is problem- or deficit-based, this makes sense. However, the solution-focused approach, the resulting curiosity stance, and the SF goal formation tools (along with scaling, relationship questions, exceptions, and other questions) are incredibly effective ways to not only supervise and manage a team but also to reinforce the SF way of working with clients. People are people. By simply using a way of interacting with staff and clients that honors and respects who they are while simultaneously grounding relationship questions in the systems perspective from which SFBT came, partnership between management and line staff is established. By modeling the questions and way of being with people when working from this model, staff members see it in action and experience the positive benefits of thinking in this different way. While subtle differences still exist between supervision and client work, SFBT has proven to be an energizing and powerful approach to use when leading a team of professionals.

7.7 How Will They Know? Solution-Focused Supervision in Counseling Adolescents with Addictions

Jayson M. Pratt

In Episode 20 of Season Three of the animated comedy show "Futurama," a dialogue takes place between the usually rude, self-serving robot known as Bender and a peaceful, patient cosmic entity that is meant to serve as a representation of God. Bender was complaining that his efforts to help others only led to disaster as those he helped quickly became dependent upon him. The cosmic entity sympathized and shared with Bender that it may be better to use a "light touch." The cosmic entity then went on to illustrate his advice by saying, "When you do things right, people won't be sure you've done anything at all."

Soon after this conversation, Bender is reunited with his friends, who have just left a monastery where they accidentally left some monks locked in a storage room. While the friends are convincing themselves that they do not need to return and free the monks because God will certainly help them, the usually selfish and lazy Bender interrupts and demands that they walk all the way back to the monastery to complete the task. Bender exclaims, "God isn't going to do anything. I talked to him and he basically told me as much. It's up to us!" As the group begins their journey back to the monastery, the camera travels up into the heavens and focuses once again on the mysterious cosmic entity, who repeats his earlier advice, "When you do things right, people won't be sure you've done anything at all." This exchange provides a wonderful introduction to what it means to be a solution-focused counselor as well as a solution-focused supervisor.

My personal experience has been in applying a solution-focused approach in working with adolescents who are dealing with issues related to addiction. As a counselor at the Right Step in Euless, Texas, I have been fortunate to serve in a variety of roles. From 2006 through 2008, I worked as a clinician in a residential, outpatient, and family therapy context, which gave me the opportunity to observe the power that solution-focused therapy has to defuse resistance in clients, to identify strengths in families who initially focused only on dysfunction, and to equip young addicts with the belief that change is possible and that their best solutions originate from within. These changes are not small miracles given that adolescent clients are typically considered to be the most difficult and challenging of all psychotherapy clients (Hanna and Hunt 1999).

From 2009 to the present, I have been director of Adolescent Services for the Right Step. These years have served as my introduction to the power of solution-focused supervision. I have been able to interact with clinicians who are currently employed as counselors and with counseling students who have been seeking opportunities to fulfill practicum requirements for master's level counseling programs. While each group offers different challenges, both groups have positively responded to solution-focused supervision efforts.

This is not to say that my approach to supervision was immediately solution-focused. Like many clinicians new to the role of supervisor, I initially struggled with ideas about what a supervisor "should" do. In *Reason and Emotion in Psychotherapy* (1994), Albert Ellis identifies the assumption that one absolutely must be competent, adequate, and achieving in all important respects or else one is an inadequate person as an irrational belief. I certainly fell into this trap as I sought to demonstrate my competence to students and employees, forgetting that it was their competence that mattered most. Clearly, this was based in fear. I believed that the supervisor must have the answers and if I did not seem as if I had the answers, I was afraid that I might not be seen as worthy of my post.

As solution-focused clinicians, the concept of entering a counseling session in a state of "not-knowing" is a fundamental skill that is practiced to the point that it becomes instinctive. Unfortunately, when clinicians advance to a position of authority, there is a risk of abandoning this respectful curiosity and assuming the role of an expert. Whether this regression is prompted by the pressures of an implicit hierarchy or in an effort to relieve the new supervisor's personal anxiety over his/her ability to lead, it limits the development of supervisees and betrays solution-focused principles.

While my graduate studies had been successfully completed, it became obvious that as a supervisor, I was entering a new type of education. Thankfully, my training as a solution-focused counselor took place under the direction of Frank Thomas, Ph.D., and Elizabeth R. (Becky) Taylor, Ph.D., at Texas Christian University. Given that TCU is in close proximity to the Right Step, I was able to communicate with Drs. Thomas and Taylor on a regular basis. Their informal supervision remained focused on what I did well and identifying the times when I experienced success with those under my supervision.

The pattern became obvious in short order. I was clearly most successful and had the most positive interactions with supervisees when I returned to the state of respectful curiosity that I employed with my clients. Instead of convincing my supervisees that I had the answers, it was exponentially more helpful to gain a deep understanding of the times in which the supervisees had experienced success. An increase in my "not-knowing" seemed to be directly correlated with an increase in supervisee confidence, comfort, and anxiety reduction.

Thomas (1996) identifies nine guiding assumptions for solution-focused supervision. While I cannot say that I went into my supervision experiences with these assumptions in mind, I can say that my successful supervision experiences certainly support several of these assumptions. Specifically, my experiences support the following assumptions: therapists know what is best for themselves, a small change is all that is necessary, and supervision should focus on what is possible and changeable (Thomas 1996). This is not to say the other six assumptions are less true. It is simply a fact that my experiences as a solution-focused supervisor provide evidence that these three assumptions have proven to be true for me.

7.7.1 Therapists Know What Is Best for Themselves

One of my greatest joys has been to offer opportunities to counselors who have recently graduated from their master's programs. There is no substitute for the energy and eagerness that a new counselor can bring to a field (addiction) that can often feel redundant and discouraging. There is also no definitive cure for the crisis of confidence that new counselors can experience when faced with resistance, lack of progress, or perceived rejection. This crisis is only elevated by a population (adolescents) who are often less than receptive to the help that a counselor tries to provide.

This combination of factors led a recently employed clinician to seek my supervision after a series of frustrating experiences with her clients had left her questioning her ability to establish rapport with newly admitted clients. While this clinician had been educated at a respected university, her diploma offered little reassurance as this counselor explained her failed attempts to connect with her clients:

Counselor: I have tried everything. I just don't know what I'm doing wrong. What should I do?
Supervisor: I doubt you have tried everything. You haven't been here long enough to try everything.
Counselor: I understand what you mean but can you tell me what you would do?
Supervisor: Let's make a deal. I will share what I would do but only after you figure out three other things that you might do differently and let me know how they work.

The temptation was certainly there to offer a few alternative strategies to a struggling clinician. However, to do so would imply that this counselor was not capable and it would also assume my way was the best way. It is also important to note that my "deal" implied that she would be able to find a solution, which gave clues as to my impression of her competence and ability.

In this particular case, the counselor researched several strategies and reported a positive experience when attempting two of the three new approaches she tried. By allowing her to determine what would be best for herself, this solution-focused supervision technique fostered a sense of competency and taught the counselor that she was capable of finding solutions if her current approaches were not working.

7.7.2 A Small Change Is All That Is Necessary

Dealing with adolescent clients can be challenging; working with clients facing addictions can be even more challenging. Doing therapy with adolescent addicts and somehow finding the energy to properly document your efforts appropriately and in a timely fashion may be the greatest challenge of all. Effective time management does not usually come to mind when people consider what it takes to be a counselor, but it is an essential skill that plays a significant role in determining the ability of a counselor to function. If a counselor cannot manage his or her time, it can have a direct impact on employee evaluations, licensing compliance, and preventing counselor burnout.

A counselor I supervised was struggling with poor time management and as a result had failed three consecutive chart audits due to late or missing documentation. I knew that this counselor had the ability to be successful in this role due to the fact that he had been transferred to our location from our central offices in Houston, TX. In facilitating this transfer, I had spoken directly with his supervisor who reported only positive outcomes in working with this counselor. Despite his previous success, he was facing serious disciplinary action within the company due to ongoing documentation deficiencies. When I met with this counselor to discuss ways to improve his performance, I was surprised at how he had attributed a behavior (slow charting) to be a part of his personality (procrastinator):

Supervisor: So tell me what I can do to help you?
Counselor: There's really nothing you can do. I've always been like this. I'm a procrastinator. It was true in high school, true in college, and it's true now. I'm pretty sure I was even born late.
Supervisor: And yet you were born, you graduated high school and college, and you're an excellent clinician. How were you able to accomplish all these things as a procrastinator?
Counselor: It's mostly about how I start. If I can focus, I can finish. It all depends on if my ADHD takes over.

Note the return to problem talk in each of the counselor's statements. The conversation was intended to devise a documentation strategy, and instead, I was now in charge of changing his identity as a procrastinator and curing ADHD. Those are big problems and I could not make changes that would come close to that scale. So, I changed his office location.

A residential unit for adolescents with addiction issues is a busy place. There is near-constant activity and every client issue is considered, by that client, to be an emergency. Also, the threat of real emergencies as adolescents struggle with internal conflicts can quickly escalate to external behavioral concerns. This is not an environment that is conducive to long, quiet, uninterrupted periods of time where it would be easy to focus.

By moving this counselor's office to the opposite side of the building and away from the adolescent unit, he would have to face a long walk to meet with his clients or to lead group. Another benefit of that distance was that when he left the chaos, he began focusing on the documentation tasks in front of him. This counselor identified himself as having problems that led to time management concerns. When I showed him the new location of his office, I asked him one question:

Supervisor: Can you focus here?
Counselor: Definitely.
Supervisor: Then you can finish.

A small change leads to a big improvement. In this case, the counselor never failed a chart audit again.

7.7.3 Supervision Should Focus on What Is Possible and Changeable

In many contexts, counselors face the dilemma of self-disclosure. While appropriate self-disclosure can enhance a therapeutic relationship and increase rapport, inappropriate levels of self-disclosure can damage the relationship between client and counselor. It is essential for novice counselors to gain an understanding of the role of appropriate self-disclosure.

In the field of addiction counseling, the role of self-disclosure is a subject of much debate. Many therapists who seek opportunities to counsel addicted clients do so because they have overcome their own addictions or have been impacted by addictions in their own families. Clients who are facing addictions may even challenge the credibility of a counselor by directly questioning the counselor's history of addiction. It is tempting to self-disclose in an effort to alleviate any questions of credibility or personal knowledge of the addict's experience. However, this type of self-disclosure also positions the counselor to function as a role model or sponsor for that client. Solution-focused therapists may find it difficult to maintain a "not-knowing" stance once they share that they actually do know what it is like to be addicted to a substance.

The solution seems to be to limit any type of self-disclosure, but that also risks the therapeutic rapport in that a counselor may seem to be evasive or dodging the client's question. A counseling student therapist I supervised during his practicum experience faced the question of self-disclosure on multiple levels. This particular student was pursuing his education while employed in the field of law enforcement. Many of the clients who are in residential addiction treatment have been ordered there by a judge or a probation officer. The student expressed a great deal of anxiety about what the clients would think if they knew about his vocation:

Student: I keep getting stumped by the clients when they ask me questions about what I do for work.
Supervisor: What do you mean when you say "stumped?"
Student: Well, they ask if I've ever done drugs or if I'm in recovery. I know they want to hear "yes" so they can trust me. However, that's not true and in fact, I work with the same people who locked them up and sent them here.

Normally, I would not encourage counselors to create a game plan for specific scenarios, as it seems to only heighten the anxiety of the supervisee. However, it did not seem possible that this therapist could be more anxious about this issue. It was also becoming a self-fulfilling prophecy: the student therapist was worried that his inability to self-disclose would impact his rapport with clients, so he was acting nervous and fearful, which, of course, impacted his rapport with clients. Therefore, we engaged in alternating role plays in which I would play the part of the client and challenge him and then he would play the role of the client and challenge me. It was during these exchanges that he became discouraged and said exactly what we both needed to hear:

Therapist: You know, we can practice this over and over and I just don't think it's going to change anything about what I do or how they think about it.

The simple brilliance of that statement was apparent to both of us. He was right; we could not change what he did or how his clients might think about that. What we could change was what he thought about it. We quickly turned our focus to his perceptions and how working for law enforcement might actually benefit him:

Supervisor: What do you wish they would see about what you do for a living?
Therapist: More than anything, I wish they would see it for what it really is. It's a resource for them. Through me, they could learn how the system really views drug abuse and what really happens to the kids who get caught. Maybe it would help strip away the illusions about that lifestyle and see that it's only going to hold them back.

After that conversation, this therapist began to see what he had to share as a resource that could help his clients as opposed to a secret that must be concealed. Although he only shared this information twice during the 6 months I supervised him, he was no longer afraid of what the clients might think if it did come up. As a result, he relaxed and presented as more approachable to his clients. His ability to build rapport improved, and his confidence increased. By focusing on what was changeable (his attitude toward possible self-disclosure), this therapist made improvements and overcame his own anxiety, which was important because the clients were actually responding to his anxiety, not his job.

7.7.4 Conclusion

In his book, *Servant Leadership: a Journey Into the Nature of Legitimate Power and Greatness* (2002), Robert Greenleaf makes the claim that "The great leader is seen as a servant first, and that simple fact is the key to his (sic) greatness" (p. 21). Greenleaf makes this statement in an effort to encourage leaders to seek opportunities to serve those that follow them and to meet their needs as opposed to a traditional view of leadership where the followers work to serve the leader.

I believe counselors who have been presented with an opportunity to teach or to supervise will face a similar choice: Will they seek to be seen as experts or will they seek to help those who they are supervising or teaching get one step closer to seeing themselves as experts? To adjust Greenleaf's statement for our purposes, the great teachers will be seen as a servant to the student and that simple choice will be the key to great teaching.

I also believe solution-focused supervision is the best way to pursue the goal of serving our supervisees. The stories I have shared are but a fraction of the successes that I have seen and the primary limitations have been experienced when I fall into the trap of diagnosing the problems or worrying about whether or not my supervisees are impressed with my level of expertise. My goal is to continue to practice and develop as a solution-focused supervisor. If I do it right, my supervisees might not be sure I've done anything at all.

7.8 Supervising Practicum Students: SF Supervision as a Cure for Negative Thinking

Marcella Stark

Supervisors take on a tremendous responsibility when they supervise. When I first began supervising practicum students as a doctoral student, I knew I had to offer more than a sounding board and occasional advice to promote the growth of my students. I wanted to be nurturing and encouraging throughout the process, but I found myself focusing on their deficits. A previous instructor in supervision (and a proponent of John Gottman's work; see Gottman and Levenson 2000) made the point that supervisors should be giving at least five positive comments for each negative one, but pointing out the negative seemed to come easier to me. I hate to admit it, but I'm naturally a "glass half empty" type of person. But focusing on a student's flaws is not helpful, and I was very aware of this. Supervisees are given the confidence and motivation to improve when feedback is positive and the emphasis is on what they are doing well. When the focus is on the negative, supervisees (particularly those counselors who are still in training) may become too anxious and inhibited to learn. I knew enough to refrain from the practice of fault-finding, but I didn't know how to both encourage my students and help them grow and develop their skills.

Typically, counseling practicum students are extremely aware of their shortcomings. According to developmental models, beginning counselors are focused on themselves and their performance (e.g., Integrated Developmental Model; Stoltenberg, McNeill, and Delworth 1998). Because the primary tool for a counselor is the *self* (i.e., the sum of his or her knowledge, experiences, and ways of being), perhaps there is no other profession where imperfection is so personalized. Many practicum students see their professional limitations as personal failures, which can make receiving constructive feedback emotionally difficult. I find this to be especially true for students who only have a professor (as opposed to those who have an additional doctoral-student supervisor) to give feedback. I had often employed a solution-focused (SF) approach in my work with clients and decided to read more about solution-focused supervision (see Juhnke 1996). When I began implementing a SF approach to supervision, my relationship with my supervisees improved dramatically. They became more open and willing to share. I was better able to see (and help them to see) their many successes. My supervisees became more confident in their counseling, and I became more confident as a supervisor.

Solution-focused supervision is also time efficient. In a practicum setting, almost all of the supervision is group supervision and time is very limited. Class time is needed to review paperwork, discuss ethical concerns, and listen to student case presentations; little time remains for talking about cases overall. During my first semester of teaching practicum without a doctoral student to assist me, I felt overwhelmed and consumed with "checking things off the list," and SF supervision fell by the wayside until midway through that semester. Once I returned to asking SF questions, our class discussions became more substantive and my students began encouraging one another, offering suggestions and pointing out strengths. In my end-of-semester evaluation, the students commented that I seemed scattered and unapproachable at the beginning of the semester, but that I seemed to change as the semester went on. I attribute these changes to use of SF supervision. It is for these reasons that I choose to use SF supervision with practicum students.

7.8.1 Techniques

In this section, I write about techniques that I use most often with practicum students. Please note that I am currently working with practicum students in a program that has a solution-focused emphasis and am writing from that perspective. However, I believe that SF supervision is appropriate for working with students of various theoretical orientations and will address this specifically in the final paragraph.

7.8.1.1 Goal Setting

Most SF techniques (e.g., scaling questions, miracle/fast-forwarding questions) are used to help practicum students set goals, both for themselves and for their clients. In my work with practicum students, I have found the keys to helping students reach their goals are to (a) help them set realistic goals and (b) remind them of the goals that they have set. Particularly early in the semester, I encourage baby steps. Objectives such as "I will not harm my client" and "I will help my client feel heard" are perfectly appropriate goals during the first few weeks of practicum. As the semester progresses, students may work toward more advanced goals (e.g., confronting discrepancies presented by the client) but should be discouraged from setting too many objectives for one session. The more goals the student has set for a single session, the more anxious and overwhelmed he or she is likely to become. One simply can't focus on more than a couple of goals and stay engaged with the client at the same time.

A second key to effective goal setting involves teaching students to remind themselves of the goals they have set. When meeting with students just before their sessions, this isn't likely to be a problem. However, supervision for supervised practicum often takes place at the end of an evening of seeing clients (after a full day of employed work), and field practicum supervision will typically take place on another day of the week. Therefore, I recommend the use of a resource and reminder clipboard. Although I discourage students from taking notes during their sessions, there is some information that can be helpful to have in the room with them. I instruct students to purchase a storage clipboard and to keep forms and handouts (e.g., self-disclosure/consent to treatment, release of information form, suicide assessment checklist, safety plan, crisis protocol for the site, resources for AA/NA, feeling word list, and a list of SF questions) inside it. On the front of the clipboard, they keep the goals they have set for the session along with a notepad for use in visual interventions (e.g., constructing genograms). For those who are opposed to students taking anything into session with them, an alternative is to have them write the goal on an index card and place it somewhere they can see it just prior to going into their client sessions.

7.8.1.2 Exception Finding

A primary SF supervision technique for use with practicum students is the exception-finding question: *What is different?* At the beginning of a semester, the question focuses on what is different about the student rather than the client. Beginning students are often unable to find exceptions in their clients. For one thing, they may not have seen the client for more than one or two sessions yet. For another, students are so focused on their own performance that they fail to observe small changes in their clients. Noting client change is a goal to be worked toward and will come more easily as they first note changes in themselves. Therefore, I begin the first supervision session with *How have you grown as a counselor between your first semester in the counseling program and today? How are these changes apparent in your work with clients?*

It is difficult to build on success when the student doesn't acknowledge having experienced any successes yet. It is essential to meet them where they are; all practicum students have experienced success as a counseling student, or they wouldn't receive approval to take the class. Sometimes this fact needs to be stated verbatim: *You would not be allowed to take this course if your previous professors did not have faith in your abilities.* Another strategy for meeting students where they are is to relate their experiences in other areas of their lives to counseling. I recall one student who felt strong in her teaching expertise but doubted her counseling abilities. I first asked the group (made up of students pursuing a school counseling track) how many others felt that way, and many of them shared the same feeling. I then asked how they felt when they first started teaching. They all agreed they didn't know what they were doing the first few weeks in the classroom either. I suggested that feeling comfortable in the counseling role takes time just as feeling comfortable in the teaching role did. The initial student offered that teaching came more naturally to her than counseling. I then asked if she was equally strong in teaching all subjects and grade levels. As expected, the answer was "no," and I made the connection that counseling has various specialties; there may be some areas that always cause a little unease and others that are an easy fit.

In subsequent early sessions, I ask: *What is different about your clients and/or yourself from last week?* Most beginning counselors focus on how they are different as counselors. Responses typically involve feeling "more confident" or "being in the zone." These responses fit with developmental models (e.g., Stoltenberg et al. 1998) suggesting that counseling students move from focusing on themselves to focusing on their clients as they grow; students begin to report that they are not as worried about their own performance and can concentrate on their clients. As this begins to happen, I know it is then safe to ask more exception questions regarding how their clients are different from previous sessions. For instance, *What positive changes have you noticed in your client?* or *What is different about the therapeutic relationship with your client?*

Even as students are able to find exceptions in their clients, they may not always be willing to take credit for their role in the change. During these times, a not-knowing approach and a bit of humor may be helpful. One particular supervisee brought up a time when her client told her the counseling was helpful, yet the supervisee remained doubtful. I inquired about the power differential which might cause the client to say something untrue to please her. She quickly shook her head and expressed disbelief that her client cared about her opinion. I suggested it was either one or the other—if the client did not care about her feelings, the client must have been telling the truth about the counseling being helpful. She smiled and admitted that she may have created an atmosphere in which her client felt safe to make positive changes. Although my supervisee continued in her tendencies toward self-deprecation, she slowly began to acknowledge her strengths and give herself credit for counseling successes.

7.8.1.3 Scaling Questions

Once counseling students gain more confidence and are able to accept that their skills are improving, scaling questions are an excellent way to help them track their progress and set goals for continued growth. That isn't to say scaling questions shouldn't be used early in the supervisory relationship; however, I find the technique to be more successful as they grow developmentally. If they are very apprehensive about their performance, they may see scaling questions as "trick questions." Their use may overemphasize the evaluator role of the supervisor and increase the student's anxiety to a debilitating level. Pointing out observed successes and giving compliments will reduce this negative effect and help them to see supervision as a tool for growth. In contrast to finding exceptions, I ask students to scale their clients more in the beginning of the semester, as opposed to focusing on themselves. In this way, they are taught to look for small changes in their clients, which complements exception finding.

As students begin to focus more on their clients, I use scaling questions to keep the student focused on his or her own growth. I typically ask students to scale themselves on a scale of 0–10 last week and this week and then process the change. Rather than asking the same scaling question each week, I try to change it up—one week I ask them to scale their relationship with their clients, another week I ask them to scale their skills using specific interventions, and in other weeks, especially during periods of summative evaluation (e.g., midterm grade conference), I ask them to scale their development as a counselor. In many practicum supervision groups, I have noticed a theme of students seeing the next higher number as "being in the zone" and "feeling more confident." In effect, they often see the next higher number as a transition from focusing on their own performance to being more present with their client, which seems to support Stoltenberg et al.'s (1998) developmental theory.

I use Nims' (2007) *wow and how* technique as a follow up to scaling and exception-finding questions. For example, *Wow, you were able to get from a 3 to a 5 in getting your child client to stay on task! How did you gain her cooperation?* or *That's fantastic! Tell me what you did to get to that higher number on the scale.* Asking supervisees to describe their successes in detail improves the likelihood of them repeating those successes. We discuss how they were able to make improvements in group supervision, and they learn vicariously from one another in ways that are not possible in individual supervision.

In such discussions, it is important to be aware of students who seem more hesitant or quiet. Hearing student peers talk about improvement may be difficult for the student who does not believe he or she is improving. During these times, I normalize ups and downs in counselor growth and use self-disclosure about my own development. I reframe how the student knows what it takes and is capable of reaching the higher number. Also, I make sure I have students describe the higher rating on the scale in detail. I make a point to consistently do this every time I use the scaling technique as a model for my students using solution-focused brief therapy (SFBT). I've noted that even students well trained in SFBT will often skip from discussing the current rating resulting from a scaling question to asking, *What will it take for you to get to a X (next higher number)?* Describing the rating in detail is vital to helping the students reach their goals.

7.8.1.4 Fast-Forwarding

The Miracle Question, another technique for setting goals, is perhaps the most well-known SF technique. However, some students are reluctant to use the Miracle Question, finding it "too canned." Although I have used it successfully during initial supervision sessions, particularly with students who were not in a program with a SF emphasis, it tends to produce sighs and eye rolling over time. I prefer the variation of forwarding questions (O'Hanlon and Weiner-Davis 1989). Typically, I ask students to fast-forward three or more sessions in the future: *Three weeks from now, when you feel more confident in using gentle confrontation with your client, what will that look like? What will tell you that your therapeutic relationship is strong enough to withstand a little discomfort?* Fewer than three sessions is too soon for some students, and they have more difficulty breaking out of their perception of the current problem reality. They are more likely to have confidence in change over a longer period of time. For instance, at least once per semester, I ask students to envision themselves at the end of the semester and ask their end-of-semester selves to give advice to their current selves. We then process what it took to get to that future scenario and what is a first step they may take to get there. Before the end of the supervision session, I make sure to get a commitment of one small step from each student.

7.8.1.5 Incorporation of Sandtray

Aside from a basic play therapy course, university classes in expressive arts are uncommon. Additionally, they are considered advanced techniques. Yet, for many practicum students, especially those who work with child and adolescent clientele, the use of expressive arts can be very helpful. Although I am not suggesting that practicum students apply such methods without proper training, employing expressive arts in the supervision process can provide a model for those students who pursue further training and an introduction for students who never considered the possibility. In my practicum courses, I incorporate the modality of sandtray because it provides a visual and tangible way for practicum students to identify their problems and explore therapeutic successes (Stark, Frels, and Garza 2011). Whereas some supervisees will embrace this experiential method wholeheartedly, others may be more hesitant. For that reason, I ask students to humor me and try sandtray as an experiment. I tell them that if they hate it, we don't have to use it again. Either way, they will learn about a possible therapeutic tool.

I ask students to use figures to make a scene in the sand of either a problem they are having with their client or their conceptualization of the client's problem. When a student has a scene of the problem laid out, he or she is better able to see ways around perceived obstacles. Once we have explored the scene, I ask the student to fast-forward to a preferred, future scenario and to move, remove, or add figures to the scene to convey his/her hopes (i.e., miracle) for the counseling relationship or for the client. We then process the differences between the two scenes, and I ask him to identify the initial steps he could take in order to make some part of the preferred scene a reality. These steps then become goals for the student. Seeing the preferred scenario in the sand may also facilitate deeper responses to follow-up relationship questions designed to motivate the student to work toward supervision goals. As mentioned earlier, the more students can describe their successes (past or future) in detail, the greater the chances that they will duplicate those successes. The modality of sandtray allows the student to create and see concrete pictures of goals that the student is working toward.

In the previous paragraph, I described the use of sandtray with an individual student. Due to the time constraints involved with practicum supervision, such activities should be limited to one or two students. It is important that there be ample time for processing sandtray scenes and it will not be possible with an entire class. I typically reserve such exercises to coincide with a student's case presentation or other times when only one student is the focus of attention for at least 40 minutes. With an entire class, I make use only of sandtray figures, as opposed to asking them to make a scene in a tray. For example, I may ask them scaling questions, using the figures rather than numbers on the scale. As with the trays, I instruct the students to describe the chosen figure in detail—*Why did you choose that figure to represent a six on your scale? Which figure might represent a seven? How are the two figures similar and different? In what ways are you already like the figure representing the seven?* One former student chose a butterfly figure to represent her current rating on a scale of where she saw herself as a counselor. She explained that she had taken breaks in her counselor program due to personal struggles and was just beginning to "get her wings." I made the observation that butterflies must spend a certain amount of time in their cocoons and that their wings will not be strong enough to support them if they are forced out too soon. The student became tearful and she shared with the class that she had felt guilty and inferior to her peers because of her time off from the program. The class then discussed the ways in which her experiences made her a better counselor, and her perceived deficit was reframed as a strength.

7.8.2 *Challenges of SF Supervision*

7.8.2.1 Evaluator Role

The grades issued to practicum students greatly impact not only their graduation from the program but also potential opportunities for employment and doctoral work. The strength-based focus of SF supervision does not preclude SF supervisors from fulfilling the role of evaluator and gatekeeper for the profession. Although rare, there are students who are overly confident. I believe these students tend to be those who don't truly understand what counseling is. They see counseling as advice giving and believe the clients will improve if they simply take the counselor's advice. In these cases, I do not support that the student knows what is best for her. I have found it helpful to use Stoltenberg et al.'s (1998) eight clinical domains (i.e., intervention skills, assessment techniques, interpersonal assessment, client conceptualization, individual differences, theoretical orientation, treatment plans and goals, and professional ethics) as a checklist for evaluation and to provide more deliberate structure to supervision while still asking SF questions to assess each domain.

My greatest challenge to applying SF supervision with practicum students is in the grading of written assignments. When I first began teaching practicum, I felt limited to giving compliments and attempting to give more positive than corrective feedback in my grading. After receiving suggestions in response to a query I made on a SF Listserv, I decided to include self-reflective questions for students to answer in addition to their case notes. I now ask students to write down one strength they noted in the session and one question they have about the case. This allows for two-way communication. Another suggestion provided by a Listserv member was to include a grading rubric that explains what made me grade their assignment at that level and what small difference(s) in their assignment would have made me grade one point higher.

7.8.2.2 Monitoring Field Practicum Students

In field practicum, as opposed to supervised practicum, there are fewer opportunities to see students in action. Coincidentally, giving compliments becomes more difficult. It is crucial to cultivate strong relationships with field site supervisors because I rely on them to provide a quality experience for my students. At the beginning of the semester, I speak with them about their goals and expectations of the practicum as well as my own. I ask about their approach to supervision, which may or may not be SF supervision, and let them know how their supervisee will be instructed in the course. In addition to making at least one site visit, touching base with the site supervisor periodically for formative feedback is a good practice. During the semester, I ask the site supervisor for specifics about what the student is doing well as well as how he or she is progressing toward supervision goals. Ongoing communication will benefit supervision of the student, in class and in the field.

Another strategy for monitoring field practicum students is the use of a formatted reflection. Logistical and time constraints typically prohibit viewing recordings of every client every week. Although a minimum number of recordings should be required, asking students to view their own tapes can also be a productive assignment. I provide students with a handout on which to respond to the SF supervision questions such as *What did I do differently in this session? What are two strengths demonstrated? On a scale of 0 to 10, with 0 being worst session ever and 10 being my best session ever, how would I rate this session and why?* and *What will I do differently in the next session with this client?* Self-reflection exercises not only help us to monitor our students, they also teach the student to self-supervise, an essential skill needed after training and licensure supervision requirements end.

7.8.3 *SFBT Versus Choose-Your-Own*

Practicum is often the culmination of counseling students' graduate training where they bring together all they have learned about theory and skills for application with clients. It is a time when students establish their theory of choice. Counselor education faculty, whether intentional or not, influence the theoretical orientation of their students. Some programs will emphasize one approach or model, such as SFBT, so that students develop competence in the practice of that approach. Although their students are exposed to other theoretical approaches in a counseling theories course at my university, SFBT is emphasized with other approaches being compared and contrasted with it. Other programs attempt to present a more unbiased view of counseling theory. Various theoretical approaches are given equal time in didactic courses, and students are encouraged to select the approach that best fits their personality, skills, setting, and clientele. Students may be given instruments, worksheets, or writing assignments to facilitate their selection of a personal approach to counseling.

Whether a program emphasizes a single approach or attempts to provide an unbiased presentation of theoretical approaches, the theoretical orientation of instructors often fosters the selection of the same counseling theory by students. This is not necessarily a bad thing. I believe it is preferable to have students get excited about a particular theory after being inspired by their mentors than to struggle on their own without a clear approach to counseling. I have supervised interns who graduated from programs that did not require them to make a choice with regard to a theoretical approach. They called themselves "eclectic," but in truth, some of these students did not understand what they were doing or why they were doing it. Although I believe beginning counselors should learn to use a variety of techniques (i.e., become technically eclectic), having a theoretical orientation or understanding of how people change will help students to better develop relationships, conceptualize cases, set goals, and effectively work with their clients.

When teaching/supervising in a program that allows students to select their own theoretical approach to counseling, practicum is the time to hold their feet to the fire and require them to decide. The decision does not need to be a lifelong choice, but they should commit to practicing one approach or model for a semester in order to truly understand it. Evaluation criteria should include demonstration of the stated theory. With both SF-only and "eclectic" practicum groups, I like to ask, *What does your theory say about this* (e.g., client conceptualization, client's motivation to change, goals for counseling, interventions)? Asking this question often gets students in the habit of using clinical judgment and helps them gain a deeper understanding of their approach (beyond "because it's what my previous instructors taught me to do").

SF supervision can be used with both types of practicum students. Students who are enrolled in a program with a SF emphasis, or who have chosen SFBT on their own, have the benefit of seeing their approach modeled through the parallel process of supervision. As the supervisor implements techniques such as exception finding, scaling questions, and a future focus in supervision, students become more confident in their abilities to utilize those same techniques with their own clients. With these students, however, it is important to help them understand that the solution focused approach is more than just techniques. As they gain confidence and experience, they may wish to incorporate techniques from other theories. I ask questions such as,

How does this technique fit within the solution focused framework? or *What is your rationale for incorporating this particular technique?* Students who have selected a different theoretical orientation may also benefit from SF supervision. For instance, a student who has chosen an Adlerian framework might be asked, *On a scale from 0 to 10, how comfortable are you using early recollections to assess your client's worldview?* A student who is practicing cognitive–behavioral therapy might be asked, *When was a time that your client completed the homework assignment you assigned, even just a little?* I find SF supervision questions to be helpful to students holding many different theoretical orientations, particularly in setting therapeutic and supervision goals. Regardless of students' theoretical emphases, SF supervision provides a time-efficient, strengths-based approach to developing practicum students.

7.9 Continuous Solution-Focused Supervision in the Workplace

Peter Sundman, B.A.

In this contribution, I will describe how solution-focused (SF) clinical supervisors can orient themselves in continuous supervision that often lasts several years. Continuous supervision is common in Scandinavian social and health care as ongoing support for mental health clinicians. In these contexts, the focus is often on support of the everyday clinical work more than on building solutions or developing specific skills and competencies. Hence, SF supervisors need to focus on what works and often "go with flow" without immediate goals and visions. They must also be prepared to reorient the supervision as the work situation changes. The "goaling" idea can be utilized more extensively than in short-term supervision, and the main challenge is to maintain the mutual engagement over time.

7.9.1 Continuous Supervision

Clinical supervision, or "work supervision" as it is called in Finnish, has been used in Finland within the fields of nursing, psychotherapy, and social work since the 1920s. It became particularly popular as a part of the case work tradition of the 1950s (Totro 2007). Since those days, clinical supervision in social and health care is, at least in Scandinavia, regarded as an important supportive aid for the professionals in their everyday work. Supervision is usually requested to relieve stress with frontline workers, to help avoid burnout, to solve problems with clients and colleagues, and to support professional development. In SF terms, continuous supervision creates many possibilities to build different kinds of solutions over time, solidly fitting with the hopes of those involved.

Sometimes supervision becomes a routine or habit, something expected regardless of the needs and situation. This poses some interesting questions for a change-oriented SF supervisor because there might not be any problems to solve or specific solutions to build.

7.9.2 Solution-Focused Supervision

From a SF perspective, clinical supervision can be defined as facilitating the development of competent professionals, enhancing the professionals' knowledge and skills, and assisting them in serving their customers (Briggs and Miller 2005; Sundman 1992). Facilitation means that the supervisor makes it easier for supervisees to apply their skills in their work. A SF supervisor can also utilize the natural desire professionals have to develop their competence, as we assume that most professionals want to do a good job and improve their performance. In addition, exposure to novel ideas is a facet of group supervision. Participants become interested in other's ideas, implementing them in their own situations even though they did not originally seek change. Individual supervision promotes personal strengths and skills to enhance development and utilization in future situations.

7.9.3 Perspectives for the Supervisor

From a process perspective, the supervisor has a threefold job:
1. To facilitate positive feelings, engagement, and trust
2. To facilitate a supportive (group) process and strengthen the group communality
3. To facilitate progress in the issues at hand

The first point refers to typical SF topics such as acknowledgement, respect, and positive feedback. In long-term supervision, I have found the concept of engagement useful because it directs attention to one's personal interests and it is a fairly behavioral term—it is easy to see when somebody is engaged.

In long-term supervision, support and communality often come through normal SF practices, although some attention should be given to ensure everybody is involved in ways that feels comfortable. Having ample supervision time makes it possible to get to know the supervisees better than in short-term supervision, especially in group supervision settings. For example, one supervisee in a group stuttered badly. In a role play that took place after the supervision group was well established, this supervisee showed a completely different side of himself: he became a tigerlike person ready for a fight, which he much preferred. After this episode, the "tiger" stood in the foreground and the stuttering moved to the background.

In longer supervision processes, changes in the supervisees' positions can be noted and used. For example, in one long-term group, a couple of key members left the organization for other positions. One member who previously had been the junior in the team suddenly realized she now was a senior member. Her realization gave us the opportunity to talk about what this meant to her and the others. A fruitful discussion about responsibility, support, learning, and teamwork emerged.

The third perspective is about handling the substance in supervision: the issues. In long-term supervision, it is possible to lend support around many issues as well as personal and team development. I have, for instance, had the opportunity to follow the "posttraumatic" growth of a leader. When we started the supervision, she had lost her leadership position. She felt humiliated and traumatized. Despite everything, she decided to stay in her position, and within 3 years, she managed to overcome her traumatic experience by learning to face and fight her humiliation and to use her newly limited position to focus on some specific development tasks. She achieved astounding results in her new position and even received national recognition for them. These results would not have been possible if she had remained in her previous position. To witness this kind of growth and such astounding results is a rewarding side of continuous supervision!

7.9.4 *Supervision in Phases*

As a SF supervisor, there are a couple of ways to work with continuous supervision processes. One is to define and work toward some goals, even small ones, to achieve something important for the supervisees. This is close to a normal SF work process. Another option is to divide the supervision into phases. Each phase builds upon the previous and adds something new. There are new issues and goals within each phase, and in group settings, new group members are often added. Each phase includes improvements from the previous one and is thus somewhat different in style. It can include new tools to keep up the engagement and fit the changed circumstances. Quite often, one experiences the new phase as deeper or more grounded to the supervisees' reality. In one long-term case work-style supervision group, we decided to include a phase in which we processed their internal relationships in support of the case work. This helped them strengthen the case work and created some much-needed variation. In another long-term supervision situation, the term "supervision" was changed to "consultation." This change in terminology helped us concentrate on one issue at a time, and they experienced more choice in the process. The adjustment also stimulated me to build more helpful responses to their questions.

Once in a while, it is useful to reorient the supervision. Checking in with supervisees at the beginning of every season often works well. This check-in can be performed like a partial "new start," with the addition of an evaluation of the previous season. Scaling the atmosphere, process, and issues (goals) generates a good discussion for a renewed contract. Being open to new possibilities helps the supervisees evaluate what they would like to gain. In one long-term supervision group, a member said that she would like to hear more diverse ideas during the supervision sessions. This was quite different from previous meetings when most ideas from certain members were supported by others without further discussion. Her suggestion was accepted, and the process changed for the better.

7.9.4.1 The Contact Phase

The supervision process usually begins with a general request for supervision through email: "We are a group of social workers looking for a new supervisor for next fall. We heard about you and wonder what the possibilities are for you to take us on for group supervision." I often answer this sort of request with some questions of what the needs, hopes, and expectations are. The answer is usually something general about either case supervision and/or relationship matters. Hopes and goals are then discussed during the first meeting. This approach works if the supervisees know my supervisory style and approach or if their hopes fit what I have to offer. If the fit is not clear, then it is important to get a sense of the possibilities for cooperation during the contract phase as described below.

Another more secure, albeit somewhat time-consuming, approach is to meet with the group before deciding to proceed. This gives the supervisor the chance to check whether the supervisees' hopes fit with what I can offer and want to be involved in. By the same token, it gives the supervisees the chance to check whether I offer what they want. This first meeting is usually best structured as a preliminary meeting because it effectively sets the stage for a SF process. People usually express the most important issues in the beginning, and these issues should be noted for future reference. Although small and often vague, some ideas for change usually emerge as well.

Next, the leader's hopes should be checked to see if they connect with the proffered supervision. This gives the supervisor the chance to hear the leader's wishes for change and consider what developments are on the way within the company. The leader's hopes might limit the supervision to some extent. However, it is usually beneficial to hear the leader's hopes because they are typically connected to company change and development and should be in line with what the supervisor does. Having this connection also helps convey ideas generated in supervision to the leaders. From a leadership point of view, it is important to get feedback to the organization. I once talked with a group of leaders about supervision praxis. They were shocked to hear that supervision might be conducted in closed groups during work hours, as they believed work was supposed to be productive time benefitting the employer, and this opened up a good discussion on the goals of supervision and how they relate to the leader and company. This is an example of how shared information can benefit leaders and supervisors.

Some supervisors stress that issues talked about in the groups are not to be discussed elsewhere to ensure confidentiality. This is necessary for people to express their problems and fears more freely, which is essential for the supervision to be useful. In my opinion, in SF supervision it is enough to make an agreement to share ideas and suggestions only when the group is together and to avoid talking about the participants' personal matters with others or outside the group meetings.

7.9.4.2 The Contract Phase

The contract phase can be described as creating a working alliance between the supervisor and the supervisees much in the same way as with clients and customers. A SF supervisor does three things in this phase: (1) forms an atmosphere in which the supervisees feel understood and competent, (2) defines and concentrates on relationships and communication, and (3) helps supervisees define goals for the supervision.

1. Forming an Atmosphere of Competence
   I usually treat the supervisees as important guests when seeing them in my office and as important customers when seeing them in their offices. It is helpful if the meeting space is somewhat like a living room rather than a regular office space, because it signals respect and something out of the ordinary. Meeting in special environments again later can raise the "level" of the supervision and change the routine.

   Paying attention to skills, news, changes, and engagement with the supervisees is another important building block in directing the supervision toward competencies. Simply asking what the supervisees like about their work can serve as a good start. In group settings, one usually gets a spectrum of different perspectives that serve as a useful base for individual goals as well as values to build on. In a group of social workers I worked with, one liked the position security, two others enjoyed the challenges of the work, a fourth appreciated the short travel to work, and the fifth loved being able to help people. At the end of the session, two of the participants said this topic helped them to understand their colleagues better, a positive contribution to their teamwork.

2. Focusing on Relationships and Communication
   There are at least four interesting relationships to focus on in supervision: supervisor/supervisee, supervisee–client/customer, supervisee/boss, and supervisee/colleagues. In the beginning it is useful to ask about what's going well and possible areas of improvement. Communication follows with questions about who does what, when, and where. I usually ask for some example of success (with Finns, of something "not too bad") from the relationship the supervisee wants to work toward improving. This serves competency and demonstrates my own orientation and style. In continuous supervision, it is also neutral enough to start with similar themes.

   Talking about the supervisor–supervisee relationship gives important information about what to do and what to avoid. "Anything else than those bloody animals!" one supervisee once said, meaning the previous supervisor had used toy animals as tools too often. Talking about this relationship gives the supervisor the chance to tell about personal preferences and competences. I have even experienced how very ordinary group supervision changed dramatically when I told about my interest in using physical activities in supervision. This group immediately wanted to try some, and we had fun with our experimentation and learning from them.

3. Defining the Goals
   The focus of continuous supervision is often on support of the everyday work more than on building solutions or developing specific skills and competencies. Hence,

SF supervisors need to focus on what works and often "go with the flow" without immediate goals and visions. They also need to be prepared to reorient the supervision as the work situation changes (Nunnally and Berg 1983). Goals can usually be defined later from themes and topics that emerge during the supervision.

As the supervisees usually have had previous supervision, it is worthwhile to check their expectations with a question such as, "How would you like to continue the supervision with me?" Sometimes it is good to be more change oriented from the beginning in order to avoid nonproductive tracks. "What could we aim for in this supervision?" and "What kind of development or results would you like to achieve?" are helpful questions in this process. Usually, these questions start a lengthy discussion of improvements, whether we go with them or not. The goaling concept fits particularly well with continuous supervision (Walter and Peller 2000). This means starting with some goals and modifying them continuously during the process. In any case, it is useful to get to know the pros and cons of the supervisees and how they decide on change. This knowledge can be used later, when the relevance of the goals comes up again.

Sometimes supervisees used to continuous supervision just want to talk about their work—"reflect on it," as it is somewhat trendily expressed. In these situations, I usually initially agree to work on what they bring up and within that conversation find out what they would like to achieve, creating a small goal for the talk. Some longer-term goals often develop from talks like this, so the goaling process continues alongside dealing with relevant issues and (hopefully) making progress. This approach often highlights issues in relation to leadership, emotions, attitudes, and identity. One supervisee in individual supervision often expressed her frustration with her work. Dealing with the specific situations didn't satisfy her. Gradually, she came to the conclusion that she needed to change not only her job but also her profession. After this huge leap, she was happy!

If the supervisees are uncertain or reluctant to set goals, one can support goals from one's own personal opinion: "That would be a great goal!" or, "That may be a bit challenging, but I could go for it!" This has to be done keeping in mind that we, as SF supervisors, are likely more change oriented than our supervisees in these relationships, and we need to remind ourselves to keep our focus on the customers' goals.

In continuous supervision, "maintenance" goals or "keeping up the good work" goals are common. These goals are about continuing to do what is working and sometimes about avoiding risks. The supervision is often seen as a means of maintaining the current quality of the work. These goals and working toward them are quite basic SF work, as described throughout this book. But supervisors can add more talk about how people think and feel about their work, how they do their work well, and how they make decisions, without forcing talk about what to do more or different. These topics typically emerge naturally from the talk as interesting ideas and possibilities.

In puzzling situations, where normal goal development and resulting questions don't lead anywhere (although they could have), the Miracle Question might fit well with supervisees, just as it does with clients. "So, if by some miracle everything suddenly changes for the better, how would you know it coming to work tomorrow morning?" After some jokes and responses about "more staff!" ideas about significant changes emerge, especially in group settings. Then the goaling discussion continues as described above.

It is quite common for hidden agendas to play a role in goal setting. The contact person might want much more from the supervision than the others. The "real" reason for supervision might not be known to all. The supervision session might be a perfect occasion for some rest or to complain about life and work. I have learned to talk about these hidden agendas as I hear or understand them. Most of them are reasonable. They might influence goals and progress and can thus be taken into account. Sometimes the wish for change is the hidden agenda. The leaders of one office ordered supervision to assist the staff in dealing with internal relationship problems. It turned out that the reason for supervision was one person's troublesome behavior. To some extent it was useful to see the behavior within all the relationships and communication; on the other hand, the hidden agenda muddled some things until it was talked about openly.

Finally, there are supervision processes and meetings where talk and goals around survival are the right things to explore. For instance, one workplace had lost several key persons along with getting assigned more work to be done. They were discouraged, angry, and tired. The closest I got to goal talk included things like, "How do you manage after all your work?" "You must be really effective to cope with this!" and "Is there anything to be done now to ease your load a little bit?" Sharing the frustration, being reminded that the bosses had the responsibility for the resources, and focusing on the core of their job—the customers—seemed to help a little. In the long run, keeping the key persons effective and managing the workload were important issues to work on.

If, at the end of the contract phase, the supervisees clearly indicate they are looking for a different kind of supervisor, it is time to talk about whether or not it would be better to stop. A supervisee once was quite unsure whether to continue supervision, so we decided to try it a couple more times. After that, she still felt I didn't understand her situation well enough. With a trial run, it was easy to terminate in a face-saving way.

7.9.4.3 The Working Phase

As continuous supervision often is about keeping things up and taking advantage of opportunities as they arise, I have found it useful to focus on (a) recognizing success and small signs of progress, (b) using engagement, and (c) staying connected to and fitting with the needs of the supervisees.

(a) Recognizing Success and Small Signs of Progress
    After starting to look for skills from the beginning, it is quite easy to create a good habit by asking, "What's gone well since we met?" or similar questions at each meeting. Of course, many start out by responding with, "nothing much," so the task is to keep digging without wearing oneself out.

Often it is useful just to be curious. One supervisee was a school assistant, who told about the failure of a remedial instruction class she should have been leading. She scheduled the classes but no one came, so after a while she went to a classroom with several pupils who could have attended the instruction class. One girl caught her attention because she hid what she was writing. The assistant skillfully moved around to see what she was writing and saw that she was lagging behind what the class was doing. The assistant knew the class was going to have an exam soon. She then managed to talk with the girl and offered her help in a way that allowed the girl to accept without others noticing. She helped the girl, and it turned out that the girl needed extensive assistance, which the teachers had not recognized before. Several remarkable skills were discovered through this episode!

I usually also ask, "What's new since last time?" to signal that changes since our last meeting are interesting to me and to become aware of changes that might influence the supervision. Sometimes engaging things come up, sometimes discouraging ones, and sometimes new possible goaling issues arise in these discussions.

(b) Using Engagement

Engagement is usually found by asking what has been or will be appealing in the near future. This is often tied to something interesting or a task to which the supervisee is looking forward. Supervision time is then used to talk about these interests generally, their meanings, emotions related to them, and the supervisee's desire for more of them. In group settings, the engaged feelings are often experienced by others and lead to interesting consequences. In a team working with money allowance cases, one worker was frustrated with a client. Another worker said she liked this kind of client. Eventually the second worker took this client on and the first worker found a different task she liked to do. This exchange strengthened the team and increased the quality of the work.

Engaged supervisees usually use the ideas and suggestions generated in the supervision between the sessions. So if the supervisees have no news since the last session, it is worthwhile to ask whether something in the supervision should be changed in order to stimulate engagement. In one such situation, a supervisee revealed that he felt hopeless to deal with the difficulties we had previously been helping him with although he liked the ideas generated. It turned out that he had to first take a leave of absence to regain some strength.

I also think it is important that the supervisor stay engaged. Although there are different ways to maintain one's interest, dealing with important supervisee questions, following their progress, and forming a creative atmosphere are important means by which I stay absorbed in the process. Using Miller's (2012) Session Rating Scale together with a personal gut feeling are the best ways for me to assess my engagement level.

(c) Staying Connected to and Fitting with the Needs of the Supervisees

Forming an alliance and thus fitting with the needs of supervisees and their workplace is usually easy using normal SF tools. As time passes, the fit often needs to be revisited to keep up the engagement and avoid unproductive routines. It is useful to introduce new ideas and methods from time to time. A new tool, activities, a different communication style, or using video recordings can renew the supervision nicely. I quite often take some props with me, such as crayons, picture cards (postcards), and plastic animals, to facilitate communication or supplement activities. My favorite habit-breaking tool is to take a walk. It is very natural and easy to do. Finns have a strong bond with nature, so a walk in the woods, on the sea shore, or in the park usually makes for different talking, feeling, and thinking. During a walk recently, a group of professionals moving past a sports facility suddenly realized they all were mothers of sporting children and had all spent a great deal of time at the hockey rink and football (soccer) field. This bonded them in a new way and created an engaged conversation about what they had experienced. Then the conversation shifted to how they had used their experiences and intended to use them professionally.

A bigger shift in the working process can be achieved with adventure kinds of activities, as they also change the goals in interesting ways. However, adventure activities need more preparation such as securing a location, additional time, and special accessories. Once I went dancing with production line workers as a supervision adventure. They were faced with a situation where some workers had difficulties in keeping up the pace of the production line, and they were not used to talking about their work. The human resources professional at the workplace suggested they all take a dance lesson together, and it seemed like a fun way to go about creating a different context. The dance teacher really gave us a workout! Afterward when we were all sitting down, one of the workers started to cry. After a while, he managed to say that he could not go on with his work. Immediately, another replied that he had experienced the same thing a year ago and was now doing better. This started a fruitful discussion of mutual support and ways to change both the production line and the way the group processed their differences and struggles.

7.9.4.4 The End Phase

The end of a meeting is a perfect occasion to check the goals, progress, methods, and relationships. In recent years, I have used the end of every meeting to do this. I also change the next meeting according to the feedback from the previous. The end of a meeting is also the time to give and take positive feedback, reflect on the issues discussed, and plan for the future.

7.9.5 Evaluation

All continuous supervisions have natural times for evaluation. Usually it is at the end of a working period or year. Many evaluation tools described in this book and elsewhere are also useful in continuous supervision. My personal preference at the moment is adapted from Miller's (2012) Outcome Rating Scale, or ORS. The ORS is a simple, focused, and fast way to keep track of the relationship, issues, progress, and process in supervision.

In general, supervisees easily give positive feedback to the supervisor. Some sort of magnifying glass is needed to figure out the dissatisfaction. For instance, one supervisee said that she had anticipated more of a solution focus in the supervision, but things had nevertheless gone very well, so she was happy. I thought I had been my normal SF supervisory self, so I asked more about what kind of SF she was talking about. She then explained she meant getting to a solution faster. I took this as a hint to use the more "mechanical" version of SF with some of her questions in an attempt to speed up the process for her.

The supervisor's feedback to the supervisees can be similar. It is also useful to look back on what kinds of issues have been dealt with and what the results were. Most people have a short memory. Putting the issues together also creates a new entity and might generate a new perspective. For instance, in a group of child protection workers looking back at all the cases discussed over time, we realized one-third of the cases were closed in good condition. This was far more than anybody had thought. The workers felt empowered, and it was rewarding to talk about what had worked!

In long-term supervision I also tend to check for when we have done enough and our work together has been completed. Sometimes direct questions such as, "Do you want to continue?" or "Are we now far from or close to ending our collaboration?" or "I have the feeling that I have started to repeat myself. What do you think?" stimulate the conversation regarding "enough."

7.9.6 Positive Feedback and Ending Rituals

Compliments and remembering success are very important in continuous supervision because supporting competent professionals is one of the main tasks. Therefore, successes and key moments are very important to remember at the end of a supervisory relationship. Some of these successes can be traced from the notes I have taken and some by talking about the mutual journey. I often use the narrative metaphor of journey to highlight competencies and engaging moments. Picture cards (postcards) are useful tools for this. In group settings, for instance, everyone can pick a card illustrating the beginning, another representing the middle, and a third symbolizing the end of the journey. Then the cards for the different phases can be combined and discussed. Sometimes I ask supervisees to summarize what they have learned from the supervision and/or work period and write it on the back of a chosen postcard. Postcards can then be put on the wall of the workplace as positive reminders of the journey and lessons learned.

7.9.7 Reflection

Reflection is a perfect tool in continuous supervision because reflecting doesn't require change or improvement. Reflection is to analyze one's actions, give them meaning, and learn from them. This comes close to finding out what works, doing more of it, defining goals, and so on. So reflection is useful during meetings and at the end of the relationship. "How was it for you today?" or "What are your conclusions of today?" are both useful reflective questions. I even use reflection questions as the main documentation of my supervision. Compiling them gives a good picture of the supervision process.

7.9.8 Follow-Up

Follow-up of previous sessions is very useful in directing the supervision. Reports of progress engage everyone and inform what to do more often or differently.

A team complained that they were lagging behind in their schedules and couldn't find time to get things done. We decided to use the supervision time for them to work on those jobs. I watched and noticed what they were doing well. They were happy with the jobs completed and my feedback. Our next meeting was very engaged as we toiled together on another work situation, like a follow-up of the previous meeting.

If the supervision has had little or no impact on the practice, it might be time to talk about whether to continue or not. This has been my Achilles' heel, because I have often talked about this topic in ways that left the supervisees feeling like I was deserting them. It is probably useful to talk about pros and cons first and then let the supervisees decide what to do.

Long-term supervision rarely has systemic follow-up after the relationship ends. Sometimes, by coincidence, I encounter former supervisees. It is quite common to get positive feedback from the supervision and hear about change that wasn't apparent at that time. One group supervision experience stands out, where we tried everything in the book to change the work situation of a social work department. The staff was engaged and really trying their best. Finally, I gave up before the end of our second "round"; I wrote a letter to the bosses explaining my understanding of the situation and regretting not being of much help. A year later, I heard that one of the bosses quit because of an impasse with the other. A new boss made the difference, and the situation started to get better.

Follow-up would be helpful with a supervision contract that ended in boredom because we could learn from it, asking questions like "Was it acceptable for the supervisees?" "What went well?" and "What could be done differently next time?"

7.9.9 Conclusion

From my experience and understanding, most of the themes and tools described in this article are common to other kinds of SF supervision. The tools simply need to be calibrated slightly and applied sensibly in continuous supervision situations. In general, more attention has to be paid to having an engaged atmosphere, to facilitating the process and using goals/goaling, to supporting practices that are working well, and to sustaining competency already present—to help the supervisees do their job as well as they can. Some ideas and tools from other approaches lend themselves well to long-term SF supervision, such as habits, facilitation, engagement, reflection, dialogues, and narratives. Some unique features characterize continuous supervision. It gives more time for change to happen, for adjustments to be made, and for follow-up on the results of these changes. During continuous supervision, there might be more and less intensive periods than in other kinds of supervision, but it is clear that the supervisor gets to know the professionals and the workplace well and can tailor the facilitation specifically to those involved and sometimes even to the whole workplace.

7.10 Solution-Focused Supervision in a College Student Affairs Setting

Jay Trenhaile and Elizabeth R. Taylor

Solution-focused supervision has many applications in the college student affairs setting, based in part on the wide variety of support positions that exist in college and university contexts. On any given campus, types and numbers of student affairs positions depend on the size and focus of the campus. For example, at larger research institutions, faculty tend to do less academic advising and college student affairs professionals (CSAPs) take on larger responsibilities for those tasks. Common positions for CSAPs involve working with college students as academic advisors, judicial representatives, housing officials, campus activities coordinators, financial aid officers, and numerous other roles.

7.10.1 The College Student Affairs Professional (CSAP) Context

Prior to discussing supervision of the CSAP, one must remember the context in which these professionals work. The clients, college, and university students come from varied backgrounds. Diversity is found in many areas, including ethnicity, age, and educational preparation. This presents unique challenges for CSAPs, as their effectiveness typically increases as they become more familiar with the backgrounds of the students they serve. For example, a 40-year-old female nursing student who is married with a local family has different needs and experiences than an 18-year-old male first-year student with no declared major who comes from a two-income family living 3 hours from campus. CSAPs' success may be compromised if they do not invest the time and effort necessary to understand students and their goals.

Theorists have been trying to capture student development in higher education for the last 50 years, which led Alexander Astin to write, "Even a casual reading of the extensive literature on student development in higher education can create confusion and perplexity" (Astin 1999, p. 518). Some CSAPs might argue that Astin's analysis is still relevant. For the purpose of this contribution, student development is viewed as theoretical beliefs outlining how college students change, grow, and develop during the course of their higher educational experiences. Perhaps McEwen (2005) described the types of development that college students experience most effectively, stating that college students will grow and change in the areas of psychosocial, social identity, and cognitive–structural development. In short, changes will occur in how students view themselves and their abilities, construct their social identities (i.e., gender, race, ethnicity, sexual orientation, etc.), and think, including their moral development.

Given these parameters, professionals in a college student affairs setting (including supervisors) should be reminded that college students' skills, needs, and abilities will often change—sometimes quickly—during their time as students. First-year students have often left home for the first time and may have concerns about adjustment to college life, mental health issues, and social skills problems. On the other hand, students in their third or fourth years have more knowledge of the expectations of the academic context and their chosen majors. These differences should be considered when making academic decisions and imposing consequences on student behaviors.

Students' growth and changes begin from the time they arrive at campus and continue until their departure. And, at times, their departure does not take place until after the completion of extended educational opportunities that may include graduate school. Students sometimes show considerable change in their perception of self throughout their time on campus. Sometimes this change is delayed and happens years after arriving. While some theorists have more clearly defined the stages they believe college students experience, the growing number of older first-time college students validates the need for a broader approach to understanding the development college students experience. Sexual orientation, gender, and ethnicity all impact the social identity that college-aged individuals develop during their time on campus. In fact, for some students from small rural communities, this may be the first time they experience interactions with someone from a diverse background, including different sexual orientations or ethnic heritages. If college CSAPs are going to be successful in working with adults in higher education settings, they must be prepared to appropriately support these students, who may be confused about how to interact with someone from a different, unfamiliar background. Finally, the CSAP should expect to see changes in cognitive development and recognize such changes in conversation and decision-making.

7.10.2 Supervision with CSAPs

Supervision in a college or university setting requires a different perspective when compared to clinical settings. First, most of the conversations between college students and CSAPs are not considered traditional "mental health therapy." Secondly, many CSAPs do not have clinical training equal to mental health professionals. In fact, many CSAPs have not taken clinical skills courses such as counseling skills or practicum. In the absence of such clinical training, supervision focusing on clinical treatment goals would not be appropriate even though the college student may be exhibiting mental health needs.

Because some CSAPs do not have clinical training and because the professional/student conversations are often not standard mental health therapy, these professionals will benefit from a supervision model that advocates for increased attention on the student. After hearing a presentation by Steve de Shazer and Harvey Ratner at the European Brief Therapy Association's Annual Conference in 2002 (de Shazer and Ratner 2002), I (Jay) proposed using four solution-focused questions to draw attention to the student in these settings (Trenhaile 2005). This focus on the students can help CSAPs identify the purpose of the relationship and provide them with an appropriate reference point even though they may not be providing actual therapeutic services.

A sample dialogue from a supervision discussion following a conversation between a CSAP and a student might be:

Supervisor: On a scale from 1 to 10, with 1 being the "pits" and 10 being pretty darn good, how would your student (client) rate your meeting?

CSAP: An 8, because he wants to come back for further discussions. He shared a number of ideas related to possible programs of study that he wants to think about. He asked me to continue to help with this decision-making process.

Supervisor: If the student were to raise his rating one or two points, what would have happened?

CSAP: Asking if there were other issues that he wanted to discuss. I've learned that issues outside of the classroom can have a large impact on academic performance and perhaps he had some things that would be helpful to discuss. Some of these issues may need to be referred to a mental health counselor, but some may not need that intervention, and then I could be more helpful.

Supervisor: What was the student doing when things were going well during the meeting?

CSAP: When he was hearing me summarize the progress he had made since the semester had started. I was using that information to compliment him. He really seemed to enjoy the opportunity to reflect on his improvement.

Supervisor: What would the student say you need to do more of?

CSAP: Be sure I am addressing what he wants, such as asking if there are other issues going on. These situations often have multiple components and I need to check on that possibility.

7.10.3 CSAP Competencies

Whether the CSAP has clinical mental health training or not, all student affairs authorities must exhibit core competencies of the profession. The American College Personnel Association (ACPA) outlined professional competencies for this profession in a 2007 document approved by the ACPA Governing Board. These included Advising and Helping; Assessment, Evaluation, and Research; Ethics; Leadership and Administration/Management; Legal Foundations; Pluralism and Inclusion; Student Learning and Development; and Teaching. This professional organization believes that all employees who enter this field must have appropriate basic skills in these areas. The first competency (and the most relevant for supervision), Advising and Helping, is described as "skills related to providing support, direction, feedback, critique, and guidance to individuals and groups" (ACPA 2007, p. 6). For some CSAPs, this list encompasses their job description. In addition, within the context of each competency identified by ACPA, skills are broken down into basic, intermediate, and advanced levels.

The basic skills in the Advising and Helping area, as outlined by ACPA (2007), include a list of those qualities and abilities that successful CSAPs must master very early in their career. These include active listening skills, establishing rapport, understanding and using appropriate nonverbal communication, strategically and simultaneously pursuing multiple objectives in conversations with students, facilitating problem solving, challenging students and colleagues effectively, facilitating individual decision-making and goal-setting, encouraging students and colleagues effectively, and knowing and using referral sources.

Supervisors can use this basic skills list for goal-setting and evaluation of CSAPs, working supportively with professionals as they hone their skills in these critical areas. For entry-level CSAPs, skills are going to vary depending on previous experience, training, and aptitude. Supervisors need to be assessing individual skill development through formal and informal means to adequately ensure professional growth. Ideally, CSAPs will enter employment with the basic skills and quickly progress to mastering the intermediate and advanced skills. When CSAPs do not enter new positions with mastery of some of the intermediate or advanced skills, they may need training beyond what supervision can provide. For example, a group processes or group-counseling course might be needed to meet the standards as identified by ACPA (2007). Or, when a new CSAP enters the field without a career counseling course, appropriate training may be more easily completed through enrollment in an actual course as opposed to using supervision alone to teach a more advanced skill.

It is also important for supervisors to be aware of developing and emerging competencies for student affairs, as college experiences transform with societal changes. Certainly one critical example is the need for CSAPs to effectively understand and utilize technological applications. Those who supervise CSAPs must also have a strong understanding of the impact of technology on students' and professionals' experiences. For example, few college students are going to respond to a written survey about services provided in the college counseling center. However, students might respond to a brief, online survey that offers a small incentive such as drawing for a tablet or other cutting-edge technology.

Supervisors need to work with CSAPs as they explore, evaluate, and utilize various resources available on the college campus, including tutorial, disability, career, and mental health services. Assisting professionals as they create lists of these referral sources and contact information allows them to quickly access services often necessary for student emergencies and student/parent inquiries.

It is also important to realize that meetings with students are often a one-time event and follow-up may not be possible or even necessary. Some students have no desire for further meetings, as the initial appointment is often viewed as a punishment or an inconvenience that they would not attend if not required. In fact, enlisting the student's attendance at the first meeting may prove to be a monumental task requiring frequent rescheduling and reminders. As a result, supervisors need to work with the CSAP to view the first meeting as a single-session conference, with every effort made to enlist cooperation in developing collaborative goals and steps toward reaching those goals. This is in line with the statement by Steve de Shazer (Hoyt 1996, p. 61) that one should meet "as few sessions as possible and not one more than necessary."

7.10.4 Strength-Based Judicial Conversations (SBJC)

One application of the solution-focused approach in the college student affairs world is in the area of judicial conversations. Students who attend college may become involved in policy violations at some point in their academic careers. There is a notable lack of models in the student affairs profession on how to have an appropriate conversation with a student who has violated university policy, so supervisors must work with CSAPs on developing approaches that meet the university's requirements and build collaboration with students for the best possible outcomes. Meetings to discuss violations of policy are often challenging and uncomfortable for students and university personnel. Students are typically defensive or even angry, and the experience is stressful for all participants. This high stress level may be a direct result of the problem-focused nature of these meetings. Understandably, when a judicial conversation does not go well, the student may walk away with frustration and negative feelings toward not only the people involved but also toward the university in general. Once a student has a negative interaction with a judicial representative, it is likely that future interactions will be met with little enthusiasm as well.

Helping the CSAP identify specific exceptions within the context of a judicial meeting can produce a significantly positive effect. The solutions-building approach (De Jong and Berg 2001) views clients, or students in this case, as the experts on their experiences. Many times, students become less defensive and more receptive to open discussion when they have the chance to relate their versions of the events instead of experiencing interaction that is only problem or blame focused.

During judicial conversations, it is often helpful to view the student as an involuntary client. De Jong and Berg (2008) provide a number of extremely useful suggestions to prepare a CSAP encountering students who have mandated meetings to discuss activities violating current university policy. Professionals who work with mandated clients describe situations when clients choose to sit silently during initial meetings as some of the most difficult moments in the counseling/interviewing process. Supervision can prove invaluable for CSAPs who need to work toward goals involving patience and varied responses to silence.

By applying some of De Jong and Berg's (2008) ideas, the CSAP can significantly increase the likelihood of success when working with difficult students. Some of the major tenets outlined by De Jong and Berg (2008) include listening for who and what, using relationship questions to address context, giving appropriate control to the clients, getting more details about the client's understandings of the situation, and asking what the client wants from the meeting. One of the biggest challenges for CSAPs is to decrease the defensiveness of the student and prompt the student to begin talking about the situation. One tool supervisors can employ in this area is assisting CSAPs with the use of relationship questions. This happens when the CSAP asks students how persons with whom they have relationships might view the students' situation. Thus, students are not directly evaluating their own individual behaviors, which some students are not ready to do during judicial meetings; instead, they are asked for indirect opinions on their situations from the viewpoint of someone trusted. For example, if Johnny has been found drinking alcohol in his residence hall room, he may be reluctant to talk much about his alcohol use. By using relationship questions, the CSAP can ask Johnny something like, "If I were to ask your friend down the hall, what might he say happened that night?" This often creates openings for students in these difficult conversations.

Seeking students' viewpoints can be as simple as asking, "When we're finished here today, what do you hope will have happened?" Though often neglected, asking for students' wishes creates a more collaborative environment even if the outcome does not align with students' best hopes for the meeting.

Strengths-Based Judicial Conversations (SBJC) is a model for judicial meetings in college settings derived from a protocol developed by De Jong and Berg (2001) when working with clients in counseling. It consists of three stages: starting, investigating exceptions, and closure.

Stage One: Starting the Meeting

At the start of the meeting, the purpose(s) and goal(s) are discussed. Shortly after this introduction, the student should be given an opportunity to discuss his or her view of the current situation or incident. It is very important that the student feels his or her statements and perceptions are heard and understood. Following student comments and a staff member's acknowledgment of the student's perspective, the university judicial officer can move ahead into the second stage, investigating exceptions.

Stage Two: Investigation of Exceptions

In judiciary meetings, an exception would be defined as any time the student could have violated university policy but did not. For example, a simple opening question such as, "Tell me about some times that you resolved a problem with your roommate without fighting. How did you do that?" can initiate positive discussion. ("When my roommate was drinking one night, instead of staying in the room, I left and spent the night with a friend who wasn't partying.") This is an excellent way to include exceptions in the discussion regarding the violating behavior, which may help everyone move away from simple discipline toward developing a viable remediation plan.

One should obtain as many relevant exception examples as possible. This part of the conversation can then be followed by, "What would the person who referred you to Judicial Affairs (perhaps the resident assistant or hall director) need to see you do differently so he or she won't send you to this office again?" Posing the question in this manner allows the student to respond less defensively. By responding to these questions, students indicate exceptions to problems and generate options within their control that may help them avoid future violations and the negative consequences that accompany such behavior. This makes future challenges seem manageable and does not assume a future of hearing after hearing or even more dire consequences (e.g., probation or suspension from the university). The process points out specific, measurable steps toward a desired state of handling problem situations in ways that will not exacerbate them.

After exceptions are thoroughly explored and noted, a version of scaling questions can be introduced (Berg and de Shazer 1993). Perhaps the first thing to check through scaling is the student's confidence that he or she will not violate policy in the future: "On a scale of one to ten, how sure are you that you will not drink with your roommate again—if one means you're not at all sure and ten means you are completely confident?" Further questions can be utilized to build on this level of confidence and check to see if it is realistic. A student's response to the scaling question may be, "Well, I think I'm at about a seven; I don't want to get in trouble for drinking again, but I'm not ready to say for sure it won't happen again." This student response can be followed by, "A seven is great! What would make you even more confident by a point or two on the scale? What could you do to make it an eight or even a nine?" The purpose of follow-up scaling questions is to elicit responses that identify concrete steps toward positive options if the problem arises in the future. This again asks students to think ahead and have good choices within their frames of reference before it becomes necessary to choose these behavioral options.

Stage Three: Closure

The end of a judicial meeting typically focuses on the penalty or consequence of the policy violation (when applicable). As the meeting enters this stage, the CSAP should remember complimenting is a solution-focused strategy that can be very reinforcing in these student affairs situations. An example of complimenting in this situation is, "Several of your comments make me believe being successful in college is very important to you, especially your comment about how your little brother looks up to you." Compliments of this sort communicate respect for the student, demonstrate that the student was heard, and reinforce the assets the student brings to the situation. Finishing the meeting on a positive note is critical to the strengths-based judicial approach. Students who enter with apprehension will hopefully leave these meetings with a sense of being heard and valued. And, perhaps most important, they will walk out with clear plans, built around their personal strengths, to avoid future policy violations.

7.10.5 Academic Action Meetings

An academic action meeting, similar to a judicial action, occurs at the program or department level and enlists mandatory student attendance to discuss adverse student behaviors, including plagiarism or cheating, inappropriate behavior in class or class assignments, and a pattern of low grades or an overall low grade point average. Consequences of the behaviors range from lowering the student's grade to dismissal from the class with a failing grade to dismissal from the program or college/university. Some students do not realize the possible consequences of the meeting and approach the meeting with indifference. Others may be contrite and nervous, crying easily and overly concerned about the consequences rather than their inappropriate actions. Supervisors can set goals with CSAPs around several skills invaluable to such encounters, including taking a not-knowing stance, staying curious, complimenting, and scaling. The following case example demonstrates these SF skills in an academic action meeting, followed by some supervision dialogue between CSAP Mark, who is using a SF approach, and supervisor Shannon, who sat in on Mark's discussion with Sue.

Sue, a first-year student majoring in education, was reported to the college dean's office for acting unprofessionally while on visit to her assigned site, a local high school. Just out of high school, she invited two high school seniors to be her Facebook friends. When the supervising teacher overheard a discussion about Sue between the high school students, he reported the incident to the principal, who contacted the professor. The professor contacted the CSAP in the dean's office for appropriate college-level action. Mark then placed a call to Sue and asked her to come into his office to "discuss communication among everyone involved in her site placement," and she agreed to the meeting despite the vague premise.

Stage One: Starting the Meeting

Mark began the meeting with Sue by asking curiosity questions about how she perceived her classes were going and her adjustment to life at the university. Taking this not-knowing stance (De Jong and Berg 2008) allowed Mark to determine if Sue was aware of the problem as well as get a sense of Sue's strengths and resources. He asked Sue what she hoped to be doing in 5 years. Sue stated she wanted to be a math teacher in New Mexico, working with Native Americans on one of the many reservations. She discussed her own Native American heritage and her desire to give back to people who had not been as fortunate. Listening carefully, Mark complimented Sue on the clarity of her future goals and her commitment to others.

Throughout this conversation, it was evident Sue that did not understand the reason for the meeting, so Mark initiated a change in the conversation. He explained the concern about "friending" the high school students and asked Sue to provide her perspective on what happened. Sue began to describe the events and admitted asking the high school students to be her Facebook friends. She stated she was only 19 years old and the students were 18, which she said was not very different from where she was a year ago. Asking curiosity questions and taking the stance of "not-knowing" allowed Mark to maintain a nonjudgmental attitude and create a more open discussion without Sue becoming defensive.

Stage Two: Investigation of Exceptions

The next step led Mark to investigate exceptions including, "Who are some people you would *not* want to ask to be your Facebook friends?" She quickly talked about people she did not know well in addition to others she did not like, explaining that such associations could create problems and even be dangerous. Sue talked about people who had taken advantage of her, mentioning she had "unfriended" them from her Facebook page. As Sue continued to talk, it became evident that she struggled to make friends and develop appropriate relationships and boundaries, even with those her own age. Sue began to cry, stating she had transferred to the university several months earlier and had tried to make friends but was having difficulty fitting in. Mark was respectful, giving her time to calm herself and validating her struggle.

Using a notepad on the table, Mark then drew several concentric circles, with one in the middle and two larger circles around the smallest one. He wrote "Sue" in the middle circle. Then he asked the student to write the names of those who were closest to her in the next concentric circle and those who were not as close in the outermost circle. Mark asked her to decide if she felt comfortable with those who were in the circle closest to her. Discussion centered on what was and was not helpful about the closer relationships. Sue quickly discerned that two of her friends (both males) took advantage of her by pressuring her to write papers for them. Mark asked Sue, "When do you feel closer to your friends?" She stated that she felt closeness when she and her friends were just talking and doing activities together, not when she wrote their papers. Sue disclosed her fear of telling her friends "no" but agreed that writing papers for them was not helpful for her or for the young men who requested her assistance.

Mark then asked Sue if there were any names in the outer circle she would like to be able to move into the inner circle. She spoke of several students in her classes whose friendship she would enjoy. When asked, "What would have to happen for them to be in the inner circle?" she replied, "I will have to think about that. It may just take time for us to know each other better."

Once again, taking the not-knowing stance and treating Sue as the expert on her problem, Mark asked, "If you were a Facebook friend with one of your students, how might this affect your interactions with the student if you were the teacher?" Sue discussed the difficulties this might pose and how perceptions might lead to further problems with parents and administration. As this dialogue continued, Sue again began to cry, as she realized her inappropriate behavior and apologized for her actions. She stated, "I never thought about it being wrong, but I understand now."

7.10 Solution-Focused Supervision in a College Student Affairs Setting 259

At this point, Mark asked her a series of scaling questions (De Jong and Berg 2008). The first question was, "On a scale of one to ten, with '10' being appropriate and '1' being not appropriate, how appropriate is it to ask a student to be a Facebook friend?" Sue immediately answered, "1, or even a 0." He complimented her on her realization of the seriousness of the situation. Mark then asked her, "On a scale of one to ten, with '1' being this type of incident will never happen again and '10' being it is very likely you will do this again, how likely are you to violate personal boundaries with high school students?" Sue stated, she was "definitely a '1'" and articulated several examples of what violations might look like.

Stage Three: Closure

The end of the meeting involved a discussion of the academic warning write-up, who would and would not have access to it, and how future warnings could affect her (after three warnings, she could be dismissed from the program). Before the meeting was adjourned, Mark used the "compliment–bridge–task" (De Jong and Berg 2008) to compliment Sue on her focus on teaching and humanitarian goals while acknowledging the difficulty of making friends in a new place and learning how to shift from being a high school student to a college student. Sue was given the task to continue setting boundaries with friends and students. She was also given the name of a counselor at the university's mental health center who she might contact in the future to address concerns.

Sue's situation required Mark to take a nonjudgmental stance, looking at Sue's strengths and resources and not just her infraction. This allowed Sue to feel more comfortable in talking about her struggles as a student, to recognize her mistake without being defensive, and to be open to doing something different. This particular example illustrates the need to consider the developmental level of the student and also be aware of campus resources.

7.10.6 SF Supervision with Academic Actions

After Sue departed, Shannon and Mark met for supervision. Shannon commonly sat in on CSAP's meetings with students and followed them with a time of debriefing and reflection. This was Mark's first such meeting, so Shannon began by getting a sense of Mark's experience and complimenting him on several specific actions he took during the meeting. In addition to noting Mark's calm and pleasant approach, Shannon told him she admired his commitment to honesty about the seriousness of the complaint and the care he took to create change with the student while protecting the college, high school professionals, and the young students. Then they discussed Mark's specific goals around finding student strengths during the interviews, staying curious, and using visuals during meetings when it was appropriate to communicate more clearly. Shannon pointed out specific instances when he maintained curiosity, including Sue's volunteering of hypothetical situations that might cross boundaries at the high school. Shannon also asked questions about Mark's "friendship circles"—how he developed the idea, when he moved from level to level, and how he and Sue used the exercise to envision a future with a different "inner circle" of friends and values. She invited Mark's feedback on this supervision time, asking what was most helpful, most supportive, and most surprising. Mark responded with specifics regarding Shannon's helpfulness on his goals. He also said he felt supported when she complimented his validation and patience with the student. Finally, Mark said he was most surprised by how pleasant it was, given past supervisors' focus on "should haves" and what they saw were errors he needed to correct.

As a supervisor with CSAPs, focusing continually on what strengths the professional sees in the student is of paramount importance. Through this lens, the questions flow smoothly and students gradually shift from seeing themselves as failing and unsuccessful to persons who can succeed. The supervisor's main focus should be on the lens through which CSAPs view the students and the successes experienced in the meetings.

7.10.7 Conclusion

Solution-focused supervision fits well in a college student affairs setting. The solution-focused principles work well with those trained to provide traditional therapy in a college or university setting. In addition, the approach works with those who serve in different capacities, such as academic advisors or housing officials, who are not typically trained to provide mental health therapy. CSAPs who provide supervision need to be knowledgeable about existing student development theories plus the skills and attributes new professionals often bring to their positions. By encouraging CSAPs to follow a strength-based model when holding judicial conversations, academic action meetings, or other student intervention encounters, a more positive outlook with collaborative short- and long-term goals can easily be developed.

7.11 Supervision Family Intervention Workers in the UK

John Wheeler

7.11.1 Historical Background

Family intervention raises many challenges in the UK, both for families and those who work with them. "An Englishman's home is his castle" is one of many culturally based and culture-defining sayings that speak to parents' expectations of privacy from state intrusion. Family intervention in the UK has mainly arisen from two concerns: concern for the safety of children and concern for their future prospects.

Unintended consequences of some early initiatives have been well documented as when large numbers of children living in poverty were sent to Canada and Australia for what were meant to be better lives. Attempts to keep children safe have evolved into legislation empowering authorities to remove children from their parents. Currently, the UK has a child protection system that has developed through several pendulum swings between the positions of keeping children safe and respecting the rights of parents. Despite attempts to promote child protection services as being there to help and support, many families living in difficult circumstances still see the "welfare" as only being interested in "taking your kids away."

Current thinking on family intervention is partly informed by professionals wanting to help children enjoy the best possible adult lives and partly informed by the way politicians decide to fund the services in which such professionals work. Market economy influences on social care have led successive governments to become increasingly aware of the cost to the economy of families who are not functioning well. Children who are not parented well are seen as being at risk of becoming adults who are a cost to the economy through, for example, criminal behavior, substance abuse, unemployability, relationship difficulties, and mental health issues. Various government initiatives at different times have led to a series of attempts to ensure that services recognize the signs of children not developing well so something can be done. The Communities and Neighbourhoods Department of the UK government has recently voiced particular concern over "troubled families," which are defined as follows:

> A troubled family is one that has serious problems - including parents not working, mental health problems, and children not in school - and causes serious problems, such as crime and anti-social behaviour. All of which costs local services a lot of time and money routinely responding to these problems. (Communities and Neighbourhoods Department 2012)

A figure of 120,000 "troubled families" has been established by using research that identified the proportion of families suffering from at least five of the following characteristics: no one in the family is employed; living in poor or overcrowded housing; no parent has any qualifications; mother has mental health problems; at least one parent has a longstanding illness, disability, or infirmity; low income; or an inability to afford a number of food or clothing items. Government data collected in October and November 2011 led to a calculation that these 120,000 families were costing the country £9 billion ($14 billion USD) a year, or £75,000 ($117,000 USD) per family. The manner in which these families have been spoken about says much about how they are viewed by those in power.

> It is unacceptable to leave the children in these families to lead the same disruptive and harmful lives as their parents. The Government believes that these and all families should have the same aspirations to education and employment. We owe it to these families and to their local communities not to excuse their behaviour but to demand that they change their ways. (Communities and Neighbourhoods Department 2012)

7.11.2 Challenges Facing Family Intervention Workers

Government expectations that the "troubled families" change fall heavily on the shoulders of those who work with them. My experience of supervising those who endeavor to do this work has brought to my attention some key challenges practitioners often face along the way.

- Early Intervention Is Not Necessarily Easy
  Many family intervention initiatives in the UK have been based on an assumption that signs of children being in difficulty can be noticed at an early stage in the development of these difficulties and that it should therefore be quite easy to bring about change. In actuality, family intervention initiatives have often brought practitioners into contact with families struggling with complex difficulties, presentations that would be a challenge to the most skilled practitioners. Family intervention services typically find they have to contend with a substantial degree of complexity.
- Families Who Don't Trust Services
  While family intervention initiatives are often seen as a new attempt to bring about change, professional involvement is often not a new experience for the families. Many describe their prior experience of professionals in negative terms: professionals who made judgments about them, professionals who criticized them, and professionals who took actions they did not like or at times even understand. Many practitioners in family intervention services have to work very hard to establish an engagement in which they are trusted and on the basis of which they can work with the family to bring about change.
- Families Who Are Not Trusted by the Services Who Know Them
  Where families have a history of involvement with services, their identity has often been constructed in negative terms. Their failure to engage with services they don't trust is often taken as evidence of their inability to change. Words and phrases such as "resistant," "in denial," and "disguised compliance" frequently attach to the families both in conversations about them and in reports on them. Family intervention workers often face the challenge of seeing beyond the labels, especially at times when family behavior seems to confirm the validity of the descriptions.
- Practitioner's Sense of Competence
  The complexity of the families' difficulties, the families' mistrust, and deficiency-focused descriptions combine to create for family intervention workers an almost impossible task. Despite this, skilled workers often know the importance of making a start in complex situations by working on what the family wants help with. They often know by being interested, respectful, and reliable, trust can sometimes be earned. Believing that people are bigger than the problems they come with is also important. However, when workers make a start on an issue the family is willing to work on, they are at risk of being criticized by other services for not dealing with what are seen to be more serious concerns. When workers begin gaining some trust, they are at risk of being seen by other services as having

been taken in. When workers discover small signs of competence, they are at risk of being seen by other services as being naïve. Workers can also be at risk of their own self-evaluations. *Am I just tinkering at the edges? Is the family really engaging with me? Is this small improvement actually significant?*

7.11.3 What Does SF Supervision Have to Offer?

As a supervisor, I carry a fervent belief and hope that supervision conversations can make a difference. I find this is more likely to happen when my supervision conversations are underpinned by the following assumptions:

"Assumptions about supervisees"

- "Supervisees want the best for their clients" (Wheeler, J. 2007, p. 353): Solution-focused supervision can help family intervention workers hold on to their best intentions.
- "Supervisees are likely to be already doing something that clients find valuable" (p. 353): Solution-focused supervision can help family intervention workers realize what this might be.
- "Supervisees are likely to have hidden talents" (p. 353): Solution-focused supervision can help family intervention workers recognize what it is they bring to the work that might be different from previous professional involvements.
- "Most supervisees underestimate the value of their work" (p. 353): Solution-focused supervision can help family intervention workers take a more balanced perspective on their work.
- "There's always more to learn" (p. 354): Solution-focused supervision can help family intervention workers continue their professional development.

"Assumptions about supervision"

- "Supervision can contribute something useful to the supervisee's practice" (p. 354): Solution-focused supervision can help family intervention workers take something back to the work that might make a difference.
- "The supervisor's focus of interest can have a big impact on the supervisee and his/her practices" (p. 354): Solution-focused supervision can help the supervisor be aware of the balance in the conversation between constructive and deficit ways of thinking about the worker's identity, the families, and colleagues.
- "Descriptions of clients can powerfully influence the supervisee's expectations of the client and his/her ability to work usefully with them" (p. 355): Solution-focused supervision can help family intervention workers be aware of how they are constructing family identities and choose frames that are more conducive to constructive engagements.

"Assumptions about therapeutic practice"

- "Therapeutic practice is worth doing" (p. 355): Solution-focused supervision can help family intervention workers remember that even if nothing has worked before, something might work now.
- "Most practitioners can adjust their style of practice to match the client's style of cooperation" (p. 355): Solution-focused supervision can help family intervention workers reflect on times they have found a good fit with a family and what they might need to do for this to happen more often.
- "Solution-focused supervision isn't just for solution-focused practitioners" (p. 355): Solution-focused supervision can equip the supervisor to support family intervention workers drawing on a range of models.

"Assumptions about clients"

- "Clients have done the best they could with their lives so far, but with finely tuned help from the supervisee, there might be more they could do" (p. 356): Solution-focused supervision can help family intervention workers engage with families on the basis that people have good reasons for doing what they've done and invite families to be more proactive in how they deal with challenges.
- "The client who keeps meeting the supervisee has some sort of an agenda for change and possibly some belief that the supervisee might be able to help" (p. 356): Solution-focused supervision can help family intervention workers identify the family's agenda and engage with what the family wants to create as a platform for change.

When supervision is underpinned by assumptions like these, supervision conversations can make a significant difference to some or all of the challenges typically facing family intervention workers, helping workers in particular to:

- Maintain and remember realistic goals for the work
- Notice exceptions to deficit-focused identities
- Evaluate the work with the family and notice signs of engagement
- Discover new frames for viewing the family which might influence how the family is viewed by other services
- Recognize their own competence

7.11.4 Options for the Supervisor

At its simplest, the supervisor who is in conversation with a family intervention worker has three options: say nothing and carry on listening, select from what the worker has said, or step in.

7.11.4.1 Say Nothing and Carry On Listening

Saying nothing and carrying on listening does not necessarily mean nothing of significance is happening. Providing workers with undivided attention can allow them to develop their thinking as they describe the family and the work to the supervisor. Accounts of practice in supervision are not just from the practitioner, they are informed uniquely by the teller and what the teller knows about the listener. The way the worker describes the family and her/his work with them to the supervisor is likely to differ from (for example) what they would say to a police officer or child protection colleague. Influenced by the first rule of brief therapy, "If it ain't broke don't fix it" (Berg and Miller 1992, p. 17), I often find myself listening in admiration to workers' descriptions of families and the work.

In the following account, a health practitioner working for a family intervention team started to describe her work with a parent who had told blatant lies to professionals but also wanted her daughter to tell the truth to her:

> The interesting work has been that, in meetings with professionals, the way that the parent communicates is through lying. So lying, and I don't like that word, there was dishonesty in absolutely everything. It's almost as though dishonesty has become part and parcel of how she communicates, so it's become an established pattern.

What do you admire about this account? For me there were signs that the practitioner was aware of the potential power of the word "lying" and how it might affect her engagement with the parent. I also saw signs she was taking an interactional perspective, a frame that might open up more possibilities of choice for the parent than an individualistic one. While I was saying nothing at the time, I hope my nonverbal communications would have been conveying, "This is very promising, keep going."

When supervising family intervention workers, I often say nothing in an encouraging sort of way when I hear language that is honest and respectful, ideas that open up possibilities of change, signs of curiosity, signs of hope, or attempts to come up with something that might work. All can make a difference to the engagement with the family, a change in how the family is viewed by other services, and the worker's sense of competence.

7.11.4.2 Select from What the Worker Has Said

De Jong, Bavelas, and Korman (in process), through microskills analysis of interviews, have noted that solution-focused interviewers select from what the client has said in a manner consistent with the assumptions underpinning the approach. Influenced by the second rule of brief therapy, "If it works do more of it" (Berg and Miller 1992, p. 17), I find solution-focused tools often help generate fresh thinking, which can make a difference to the engagement with the family, the work with the family, how the family is seen by other services, and workers' sense of their own competence.

The solution-focused approach provides a number of tools that can be very relevant to the supervision of family intervention workers:

- Clarifying realistic outcomes that make sense to the family, other services, and the worker.

  What do the family members want from their involvement with the service? How would other services be able to tell that sufficient change has happened in the family?

How would you be able to tell that your work with the family has been worthwhile?

- Noticing strengths in the family, the worker, the work they do together, and small signs of other services seeing family strengths.
- Exceptions that exemplify family strengths, what the worker does well, what is going well in the work, and what other services do well.

    What do the family/parents do well?
    What's the best you've managed so far in your work with the family?
    What would the family or you say have been the best parts of the work so far?
    Which service has been able to contribute something useful to how the family is managing?

- The Miracle Question, which can identify small changes that would make a difference in the family, the work with the family, the worker's sense of competence, and the connections between the family and other services.

    Suppose a miracle happened in the family; what would be the first sign?
    Suppose a miracle happened in your work with the family; next time you see them, how would you be able to tell?
    Suppose a miracle happened for you; what would be different in your work?
    Suppose a miracle happened and the connections between the family and other services were transformed for the better; what would be the first sign this had happened?

- Scaling questions which help offer a perspective on how the family is functioning, the worker's sense of competence, and the connections between the family and other services. Diagram 7.1 shows how scaling was used to help a worker evaluate variations with a family over a number of sessions. At a time when the worker was preoccupied by difficulties in engagement, the wider view gave an opportunity to reflect on what had contributed to the better engagement at an earlier stage in the work, which in turn generated ideas about how to address the current challenge.

    On a scale of 0 to 10, how would you say the family is managing now? How has this varied since you've known them? What helps to explain the highest number? If the number was one higher now, how would you be able to tell?
    On a scale of 0 to 10, how capable do you feel of being able to help the family bring about change? How has this number changed over time? What helps to explain the highest number? If the number was one higher, how would you be able to tell?
    On a scale of 0 to 10, how do other services evaluate how the family is managing?

Different services can have different numbers and this can be mapped out.

What do the highest numbers correspond to? What would services need to see for them to believe the number was one higher?

As the supervision developed, the practitioner reflected on a meeting with professionals in which the mother denied something that was clearly true:

She completely constructs this differently, which led to professionals continuing to think that she can't change.

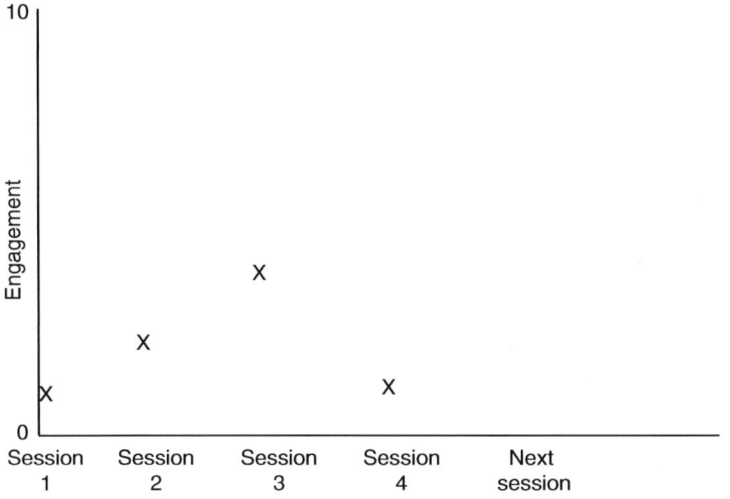

Diagram 7.1 Worker's evaluation of engagement with family over time

Seeing this as the recognition of a pattern, I commented:

So this is a pattern you see, that when she constructs it this way, this is what happens.

This prompted her to reflect:

This is what happens, professionals don't believe her. And then it's, well, can she change? And I thought, well that's a great pity for the amount of work we've done, and then I thought, this presents a golden opportunity because I've seen it in action. It's something I've been party to.

At this stage of the supervision it was unclear where recognition of this pattern of interaction would take us; nonetheless, I judged that viewing the mother this way rather than as a liar was more likely to contribute to the practitioner's engagement, a difference in how the mother was viewed by professionals, and perhaps even a way of bringing about change. I complimented with this in mind, hoping it would help sustain this novel way of thinking about what had been observed:

Yes, indeed. And it also strikes me that you are naming that sequence in a very open way ... she constructs this event that way and that results in those responses by the professionals and that then leads into the question of whether she can change.

7.11.4.3 Step In

Influenced by the third rule of brief therapy, "If it doesn't work, do something different" (Berg and Miller 1992, p. 17), on occasion I find myself stepping in when supervising family intervention workers, hoping to take the conversation in a different direction. I typically do this for the following reasons:

- The way the worker is talking is likely to reduce her/his sense of competence.
- The description of what's happening in the family has raised concerns for me over the safety of children.
- The way the worker is constructing the family's identity is likely to compound difficulties in engagement.
- The way the worker is talking about other services is likely to position the intervention efforts in opposition to other services and reduce the likelihood of the intervention efforts contributing to a different viewing of the family by other services.

The practitioner went on to reflect on the challenge of making sure the work she does with the mother actually makes a difference to how she engages with other services and how she is viewed by them. I commented:

It's a challenge, isn't it?

To which she replied:

It's a real challenge. It just seems so massive; at times it feels overwhelming.

What ideas do you think the practitioner might have been having about her professional competence at this point in the conversation? I was worried that if we didn't find a way to move forward, the practitioner who left the supervision to continue her work might have less to draw on to believe that she could make a difference. While it was clearly difficult to figure out a way forward in the complexity of the work, I assumed we might at least be able to do something in the supervision that could turn out to be useful and asked: *So what else might you get from supervision around this that might be useful?*

This prompted her to reflect:

I think as I'm talking about it, it seems that the work we are doing is systemic work, it's trying to think about... it's not just about this bit of work we are doing, it's about thinking about it in a wide way, and it's about relationships and communications. But the helpful bit would be, it's almost like honest communication from us to her, but also how she sees honesty. What is honesty?

The change in the practitioner's energy was evident, giving me a sense that curiosity, creativity, and hope had returned to the conversation.

Sometimes the family intervention worker is the only person external to the family who is aware that children are at significant risk of harm. Risk of harm is not an either/or phenomenon, however. Solution-focused supervision can help provide a frame for workers to locate their concerns on a spectrum ranging from "so worrying that a referral to child protection services must be made straight away" to "this is worrying but referral is not needed and further work might improve matters." A well-established framework for assessing safety and planning work with families, drawing on solution-focused thinking, has been developed by Turnell and Edwards (1999). The key elements of the Signs of Safety framework are shown in Diagram 7.2.

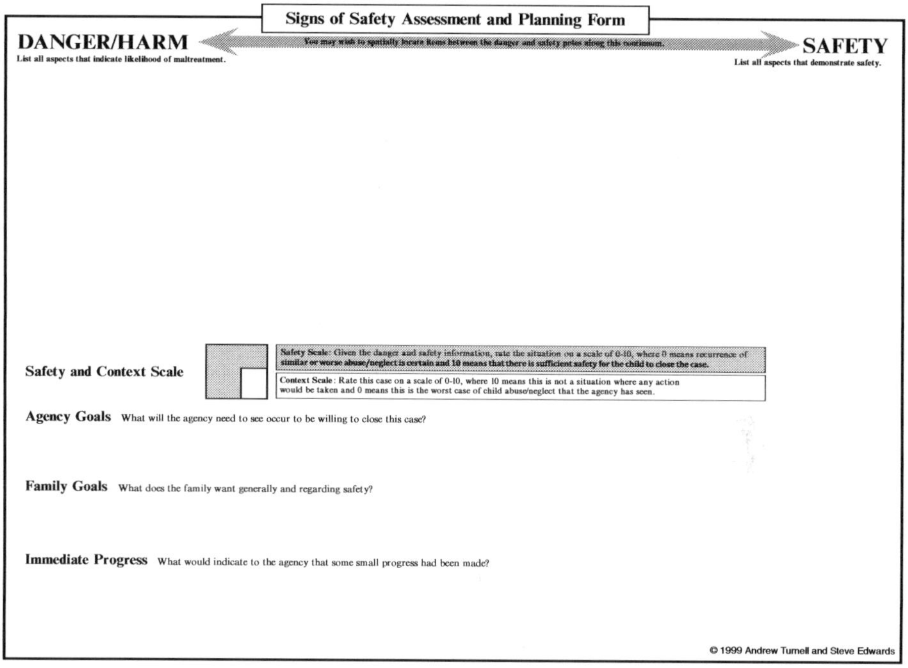

7.11 Supervision Family Intervention Workers in the UK

Diagram 7.2 Signs of Safety Assessment and Planning Form (©1999 Andrew Turnell and Steve Edwards, used with permission)

The Danger/Harm part of the framework gives practitioners an opportunity to identify why they are concerned now, in factual terms that could be explained to the carers.[8] In complex presentations, practitioners are easily overwhelmed by worrying information. Turnell has found in practice, however, that some of the information is best understood as "complicating factors." "What in particular is causing you to be worried about this child now?" can sometimes help the practitioner isolate the most significant source of his/her concern.

The safety aspect of the framework provides an opportunity for the supervisor to help the worker identify strengths in the family, its support network, and connections to services. Asking, "What are the strengths that contribute to safety in this family?" helps the practitioner notice strengths that are in place and helps workers be clear about whether a particular strength actually contributes to safety. A parent taking medication for mental health issues, for example, may or may not contribute to safety depending on the effect it has on parenting.

When dangers and strengths have been mapped out, the practitioner is then presented with two scales. The context scale helps the practitioner take account of how familiar she/he is with the presentation. The safety scale helps the practitioner

---

[8] Carers is the term conventionally used in the UK as an inclusive wording to cover parents, grandparents, and so on.

locate her/his concerns between two extreme points where 10 represents enough safety to close the case and 0 represents a judgment that the dangers will continue. Asking what services need to see to close the case helps generate ideas about positively defined outcomes. Asking what the family wants reminds the practitioner to seek family members' views. Asking what would be a first sign of progress helps the practitioner think in a focused and realistic way about action planning with the family to identify changes that could increase other services' confidence in the family.

Practitioners working in services involved with families who experience multiple challenges develop many ways of naming the families and how they act. Naming contributes to identity construction in ways that may or may not keep a space open to engage with curiosity and attend to client accounts with what Eve Lipchik (1988) has called a constructive ear. Negative namings can easily change from being a way of thinking to incontrovertible truths that close down the possibility of change. Mindful of such possibilities, I step in when I hear words such as "manipulative," "attention seeking," "damaged," and "dysfunctional."

Supervision offers an opportunity for practitioners to generate a choice of ways of viewing families and a richer vocabulary to draw on when talking about them:

When the parent acts in ways that people would call manipulative, what do you think she is hoping to achieve? What do you think might be some good reasons for acting in these ways, from her point of view? If you were in her shoes and acted in such ways, how might you explain yourself to someone who was sympathetic?
What other words could be used to describe a parent who acts in these ways for these reasons? Out of all the words we might use, which one would most help you engage with the family with curiosity and some degree of hope?

When practitioners engage constructively with families who have had a negative experience of other services, there is a risk of positioning themselves in stark opposition to other services who are still seeing the family in negative terms. At worst this can lead to practitioners becoming champions for the family or trying to convince other services their evaluations of the family are wrong. In my experience, this seldom leads to positive change and often makes matters worse, especially if the practitioner's behavior is understood by other services as further evidence of the family's manipulation. Given that assessment can be thought of as a dynamic process, I am much more interested in helping practitioners help families make changes that make a difference to how they are viewed by other services.

What would be the smallest sign to the child protection worker that something is changing for the better in the family?
Which service would take most convincing that the family is making progress in their work with you? What would they need to see to believe this?
Which service is starting to notice changes that are happening in the family as a result of the work you have been doing together? What could you and that service contribute to meetings with other services that might catch people's attention and perhaps even make them curious?

7.11.5 Conclusion

Family intervention workers can face difficult challenges when working with families with multiple difficulties. Supervision provides an essential opportunity for workers to reflect on the work and plan ways to move forward. The solution-focused approach provides supervisors with many possibilities for helping workers do the best they can.

The supervision with the practitioner continued as follows with me as supervisor saying nothing or selecting and stepping in at various points and both of us struggling together until something useful emerged.

JW: *My instincts are taking me into wondering how this might be named differently. Is there a terminology that might be useable that she would be comfortable with and that would help other professionals think, yes this is another way of understanding what's going on here....*

Practitioner : *Oh yeah.*

JW: *But you've got this interactional take on what happens there. You've seen the patterns. I don't know what the naming would be, but if there could be a lighter way of naming it, that nonetheless speaks to what is happening, so it's honest, but it might make it easier for her to say, "Oh, I've done such and such again, if that happened it would take me straight to doing such and such." And perhaps for professionals, the services allied with you over this work, another way of viewing what would otherwise be called lying.....*

P: *And I quite like that idea... I suppose I got quite caught up in that idea that it's her relationship with how she communicates and the way she communicates when she's under duress is that she needs to cover up things.*

JW: *Like a stress reaction you could say? When she feels under attack, which makes lying more of an attraction. And it's a pattern which mainly happens in these situations. ...*

P: *Yeah, and I think it's about being mindful of the process of change as well. In that different ways of communicating can take a little while to embed in, because she's been so used to...*

JW: *So for this mother she would have to develop different ways of dealing with stress or different ways of dealing with being criticized?... There could be a scale, 10 would be acceptable ways of responding to stress and criticism and 0 is completely unacceptable. Just to give us a bit of play with the scale, where do you feel she is on this scale, given the whole range of things parents have done when they've felt under stress or felt criticized, given that some parents have done more extreme things than tell lies, some have taken workers hostage or attacked someone with a knife and so on.*

P: *I'm thinking of three.*

JW:	*So, we know that although this is frustrating enough, problematic enough, there are worse things parents do. So there might be small steps forward, because you were saying it would take a while to develop new ways.*
P:	*And she has developed, she is thinking about it. Whereas when I first started working with her, she would fill the space with anything and everything. So the process of her thinking has slowed right down and she can identify; she's starting to be able to reflect and identify times when she's felt under stress and I think that shows insight.*
JW:	*I think what that's taking you into is, I think you are sensitive to small signs of progress. Instead of blurting out a blatant lie, she stops and thinks and that's different from just blurting out a blatant lie… She's at least thinking about interaction and the implications of interaction. "Other people are going to react to what I say next, so I'd better stop and think about this." So I don't know how a frame like that might be useful in your work with her or indeed with other professionals. You know how in Signs of Safety there's the question, "What's the smallest sign of progress?"*
P:	*Yes, I think that's a really good question. And that could be good to use with another service with the mother there….I met with a colleague who used to know the mother a long time ago and she felt for her just to stop and consider her lying was an absolutely massive improvement.*
JW:	*So she's seen the significance of that. So maybe there's something of a project here that other professionals can be recruited to work on with you and the mother.*

As the discussion drew to a natural conclusion, the practitioner decided she was in a better place to continue her work with the family and other services. What do you think are the differences that might have made a difference in the practitioner's work with the family and connection to other services?

When the practitioner looked back on the supervision, she reflected that the conversation had made a difference for her in the following ways:

> Supervision provided me with the reflective space to consider the meanings and use of language within a therapeutic relationship between the client, myself (as a therapist) and the wider professional system (Anderson 1997; Anderson and Goolishian 1992). The exploration of the word "lying" helped me to consider the client's position and the importance of contextualising language and sharing the meaning within the therapeutic relationship, family and professional system (McNamee and Gergen 1992). Through the course of supervision I became more attuned to the importance of ethical practice and my ethical positioning (Tomm 1992). Attention to the detail of ethics and ethical posturing helped me to think systemically and provided me with a scaffold for ethical practice (White 2007). Supervision opened up my thinking to the wider context of our work, increasing my learning and development, particularly within the use of language with family, community and professional systems (Vygotsky 1986). The scaling question was taken back to the team and led to lively discussions about how language is used and the influence this may have. We discussed in

particular how scaling questions can be used within our conversations rather than as a stand-alone technique, to enrich and create different conversations (Burnham 1993). The scale enabled us to think about how we talk, in particular with other professionals in these highly complex situations, and how our conversations can assist in opening rather than closing down possibilities for families (White and Epston 1990).

Having now heard from supervisor and supervisee, what will you take from your reading of this contribution into the supervision you offer?

Chapter 8
Concluding Thoughts on SF Supervision

> *"Beauty is truth, truth beauty,"* - that is all ye know on earth, and all ye need to know.
>
> ~ John Keats

8.1 Whither Supervision

The influence of SF approaches is underestimated. In many ways it has become mainstream, showing up in best-selling books on change being read by the leadership in Washington, DC (Heath and Heath 2010), as well as being cited in runaway best-selling novels:

> …I am much more concerned with the future and getting Christian to a place where he wants to be. The technical term is SFBT…that stands for Solution-Focused Brief Therapy. Essentially, it's goal oriented. We concentrate on where Christian wants to be and how to get him there…There's no point in breast-beating about the past - all that's been picked over by every physician, psychologist, and psychiatrist Christian's ever seen. We know why he's the way he is, but it's the future that's important. (James 2012, p. 412)

But popularity is not truth, nor does it determine value. I believe people overreach many times when promoting models or approaches. Some commit their professional (or even personal) lives to endorsing particular ways of thinking, resulting in their credibility being stretched thin. Others even act deceptively, directing us to watch the staged presentation but bristling when we try to look behind the curtain. Whether one is postmodernist or modernist, evidence based or experiential, promoting a viewpoint should not involve prohibiting careful examination by others. At the same time, proponents of opposing views should not dismiss my own based only on their private evaluative criteria. Before you leave this paragraph completely confused, let me attempt to clarify with a few examples and then bring it back to SF supervision.

Research supports the idea that therapists who believe in their model or approach are more likely to positively impact their clients' process of change (Duncan, Miller, and

Sparks 2004). In addition, SFBT has shown effectiveness in an increasing number of research studies (Franklin, Trepper, McCollum, and Gingerich 2012). However, to claim SFBT is just as or even more effective than other psychotherapy models simply invites criticism—it cannot be supported by evidence the scientific community would accept. "Despite strong beliefs to the contrary,…currently the evidence indicates that solution-focused therapy is only modestly effective" (Sommers-Flanagan 2012). The best we can say is that SFBT has demonstrated effectiveness in certain studies… period. So, to overreach and promote SF practices as "more" or "better" or "proven to be" gives critics the ammunition they need to dismiss these approaches entirely.

It is also disingenuous to ignore or reject honest questioning. I'm not talking about attacks on a person or approach, which should be handled as attempts to provoke rather than addressed as authentic inquiry; I'm referring to sincere curiosity from inside and outside the SF circle. An honorable response to inquiry is dialogue, not control or suppression. Unless one believes in a received view of truth regarding mental health, change, or psychotherapy, which cannot be questioned (e.g., the source of one's perspective is divine), responses to those questioning our assumptions and practices should be marked by hospitality.

Supervision practices and their importance in the field of psychotherapy have been built on ideas more than research. To dismiss these formative concepts simply because some person or group declares there isn't enough empirical evidence to support the premises must be viewed as a promotion of a philosophy, not as a statement of truth. I am in agreement with Slife and his colleagues: "Although we favor evidence-based research to justify the use of therapeutic treatments, we dispute the notion that there is only one particular philosophy of science to provide this evidence" (Slife, Wiggins, and Graham 2005, p. 84). Although they are writing about therapy, I believe the same premise applies to examining supervision. "The philosophy of empiricism has served science well" (Slife et al. 2005, p. 85), but promoting empiricism as the final arbiter of truth while relegating all other approaches of inquiry to the fringes significantly reduces the variety of potentially useful notions about supervision and the data we can examine. In dynamic tension with the idea that there are many paths to evaluating therapeutic and supervisory competence is the rejection of "anything goes." The ethical standards of nonmaleficence ("do no harm") and beneficence ("benefitting the other") must prevail in supervision (Kitchener 1984). Simply assuming an educational or training program provides "enough" to ensure therapist competence is wrong and dangerous. Holding firmly to a philosophical position does not establish truth, and merely declaring someone capable based on a certificate or diploma will not stand up to scrutiny from the profession, regulatory bodies, government, or the public.

8.2 SF Supervision and Ethics (See Sects. 3.5 and 6.2.1)

Supervision is not therapy, but it is also neither a consultation business nor training. Most supervision of mental health professionals is regulated by national, state, or provincial governments and subject to oversight, and regulation almost always designates appropriate and inappropriate behavior. In addition to minimal ethical standards required by governing bodies (what one must or cannot do in this role), each supervisor has personal notions regarding ethical behavior for the supervision context. This may include assumptions about one's obligations, such as serving as a role model for the novice therapist. A personal ethical stance may also address confidentiality, informed consent, and managing multiple roles as well as other requirements beyond minimum standards (Barnett, Cornish, Goodyear, and Lichtenberg 2007; Pettifor, McCarron, Schoepp, Stark, and Stewart 2011).

One aspect of supervision that is not isomorphic to therapy is evaluating or assessing competence (Morgan and Sprenkle 2007). "If therapists have 'no privileged position or neutral vantage point from which to observe or practice' (Parry 1991, p. 39), then the same is true for supervisors" (Flemons, Green, and Rambo 1996, p. 45). If one's supervision context requires evaluation, then an ethical SF supervision approach to assessing competence would align with its guidelines and practices. Since I believe a thorough examination of therapeutic competence is beyond the scope of this book, I will reference some ideas here and direct attention to a few excellent resources that may assist in the development of assessment approaches consistent with a SF supervision stance.

First, Flemons et al. (1996) carefully created and researched an evaluation schema for university settings that can inform many contexts. Their intent was to form an approach that could be valuable to therapists and supervisors rather than simply attempting to maintain objectivity and meet external standards. Their relational method outlined key values regarding context, responsibility, and sensitivity. They also took experience into account, tailoring the evaluation to each therapist's level of expertise. Finally, they committed themselves to continual examination of the evaluation scheme itself, using several highly regarded qualitative research methodologies to "help us in the ongoing process of assessing the *trustworthiness* of our evaluation method" and "make our evaluation method more *credible, transferable, dependable, and confirmable*" (p. 48, emphasis in original). The results of their work cover such varied areas of practice as professionalism, sensitivity, and larger system issues. This scheme also includes evaluation ideas very relevant to SF supervision addressing curiosity, being tentative, promoting respect, avoiding pathologizing, acting systemically, setting goals, and developing skills. I refer the reader to this wonderfully crafted article for ideas to inform assessment and evaluation, whatever your context.

Second, Fine and Turner (Fine and Turner 1997; Turner and Fine 1995) have written clear and comprehensive publications on collaborative postmodern supervision that include evaluation concepts and practices. Their discussion of power in the supervisory relationship (Fine and Turner 1997) outlines premises regarding hierarchy and judgment that are quite applicable to SF supervision. (I adapted their distinctions on power from the 1997 chapter to create the overlapping systems diagram found in Sect. 2.1.) Practices found in both of their documents include the consideration of relative talk time (to reduce hierarchy), parallel goal setting, transparency in the process, disclaimers, and notions on offering ideas tentatively but as clearly as possible. The entire Fine and Turner (1997) chapter is framed by ethical considerations and is worthy of consideration as SF supervisors develop assessment procedures and policies, and the Turner and Fine (1995) article is written to assist postmodern supervisors as they juxtapose evaluation and expertise.

8.3 Cautions Regarding SF Supervision

Inspired by Cade's (1992) article, "I Am an Unashamed Expert," I have come to view myself as somewhat of an expert on what does *not* work in supervision and what can become dangerous practices in SF supervision. This list did not come without someone's pain and suffering—mine, other supervisors, and therapists—because, like so many things in life, it sometimes takes hammering your thumb or stepping on a Lego© to really solidify one's learning. Being a second-born child, I also learn from watching others' successes and failures—I'm certain my older brother, Mark, had many more scars by age eighteen than I because I had the luxury of secondhand learning. There may be easier paths to enlightenment regarding what doesn't work in supervision, but these are some of the lessons I have gathered on the path I have walked and observed. Here is my brief list of limitations and erroneous assumptions in SF supervision (or, in most cases, any approach to supervision).

8.3.1 "Delusions of Certainty" (Hubble and O'Hanlon 1992) or, "SF Is the Answer—What's the Question?"

> *All theoretical models and therapeutic strategies are inherently limited and will generate their share of impossibility when repetitively applied.*
>
> ~ Duncan, Hubble, and Miller 1997, p. 10

Early in my psychotherapy education, I began employing principles from the therapy context in conversations with my wife. It didn't take long for Lori to tire of my overextension. She once (and only once) said, "No shrink stuff in this house"…and we've lived more authentic lives because of it.

Some professionals overextend the SF metaphor, liberally using superlatives ("best," "most," etc.) in their descriptions. Some even attempt to generalize the approach far beyond the contexts in which it was created and developed. Every philosophy, model, theory, and approach has limitations. Every. Single. One. Life will not be reduced to SF constructs—love, relationship, faith, art, and goodness cannot be diminished and understood using SF ideas alone. The SF approach is not a way of living, although one might apply principles of SF in some areas of day-to-day life. SF approaches have limits because some aspects of life are not amenable to influence—some things simply cannot be controlled or persuaded toward change. In addition, not everything in life *should* be questioned or deconstructed (Ellis 1989). A SF approach is not the "best" way to live because (1) no such approach exists, and (2) every model or philosophy has limitations.

> While solution-focused therapy involves socially constructing new stories for clients' lives, it does not require—or even emphasize—that the new stories address and explain *every* aspect of clients' lives. Questions about the intellectual and political concerns of therapy

and about actual therapy practice involve very different issues. It is important that we keep these differences in mind. Practical questions about therapy focus on clients' desires for change, and therapists' responsibility to work with clients in constructing change. This is what clients pay their therapists to do. It is the therapists' job (Miller and de Shazer 1998, pp. 365–367, emphasis added).

Miller and de Shazer's ideas about therapy apply to supervision as well. Changes take place in therapists' lives that cannot be addressed by SF approaches, and SF has no theory to account for or influence such changes. These include physical changes due to aging or disease, existential struggles, and other aspects of living that cannot be reduced to ideas around scales, miracles, or exceptions. No approach to therapy or supervision—SF or other—should be forced on anyone as a life philosophy or cure-all. It has usefulness within certain contexts and that makes it potentially valuable, but the SF approach, including supervision, is not the Holy Grail.

8.3.2 *"The Unsolicited Lecture (Especially When Given 'for Your Own Good!')" (Cade 1992, p. 30)*

Captive audiences often suffer unsolicited lectures. Many contexts support such behavior by those in power, including military boot camp, church catechism lessons or Sunday school, university courses (where you are warned that there will be "lectures" before you pay money for a seat in the class), soccer practice, criminal court, and (of course) parent/child interaction. Wherever power is unequal, the temptation to lecture will emerge.

Supervisors can exploit power in many ways, but a common mishandling comes in the form of unwanted monologue. When captive, the therapist rarely welcomes the lesson. Since mental health professionals are trained listeners, supervisors may mistake politeness for attention and silence for agreement. "No imposition without permission" is my standard—if I wish to offer the therapist the "benefit" of my wisdom, knowledge, or experience, I should ask if the timing is appropriate and check to see if what I offered was relevant. For those who wish to further contemplate power in supervision, Fine and Turner's (1997) wonderful essay is well worth reviewing.

8.3.3 *Minimalism Rules, Except When It Shouldn't*

De Shazer and his colleagues make a statement with which I must disagree. They wrote, "*If it works, do more of it*…SFBT therapists do not judge the quality of a client's solutions, only whether a solution is effective" (2007, p. 2). Personally, I *do* judge the "quality of a client's solutions." Because most understandings of this statement terminate with the *client's* view of "effective" (which implies "good"), I promote a view that is more encompassing. Supervisors must attend to therapists' "orbit of care" (Doherty 1999), a broader context than the immediate therapist–client relationship and agreed-upon goals. A solution that "works" for the individual client must take its impact on (at least) significant others into account or it is not "good" (Wong 2006).

I realize I have lifted a single quotation out of a book I greatly admire (de Shazer et al. 2007), but too often professionals invest themselves in defending positions that fall short of *optimal* practice. Although I think the creation/identification of success is necessary in the supervisory relationship, I don't believe only doing more of "what works" is sufficient. I think the optimal is superior to either the minimal or maximal. SFBT and other SF practices have historically emphasized minimalism, citing Ockham's razor ("never introduce complexity when simplicity will do") as an unquestionable SF tenet rather than acknowledging minimalism as a philosophical bias. Solution-focused supervision is not solution-focused *brief* supervision—there is no "brief" in the description because the supervision relationship is not a one-to-one match with SFBT. SF supervision can be practiced isomorphically, but minimalism is not a requirement for success, nor is it always "enough." Others are affected by a single person's change, and the impact of one person's change on significant others must be considered in supervision.

Being a minimalist has a different value in SF supervision, since supervision involves more than solution building related to a problem or complaint. I still believe the foundational aspects of this unique approach should be practiced in SF supervision. These include centering on the therapists' goals, honoring their knowledge and experience, maintaining a future focus, and developing skills that work. We should not create complexity; we should keep it simple whenever possible. *In addition*, we have obligations to educate therapists, assess their competence, oversee their cases as administrators, and ensure adherence to wider system obligations (agency, licensure, legislative). A quote from Albert Einstein balances Ockham's razor for me: "Everything should be as simple as it is, but not simpler" (Einstein 2012). This is optimal practice.

8.3.4 Therapy-Once-Removed Supervision (see Sects. 3.5 and 6.2.1)

"What you need to do is this:…" takes many forms. At times, it is necessary for the supervisor to intervene in a case to avert catastrophe. Other times, the supervisor is wearing an administrative hat, giving directives to ensure policy is maintained or correcting a moment of ignorance before things deteriorate. Also, on occasion, supervisors draw an ethical line and do not allow therapists with whom they share clinical responsibility to cross it. But I believe these occurrences are rare; most of the time when such an intervention is used, supervisors are attempting to be the director and the primary (clinical) actor in the same stage play.

There are several faults in performing therapy-once-removed, but the primary error is thinking that one can predict the future. Embedded in a directed action is the belief that one can know the result of such an action: "If you do what I tell you to do, the outcome will be better than if you carry out the action you planned." This is closely related to 20/20 hindsight: "If you *would* have done what I am telling you to do, it *would* have turned out better." There is simply no way to prove therapy-once-removed is superior or inferior, but the power differential that resides in the supervisor's position infers superiority and requires compliance. Most of the time, this line of thinking is merely wishful and results in discouragement (and/or shame) for therapists.

A major practice within my group supervision work is developing alternatives to therapy-once-removed. When viewing one therapist's video with a group of therapist peers, two things happen if rules of conversation are not discussed. First, the peers offer 20/20 hindsight, what I call the tyranny of the "shoulda/coulda/woulda"— "You should have….", or "You could have….", or, "If only you would have…" The fictional results of shoulda/woulda/coulda are always favorable: "the situation would have been better than what actually took place if you had done what I am proposing." If the group process is allowed to take this course, the therapist's response is fairly predictable: she or he will ask the group (and the supervisor), "So, what should I do next?" In addition to discouragement and shame, therapists often encounter self-doubt and feel judged by group experiences that are masked as "suggestions" or "feedback" but are generally critical or even negative. As the (SF) supervisor, I firmly believe group supervision should be supportive and generative; therefore, it is my responsibility to do what I can to ensure supervision avoids destructive outcomes and stimulates viable possibilities.

An alternative process involves establishing a fine-tuned rule to practice "what is helpful to the therapist" in supervision, guided by the SF tenet of staying tentative. I ask each therapist presenting a case to bring two or three written items to guide the group, responding to this question: "What would be most helpful for you today as you present?" I also block shoulda/woulda/coulda responses from the group as possible "most helpful" practices, transparently explaining my views and negative experiences that guide this supervisory concept. If the therapist asks for alternative ideas, we talk about future encounters rather than this past clinical session, always using a tentative approach. "What might one do in such a situation?" is quite different from "What should have/could have been done in this situation?" As the group members share views that might be helpful but are not corrective, therapists tend to relax and consider each idea's potential value for the present case and future practice.

With more seasoned therapists, shoulda/woulda/coulda tends to ignite debate and defense:

Group Supervision Peer: "You should have…"
Presenting Therapist: "Well, I didn't do that because…"

or

Group Supervision Peer: "If you would have…"
Presenting Therapist: "Here's why I did what I did:…You weren't there, so you don't know…"

Many experienced therapists have commented on how this fairly simple rule/practice eliminates speculation, reduces discussions attempting to correct past events, and honors the presenting therapist's experience and autonomy. Competition is decreased, and group cohesion is improved.

For one-on-one supervision, I have found this guiding idea reduces the power differential and promotes therapist confidence. Rarely am I asked, "What should I do next?" because the two of us generate options as involved, competent professionals. Whether the therapist applies an option I have generated is usually unimportant; what takes precedence is the client's well-being and goals, with resulting therapist confidence in his or her abilities to make difficult decisions and learn from both positive and less-than-positive outcomes.

Supervisors cannot shield therapists from making mistakes. One of my preferred metaphors for supervision is the concept of an area surrounded by a fence. The fence represents the boundary placed on therapists' practices. This boundary includes limits the supervisor places on clinical decisions therapists can make as well as legislative restrictions, agency policies, and ethical requirements. Inside the perimeter, therapists are free to explore and make decisions. As a therapist gains experience, supervision promotes discussion on expanding the boundary so there is more room to "roam." Everyone is bound by limits, supervisor and therapist alike; open dialogue displaces therapy-once-removed and replaces it with generative options and respect for everyone's abilities to contribute.

8.4 SF Supervision Research: What's Next?

Here are two statements that represent what must be addressed as one considers the future of SF supervision research:

1. What matters is what *works*, and what works can only be discovered by careful quantitative measurement and by controlled clinical trials (Joiner, Sheldon, Williams, and Pettit 2003, p. 318, emphasis in original).

    Joiner and his colleagues argue for the value of empirical studies while acknowledging the importance of more humanistic approaches to understanding the process of therapy. They are in the mainstream of research: the importance of a particular study is evaluated on its design as well as its results. Generalizability and prediction are valued highly—what we can know and use to predict about groups of people is more important than knowledge confined to a single person or context.

2. We, of course, do not want to lose the integrity of SFBT. As we see it, there is a danger that research, with its usual focus on aggregates, will lose the individual client and thus ignore the client's goals, the client's evaluation of the therapy and the client's own life; all of which are so important to Solution-Focused Brief Therapy (de Shazer and Berg 1997, p. 123).

This quote, from de Shazer and Berg's article, "'What works?' Remarks on research aspects of solution-focused brief therapy" (1997), supports the importance of general knowledge ("aggregates") while maintaining the significance of the single case. In the SF world, what works generally *and* locally are both important in the discussion. Bateson once wrote, "The generic we can know, but the specific eludes us" (1979, p. 43)—this highlights what we can know but does not diminish the value of seeking knowledge of "the specific."

I see the future of SF supervision attending to both the general and the specific. Because SF approaches highly value "what works" for the individual, single-case studies and qualitative inquiry with small samples are and should remain prominent in our exploration. Research has informed SF supervision practice, as outlined in Chap. 6. Single-case studies (Wheeler and Greaves 2005) and small-group experiences (Trenhaile 2005) are excellent beginnings, informing ways of thinking about supervision research as well as the questions researchers raise. The work of Hsu and her colleagues (Hsu 2007, 2012; Hsu and Sun 2008; Hsu and Tsai 2011) has opened doors to more complex analysis of SF supervision experiences. Others have brought questions from general supervision research to the study of SF supervision. These questions, including therapist self-efficacy (Koob 1999, 2002), offer fruitful directions for future research. One particular study, Lehrman-Waterman and Ladany (2001), could be replicated with therapists experiencing SF supervision and contribute significantly to what we generally know about alliances, self-efficacy, and satisfaction levels of these therapists.

I personally hope studies like Triantafillou's (1997) that examine the influence of supervision on client outcome will emerge to bolster the image of SF practices and provide direction for supervision, but it is unlikely. Supervision remains more theory than research driven, and unless funding sources create a market for complex research studying client–therapist–supervisor factors and outcomes, such studies will be rare indeed.

My personal bias is to encourage research utilizing qualitative methodologies that intensely investigate the question, "What do therapists and supervisors do together that is useful?" Microanalysis has been applied to SFBT (Bavelas 2012) and offers a promising methodology for SF supervision research because of its broad acceptance within the SF world. In addition, qualitative inquiries using a grounded theory approach (Gazzola and Theriault 2007) or open-ended survey questions (Heath and Tharp 1991; Thomas, Coffey, Scott, and Shappee 2000a, b; Thomas and Shappee 2001) are especially informative.

Research goals vary with philosophy. I happen to appreciate all inquiries if it generatively influences my thinking, allows me to form better questions, or gives me tools with which to experiment with the goal of improving supervision, one therapist at a time.

8.5 What Matters in a SF Supervisory Relationship

Here is my short list of what matters:
- Therapist/supervisee perspectives and influence matter in the supervisory relationship (Lowe and Guy 2002; Thomas et al. 2000b). If I discount therapists' experiences, the impact on the relationship is always harmful. It is rare to find

someone who likes being told what to do, and one of the prominent themes in SF approaches is its commitment to the importance of others' voices and respecting experiences. I tell supervision workshop attendees they may adopt SF supervision techniques freely, but using techniques does not make their supervision solution-focused. Logic endorsing action without a concurrent adoption of philosophy would be akin to saying that wearing a military uniform and marching up and down the street makes one a soldier or singing songs and reciting liturgy at a worship service makes one a Christian. Action and identity are not synonymous. Although others in the SF world may disagree, adopting a SF stance *and* utilizing SF techniques allows SF practice to emerge.
- Client perspectives matter and influence the supervisory relationship (Shilts, Rambo, and Hernandez 1997; Sparks, Kisler, Adams, and Blumen 2011). Supervision without client feedback lacks a SF orientation. Although supervision models exist that focus on therapist development, a SF approach to supervision works to identify "what works" with therapists and clients. Researching clients' views on what works for them in therapy should be a top priority for supervisors and therapists, using methods that sample and enhance clients' experiences (Duncan et al. 2004; Miller and Hubble 2006).
- Research matters and should inform the supervisory relationship (Cunanan and McCollum 2006). Based on my comments above, I hope readers gain a sense of the value I place on research. Whether it is a large controlled study or a single-case reflection, research informs our work. Supervisors who ignore research do so at their own peril, as myopia comes quickly to those who believe their views are beyond improvement.
- Ethics matter and guide the supervisory and therapeutic relationships (Flemons et al. 1996; Haber 1996; Pettifor et al. 2011). "[T]here is no way to escape the responsibility of making moral decisions" (Epstein and Loos 1989, p. 418), which certainly applies to supervision. Whatever emphasis SF approaches place on the pragmatic, all must be considered within an ethical framework. As I wrote on the idea of minimalism (see above), such stances have biases and consequences. Ethical concerns must take precedence over philosophical commitments to the model or approach one uses.

8.6 Closing Thoughts

Participation precedes learning.

~ Mary Catherine Bateson 1992, p. 41

Standards for becoming a psychotherapy supervisor are minimal, and supervisors often practice in positions of influence with little oversight. Their expertise is assumed and unquestioned, and status is often conferred with no qualifying examination or internship to promote the development of expertise. In many states in the USA, a single graduate-level course and minimal clinical experience are the only requirements for achieving supervisory status within the licensure process. Unless there is evidence to the contrary, therapists usually assume mental health professionals with the "supervisor" title are competent and so do supervisors. Improving one's supervisory practice requires purpose, diligence, feedback, and time. How one gained supervisor status is less important than improving performance to benefit therapists and clients.

Harry Korman (2012), one of the world's leading SF therapists and trainers, recently wrote this about language and therapy: "I think it's essential that clients really, really know that you are really, really trying to understand what they are going through, and the emphasis is on trying." The same principle applies to SF supervision. As a postmodern approach, SF supervision cannot know the exact meaning of others' experiences, but we must try. Struggling to understand therapists' efforts, successes, and questions is the best we can do, and we owe them the best we can do.

Finally, those who apply SF supervision ideas and practices in their work *will be changed*. There is no objective place from which to observe and influence in supervision. Behavior affects perception (Powers 1973), so acting from SF assumptions will affect your experiences as well as those touched by your supervision. My goal for this book is to provide a resource for supervisory excellence. It can only be realized if one acts—"Act always so as to increase the number of choices" (von Foerster 1984, p. 308).

Appendix A
Supervision and Informed Consent

Creating a supervisory information document sets the tone for freer disclosure by both parties regarding expectations, guidelines, and those nonnegotiable obligations with which all supervisors must live. These obligations which cannot be altered include state and federal laws, licensure requirements, agency policies, and personal ethical limitations. Although the number is limited, these fixed standards need to be stated and discussed not only at the start of a supervisory relationship but also during the course of the contract relationship. This is a best practice standard in therapeutic work: periodically reviewing expectations, limitations, and obligations clarifies the freedoms and constraints with which all mental health professionals contend.

Appendix A is an example of a SF supervision informed consent document. Please consider this appendix to be a suggested outline rather than a copy-and-use document, as many items can be included in an informed consent agreement that are not included in this appendix example.

A.1. Supervision "Informed Consent" Example

I believe supervision is potentially a unique career-enhancing process for the therapist and a rewarding professional relationship, and my initial commitment is to nurture the development of both these aspects of supervision.

Many documents regarding supervision contracts and "informed consent" have been written over the decades. To help you understand more about how I think and act as a supervisor, I will provide you with a few short readings I have authored. I welcome any and all responses and questions, as no written material can be as responsive as a conversation.

I draw my inspiration for this document from three specific ideas. First, supervision should fit *you* well.[1] Second, supervision works best for most people when there are clearly defined goals for the therapist and for the relationship.[2] Finally, continuous feedback—from you, me, and your clients—should be a central aspect of supervision.[3, 4, 5]

A.1.1. Fit

Whenever possible, I attempt to fit my supervision style and practices to the therapist's needs and desires. Of course, there are limits—some are my own limits based on my skills as well as my personal ethics. But there are also larger systems that place requirements on what we do and how we interact. The state licensing boards, state and federal law, and this institution's policies and procedures all restrict the supervision process. However, the good news is there is a great deal of room to roam within these fences!

To assist me in fitting with you, you will be engaged in an active goal-setting and evaluation processes. This is described more below, but my aim is to provide what AAMFT calls a "sustained and intense" learning experience that fits well with your current abilities, learning styles, strengths, and resources. You will need to guide me on how I can best help you meet these goals—I can't do it without your assistance. As you and I set goals and you make strides toward achieving them, we will continually collaborate to create a process that is rewarding and challenging.

A.1.2. Thinking About, Setting, and Evaluating Goals

Not everything important in supervision is tied to a goal-setting process. There are qualitative shifts and personal growth experiences that cannot be predicted or measured; in fact, some of the changes you go through during supervision will be unexpected and potentially life altering. But the supervision literature supports the idea that therapists are more satisfied with the supervision experience when goals are clear and feedback is positive and challenging,[6] so we will set goals and assess progress throughout our time together.

---

[1] Atkinson (1997).
[2] Lehrman-Waterman and Ladany (2001).
[3] Kilminster and Jolly (2000).
[4] Sparks et al. (2011).
[5] Worthen and Lambert (2007).
[6] Lehrman-Waterman and Ladany (2001).

Appendix A Supervision and Informed Consent

I believe there are several areas of goal setting and evaluation that are crucial for the therapist, and one particular area is important to the therapist and mandated by the institution. You will create goals in these skill areas: *case management, therapeutic relationships, perception, conception*, and *participation*. This institution believes it is important for everyone to acquire and practice specific case management skills, including case notes, file organization and maintenance, billing, time accountability, and reporting. You and I will assess your current knowledge and skills in this area and then set goals so you will meet the institution's requirements within the first 90 days. Intermittent monitoring is a requirement of employment, and I will be working with you to maintain a high level of professionalism in this area as long as you are employed here.

The other four areas cover what the expertise development literature says is important.[7] The "Goal-Setting Template," attached to this document, outlines the content of these four skill areas along with some examples to organize your thoughts around the concepts. There is a great deal of freedom for us in this process—your goals need to be meaningful to you—and the structure of the goal-setting activity almost always assists faster acquisition by keeping us focused on your aims and progress.

A.1.3. Feedback

The concept of feedback is often understood as unidirectional and final. "Let me give you some feedback" usually means, "I'm going to tell you what I think, and that's the end of the conversation—do whatever you want with the information." However, since I come from a systems/cybernetic background, feedback has a very different meaning. In my interaction, feedback is "output returned to the system as input." That is, what I do and say to you will have an influence, and your behavior and responses to me will influence me as well. In addition, feedback from your clients will become a part of our supervision system, influencing you and me as we consider the information. Feedback guides and recycles, and it is a necessary part of supervision.

I will provide feedback on your work and progress every time we meet. You can request the form of feedback, but I may choose additional forms depending on the content and urgency of my responses. I will also request that you provide me with your impressions of how I am performing and how our interaction is progressing, using both forms[8] and conversation. My commitment is to make this process as helpful, responsive, and safe as possible.

---

[7] Dreyfus and Dreyfus (2005).

[8] We will use the LASS (Leeds Alliance and Supervision Scale) developed by Nigel Wainwright (2010) as one of the formal ways you provide me with feedback. This form, one of the performance measures free for single-supervisor use, can be downloaded from http://scottdmiller.com/?q=node/6. I also have other feedback tools that draw from the work of Lehrman-Waterman and Ladany (2001) that I will ask you to complete periodically so I can learn more about your views of our goal-setting and feedback processes.

A.1.4. Rules, Regulations, and Limitations

I prefer to clearly outline the requirements of supervision with therapists. These are outside of our influence to change, so any discussion will focus on how we comply while maintaining safety for our clients and the integrity of our relationship and this institution.

The law—federal and state—requires the following:

1. We must meet at least every other week for individual (1–2 therapists) or group (3–6 therapists) supervision, and we must operate under an approved supervision contract.
2. We have "joint responsibility" for your clients, according to my licensure board's regulations. This means I am held equally accountable for the progress and well-being of your clients.
3. Both you and I are bound by the codes of ethics of my license, your temporary license, and the professional associations to which we belong.
4. Many state laws relating to "professionals" apply to us. The most common of these involve client confidentiality, orders from the courts, and child or elder abuse. I will provide you with readings that outline other laws that we must uphold as a condition of our employment with this institution.

A.1.5. Our Commitments to Each Other and the Supervisory Relationship

1. Collaboration is the process and the goal of this supervisory relationship. Whenever possible, we will make shared decisions following careful independent thought and professional deliberation.
2. I take supervisory responsibilities seriously. Therefore, I will monitor all your cases and treatment planning, assist in your goal development, address conflict, and support you to the best of my ability in this collegial relationship. Your responsibility in this area is to prepare for our supervision meetings so you get the most out of each hour, consult with me on all emergencies, risks, and liabilities in a timely manner, and initiate conversations about conflicts to seek resolution.
3. Our supervisory conversations contain confidential material, but confidentiality in this state is reserved for clients and does not extend to supervision relationships in the same way. We should be discreet with information you and I share whenever possible to protect our reputations and relationship.
4. I will consult you regarding your clients whenever we have a difference of opinion regarding laws, rules, and regulations; however, I may take independent action if we disagree, but I still believe the best course of action differs from your opinions. For example, your best judgment may be to maintain client confidentiality when there is threat of harm, but I may take action to reveal information to law enforcement or medical professionals if I conclude this to be the best course of action.

Appendix A Supervision and Informed Consent

5. As your supervisor, I cannot provide personal counseling for you; all of the applicable regulations and ethics codes clearly state this. I will work to bring up any confusion I have in this area, and I hope you will do the same.
6. I pledge to maintain my state licensure, state licensure supervision status, and my AAMFT Approved Supervisor designation for the entire period of our contract. This includes being up-to-date in all my continuing education requirements as I strive to be the best-informed supervisor possible. You must maintain your temporary licensure status and immediately inform me if there are any changes or challenges in this status.
7. Honesty and respect are hallmarks of good relationships. Therefore, we should communicate ideas and concerns in a way that conveys information and supports our relationship. There are rare times when I may decide not to disclose my views or certain information (e.g., if my assessment of your progress differs significantly from your own and I require more time to reflect on this difference before discussing it with you), but I will always be as transparent as I can. I ask that you be as transparent as possible, given the power difference in our relationship, and bring conflicts to our attention so we can attempt to resolve them prior to the involvement of any third party. Also, I use a wide range of communication styles, from very indirect to direct. If at any time you feel I need to move up or down this continuum, I will do my best to accommodate your request.

A.1.6. About My Qualifications

I received my doctoral degree from Texas Tech University's Family Therapy Program in 1988. I began my supervision career in the Family Therapy Clinic at TTU in 1986 and have continuously provided supervision at three other universities and several major not-for-profit mental health agencies and clinics over the past 25 years. I have been involved in counseling in a variety of settings since 1976, as I also hold a B.S. in Sociology/Social Work and have a seminary degree (M.Div.) that provided me with psychotherapy training. I hold a license to practice as a Texas Licensed Marriage and Family Therapist (LMFT), and I have earned the supervisor designation from this state licensing board (LMFT-S). This license meets state qualifications for treating individual, marital, family, and other interpersonal problem conditions. I am also a Clinical Fellow and Approved Supervisor of the American Association for Marriage and Family Therapy (AAMFT), the only national accrediting body in the field of marriage and family therapy (MFT).

I am a tenured full professor in the counseling program at Texas Christian University where I teach and supervise master's and doctoral counseling students. I have written and published over 80 professional articles and book chapters as well as five books directly related to the practice of counseling. One of my specialties is in solution-focused approaches to therapy and supervision. I have published over 50 books, articles, and chapters and given over 100 professional presentations on solution-focused approaches. Additionally, I have written more than a dozen publications and given over 30 presentations on the topic of supervision (15 at international conferences). Overall, I have made a serious commitment to contributing to the body of knowledge regarding supervision and trained hundreds of supervisors in the art.

A.1.7. Final Thoughts

My desire is to provide you with the most rewarding supervision experience I can. I will take on different roles at different times, including administrative supervisor, supporter, teacher, clinical supervisor, case consultant, coach, mentor, or even advocate. But through all our shifts and transitions, my goal is to support your goal of becoming the finest clinician you can be. Every idea in this document is open for clarifying discussion—raise questions and ask them freely.

Appendix B
Systems/Cybernetics Reading List

(*=psychotherapy-related reading)

Bateson, G. (1979). *Mind and nature: A necessary unity*. New York: Dutton.
Bateson, G. (1972). *Steps to an ecology of mind*. Northvale: Jason Aronson.
Becvar, D. S., & Becvar, R. J. (2008). *Family therapy: A systemic integration* (7th ed.). Boston: Pearson.*
Beer, S. (1975). *Platform for change*. Wiley: London.
Charlton, N. G. (2008). *Understanding Gregory Bateson: Mind, beauty, and the sacred earth*. Albany: SUNY Press.
Checkland, P. (1981). *Systems thinking, systems practice*. Wiley: New York.
Flemons, D. (2005). May the pattern be with you. *Cybernetics and Human Knowing, 12*(1–2), 91–101.*
Flood, R. L. (2006). The relationship of 'systems thinking' to action research. In P. Reason & H. Bradbury (Eds.), *Handbook of action research* (pp. 117–128). London: Sage.
Gharajedaghi, J. (2006). *Systems thinking: Managing chaos and complexity* (2nd ed.). Burlington: Butterworth-Heinemann.
Gladwell, M. (2000). *The tipping point: How little things can make a big difference*. New York: Little, Brown & Co.
Hanson, B. G. (1995). *General systems theory: Beginning with wholes*. Washington, DC: Taylor & Francis.
Heylighen, F., & Joslyn, C. (2001). Cybernetics and second order cybernetics. In R. A. Meyers (Ed.), *Encyclopedia of physical science & technology, volume 4* (3rd ed.) (pp. 155–170). New York: Academic.
Keeney, B. P. (2005). Confessions of a cybernetic epistemologist. *Kybernetes, 34*(3/4), 373–384.*
Keeney, B. (1983). *Aesthetics of change*. New York: Guilford.*
Keeney, B. P., & Thomas, F. N. (1986). Cybernetic foundations of family therapy. In F. Piercy, D. Sprenkle, & Associates (Eds.), *Family therapy sourcebook* (pp. 262–287). New York: Guilford.*
Keeney, H., & Keeney, B. (2012). *Circular therapeutics: Giving therapy a healing heart*. Phoenix: Zeig, Tucker, & Theisen.*
Keeney, H., & Keeney, B. (2012). What is systemic about systemic therapy? Therapy models muddle embodied systemic practice. *Journal of Systemic Therapies, 31*(1), 22–37.*
Marshall, J. (2004). Living systemic thinking: Exploring quality in first-person action research. *Action Research, 2*(3), 309–329.
Maturana, H. R., & Varela, F. (1987). *Tree of knowledge*. Boston: Shambala.

Morin, E. (2008). *On complexity* (trans: Postel, R.). Cresskill: Hampton Press.
O'Connor, J., & McDermott, I. (1997). *The art of systems thinking: Essential skills for creativity and problem solving*. London: Thorsons.
Pinker, S. (2009). *How the mind works*. New York: Norton.
Powers, W. T. (1973). *Behavior: The control of perception*. Chicago: Aldine.
Rawson, M. (2000). Learning to learn: More than a skill set. *Studies in Higher Education, 25*(2), 225–238.
Thomas, F. N. (2005). I see that I see: A hero's impact on a family therapist. *Kybernetes: The International Journal of Systems & Cybernetics, 34*(3/4), 343–352.*
Thomas, F. N., Waits, R. A., & Hartsfield, G. L. (2007). The influence of Gregory Bateson: Legacy or vestige? *Kybernetes: The International Journal of Systems & Cybernetics, 36*(7–8), 871–883.*
Volk, T., Bloom, J. W., & Richards, J. (2007). Toward a science of metapatterns: Building upon Bateson's foundation. *Kybernetes: The International Journal of Systems & Cybernetics, 36*(7–8), 1070–1080.
von Foerster, H. (Ed.). (1981). *Observing systems*. Seaside: InterSystems.
von Foerster, H., & Krippendorf, K. (Eds.). (1995). *Cybernetics of cybernetics*. New York: Gordon and Breach.
Watzlawick, P., Beavin Bavelas, J., & Jackson, D. (1967). *Pragmatics of human communication: A study of interactional patterns, pathologies and paradoxes*. New York: Norton.*
Watzlawick, P., Weakland, J., & Fisch, R. (1974). *Change: Principles of problem formation and problem resolution*. New York: Norton.*
Wiener, N. (1950). *The human use of human beings: Cybernetics and society*. New York: Houghton Mifflin.

Appendix C
Goal-Setting Template and Examples

C.1 Goal Setting

Name:_____   Date: _____

I have set some goals for you this semester and you need to set goals for your learning as well. These are to be computer generated and turned in to me on the assigned date. Retain a copy, as we will use this as part of your evaluation at semester's end. Feel free to discuss altering your goals at any time—I want this to be useful for you!
Respond to each of these numbered items:

1. Whenever possible, please make your goals MEASURABLE, ATTAINABLE, and OBSERVABLE. This will aid the supervision/learning process because others—including your instructor—will be able to witness your progress. Write your INITIAL GOALS in regular text, *MIDTERM GOALS/CHANGES in italics,* and FINAL ASSESSMENT using underlined text.
2. Set goals in the following areas:
3. *Case Management*: Writing consistent case notes, complying with ISD policies
   Example: "I will attain consistency in my case notes with the SFBT model by the end of the semester in 90% of my cases."
4. *Therapeutic Relationships*: Conveying warmth, respect; use of self
   Example: "I will convey 'respect' to my clients in 50% of my cases, depending on peer, supervisory, and client feedback for evaluation."
5. *Perceptual Competencies*: Ability to observe pattern, see nonverbal behavior, distinguish content/process, self-awareness
   Example: "I will be able to identify relevant nonverbal behavior in each session, to be evaluated through the progress notes and feedback from clients and supervisors."
6. *Conceptual Competencies*: Ability to think within the assumptions of your model, ability to base clinical work (goals, interventions, termination) on

model/theory, SFT thinking skills, ability to incorporate idiosyncratic, gender, and cultural aspects

Example: "I will assess cultural factors in 75% of my first sessions and report these factors in supervision the next supervisory session."

7. *Participatory Competencies*: Changing your approach when stuck, controlling when exchanges are nonproductive or chaotic, terminating sessions, follow through with homework

    Example: "I will check on homework assignments on 90% of my cases in which homework is assigned."

8. Decide and outline how you will gain client feedback on your cases plus other ways you will use to acquire a better sense of clients' perspectives. I expect you to seek direct client responses to your work and also take advantage of third-party (i.e., peer and on-site supervisor) feedback and review of video recordings, starting immediately.
9. How can I best help you meet your goals? How can peers in this context best help you?
10. How do you best learn?
11. What is your best therapeutic model at this point in your career? Why?
12. What is your top interpersonal strength?
13. What is your greatest systemic strength?
14. What do you need to get from this time period of supervision with me to call it a "success"?

Goal-Setting Example #1

Haley Bunch Cox   EDGU 70103 and 70203, Practicum I and II
Master's in Education (MEd) Counseling Program
College of Education, TCU

<u>Haley Bunch Cox, MEd</u> *is an elementary school counselor in an east Texas independent school district. This was her second semester of practicum, and her site was a north Texas public ISD elementary school where she provided individual and group counseling services as well as classroom guidance lessons.*

1. Whenever possible, please make your goals MEASURABLE, ATTAINABLE, and OBSERVABLE. This will aid the supervision/learning process because others—including your instructor—will be able to witness your progress. Write your INITIAL GOALS in regular text, *MIDTERM GOALS/CHANGES in italics,* and <u>FINAL ASSESSMENT using underlined text.</u>
2. Set goals in the following areas:
3. *Case Management:* Writing consistent case notes, complying with ISD policies

    #1 –

    INITIAL: I will write 75% of my progress notes immediately following an individual client or small group session. The other 25% of my progress notes will be written within 24 hours of having counseled the clients.

Appendix C   Goal-Setting Template and Examples

MIDTERM: As you and I agreed, I will not be writing progress notes starting next week but instead helping other students in the class. I will keep some type of notes about my cases with them, though, so that I can read up on the students' work before I meet with them. I have noticed that I meet with so many different students it can be difficult to remember specific details about some of the cases.

FINAL: I feel like I have reached this goal because I held myself accountable to recording some kind of brief note about each student I met with at my sites. It is easy to forget what you talk about with students because there are so many different ones every week. Just taking brief notes about who and what was discussed helped spark my memory when I met with students over and over again.

#2 –

INITIAL: I will begin working on my first case study within 3 weeks of beginning my practicum. I plan to gather a lot of data about my client from cumulative files, speaking with his/her teacher, parents, counselors, etc.

MIDTERM: I have completed both my first case study and case study for oral examinations at this point. I have one more case study to type up and plan to finish it within a week. I would like to continue video recording about half of my sessions to play back and observe how they go.

FINAL: I video recorded several sessions other than just my case studies. I reviewed them but did not do transcripts for the sessions. I just needed to have something to look over in order to improve my skills. I have found that it really helps to watch my videos.

#3 –

INITIAL: I will speak with my supervisor about any major ISD policies that I need to be aware of within the first 2 weeks of starting my practicum. I will review emergency situations with my supervisor that I will bring to class.

FINAL: I completed this goal and know the ISD policies that a counselor should be aware of in case of an emergency.

4. *Therapeutic Relationships*: Conveying warmth, respect; use of self

#1 –

INITIAL: I will take time in 60% of my cases to find out exactly what it is the client wants to work on regardless of what their teachers/parents want the goal to be. I am curious as to what they perceive to be the "problem."

MIDTERM: I feel like I am working on this goal constantly for a few different reasons. I decided to ask my latest case study what she wanted to work on. The counselor told me that the client had one problem, but I wanted to check with the child/client about what she thought we should talk about during our time together. She came up with another challenging goal for herself that I went with.

<u>FINAL: I will always be working hard on this goal as a counselor. I have found that teachers and parents really want you to work on specific issues with students while the students may have somewhere else they want to go with the session. I am trying to learn how to work on both sets of goals but still find it very difficult.</u>

#2 –

INITIAL: I will compliment every client during individual counseling at least twice during a session. I will find at least one compliment to give to an entire class during a guidance lesson in every class. I will compliment 50% of the students in a small group session. I am hoping that the group members will find ways to compliment each other as well.

MIDTERM: I feel like I need to really improve on my complimenting during small group sessions. I am getting ready to participate in five different small groups starting next week so I can really test this out. I feel like I have been meeting my goals when it comes to complimenting individual students and after guidance lessons.

<u>FINAL: I have given compliments during our small group sessions, but occasionally I forget. It is challenging to remember to do everything in just 30–45 minutes of group time. I probably gave compliments 70% of the time during and after small group sessions.</u>

#3 –

INITIAL: I will make a point to introduce myself to at least ten people whenever I have lunch duty and try to build rapport with students.

MIDTERM: I feel like I have done an okay job on this goal. I usually meet 6–8 people during lunch duty now. I have met so many students at this point that I spend a lot of time talking to those that I have previously met. I am not going to focus on this goal as much as I had in the past.

<u>FINAL: I probably have met 100 different students during my days on lunch duty. I have not had lunch duty quite as much the second half of the semester as I did in the beginning.</u>

5. *Perceptual Competencies*: Ability to observe pattern, see nonverbal behavior, distinguish content/process, self-awareness

#1 –

INITIAL: I will look for patterns when talking with reoccurring students and begin trying new things that I might not have observed the first time I talked with them.

MIDTERM: This goal is still a challenge for me. I plan to meet with my supervisor more and ask for suggestions. I am really struggling to notice pat-

Appendix C   Goal-Setting Template and Examples

terns during our sessions. I feel like I have so many other things to look for that I have room for improvement here.

FINAL: I met with my supervisor on how to notice patterns with students. She observed me counseling a few students and pointed out some things I had missed. I learned how to take note of students' body language.

#2 –

INITIAL: I will receive feedback from my supervisor/peers and learn to ask questions that I might not have thought to ask in the past at certain points of therapy.

FINAL: I have received lots of feedback from both of my supervisors. I feel very fortunate to have worked with these counselors during my practicum experience. I feel comfortable asking them questions after a session with a student.

6. *Conceptual Competencies*: Ability to think within the assumptions of your model, ability to base clinical work (goals, interventions, termination) on model/theory, SFT thinking skills, ability to incorporate idiosyncratic, gender, and cultural aspects

#1 –

INITIAL: I will use the EARS practice with 90% of my clients after I hear an exception.

MIDTERM: I will continue to use the EARS practice during my sessions. I would like to spend a little more time discussing this technique with both of my supervisors and see if they have any good suggestions for me. I feel like I say a lot of the same things and would like to try to reword some of my phrases.

FINAL: I am continuing to get better at using the EARS practice. I feel like I use this approach with just about every case I have that brings up an exception.

#2 –

INITIAL: I will search for new interventions to try with clients that can be useful in a school environment. I will locate ten interventions by midterm that relate directly to school counseling and that can be used in a school environment.

MIDTERM: I feel like I have met this goal in the fact that I talked with Dr. Thomas about finding some new interventions. I have tried out several of the interventions that he sent us in the drop box.

FINAL: I still need to continue to look for interventions. I think it might be helpful to read the book about Erickson again that I read in my interventions class. I really need a refresher on some interventions and found this book to be very helpful.

#3 –

INITIAL: I will practice the skills for "not knowing" in at least 75% of my cases.

MIDTERM: I feel like I practice the skills for "not knowing" in more than 75% of my cases at this point. I plan on using these skills in all of my cases now. I really do not have to spend nearly as much time thinking about the skills as I previously had because they often come out naturally.

FINAL: I am still making gains on this goal. I probably use the skills for not knowing in 90% of my cases at this point. I am continuing to paraphrase, summarize, use silence, compliment, etc. I like to work with my students on goal-setting as well.

7. *Participatory Competencies*: Changing your approach when stuck, controlling when exchanges are nonproductive or chaotic, terminating sessions, follow through with homework

#1 –

INITIAL: I will assign a task for 70% of my cases that will meet with me again and check with them all to see whether or not they have completed it.

MIDTERM: I am still struggling to assign tasks with all of my cases. I think I need to remember to at least ask my students to notice when things are different or better. This is still a form of a task and would be something easy for them to try to do.

FINAL: I have given most of my students tasks, but I realized that I have not always been as good about checking back with them to see if they have completed their tasks. I just feel like there is never enough time in the day to get everything accomplished that I need to at my sites.

#2 –

INITIAL: I will consult with my supervisor within 1 week of being "stuck" on all of my cases.

FINAL: I definitely consult my supervisors when I have a challenging or difficult case. They are both eager to help me and offer up great suggestions on what I might consider trying to do next.

#3 –

INITIAL: I will check for feedback from my clients 80% of the time we meet to see if they feel they are reaching their goals.

MIDTERM: I think this goal is something that I need to work more on. Honestly, I forgot that I set this goal for myself and now that I remember I plan on being more persistent with searching for feedback from clients.

FINAL: I have received feedback from several clients the past few weeks. I meant to create a quick questionnaire for my students to complete, but I never got to do that. However, my students are honest and always provide me with excellent feedback.

8. Decide and outline how you will gain client feedback on your cases. I expect you to seek direct client responses to your work, through third-party (i.e., peer and on-site supervisor) feedback, on tape, and/or in your notes on 50% of your cases, starting immediately.

INITIAL: I will ask my clients at the end of sessions what they thought about how things went for the day. I will video record my cases 25% of the time to go back and watch for things I missed during the session. I will pose questions to my supervisor about what she thought of a session that she sat in on. I will ask for particular things that she feels I need to work on. I will revisit these goals to see how well I am achieving them. I plan to evaluate myself both at midterm and final to see how I am improving my counseling skills.

MIDTERM: I plan on showing my supervisors the videos of me working with their students. I would like to receive feedback on what they thought about how the sessions went. I realize they will not have time to watch the entire videos, but I think they might have a few minutes to watch a few of them.

FINAL: Unfortunately, I was not able to show my supervisors the videos because I have turned them all in before they got a chance to see them. I did talk about the sessions and provide my supervisors with transcripts. I did ask students directly how they felt the sessions went and what might be different in the future if we worked together.

9. How can I best help you meet your goals? How can others in the practicum help you?

INITIAL: I think by just asking me how my goals are going will help me to meet them in the coming weeks. I need to be held accountable by having my supervisors check to see how everything is going. I would like to be able to talk about our goals at least once a month in class. I think that constructive criticism during my videos will help me to accomplish even more goals than maybe I first came up with. I am hoping that others will notice and point out things that I need to work on.

MIDTERM: I still feel the same way about receiving feedback on my goals. I am curious to see how you feel about I am doing when it comes to meeting my goals after you read my midterm goal sheet. I would like to partner up with a student in our practicum and take time in class to discuss our goal sheets and compare them. It helps me reach my goals when I verbalize them and take time to explain what they are to others.

FINAL: I feel like you as well as others have helped me a lot this semester. I really enjoyed watching the videotapes that we did in class. It also just helped discussing specific cases in class. I felt like I got a lot out of the classes that we discussed bullying, suicide, and anxiety. I tried to take detailed notes to go back and review in the future.

10. How do you best learn?

INITIAL: I am a visual learner for the most part, but I have realized that it is extremely helpful for me to practice different techniques. I really need to try certain things out to see how they go or what I need to change in the future. The helping class really taught me a lot because we had a chance to practice our skills with a partner after going over them. I also learn a lot from watching others during a counseling session. I enjoy when you demonstrate a particular intervention, technique, etc. to the entire class.

MIDTERM: I enjoyed having (guest supervisor) come into our practicum the other day just to get another perspective on my case study. She asked some really great questions and thought of ways that I might have brought up issues in other ways than what I did. I also like having the questions at the end of our cases that we discuss with the class.

FINAL: I still believe I am a visual learner. I realize I learned the most from reviewing my videos as well as others in the class. I also like to watch videos from professionals in the field that are on file at the TCU library.

11. What is your best therapeutic model at this point in your career? Why?

INITIAL: My best therapeutic model thus far is solution-focused therapy. I have spent quite a lot of time reading about it and applied some aspects of it last semester during practicum one. I just feel the most comfortable when applying this model in a school counseling session. I would love to try out some other models, but I really do not know how to go about that in a session. I have practiced doing a little play therapy with a sand tray. My supervisor last semester used that quite a lot, which was helpful in the long run.

MIDTERM: I still believe I feel the most confident in solution-focused therapy. However, I am gradually trying out a few other techniques in small ways. I used role-playing the other day, and I felt like it went pretty well. I would like to try to use more narrative therapy the second half of the semester.

FINAL: I prefer solution-focused therapy, but I am open to other types of therapy. I am excited about taking a play therapy class this summer at Texas A&M Commerce. I did not get to use quite as much narrative therapy as I had hoped to use but will still try it out whenever I get a chance.

12. What is your top interpersonal strength?

INITIAL: My top interpersonal strength is probably active listening. I try hard to really pay attention to what a student is telling me. One way I do this is by clarifying with them when I am confused about something they might have just said. I try to get them to use their own words so that I know exactly what it is they are talking about. I try my best to convey to them that I care about them

Appendix C   Goal-Setting Template and Examples   303

and that I want to hear what it is they have to say. I believe it is extremely important to give them the attention they ask for without daydreaming about other things. I really try hard to be in the moment with each and every student I work with.

MIDTERM: I still believe this is a strength of mine, but I feel like there has even been growth in the past few weeks when it comes to clarifying with students. It is easy to misunderstand them, but I am learning how to paraphrase and summarize what they have said in order to make sure that I know what they mean.

<u>FINAL: I believe my top interpersonal strength is active listening because I really do care what they have to say. I try to get plenty of rest before I go to my practicum sites so that I can give my clients my undivided attention while I am working with them. I know that they can tell whether or not someone is really listening to what they have to say.</u>

13. What is your greatest systemic strength?

    INITIAL: I believe one of my greatest systemic strengths is the fact that I try my best to be a peacemaker. I'm not sure that is always a good thing, but it definitely can be helpful in most situations. I do not want to see students upset with their teachers, parents, etc. so I look for ways that I can help them discover ways to improve their relationships with others. I have never enjoyed confrontation so I think that is why I try so hard to find peace within a situation. I hope that it has a calming effect on those around me.

    MIDTERM: I found myself trying to help a teacher and student who were not getting along the other day. I felt like I did a good job at hearing both sides of the story and was just someone they could talk to. I felt like both parties wanted to be heard. I was able to help them come up with a few strategies to try out in the classroom in order to resolve some of their conflicts.

    <u>FINAL: I consider myself a team player and always work hard to achieve peace between others. I think sometimes I put too much responsibility on myself when it comes to helping others get along. I have to remind myself daily that I can only help students look for solutions, but ultimately they must be the ones to take responsibility for their actions.</u>

14. What do you need to get from supervision with me this semester to call it a "success"?

    INITIAL: I feel like there is still so much to learn from you, but I would really like to focus on at least a few things I can do better during my counseling sessions. I know that from watching my first video you will have things that I can improve on. For this semester to be a success, I would like to do better on whatever you point out during my second video. I just want to see overall improvement in each session with my students. I am really looking forward to having you as my supervisor this semester!

MIDTERM: I think I need to continue to receive feedback on things that I can work on as a counseling intern. I want to be able to notice that I am taking what I hear from other practicum students as well as yourself and applying it during my sessions.

<u>FINAL: I feel like this semester has been a success. I hope that you can tell I have grown from the beginning of my practicum to this point. I know I still have so much to work on, but I am gradually getting better in my counseling sessions. I'm excited about graduating next weekend! Thank you for everything you have helped me with the past 2 years!</u>

Goal-Setting Example #2

<u>Kimberly Grigg</u>   EDGU 70103 and 70203, Practicum I and II
Master's in Education (MEd) Counseling Program
College of Education, TCU

Kimberly Grigg, MEd is a counselor at a private prekindergarten through grade-12 school in north central Texas and a student in the Ph.D. Program in Counseling and Counselor Education at TCU. Ms. Grigg has over 15 years' experience as an elementary school teacher and several years' experience as a private school counselor. Her practicum experience was in a private school where she also taught, and she provided individual and group counseling services as well as classroom guidance lessons.

1. Whenever possible, please make your goals MEASURABLE, ATTAINABLE, and OBSERVABLE. This will aid the supervision/learning process because others—including your instructor—will be able to witness your progress. Write your INITIAL GOALS in regular text, *MIDTERM GOALS/CHANGES in italics,* and <u>FINAL ASSESSMENT using underlined text.</u>
2. Set goals in the following areas:
3. *Case Management:* Writing consistent case notes, complying with ISD policies

   INITIAL: I will strive to maintain accurate and timely case notes. I will utilize the notes as tools for learning rather than viewing them as paper work. During the first few weeks of practicum, I found them to be time-consuming and a bit overwhelming. Consequently I didn't use the notes effectively, and I plan to use them to guide future sessions more thoughtfully.

   MIDTERM: I have made progress in this area; however, I'm still struggling with finishing the case notes the same day of the session. I usually begin the paperwork, but I end up finishing it the next day or two. I'm getting more comfortable with each section, and I'm still working on understanding and conveying the intervention section. On March 24, we will have a session in class with more specific help in this area, and I'm looking forward to learning more about the interventions and descriptions. In regard to the ISD policies, I've had a relatively smooth transition in this area due to my experience at this same private school as a teacher.

Appendix C Goal-Setting Template and Examples   305

FINAL: In regard to complying with ISD policies, I was successful due largely to my experience as a teacher in this school and my familiarity with the policies. I also wrote more consistent case notes once I gained a better understanding of interventions. I still need to work on succinct case notes as I tend to write in complete sentences. I also need to be more specific in writing clear client goals that are measureable.

4. *Therapeutic Relationships*: Conveying warmth, respect; use of self

   INITIAL: I will value and respect individuals with warmth and respect. After teaching for 12 years, this has been the greatest asset noted by my administration in my annual reviews, and I think that I'll be able to continue this in counseling.

   MIDTERM: I am comfortable with the rapport that I've established with my clients thus far. In many cases, I already know the students since I've been teaching at this school for 7 years. However, with a new role in the school, I've been successful in conveying warmth and respect to the clients.

   FINAL: The therapeutic relationship seemed to be an area that felt natural and came relatively easily for me. Again, I was at an advantage since I have been teaching at this site and know most of the students. I enjoyed building rapport with the students in a new context. I especially enjoyed visiting each of the grade levels and classrooms for guidance lessons, and I've received encouraging feedback from students on my visits to the classrooms.

5. *Perceptual Competencies*: Ability to observe pattern, see nonverbal behavior, distinguish content/process, self-awareness

   INITIAL: I will observe pattern, see nonverbal behavior, and distinguish content/process by attending. Rather than focusing on my technique, I'll try to avoid being conscious of my own questions and really notice my client's needs. With experience, I plan to move from being self-conscious to attending my client.

   MIDTERM: As I've had more sessions, I've noticed that I'm making significant progress in this area. I've been able to attend to my clients with more experience and confidence. I'm finally starting to see how the SFT questions lead clients away from problem talk to solution talk with my guidance. I still have work to do, but I've noticed progress in this area.

   FINAL: As the semester went on, I attended to my clients more successfully. With experience, I gained more confidence. Although I made progress in this area, I also realize that I will continue to learn with more client contact, and I still have plenty of room for growth. Experience with a variety of clients will enable me to distinguish unique circumstances more readily. Intuition is definitely an important element, but experience will be the best teacher.

6. *Conceptual Competencies*: Ability to think within the assumptions of your model, ability to base clinical work (goals, interventions, termination) on

model/theory, SFT thinking skills, ability to incorporate idiosyncratic, gender, and cultural aspects

INITIAL: I will assess my student's cultural background and experiences in 50% of my first sessions and utilize these factors in deciding on interventions. I will continue to assess cultural factors in my second session with more success and confidence. Presently, my first sessions are moving more slowly due to my cautious approach from inexperience. Consequently, I think my goal will be more realistic if I set more progress for future sessions.

MIDTERM: I'm making progress with moving slowly from too much caution to a more comfortable pace. I'm gaining confidence with my therapeutic approach, and this enables me to incorporate other aspects outside of my comfort zone. For instance, I had a session with a first-time client, and I asked him the Miracle Question in the first session. I wasn't sure how he'd respond because he's quiet, but he really shared his miracle day openly. I felt encouraged as the session progressed naturally with the exception and scaling questions as well.

FINAL: I realized that my experience in my particular school setting is a bit limiting in this area. I didn't really have to understand a variety of cultural aspects since the demographic at this private school isn't very diverse. I did, however, make progress with incorporating goals and interventions more effectively. I was able to use a goal-setting sheet effectively for clients. I adopted a form that was used in my small group's course, and it enabled me to put more direction into the hands of the clients. I also used SFT questions to move clients from problem to solution talk more successfully. For instance, I redirected changes to the client rather than focusing on the changes of others.

7. *Participatory Competencies*: Changing your approach when stuck, controlling when exchanges are nonproductive or chaotic, terminating sessions, follow through with homework

INITIAL: I will practice more techniques when I am stuck. If my SFT process is not moving forward, I will integrate cognitive/CBT interventions into my therapeutic approach. I will also try to utilize concepts from narrative and family systems theories when applicable. I will need to actually practice these skills to gain confidence with integrating various theories for more productive sessions.

MIDTERM: Quite frankly, I've concentrated on SFT so much that I've not made progress with other therapeutic approaches. I've wanted to gain as much experience as possible with SFT, and I've felt it necessary to continue using it in my sessions as my primary therapeutic model. Again, I will venture out into other approaches as I gain experience and confidence.

FINAL: I discussed with my supervisor a certain client who was having trouble relating to the scaling questions. Since math is a source of stress to this client, the numbers on the scale tended to make her uneasy. My supervisor

Appendix C Goal-Setting Template and Examples   307

suggested using the facial expression scale to better connect with the client. The client did respond better to this method. I learned that I have to alter the recipe from time to time to tend to the client's specific needs! I've been terminating sessions successfully in most cases. A couple of clients wanted to start sessions again in the fall, but I told them that I would be leaving this school. I referred them to the school counselor for the fall semester.

8. Decide and outline how you will gain client feedback on your cases. I expect you to seek direct client responses to your work, through third-party (i.e., peer and on-site supervisor) feedback, on tape, and/or in your notes on 50% of your cases, starting immediately.

   INITIAL: I will gain client feedback on my cases through various methods. First, I will utilize my on-site supervisor's experience and request that she observe me in both guidance and small group counseling. I will also share my video-recorded sessions with her to give her more chances for mentoring. Additionally, I will get feedback from my peers in practicum as we view taped sessions. Dr. Thomas will give me feedback on my progress notes and in other relevant areas.

   MIDTERM: My on-site supervisor has observed my work in small groups and through video-taped sessions. She has been quite encouraging. She has given me advice on a few areas. For instance, she noticed that I had told a small group member that her definition for "weathered" wasn't correct, and she suggested that I might say something like, "Let's see if you think it still means that after our activity." As a teacher, my principal has always encouraged the teachers to let students know if they are incorrect, so this was my natural tendency. It was helpful to view this from a counselor perspective vs. an educator perspective.

   FINAL: I realize that I gained consistent feedback from my on-site supervisor throughout the semester. I shared my videos and progress notes with her, and she was able to give me direction for growth. During my oral examination, the committee also gave helpful and constructive criticism that will promote growth in this area. During my small group session, I sought the client's opinions of what helped during our meetings, and each of the clients shared what worked for them and what didn't. I had used a nine-session format with an activity booklet to promote discussion; however, the booklet required a bit too much construction and we ended up putting it aside to focus more on group discussion. After hearing the client's comments, I altered the program to fit their needs.

9. How can I best help you meet your goals? How can others in the practicum help you?

   INITIAL: Dr. Thomas can best help me meet my goals through providing samples and examples of exemplary work that I can gain insight from. My peers in practicum will help me meet my goals by sharing their struggles and successes.

Their support will help to encourage me with my own struggles and successes. As Dr. Thomas had once noted in one of his books, sharing sufferings and celebrations will make for a more meaningful journey.

MIDTERM: Viewing the videos is very beneficial, and I'm looking forward to seeing more work from my peers. As my video was viewed, it was helpful to hear the feedback from my peers and Dr. Thomas. Since I tend to be critical of myself, the positive comments gave me encouragement and confidence that I'm on the right track to making progress.

<u>FINAL: My peers in practicum helped me through common experiences of both struggles and achievements. I especially felt support from other teachers who tried to balance a full time job with the practicum requirements. I appreciated the support I received from Dr. Thomas and his sense of when assignment requirements needed to be adjusted due to unforeseen circumstances.</u>

10. How do you best learn?

    INITIAL: I best learn from observing visual examples and then actually practicing and participating in the learning process.
    MIDTERM: As previously mentioned, the video-recording experience is invaluable. Although it's certainly uncomfortable, seeing and hearing "play-by-play" calls is enlightening. Also, transcribing the session allowed me to see what was working and what still needs work.

    <u>FINAL: The best learning tool was the actual experience gained from direct client contact. This experience moved me from cautious approach to a more purposeful approach. In other words, I went from going through the motions to guiding my clients toward solutions more consistently.</u>

11. What is your best therapeutic model at this point in your career? Why?

    INITIAL: I just completed an online course on Counseling Theories, and I chose SFT as most influential in my personal counseling theory. My training and experience at TCU has been with SFT, and it is the therapeutic model that I most identify with. I appreciate SFT for its optimistic approach and for its focus to make change relevant and long lasting for the client. I also value SFT for its ability to integrate other techniques into its therapeutic process.

    MIDTERM: As mentioned earlier, I've consciously worked on SFT because I've needed the experience in this area. I really haven't had much practice since "Helping Relationships," and I learn best by doing. I've made improvement in this area, but I need to keep working on these skills.

    <u>FINAL: The SFT model of therapy works very well in a Christian school setting because it lends itself to incorporating faith into the therapeutic session. I will also utilize prayer in my sessions, and I plan to further study other theological models of therapy that might supplement the SFT therapeutic approach.</u>

Appendix C Goal-Setting Template and Examples   309

12. What is your top interpersonal strength?

    INITIAL: I consider my top interpersonal strength to be consideration and respectfulness. I value individuals and their opinions, and I try to listen with respect as others share their experiences with me.

    MIDTERM: I'm comfortable that I've been able to utilize my strengths to develop rapport with my clients. It is easy for me to be considerate and respectful to my diverse students and clients because of my experiences growing up on air force bases with different cultures and backgrounds.

    FINAL: Thankfully, I am pleased with how I treat my clients with respect. As a result, the sessions were rewarding because the clients appeared to sense my consideration for their unique set of circumstances.

13. What is your greatest systemic strength?

    INITIAL: Again, due to my consideration of others, I work hard to communicate effectively. Consequently, I strive to improve various situations for the best outcome for all those involved.

    MIDTERM: I've had the advantage of working within previously established relationships in the school. However, I've had to be very flexible with working around teachers' schedules, and I have a clear understanding of the importance of considering the academic scheduling. One day, I received a call from a teacher who said I had one of her students for 2 weeks in a row and she needed that student in class. I had neglected to inform the teacher of our sessions. I had talked to both the parents and the homeroom teacher, but I overlooked the needs of the music teacher. It was a learning experience! I apologized and we made an adjustment to the student's schedule that wouldn't affect that teacher. My supervisor enjoyed hearing about this since she deals with scheduling issues on a regular basis.

    FINAL: I used my consideration of others and their demanding schedules effectively to schedule guidance lessons with every teacher in each grade level. It was challenging and wasn't always easy, but it was rewarding.

14. What do you need to get from supervision with me this semester to call it a "success"?

    INITIAL: Since I've had direction from you in several other courses, I'm sure that you'll provide successful supervision in practicum. I've learned effectively from you in each previous course, and I value your judgment and experience. I will need your advice and suggestions on how to work on moving away from a teaching stance and assume the "not knowing" stance more naturally in my counseling.

    MIDTERM: Although our class times have been limited due to the snowstorms, etc., I learn well from your feedback and classroom role play. As I'm going through my therapy sessions, I often refer back to the "Helping

Relationships" course and try to utilize the skills you taught the class through example.

FINAL: The committee's feedback during the oral examination helped me to feel successful. Likewise, I always appreciate your guidance in helping me to improve with your unique style of constructive criticism with a dose of encouragement. I learned many invaluable lessons from your nonjudgmental and discerning lessons. I will carry those lessons with me as I continue to understand the intricate considerations of counseling.

Appendix D
Weekly Risk/Goal Chart Example

This is an example of a weekly reporting form, completed by the therapist/supervisee and turned in with case notes or files to appropriate supervisors. This can be created in Microsoft Word or Excel and used in printed or electronic form, depending on agency policies and supervisor preferences. It is cumulative, adding columns and rows as needed, and usually covers a fiscal year or university practicum semester in length.

Prior to the beginning of a supervision session, supervisors can take a quick look at this chart to inform the course of the meeting. It was created as shorthand, not a substitute for case file review.

At a glance, this summary sheet communicates several items:

1. Client code: In this case, a combination of each client's initials and age to protect confidentiality; institutional procedures and policies should determine how these codes are created and disseminated.
2. Date: Exact date of sessions.
3. Risk: As assessed by therapist (0–10, 10 being "high" or negative).
4. Goal: As assessed by therapist with client (0–10, 10 being "perfect" or positive).
5. !!: Symbols used by therapist to draw supervisor's attention to the case and/or session.
6. SUPV: Denotes therapist received supervision on this session.
7. Term: Denotes termination of the case (in both client column and date of last session).
8. Total case load: (Client column total) minus (term, or terminated).
9. Total sessions for a particular week: (DATE column).

Appendix D Weekly Risk/Goal Chart Example

Client code	Date risk/goal	Date risk/goal	Date risk/goal	Date risk/goal	Date risk/goal	Date risk/goal
BAP12	1/15/2012 2/3	1/22/2012 2/5		2/5/2012 2/6		
GAR10 (term)	1/15/2012 1/6		1/29/2012 1/8 term			
SMP16 !!	1/15/2012 5/3 !!	1/22/2012 5/2 !!	1/29/2012 5/3 !! SUPV	2/5/2012 4/6		
JML32		1/21/2012 2/4	1/28/2012 2/6			
HEB15 (term)		1/21/2012 2/6	1/28/2012 2/7	2/6/2012 2/8 term		
FRT14		1/23/2012 3/5	1/30/2012 3/6	2/6/2012 3/6		
DRW12			1/28/2012 2/2	2/6/2012 2/2 SUPV		
PMJ15			1/29/2012 6/2 !!	2/6/2012 4/5		

Appendix E
Berg Japan Supervision Workshop

Insoo Kim Berg, MSSW

(SFBTA Archive Video, Item #10128-0064)

Location: Japan   Date: unknown

The following outline is a handout recreation based on a video of Insoo Kim Berg, MSSW presenting a workshop entitled, "Solution-Focused Supervision." Whenever possible, the words used are verbatim.

Opening Ideas About Supervision:

1. Just like a client and therapist, the supervisee and the supervisor relationship is unequal and hierarchical:
    a. Learning theory: people learn better when they are more self-motivated.
    b. When we are more equal, we learn better.
    c. As a supervisor, one should think about how to reduce the hierarchy so that therapist and supervisor become more or less equal, which will help the supervisee learn better.
2. Supervision happens in the context of language, so it's very important for us to pay attention to how we conduct the conversation of supervision.
3. Cantwell and Holmes (1994) says that we as supervisors lead from one step behind; that is, we are leading because supervision is hierarchical, so supervisors have to lead; but, when you lead from one step behind, then the supervisee takes responsibility for his or her own learning; when you have power, you have to follow in order to lead.
4. Supervision has two tasks or functions: teaching and evaluation.

Techniques of Supervision: "How to Reduce the Power Difference in Supervision"

1. Use a very conversational style of language. Like talking with a client, you also want to use everyday conversational language rather than using really professional jargon. Imagine sitting in the kitchen of your home, having a conversation with someone.
2. Share your power. You have a power difference and as much as possible, think about how you can share that eliciting the supervisee's ideas rather than my telling him/her what I'm thinking. Help the supervisee self-evaluate.
3. Let the supervisee generate the topic. "What topic do you want to talk about this time, this meeting, this time?"
4. Just as you would take a client's perspective of his or her concerns, we also need to take the supervisee's perspective on his or her way of looking at things.
5. Avoid showing off how much you know.

Supervision and Evaluation:

1. A good supervisor always gives a positive evaluation. Because when you give a positive evaluation, you are giving suggestions for what to do more of.
2. "Don't" is not a good way to teach. And "stop" is not a good way to teach. So don't use these two words. Always use "do this" or "try this" or "that was good," "that worked very well," "so what do you need to do so that you can do it again?"
3. Just as in therapy, we are creating a whole different reality for the supervisee. Our job is to change that reality so the supervisee feels more in control, competent, and successful.
4. Supervision is a constructing process. That means that the supervisor contributes something, and the supervisee contributes something, and through this interaction, we are creating a whole different sense of how the supervisor is as a therapist. And of course it is very, very trustful and respectful. We ask questions and answer, and ask questions and answer, back and forth in dialogue.
5. Important: I as a supervisor learn from supervision. I take away something from this interaction as well as the supervisee learns something from this. So we contribute, we both contribute, and we both learn and take new things away from this interaction.
6. As much as possible, we want the supervisee to generate his or her ideas. From discourse analysis (of supervision?), I have noticed lots of "hedging" and tentative language. Tentative language invites the supervisee to generate his or her own ideas. It invites a discussion and feedback:
    a. Supervisee/therapist: "Well, I talk a lot during the session because, because the client wasn't saying anything!"
    Supervisor/IKB: "OK, so talking a lot is one way." I may ask then, "So, what else can you do next time when the client doesn't talk?"
    b. This invites the supervisee to generate his own ideas of "what else can I do?"
    c. Using a tentative language: "it seems…" or "it seems like…"

7. Use scaling questions a lot in supervision:
   a. Supervisee talks about a case, and then I would say: "On a scale of 1 to 10, if I were to ask your client, what would he say how much you were helpful to him?"
   b. Or: "On a scale of 1 to 10, how much progress would your client say she is making?"
   c. Or: "On a scale of 1 to 10, how much progress would your client say he has made since he has started therapy with you?"
8. Consult the client: You can also ask, "What would the client say you could do to be more helpful to the client?"
9. "Many supervisors make the mistake of thinking the supervisees don't know anything. Supervisor believes that supervisee don't know anything. And so we keep telling. But just as I do about clients, ...I absolutely believe that all supervisees have lots of abilities. And my job is to bring it out. So, for example, (a supervisee) who talks about (a client) who doesn't talk a lot, my job is to help (the supervisee) use his or her tendency to talk a lot, to use it to be helpful to the client."
10. Criticism: When supervisees present a case, they receive lots of criticism about what you do wrong. This does not help.
11. Client-driven supervision: When using a one-way mirror, after the session is finished, "the supervisor goes in and asks the client right after the session, 'What did this therapist do that was helpful for you?'"
12. Supervision, (case) consultation, and teaching: "Do you make a distinction among the three? They are very different activities...Usually in case discussion, (one) tends to focus on what did you do or what didn't you do. Instead of (an) emphasis on what, maybe you are to pay attention to how... Anybody can get concrete information. That's not hard. What's difficult is how to use the "what," the information you have" ...and that's where we are useful to the supervisee.

References

Cantwell, P. & Holmes, S. (1994). Social construction: A paradigm shift for systemic therapy and training. *Australia and New Zealand Journal for Family Therapy, 15*(1), 17–26.

References

AAMFT. (2005). *Commission on accreditation for marriage and family therapy education accreditation standards*. Retrieved June 7, 2012 from http://www.aamft.org/imis15/Content/COAMFTE/Accreditation.aspx

AAMFT. (2007). *Approved supervisor designation standards and responsibilities handbook*. Retrieved June 7, 2012 from http://www.aamft.org/imis15/content/supervision/Becoming_Supervisor.aspx.

AAMFT. (2012, June). Federal department of veteran affairs announces ten percent clinical mental health staffing increase; will include MFTs. *Family Therapy Magazine, 11*(4), 5.

Abidin, R. R. (2012). *The parenting stress index* (4th ed.). Lutz: Psychological Assessment Resources.

Ahn, H., & Wampold, B. E. (2001). A meta-analysis of component studies: Where is the evidence for the specificity of psychotherapy? *Journal of Counseling Psychology, 48*, 251–257.

American College Personnel Association. (2007). *Professional competencies: A report of the steering committee on professional competencies*. Retrieved July 31, 2012, from www.myacpa.org/au/governance/docs/ACPA_Competencies.doc

American Psychological Association. (2010). Guidelines for child custody evaluations in family law proceedings. *American Psychologist, 65*(9), 863–867.

Amundson, J., Stewart, K., & Valentine, L. (1993). Temptations of power and certainty. *Journal of Marital and Family Therapy, 19*(2), 111–123.

Andersen, T. (1987). The reflecting team: Dialogue and meta-dialogue in clinical work. *Family Process, 26*, 415–428.

Andersen, T. (1991). *The reflecting team: Dialogues and dialogues about the dialogues*. New York: Norton.

Anderson, H. (1997). *Conversation, language, and possibilities: A postmodern approach to therapy*. New York: Basic.

Anderson, H. (2003). Feet planted firmly in midair: A spirituality for family living. In F. Walsh (Ed.), *Spiritual resources in family therapy* (pp. 157–178). New York: Guilford.

Anderson, H. (2005). Myths about "not-knowing.". *Family Process, 44*(4), 497–504.

Anderson, H., & Gehart, D. R. (Eds.). (2006). *Collaborative therapy: Conversations and relationships that make a difference*. New York: Brunner-Routledge.

Anderson, H., & Goolishian, H. (1992). The client is the expert: A not-knowing approach to therapy. In S. McNamee & K. J. Gergen (Eds.), *Therapy as social construction* (pp. 25–39). London: Sage.

Association of Family and Conciliation Courts. (2006). *Model standards of practice for child custody evaluation*. Madison: Association of Family and Conciliation Courts.

Astin, A. W. (1999). Student involvement: A development theory for higher education. *Journal of College Student Personnel, 40*(5), 518–529.

Atkinson, B. J. (1997). Informed consent form. In C. L. Storm & T. C. Todd (Eds.), *The reasonably complete systemic supervisor resource guide* (pp. 11–15). Boston: Allyn & Bacon.

Atkinson, B. J., & Heath, A. W. (1990). Further thoughts on second-order family therapy – This time it's personal. *Family Process, 29*, 145–155.

Baker, E. N. (2006). *The relationship between perceived self-efficacy and clinical supervision among student therapists*. Unpublished master's thesis, California State University, Long Beach.

Bambling, M., King, R., Raue, P., Schweitzer, R., & Lambert, W. (2006). Clinical supervision: Its influence on client-rated working alliance and client symptom reduction in the brief treatment of major depression. *Psychotherapy Research, 16*(3), 317–331. doi:10.1080/10503300500268524

Barnard, C. P., & Kuehl, B. P. (1995). Ongoing evaluation: In-session procedures for enhancing the working alliance and therapy effectiveness. *American Journal of Family Therapy, 23*, 161–172.

Barnes, D., Carlisi, J., Peterik, J. M. (1981). *Hold on loosely [Recorded by 38 Special]. On Hold on loosely [vinyl single]*. Netherlands: A&M Records.

Barnett, J. E., Erickson Cornish, J. A., Goodyear, R. K., & Lichtenberg, J. W. (2007). Commentaries on the ethical and effective practice of clinical supervision. *Professional Psychology: Research and Practice, 38*(3), 268–275.

Barrera, I. (2003). *The impact of solution-focused supervision and social workers*. Unpublished master's thesis, California State University, Long Beach.

Barretta-Herman, A. (2001). Fulfilling the commitment to competent social work practice through supervision. In L. Beddoe & J. Worrall (Eds.), *Supervision conference from rhetoric to reality: Keynote address and selected papers* (pp. 1–10). Auckland: Auckland College of Education.

Bateson, G. (1972). *Steps to an ecology of mind*. Northvale: Jason Aronson.

Bateson, G. (1979). *Mind and nature: A necessary unity*. New York: Dutton.

Bateson, M. C. (1992). *Peripheral visions: Learning along the way*. New York: HarperCollins.

Bavelas, J. B. (2012). Connecting the lab to the therapy room: Microanalysis, co-construction, and solution-focused brief therapy. In C. Franklin, T. S. Trepper, W. J. Gingerich, & E. E. McCollum (Eds.), *Solution-focused brief therapy: A handbook of evidence-based practice* (pp. 144–162). New York: Oxford University Press.

Beck, A. T. (1993). *The Beck anxiety inventory*. San Antonio: Pearson Assessment.

Beck, A. T., Steer, R. A., & Brown, G. K. (1996). *The Beck depression inventory* (2nd ed.). San Antonio: Pearson Assessment.

Becvar, D. S., & Becvar, R. J. (2008). *Family therapy: A systemic integration* (7th ed.). Boston: Pearson.

Benner, P. (1984). *From novice to expert: Excellence and power in clinical nursing practice*. Reading: Addison-Wesley.

Berg, I. K. (1994). *Family-based services: A solution-focused approach*. New York: Norton.

Berg, I. K. (1995). *Irreconcilable differences: A solution-focused approach to marital therapy* [videorecording]. (Available from www.SFBTA.org).

Berg, I. K. (1999a). *Questions lead-in for supervisors*. Unpublished manuscript. Fort Worth: SFBTA Archive.

Berg, I. K. (1999b). *Supervision consult at the Bridge (Item #10546-0129)*. Fort Worth: SFBTA Archive.

Berg, I. K. (2000). *20 minute interview*. Unpublished manuscript.

Berg, I. K. (2002). *Case presentation/consultation outline*. Unpublished manuscript.

Berg, I. K. (2003). *Supervision and mentoring in child welfare services*. Unpublished manuscript. Retrieved July 31, 2012 from http://www.sfbta.org/trainingLinks.html.

Berg, I. K. (2005). The state of miracles in relationships. *Journal of Family Psychotherapy, 16*(1/2), 115–118.

Berg, I. K. (n.d.). *For students only*. Unpublished manuscript.

References

Berg, I. K. (n.d.). *Hot tips III: Application of SFBT in supervision and management.* Unpublished manuscript.

Berg, I. K. (n.d.). *Japan supervision workshop* (video). SFBTA Archive Item 10128–0064. Fort Worth: SFBTA Archive.

Berg, I. K. (n.d.). *Supervision consultation.* SFBTA Archives Item 10173–0092. Fort Worth: SFBTA Archive.

Berg, I. K., & De Jong, P. (1996). Solution-building conversations: Co-constructing a sense of competence with clients. *Families in Society: The Journal of Contemporary Human Services, 77*(6), 376–391.

Berg, I. K., & De Jong, P. (2005). Engagement through complimenting. *Journal of Family Psychotherapy, 16,* 51–56.

Berg, I. K., & de Shazer, S. (1993). Making numbers talk: Language in therapy. In S. Friedman (Ed.), *The new language of change: Constructive collaboration in psychotherapy* (pp. 5–24). New York: Guilford.

Berg, I. K. (n.d., circa 1997). *Supervision conversation.* SFBTA Archive Item #10149-0074. Fort Worth: SFBTA Archive.

Berg, I. K., & Miller, S. D. (1992). *Working with the problem drinker: A solution-focused approach.* New York: Norton.

Berg, I. K., & Szabó, P. (2005). *Brief coaching for lasting results.* New York: Norton.

Berg, I. K., & Wheeler, J. (2006). Riding the underground railroad. *Solution News, 2*(3), 3–6.

Berg, I. K., Friedman, E., Liddle, H., & Todd, T. (1991). *Fielding supervision impasses [video recording].* Alexandria: AAMFT.

Bernard, J. M., & Goodyear, R. K. (2009). *Fundamentals of clinical supervision* (4th ed.). Upper Saddle River: Pearson.

Berne, E. (1964). *Games people play: The psychology of human relationships.* New York: Ballantyne.

Bertrando, P. (2000). Text and context: Narrative, postmodernism and cybernetics. *Journal of Family Therapy, 22,* 83–103.

Beyebach, M. (2000). *European Brief Therapy Association outcome study: Research definition description of the treatment.* Retrieved July 9, 2012 from http://www.ebta.nu/page2/page30/page30.html

Beyebach, M., & Herrero, M. (2004). *The Salamanca research project on stuck cases: A measure of treatment integrity.* European Brief Therapy Association Conference, Amsterdam.

Bidwell, D. R. (2000). Hope and possibility: The theology of culture inherent to solution-focused brief therapy. *American Journal of Pastoral Counseling, 3*(1), 3–21.

Bidwell, D. R. (2007). Miraculous knowing: Epistemology and solution-focused therapy. In T. S. Nelson & F. N. Thomas (Eds.), *Handbook of solution-focused brief therapy: Clinical applications* (pp. 65–87). New York: Haworth.

Bliss, E. V., & Bray, D. (2009). The smallest solution focused particles: Towards a minimalist definition of when therapy is solution focused. *Journal of Systemic Therapies, 28*(2), 62–74.

Bobele, M., Gardner, G., & Biever, J. (1995). Supervision as social construction. *Journal of Systemic Therapies, 14,* 14–25.

Bordin, E. S. (1983). Contemporary models of supervision: A working alliance based model of supervision. *The Counseling Psychologist, 11,* 35–41.

Brickman, P., Coates, D., & Janoff-Bulman, R. (1978). Lottery winners and accident victims: Is happiness relative? *Journal of Personality and Social Psychology, 36,* 917–927.

Briggs, J. R., & Miller, G. (2005). Success enhancing supervision. *Journal of Family Psychotherapy, 16*(1/2), 199–222.

Brodsky, S. L., Hendricson, S., & Scott, M. (1991). *Testifying in court: Guidelines and maxims for the expert witness.* Washington, DC: American Psychological Association.

Bucknell, D. (2000). Practice teaching: Problem to solution. *Social Work Education, 19*(2), 125–144.

Burnham, J. (1993). Approach, method and technique: Making distinctions and creating connections. *Human Systems, 3,* 3–27.

Butcher, J. N., Dahlstrom, W. G., Graham, J. R., Tellegen, A., & Kaemmer, B. (1989). *The Minnesota Multiphasic Personality Inventory* (2nd ed.). Minneapolis: University of Minnesota Press.

Cade, B. (1992). I am an unashamed expert. *CONTEXT: A News Magazine of Family Therapy, 11*, 30–31.

Callahan, J. L., Almstrom, C. M., Swift, J. K., Borja, S. E., & Heath, C. J. (2009). Exploring the contribution of supervisors to intervention outcomes. *Training and Education in Professional Psychology, 3*(2), 72–77.

Cantwell, P., & Holmes, S. (1994). Social construction: A paradigm shift for systemic therapy and training. *Australia and New Zealand Journal for Family Therapy, 15*(1), 17–26.

Cantwell, P., & Holmes, S. (1995). Cumulative process: A collaborative approach to systemic supervision. *Journal of Systemic Therapies, 14*(2), 35–46.

Carlson, T. D., & Erickson, M. J. (2001). Honoring and privileging personal experience and knowledge: Ideas for a narrative therapy approach to the training and supervision of new therapists. *Contemporary Family Therapy, 23*(2), 199–220.

Casemore, R. (2009). It is all in the relationship: Exploring the differences between supervision training and counselling training. In P. Henderson (Ed.), *Supervisor training: Issues and approaches* (pp. 15–25). London: Karnac.

Chang, J. (1998). Children's stories, children's solutions: Social constructionist therapy for children and their families. In M. F. Hoyt (Ed.), *Handbook of constructive therapies* (pp. 251–275). San Francisco: Jossey-Bass.

Chang, J. (2010). Hermeneutic inquiry: A research approach for postmodern therapists. *Journal of Systemic Therapies, 29*(1), 19–32.

ChangingMinds.org. (2005, June 20). *Yes-set close technique*. Retrieved from http://changingminds.org/disciplines/sales/closing/yes-set_close.htm

Chenail, R. J. (1995). Recursive frame analysis. *The Qualitative Report, 2*(2). Retrieved June 20, 2012 from http://www.nova.edu/ssss/QR/QR2-2/rfa.html

Cheon, H. S., Blumer, M. L. C., Shih, A. T., Murphy, M. J., & Sato, M. (2009). The influence of supervisor and supervisee matching, role conflict, and supervisory relationship on supervisee satisfaction. *Contemporary Family Therapy, 31*, 52–67.

Cigrand, D. L., & Wood, S. M. (2012, July 8). *School counseling and solution-focused site supervision: A theoretical application and case example*. Retrieved from www.jsc.montana.edu/articles/v9n6.pdf

College of Alberta Psychologists. (2005). *Standards of practice*. Edmonton: Author.

College of Alberta Psychologists. (2006a). *Professional guidelines for psychologists: Child custody assessment*. Edmonton: Author.

College of Alberta Psychologists. (2006b). *Professional guidelines for psychologists: Psychological evaluations for child protection decisions*. Edmonton: Author.

Communities and Neighbourhood Department. (2012). Accessed April 18, 2012 from http://www.communities.gov.uk/communities/troubledfamilies

Conoley, C. W., Graham, J. M., Neu, T., Craig, M. C., O'Pry, A., Cardin, S. A., Brossart, D. F., & Parker, R. I. (2003). SFBT treatment integrity information: Solution-focused family therapy with three aggressive and oppositional-acting children: An N = 1 empirical study. *Family Process, 42*(3), 361–374.

Constantine, J. A., Piercy, F. P., & Sprenkle, D. H. (1984). Live supervision-of-supervision in family therapy. *Journal of Marital and Family Therapy, 10*, 95–97.

Cooper, R. J. (2009). Solo doctors and ethical isolation. *Journal of Medical Ethics, 35*, 692–695.

Corcoran, K. B. (2001). *An ethnographic study of therapist development and reflectivity within the context of postmodern supervision and training*. Unpublished doctoral dissertation, University of Akron.

Crocket, K., Pentecost, M., Cresswell, R., Paice, C., Tollestrup, D., de Vries, M., & Wolfe, R. (2009). Informing supervision practice through research: A narrative inquiry. *Counselling and Psychotherapy Research, 9*(2), 101–107.

Cullin, J. (2005). The ethics of paradox: Cybernetic and postmodern perspectives on non-direct interventions in therapy. *Australian and New Zealand Journal of Family Therapy, 26*(3), 138–146.

Cunanan, E. D. (2003). *What works when learning solution focused brief therapy: A qualitative analysis of trainees' experiences.* Unpublished master's thesis, Virginia Tech University.

Cunanan, E. D., & McCollum, E. E. (2006). What works when learning solution-focused brief therapy: A qualitative study of trainees' experiences. *Journal of Family Psychotherapy, 17*(1), 49–65.

Curtin, L. L. (1996). Why good people do bad things. *Nursing Management, 27*(7), 63–65.

De Jong, P., Bavelas, J. B., & Korman, H. (2012). *Using microanalysis to observe co-construction in psychotherapy.* Unpublished manuscript.

De Jong, P., & Berg, I. K. (2001). *Interviewing for solutions* (2nd ed.). Pacific Grove: Brooks/Cole Publishing.

De Jong, P., & Berg, I. K. (2005). Engagement through complimenting. *Journal of Family Psychotherapy, 16*(1/2), 51–56.

De Jong, P., & Berg, I. K. (2008). *Interviewing for solutions* (3rd ed.). Belmont: Thomson Brooks/Cole.

De Jong, P., & Berg, I. K. (2012). *Interviewing for solutions* (4th ed.). Belmont: Thomson Brooks/Cole.

De Jong, P., & Cronkright, A. (2011). Learning solution-focused interviewing skills: BSW student voices. *Journal of Teaching in Social Work, 31*, 21–37.

De Jong, P., Kelly, S., Berg, I. K., & Gonzales, L. (2012). *Building strengths-based tools for child protection practice: A case of "parallel process."* Unpublished manuscript. Retrieved July 31, 2012 from http://www.sfbta.org/trainingLinks.html

de Shazer, S. (1979). Brief therapy with families. *American Journal of Family Therapy, 7*(2), 83–95.

de Shazer, S. (1982). *Patterns of brief family therapy: An ecosystemic approach.* New York: Guilford.

de Shazer, S. (1985). *Keys to solution in brief therapy.* New York: Norton.

de Shazer, S. (1988). *Clues: Investigating solutions in brief therapy.* New York: Norton.

de Shazer, S. (1991). *Putting difference to work.* New York: Norton.

de Shazer, S. (1994). *Words were originally magic.* New York: Norton.

de Shazer, S., & Berg, I. K. (1994). *A tap on the shoulder: Six useful questions in building solutions (audio recording).* Milwaukee: Brief Family Therapy Center.

de Shazer, S., & Berg, I. K. (1997). "What works?" Remarks on research aspects of solution-focused brief therapy. *Journal of Family Therapy, 19*(2), 121–124.

de Shazer, S., & Ratner, H. (2002). *"I've tried that!" Supervising the solution-focused practitioner.* Presentation at the European Brief Therapy Association, Cardiff.

de Shazer, S., Berg, I. K., Lipchik, E., Nunnally, E., Molnar, A., Gingerich, W., & Weiner-Davis, M. (1986). Brief therapy: Focused solution development. *Family Process, 25*, 207–222.

de Shazer, S., Dolan, Y., Korman, H., Trepper, T., McCollum, E., & Berg, I. K. (2007). *More than miracles: The state of the art of solution-focused brief therapy.* New York: Haworth.

Dishion, T. J., & Stormshak, E. A. (Eds.). (2007). *Intervening in children's lives: An ecological, family-centered approach to mental health care.* Washington, DC: American Psychological Association. doi:10.1037/11485-008

Doherty, W. J. (1999). *If most therapies are equally effective, why be an MFT? A workshop presented at the American Association for Marriage and Family Therapy Annual Conference,* Chicago.

Dreyfus, H. L., & Dreyfus, S. E. (2005). Expertise in real world contexts. *Organizational Studies, 26*(5), 779–792.

Duncan, B. L., Hubble, M. A., & Miller, S. D. (1997). *Psychotherapy with "impossible" cases: The efficient treatment of therapy veterans.* New York: Norton.

Duncan, B., Miller, S., & Sparks, J. (2004). *The heroic client: A revolutionary way to improve effectiveness through client-directed, outcome-informed therapy.* San Francisco: Jossey-Bass.

Durrant, M. (2012). *Supervision: Building strengths, developing competence*. Unpublished workshop handout. Sydney: Brief Therapy Institute of Sydney.

Einstein, A. (2012). *Quotations*. Retrieved June 15, 2012 from http://www.brainyquote.com/quotes/quotes/a/alberteins103652.html

Ellis, J. M. (1989). *Against deconstruction*. Princeton: Princeton University Press.

Ellis, A. (1994). *Reason and emotion in psychotherapy*. New York: Birch Lane Press.

Ellis, M. V., D'Iuso, N., & Ladany, N. (2008). State of the art in the assessment, measurement, and evaluation of clinical supervision. In A. K. Hess, K. D. Hess, & T. H. Hess (Eds.), *Psychotherapy supervision: Theory, research, and practice* (2nd ed., pp. 473–499). New York: Wiley.

Epstein, R. M., & Hundert, E. M. (2002). Defining and assessing professional competence. *Journal of the American Medical Association, 287*(2), 226–235.

Epstein, E. S., & Loos, V. E. (1989). Some irreverent thoughts on the limits of family therapy: Toward a language-based explanation of human systems. *Journal of Family Psychology, 2*, 405–421.

Erford, B. T. (2012). *Assessment for counselors* (2nd ed.). Boston: Cengage Learning.

Ericsson, K. A., Krampe, R. T., & Tesch-Römer, C. (1993). The role of deliberate practice in the acquisition of expert performance. *Psychological Review, 100*, 363–406.

Etringer, B. D., & Hillerbrand, E. (1995). The transition from novice to expert counselor. *Counselor Education & Supervision, 35*(1), 14. Accessed January 2, 2011 from Academic Search Complete.

Falender, C. A., & Shafranske, E. P. (2004). *Clinical supervision: A competency-based approach*. Washington, DC: American Psychological Association.

Fine, M., & Turner, J. (1997). Collaborative supervision: Minding the power. In T. C. Todd & C. L. Storm (Eds.), *The complete systemic supervisor: Context, philosophy, and pragmatics* (pp. 229–240). Boston: Allyn & Bacon.

Flemons, D. G., Green, S. K., & Rambo, A. H. (1996). Evaluating therapists' practices in a postmodern world: A discussion and scheme. *Family Process, 35*, 43–56.

Fowers, B. J., & Tjeltveit, A. C. (2003). Virtue obscured and retrieved: Character, community, and practices in behavioral science. *American Behavioral Scientist, 47*(4), 387–394.

Franklin, C., & Streeter, C. L. (2003). *Solution-focused accountability schools for the twenty-first century: An evaluation of Garza High School*. The University of Texas at Austin: Hogg Foundation for Mental Health.

Franklin, C., Corcoran, J., Streeter, C. L., & Nowicki, J. (1997). Using client self-anchored scales to measure outcomes in solution-focused therapy. *Journal of Systemic Therapies, 16*(3), 246–265.

Franklin, C., Trepper, T. S., McCollum, E. E., & Gingerich, W. J. (2012). *Solution-focused brief therapy: A handbook of evidence-based practice*. New York: Oxford University Press.

Freitas, G. J. (2002). The impact of psychotherapy supervision on client outcome: A critical examination of 2 decades of research. *Psychotherapy: Theory, Research, Practice, Training, 39*(4), 354–367.

Furman, B., & Ahola, T. (1992). *Solution talk: Hosting therapeutic conversations*. New York: Norton.

Gadamer, H. G. (1989). *Truth and method* (trans: Weinsheimer, J., & Marshall, D. G.). New York: Crossroads Press (Original work published 1960).

Gardner, G. T., Bobele, M., & Biever, J. L. (1997). Postmodern models of family therapy supervision. In T. C. Todd & C. L. Storm (Eds.), *The complete systemic supervisor: Context, philosophy, and pragmatics* (pp. 217–228). Boston: Allyn & Bacon.

Gazzola, N., & Theriault, A. (2007). Super- (and not-so-super-) vision of counsellors-in-training: Supervisee perspectives on broadening and narrowing processes. *British Journal of Guidance and Counselling, 35*(2), 189–204.

Gerard, A. B. (2005). *The parent–child relationship inventory*. Los Angeles: Western Psychological Services.

Gergen, K. J. (1990). Therapeutic professions and the diffusion of deficit. *The Journal of Mind and Behavior, 11*(3/4), 353–368.

Gergen, K. J. (1999). *An invitation to social construction*. London: Sage.
Gergen, K. J. (2001). Psychological science in a postmodern context. *American Psychologist, 56*, 803–813.
Gergen, K. J., Hoffman, L., & Anderson, H. (1996). Is diagnosis a disaster? A constructionist trialogue. In F. W. Kaslow (Ed.), *Handbook of relational diagnosis and dysfunctional family patterns* (pp. 102–118). Oxford: Wiley.
Gershenson, J., & Cohen, M. S. (1978). Through the looking glass: The experiences of two family therapy trainees with live supervision. *Family Process, 17*, 225–229.
Godard, G. J. (2006). *Positioning and intentionality in collaborative counselling relationships*. Unpublished manuscript.
Gorsuch, N. (2001). Collaborative pastoral conversation. In H. W. Stone (Ed.), *Strategies for brief pastoral counseling* (pp. 30–45). Minneapolis: Fortress Press.
Gottman, J., & Carrere, S. (2000). Welcome to the love lab. *Psychology Today, 33*(5), 42, 7.
Gottman, J. M., & Levenson, R. W. (2000). The timing of divorce: Predicting when a couple will divorce over a 14-year-period. *Journal of Marriage and Family, 62*(3), 737–745. doi:10.1111/j.1741-3737.2000.00737.x
Greenleaf, R. K. (2002). *Servant leadership: A journey into the nature of legitimate power & greatness*. Mahwah: Paulist Press.
Haber, R. (1996). *Dimensions of psychotherapy supervision: Maps and means*. New York: Norton.
Haley, J. (1968). An interactional explanation of hypnosis. In D. D. Jackson (Ed.), *Therapy, communication, and change* (pp. 74–96). Palo Alto: Science and Behavior Books.
Haley, J. (1976). *Problem solving therapy*. San Francisco: Jossey-Bass.
Hanna, F. J., & Hunt, W. P. (1999). Techniques for psychotherapy with defiant, aggressive adolescents. *Psychotherapy: Theory, Research, Practice, Training, 36*(1), 56–68.
Harwood, T. M., Beutler, L. E., & Groth-Marnat, G. (2011). *Integrative assessment of adult personality* (3rd ed.). New York: Guilford Press.
Heath, C., & Heath, D. (2010). *Switch: How to change things when change is hard*. New York: Broadway Books.
Heath, A., & Tharp, L. (1991). *What therapists say about supervision*. Dallas: AAMFT.
Heilemann, J., & Halperin, M. (2010). *Game change: Obama and the Clintons, McCain and Palin, and the race of a lifetime*. New York: HarperCollins.
Henden, J. (2011). *Beating combat stress: 101 techniques for recovery*. West Sussex: Wiley-Blackwell.
Henderson, P. (Ed.). (2009). *Supervisor training: Issues and approaches*. London: Karnac.
Hess, A. K. (Ed.). (1980). *Psychotherapy supervision: Theory, research, and practice*. New York: Wiley.
Heylighen, F. (1997). *Occam's razor*. Retrieved May 12, 2012 from Principia Cybernetica Web at http://pespmc1.vub.ac.be/OCCAMRAZ.html
Hofstadter, D. R. (1999). *Gödel, Escher, Bach: An eternal golden braid*. New York: Basic Books.
Holloway, E., & Neufeldt, S. (1995). Supervision: Its contributions to treatment efficacy. *Journal of Consulting and Clinical Psychology, 63*, 207–213.
Homrich, A. M. (2005). *Solution-focused supervision in clinical training*. Solution Focused Brief Therapy Association Conference, Fort Lauderdale.
Hooks, B. (2003). *Teaching community: A pedagogy of hope*. New York: Routledge.
Horsfall, D. (2008). Bearing witness: Toward a pedagogical practice of love? *Reflecting Practice, 9*(1), 1–10.
Horvath, A. O., Del Re, A. C., Flückiger, C., & Symonds, D. (2010). Alliance in individual psychotherapy. In J. C. Norcross (Ed.), *Evidence-based therapy relationships* (pp. 5–6). Washington, DC: SAMHSA.
Hoyt, M. (1996). Solution building and language games: A conversation with Steve de Shazer. In M. Hoyt (Ed.), *Constructive Therapies 2* (pp. 60–86). New York: Guilford Press.
Hoyt, M. (2001). *Interviews with brief therapy experts*. Philadelphia: Brunner-Routledge.

Hsu, W. (2007). Effects of solution-focused supervision. *Bulletin of Educational Psychology, 38*(3), 331–354.
Hsu, W. (2009). The components of solution-focused supervision. *Bulletin of Educational Psychology, 41*(2), 475–496.
Hsu, W. S. (2012). *Solution-building: Solution-focused brief therapy (in Chinese)*. Ningbo: Ningbo Press.
Hsu, W., & Sun, S.-T. M. (2008). *Study on the components of solution-focused supervision*. Workshop presented at the International Counseling Psychology Conference, Chicago.
Hsu, W., & Tsai, S. (2008). The effects of solution-focused group supervision on school counselors. *Bulletin of Educational Psychology, 39*(4), 603–622.
Hsu, W. S., & Tsai, S. L. (2011). The effect of learning of solution-focused brief therapy for junior high school counselors (in Chinese). *Global Mental Health E-Journal, 2*(1), 1–19.
Hubble, M. A., & O'Hanlon, W. H. (1992). Theory countertransference. *Dulwich Centre Newsletter, 1*, 25–30.
Hyland, K. (1996). Writing without conviction? Hedging in science research articles. *Applied Linguistics, 17*(4), 433–454.
Inman, A. G., & Ladany, N. (2008). Research: The state of the field. In A. K. Hess, K. D. Hess, & T. H. Hess (Eds.), *Psychotherapy supervision: Theory, research, and practice* (2nd ed., pp. 500–517). New York: Wiley.
Iveson, C. (2005). Teaching the difficult craft of not knowing. *Solution News, 1*(3), 3–5.
Jackson, D. D. (1968). Family interaction, family homeostasis and some implications for conjoint family psychotherapy. In D. D. Jackson (Ed.), *Therapy, communication, and change* (pp. 185–203). Palo Alto: Science and Behavior Books.
Jackson, P. Z., & McKergow, M. (2007). *The solutions focus: Making coaching & change SIMPLE* (2nd ed.). London: Nicholas Brealey Publishing.
James, E. L. (2012). *Fifty shades darker (Fifty shades, book 2)*. New York: Vintage.
Joiner, T. E., Jr., Sheldon, K. M., Williams, G., & Pettit, J. (2003). The integration of self-determination principles and scientifically informed treatments is the next tier. *Clinical Psychology: Science and Practice, 10*, 318–319.
Jordan, A. E., & Meara, N. M. (2008). Ethics and the professional practice of psychologists: The role of virtues and principles. In D. N. Bersoff (Ed.), *Ethical conflicts in psychology* (4th ed., pp. 139–143). Washington, DC: American Psychological Association.
Juhnke, G. A. (1996). Solution-focused supervision: Promoting supervisee skills and confidence through successful solutions. *Counselor Education and Supervision, 36*, 49–57.
Kahneman, D., & Klein, G. (2009). Conditions for intuitive expertise: A failure to disagree. *American Psychologist, 64*(6), 515–526.
Keeney, B. P. (1983). *Aesthetics of change*. New York: Guilford.
Keeney, H., & Keeney, B. (2012). *Circular therapeutics: Giving therapy a healing heart*. Ithaca: Zeig, Tucker, & Theisen.
Keeney, B. P., & Thomas, F. N. (1986). Cybernetic foundations in family therapy. In F. Piercy & D. Sprenkle (Eds.), *Family therapy sourcebook* (pp. 262–287). New York: Guilford.
Ketonen, Y., & Korhonen, M. (toim). (2007). *Työnohjaus, Suomen Työnohjaajat ry:n 25-vuotisjuhlakirja*. Suomen Työnohjaajat ry.
Keyes, R. (2006). *The quote verifier: Who said what, where, and when*. New York: St. Martin's Griffin.
Kilminster, S. M., & Jolly, B. C. (2000). Effective supervision in clinical practice settings: A literature review. *Medical Education, 34*, 827–840.
Kitchener, K. S. (1984). Ethics in counseling psychology: Distinctions and directions. *The Counseling Psychologist, 12*(3), 15–18.
Klinger, R. S., Ladany, N., & Kulp, L. E. (2012). It's too late to apologize: Therapist embarrassment and shame. *The Counseling Psychologist, 40*(4), 554–574. doi:10.1177/0011000011416372
Knight, C. (2004). Modeling professionalism and supervising interns. In M. J. Austin & K. Hopkins (Eds.), *Supervision as collaboration in the human services* (pp. 110–124). Thousand Oaks: Sage.

Knight, C. (2005). Integrating solution-focused principles and techniques into clinical practice and supervision. *The Clinical Supervisor, 23*(2), 153–173.

Koltz, R. L., Odegard, M. A., Feit, S. S., Provost, K., & Smith, T. (2012). Parallel process and isomorphism: A model for decision making in the supervisory triad. *The Family Journal, 20*(3), 233–238. doi:10.1177/1066480712448788

Koob, J. J. (1999). *The effects of solution-focused supervision on the perceived self-efficacy of developing therapists.* Unpublished doctoral dissertation, Marquette University.

Koob, J. J. (2002). The effects of solution-focused supervision on the perceived self-efficacy of therapists in training. *The Clinical Supervisor, 21*(2), 161–183.

Korinek, A. W., & Kimball, T. G. (2003). Managing and resolving conflict in the supervisory system. *Contemporary Family Therapy, 25,* 295–309.

Korman, H. (2012). *Language and therapy.* Posted August 24, 2012 on SFT-L (Solution Focused Therapy Listserv, SFT-L@LISTSERV.ICORS.ORG).

Korman, H., & Söderquist, M. (1999). *"Talk about a miracle!" Cooperating with addicts and their networks.* Unpublished manuscript, Malmö, Sweden. Retrieved August 3, 2009 from http://www.sikt.nu/Articl_and_book/eng%20articles.htm

Kuehl, B. (2008). Geogram of family therapy. *Family Therapy Magazine,* September/October, 12–21 ff.

Ladany, N., & Lehrman-Waterman, D. E. (1999). The content and frequency of supervisor self-disclosures and their relationship to supervisor style and the supervisory working alliance. *Counselor Education and Supervision, 38,* 143–160.

Ladany, N., Hill, C. E., Corbett, M., & Nutt, L. (1996). Nature, extent, and importance of what therapy trainees do not disclose to their supervisors. *Journal of Counseling Psychology, 43,* 10–24.

Lakoff, G. (1973). Hedges: A study in meaning criteria and the logic of fuzzy concepts. *Journal of Philosophical Logic, 2,* 458–508.

Lambert, M. J., & Hawkins, E. J. (2001). Using information about patient progress in supervision: Are outcomes enhanced? *Australian Psychologist, 36,* 131–138.

Lee, M. Y., Sebold, J., & Uken, A. (2003). *Solution-focused treatment with domestic violence offenders: Accountability for change.* New York: Oxford University Press.

Lehrman-Waterman, D., & Ladany, N. (2001). Development and validation of the Evaluation Process within Supervision Inventory. *Journal of Counseling Psychology, 48*(2), 168–177.

Levenson, E. A. (1984). Follow the fox. In L. Caligor, P. M. Bromberg, & J. D. Meltzer (Eds.), *Clinical perspectives on the supervision of psychoanalysis and psychotherapy* (pp. 153–167). New York: Plenum Press.

Lichtenberg, J. W. (2006). What makes for effective supervision? In search of clinical outcomes. *Professional Psychology: Research and Practice, 38*(3), 275.

Liddle, H. A., & Saba, G. W. (1983). On context replication: The isomorphic relationship of training and therapy. *The Journal of Strategic and Systemic Therapies, 2*(2), 3–11.

Liddle, H. A., Breunlin, D. C., Schwartz, R. C., & Constantine, J. A. (1984). Training family therapy supervisors: Issues of content, form and context. *Journal of Marital and Family Therapy, 10*(2), 139–150.

Liddle, H. A., & Saba, G. W. (1985). The isomorphic nature of training and therapy: Epistemologic foundation for a structural-strategic training paradigm. In J. Schwartzman (Ed.), *Families and other systems: The macrosystemic context of family therapy* (pp. 27–47). New York: Guilford.

Lipchik, E. (1988). Purposeful sequences for beginning the solution-focused interview. In E. Lipchik (Ed.), *Interviewing* (pp. 105–116). Rockville: Aspen.

Lipchik, E. (2002). *Beyond technique in solution-focused therapy: Working with emotions and the therapeutic relationship.* New York: Guilford Press.

Lipchik, E., Walter, J., Miller, G., Gingerich, W., Gallagher, D., & Cade, B. (2010). *The SFBT founders group.* A plenary presented at the annual conference of the European Brief Therapy Association (EBTA), Malmö.

Lloyd, H., & Dallos, R. (2008). First session solution-focused brief therapy with families who have a child with severe intellectual disabilities: Mothers' experiences and views. *Journal of Family Therapy, 30*, 5–28.

London, S., & Tarragona, M. (2007). Collaborative therapy and supervision in a psychiatric hospital. In H. Anderson & D. Gehart (Eds.), *Collaborative therapy: Relationships and conversations that make a difference* (pp. 251–267). New York: Routledge/Taylor & Francis.

Lowe, R. (2000). Supervising self-supervision: Constructive inquiry and embedded narratives in case consultation. *Journal of Marital and Family Therapy, 26*(4), 511–521.

Lowe, R., & Guy, G. (2002). Solution oriented inquiry for ongoing supervision: Expanding the horizon of change. In M. McMahon & W. Patton (Eds.), *Supervision in the helping professions: A practical approach* (pp. 66–77). French Forrest: Pearson Education Australia.

Macdonald, A. J. (2007a). Applying solution-focused brief therapy in mental health practice. In T. S. Nelson & F. N. Thomas (Eds.), *Handbook of solution focused brief therapy: Clinical application* (pp. 267–294). Binghamton: Haworth.

Macdonald, A. J. (2007b). *Solution-focused therapy: Theory, research & practice*. Los Angeles: Sage.

Madanes, C. (1981). *Strategic family therapy*. San Francisco: Jossey-Bass.

Magic Eye. (2012, July 7). Retrieved from www.magiceye.com/faq_example.htm

Malinen, T., Cooper, S. J., & Thomas, F. N. (Eds.). (2011). *Masters of collaborative and narrative therapy: The voices of Tom Andersen, Harlene Anderson, and Michael White*. New York: Routledge.

Marek, L. I., Sandifer, D. M., Beach, A., Coward, R. L., & Protinsky, H. O. (1994). Supervision without the problem: A model of solution-focused supervision. *Journal of Family Psychotherapy, 5*, 57–64.

Marovic, S., & Snyders, F. (2010). Cybernetics of supervision: A developmental perspective. *The Clinical Supervisor, 29*, 35–50.

Maturana, H. R., & Poerksen, B. (2004). The view of the systemicist: A conversation. *Journal of Constructivist Psychology, 17*, 269–279.

McCollum, E., & Wetchler, J. (1995). In defense of case consultation: Maybe "dead" supervision isn't dead after all. *Journal of Marital and Family Therapy, 21*(2), 155–166.

McEwen, M. K. (2005). The nature and uses of theory. In M. E. Wilson & L. E. Wolf-Wendel (Eds.), *ASHE Reader on College Student Developmental Theory* (pp. 5–23). New York: Pearson.

McGee, D., Del Vento, A., & Bavelas, J. B. (2005). An interactional model of questions as therapeutic interventions. *Journal of Marital and Family Therapy, 31*(4), 371–384.

McKergow, M., & Clarke, J. (2007). *Solutions focus working: 80 real-life lessons for successful organisational change*. Cheltenham: SolutionsBooks.

McKergow, M., & Korman, H. (2009). Inbetween—neither inside nor outside: The radical simplicity of solution-focused brief therapy. *Journal of Systemic Therapies, 28*(2), 34–49.

McNamee, S., & Gergen, K. (1992). *Therapy as social construction*. London: Sage.

Mee-Lee, D., McLellan, A. T., & Miller, S. D. (2010). What works in substance abuse and dependence treatment. In B. L. Duncan, S. D. Miller, B. E. Wampold, & M. A. Hubble (Eds.), *The heart and soul of change: Delivering what works in therapy* (2nd ed.). Washington, DC: American Psychological Association.

Metcalf, L., Thomas, F. N., Miller, S. D., Hubble, M. A., & Duncan, B. (1996). Client and therapist perceptions of solution focused brief therapy: A qualitative analysis. In S. D. Miller, M. A. Hubble, & B. L. Duncan (Eds.), *Handbook of solution focused brief therapy: Foundations, applications, and research* (pp. 335–349). San Francisco: Jossey Bass.

Miller, G. (1997). Systems and solutions: The discourses of brief therapy. *Contemporary Family Therapy, 19*(1), 5–22.

Miller, S. D. (2012). *Performance metrics*. Retrieved July 23, 2012 from http://scottdmiller.com/?q=node/6

Miller, G., & de Shazer, S. (1998). Have you heard the latest rumor about…? Solution-focused therapy as a rumor. *Family Process, 37*(3), 363–377.

References

Miller, S. D., & Hubble, M. A. (2006). Further archeological and ethnological findings on the obscure, late 20th century, quasi-religious earth group known as "the Therapists" (a fantasy about the future of psychotherapy). *Journal of Psychotherapy Integration, 14*(1), 38–65.

Miller, G., & McKergow, M. (2012). From Wittgenstein, complexity and narrative emergence: Discourse and solution-focused brief therapy. In A. Lock & T. Strong (Eds.), *Discursive perspectives in therapeutic practice* (pp. 163–183). Oxford: Oxford University Press.

Millon, T., Millon, C., Davis, R., & Grossman, S. (1994). *The Millon Multiaxial Clinical Inventory* (3rd ed.). San Antonio: Pearson Assessment.

Mills, S. D., & Sprenkle, D. H. (1995). Family therapy in the postmodern era. *Family Relations, 44*, 368–376.

Milne, D. L., Pilkington, J., Gracie, J., & James, I. (2003). Transferring skills from supervision to therapy: A qualitative and quantitative N=1 analysis. *Behavioural and Cognitive Psychotherapy, 31*, 193–202.

Milne, D., Aylott, H., Fitzpatrick, H., & Ellis, M. V. (2008). How does clinical supervision work? Using a "best evidence synthesis" approach to construct a basic model of supervision. *The Clinical Supervisor, 27*(2), 170–190.

Monk, G., & Sinclair, S. L. (2002). Toward discursive presence: Advancing a social constructionist approach to self-supervision. *The Clinical Supervisor, 21*(2), 109–128.

Morgan, M. M., & Sprenkle, D. H. (2007). Toward a common-factors approach to supervision. *Journal of Marital and Family Therapy, 33*(1), 1–17.

Nash, J. (1999). Developing and refining supervisory skills: An application of solution-focused thinking. *Educational Psychology in Practice, 15*(2), 108–115.

Nelson, M. L., & Friedlander, M. L. (2001). A close look at conflictual supervisory relationships: The trainee's perspective. *Journal of Counseling Psychology, 48*, 384–395.

Nelson, M. L., Gray, L. A., Friedlander, M. L., Ladany, N., & Walker, J. (2001). Toward relationship-centered supervision: Reply to Veach (2001) and Ellis (2001). *Journal of Counseling Psychology, 48*(4), 407–409.

Nims, D. R. (2007). Integrating play therapy techniques into solution-focused brief therapy. *International Journal of Play Therapy, 16*, 54–68. doi:10.1037/1555-6824.16.1.54

Norcross, J. C. (2003). Empirically supported therapy relationships. In J. C. Norcross (Ed.), *Psychotherapy relationships that work* (pp. 3–16). New York: Oxford University Press.

Norcross, J. C., & Halgin, R. P. (1997). Integrative approaches to psychotherapy supervision. In C. E. Watkins Jr. (Ed.), *Handbook of psychotherapy supervision* (pp. 203–222). Chichester: Wiley.

Norman, H. (2003). Solution-focused reflecting teams. In B. O'Connell & S. Palmer (Eds.), *Handbook of solution-focused therapy* (pp. 156–167). London: Sage.

Nunnally, E., & Berg, I. K. (1983). We tried to push the river. *The Journal of Strategic and Systemic Therapies, 2*(1), 63–68.

Nyland, D., & Corsiglia, V. (1994). Becoming solution-focused forced in brief therapy: Remembering something important we already knew. *Journal of Systemic Therapies, 13*(1), 5–12.

O'Connell, B., & Jones, C. (2001). Solution-focused supervision. In S. Palmer & J. Milner (Eds.), *Counselling, 2*, 402–408.

O'Connor, J., & McDermott, I. (1997). *The art of systems thinking: Essential skills for creativity and problem solving*. London: Thorsons.

O'Donoghue, K. (2012). Windows on the supervisee experience: An exploration of supervisees' supervision histories. *Australian Social Work, 65*(2), 214–231.

O'Hanlon, W. H., & Weiner-Davis, M. (1989). *In search of solutions: A new direction in psychotherapy*. New York: Norton.

O'Hanlon, W., & Wilk, J. (1987). *Shifting contexts: The generation of effective psychotherapy*. New York: Guilford.

Olk, M. E., & Friedlander, M. L. (1992). Trainees' experiences of role conflict and role ambiguity in supervisory relationships. *Journal of Counseling Psychology, 39*(3), 389–397.

OQ Measures. (2012). *OQ®-45*. Retrieved June 12, 2012 from www.oqmeasures.com

Pakrosnis, R., & Čepukienė, V. (2011). *Solution-focused self-reflection for personal growth: An outcome study*. Research poster presented at the Solution-Focused Brief Therapy Association Conference, Bakersfield.

Parker, I. (2004). *Qualitative psychology: Introducing radical research*. Buckingham: Open University Press.

Parry, A. (1991). A universe of stories. *Family Process, 30*, 37–54.

Pearce, J., & Pezzot-Pearce, T. (2004). *Parenting assessments in child welfare cases: A practical guide*. Toronto: University of Toronto Press.

Pearson, Q. M. (2006). Psychotherapy-based supervision: Integrating counseling theories into role-based supervision. *Journal of Mental Health Counseling, 28*, 241–252.

Pettifor, J., McCarron, M. C. E., Schoepp, G., Stark, C., & Stewart, D. (2011). Ethical supervision in teaching, research, practice, and administration. *Canadian Psychology, 52*, 198–205.

Philp, K., Guy, G., & Lowe, R. (2007). Social constructionist supervision or supervision as social construction? Some dilemmas. *Journal of Systemic Therapies, 26*(1), 51–62.

Pichot, T., & Dolan, Y. M. (2003). *Solution-focused brief therapy: Its effective use in agency settings*. New York: Haworth.

Pond, C. (1997). Highlighting success in groups: Empowering and energizing supervisees. In C. L. Storm & T. C. Todd (Eds.), *The reasonably complete systemic supervisor resource guide* (pp. 165–167). Boston: Allyn & Bacon.

Pope-Davis, D. B., & Coleman, H. L. K. (Eds.). (1997). *Multicultural counseling competencies: Assessment, education and training, and supervision*. Thousand Oaks: Sage.

Powers, W. T. (1973). *Behavior: The control of perception*. Chicago: Aldine de Gruyter.

Presbury, J., Echterling, L. G., & McKee, J. E. (1999). Supervision for inner vision: Solution-focused strategies. *Counselor Education and Supervision, 39*, 146–152.

Prince, E. F., Frader, J., & Bosk, C. (1982). On hedging in physician-physician discourse. In R. di Pietro (Ed.), *Linguistics and the professions: Proceedings of the second annual Delaware symposium on language studies* (pp. 83–97). Norwood: Ablex.

Ratner, H., George, E., & Iveson, C. (2012). *Solution focused brief therapy: 100 key points and techniques*. London: Routledge.

Ray, W. A., & Nardone, G. (2009). *Paul Watzlawick: Insight may cause blindness and other essays*. Ithaca: Zeig, Tucker & Theisen.

Reese, R. J., Usher, E. L., Bowman, D. C., Norsworthy, L. A., Halstead, J. L., Rowlands, S. R., & Chisholm, R. R. (2009). Using client feedback in psychotherapy training: An analysis of its influence on supervision and counselor self-efficacy. *Training and Education in Professional Psychology, 3*(3), 157–168.

Reichelt, S., Gullestad, S., Hansen, B., Rønnestad, M., Torgersen, A., & Jacobsen, C., et al. (2009). Nondisclosure in psychotherapy group supervision: The supervisee perspective. *Nordic Psychology, 61*(4), 5–27. doi:10.1027/1901-2276.61.4.5

Roe v. Wade, 410 U.S. 113 (1973).

Roffman, M. S. (2007). *Supervisee perceptions of supervisory focus on strengths and constructive focus on deficits: Development and validation of a measure*. Dissertation, University of Maryland.

Rogers, C. (1951). *Client-centered therapy*. Boston: Houghton Mifflin.

Rosenthal, R. (2002). Experimenter and clinician effects in scientific inquiry and clinical practice. *Prevention & Treatment, 5*, 12.

Ross, L. R. (2011). Attachment "disorders": Capitalizing on misfortune. *Atlantis: A Women's Studies Journal, 35*(2), 51–61.

Rudes, J. (1992). *Language games in focused supervision: A post-structural analysis*. Unpublished dissertation, Nova Southeastern University.

Rudes, J., Shilts, L., & Berg, I. K. (1997). Focused supervision seen through a recursive frame analysis. *Journal of Marital and Family Therapy, 23*(2), 203–215.

Schröder, T., & Davis, J. (2004). Therapists' experience of difficulty in practice. *Psychotherapy Research, 14*, 328–345.

Selekman, M. D., & Todd, T. C. (1995). Co-creating a context for change in the supervisory systems: The solution-focused supervision model. *Journal of Systemic Therapies, 14*(3), 21–33.

Selvini-Palazzoli, M., Boscolo, L., Cecchin, G.-F., & Prata, G. (1978). *Paradox and counterparadox: A new model in the therapy of the family in schizophrenic transaction.* New York: Jason Aronson.

Shilts, L., Rambo, A., & Hernandez, L. (1997). Clients helping therapists find solutions to their therapy. *Contemporary Family Therapy, 19*, 117–132.

Shotter, J. (1993). *Conversational realities: Constructing life through language.* London: Sage.

Skott-Myhre, H. A. (1994). Competency based counseling: Some reflections on stance. *News of the Difference, 3*(1), 3–6.

Skovholt, T. M. (2001). *The resilient practitioner.* Boston: Allyn & Bacon.

Skovholt, T. M., Rønnestad, M. H., & Jennings, L. (1997). Searching for expertise in counseling, psychotherapy and professional psychology. *Educational Psychology Review, 9*, 361–369.

Slife, B. D. (2004). Theoretical challenges to therapy practice and research: The constraint of naturalism. In M. Lambert (Ed.), *Handbook of psychotherapy and behavior change* (pp. 44–83). New York: Wiley.

Slife, B. D. (2005). Testing the limits of Henriques' proposal: Wittgensteinian lessons and hermeneutic dialogue. *Journal of Clinical Psychology, 61*, 1–14.

Slife, B. D., & Gantt, E. (1999). Methodological pluralism: A framework for psychotherapy research. *Journal of Clinical Psychology, 55*(12), 1–13.

Slife, B. D., Wiggins, B. J., & Graham, J. T. (2005). Avoiding an EST monopoly: Toward a pluralism on philosophies and methods. *Journal of Contemporary Psychotherapy, 35*(1), 83–97.

Sluzki, C. E. (1990). Negative explanation, drawing distinctions, raising dilemmas, collapsing time, externalisation of problems: A note on some power conceptual tools. *Residential Treatment for Children & Youth, 7*(3), 33–37.

Smith, J. D., & Dumont, F. (2002). Confidence in psychodiagnosis: What makes us so sure? *Clinical Psychology & Psychotherapy, 9*, 292–298.

Smock, S. A., McCollum, E. E., & Stevenson, M. L. (2010). The development of the solution building inventory. *Journal of Marital and Family Therapy, 36*(4), 499–510.

Snyder, C. R. (2002). Hope theory: Rainbows in the mind. *Psychological Inquiry, 13*(4), 249–275.

Solution-Focused Brief Therapy Association (SFBTA). (2012). *Proposal guidelines.* Retrieved July 9, 2012 from http://www.sfbta.org/confProps/proposal_guidelines.html

Sommers-Flanagan, J. (2012). *The miraculous (or not) efficacy of solution-focused therapy.* Retrieved July 12, 2012 from http://www.psychotherapy.net/blog/title/the-miraculous-or-not-efficacy-of-solution-focused-therapy

Sparks, J. A., Kisler, T. S., Adams, J. F., & Blumen, D. G. (2011). Teaching accountability: Using client feedback to train effective family therapists. *Journal of Marital and Family Therapy, 37*, 452–467.

Sparrer, I. (2007). *Miracle, solution and system: Solution-focused systemic structural constellations for therapy and organizational change.* Cheltenham: SolutionsBooks.

Sperry, L. (2005). Case conceptualization: A strategy for incorporating individual, couple, and family dynamics in the treatment process. *American Journal of Family Therapy, 33*(5), 353–364. doi:10.1080/01926180500341598

Spiegel, A. (2005, January 3). The dictionary of disorder: How one man revolutionized psychiatry. *The New Yorker*, 56–63.

Stark, M. D., Frels, R. K., & Garza, Y. (2011). The use of sandtray in solution-focused supervision. *The Clinical Supervisor, 30*(2), 277–290. doi:10.1080/07325223.2011.621869

Steinhelber, J., Patterson, V., Cliffe, K., & LeGoullon, M. (1984). An investigation of some relationships between psychotherapy supervision and patient change. *Journal of Clinical Psychology, 40*(3), 1346–1353.

Stewart, K. (2003). *Certainty in couples therapy*. American Association for Marriage and Family Therapy, Long Beach.

Stewart, K., & Amundson, J. (1995). The ethical postmodernist: Or not everything is relative all at once. *Journal of Systemic Therapies, 14*(2), 70–78.

Stith, S. M., McCollum, E. E., Rosen, K. H., Locke, L. D., & Goldberg, P. D. (2005). Domestic violence-focused couples treatment. In J. L. Lebow (Ed.), *Handbook of clinical family therapy* (pp. 406–430). Hoboken: Wiley.

Stoltenberg, C. D., & McNeill, B. W. (2010). *IDM supervision: An integrative developmental model for supervising counselors and therapists* (3rd ed.). New York: Routledge.

Stoltenberg, C. D., McNeill, B., & Delworth, U. (1998). *IDM supervision: An integrated developmental model for supervising counselors and therapists*. San Francisco: Jossey-Bass.

Storm, C. L., Todd, T. C., McDowell, T., & Sutherland, T. (1997). Supervising supervisors. In T. C. Todd & C. L. Storm (Eds.), *The complete systemic supervisor: Context, philosophy, and pragmatics* (pp. 373–388). Boston: Allyn & Bacon.

Strong, T. (2007). Accomplishments in social constructionist counseling: Micro-analytic and retrospective analyses. *Qualitative Research in Psychology, 4*(1/2), 85–105.

Strong, T., Pyle, N. R., & Sutherland, O. (2009). Scaling questions: Asking and answering them in counselling. *Counselling Psychology Quarterly, 22*(2), 171–185.

Sundman, P. (1992). Ratkaisukeskeisellä työnohjauksella ripeästi muutostyön alkuun (A rapid start in supervision with the solution focused approach). *Sosiaaliturva, 16*, 19–23.

Tarasoff v. Regents of the University of California, 17 Cal. 3d 425, 551 P.2d 334, 131 Cal. Rptr. 14 (California Supreme Court, 1976).

Taylor, L. (2010). *Workshop manual for training trainers and supervisors*. SFBTA Conference, Banff, Canada.

Ten Tips for Comforting Colic. (2012). Retrieved July 14, 2012 from http://www.askdrsears.com/topics/fussy-baby/coping-colic/10-tips-comforting-colic

Texas Family Code Chapter 261: Investigation of report of child abuse or neglect. Retrieved July 22, 2012 from http://www.statutes.legis.state.tx.us/Docs/FA/htm/FA.261.htm

Tharpar v. Zezulka, 994S.W.2d 635 (Texas Supreme Court 1999).

Thomas, F. N. (1990). *The coaxing of expertise: Solution focused supervision*. American Association for Marriage and Family Therapy Conference, Washington, DC.

Thomas, F. N. (1992). *Solution oriented supervision*. American Association for Marriage and Family Therapy Annual Conference, Miami.

Thomas, F. N. (1994a). The experience of solution oriented therapy: Post therapy client interviewing. *Case Studies in Brief and Family Therapy, 8*(1), 47–58.

Thomas, F. N. (1994b). Solution oriented supervision: The coaxing of expertise. *The Family Journal: Counseling and Therapy for Couples and Families, 2*(1), 11–18.

Thomas, F. N. (1996). Solution-focused supervision: The coaxing of expertise. In S. D. Miller, M. A. Hubble, & B. L. Duncan (Eds.), *Handbook of solution-focused brief therapy* (pp. 128–151). San Francisco: Jossey-Bass.

Thomas, F. N. (2000). Mutual admiration: Fortifying your competency-based supervision experience. *RATKES: Journal of the Finnish Association for the Advancement of Solution and Resource Oriented Therapy and Methods, 2*, 30–39.

Thomas, F. N. (2007a). Possible limitations, misunderstandings, and misuses of solution-focused brief therapy. In T. S. Nelson & F. N. Thomas (Eds.), *Handbook of solution-focused brief therapy: Clinical applications* (pp. 391–408). Binghamton: Haworth.

Thomas, F. N. (2007b). Simpler may not be better: A personal journey with and beyond systemic and solution-focused practices. *Journal of the Texas Association for Marriage and Family Therapy, 12*(1), 4–29.

Thomas, F. N. (2007c). *Solution-focused supervision: Coaxing expertise*. Workshop presented for the University of Pittsburgh School of Social Work, Pittsburgh.

Thomas, F. N. (2008). The hurried therapist: Ethics and the pressure toward mastery. *CONTEXT: The Magazine for Family Therapy and Systemic Practice, 46*, 33–35.

References

Thomas, F. N. (2010a). *The consultation style of Insoo Kim Berg: Themes and techniques from the SFBTA/BFTC Archive*. European Brief Therapy Association, Malmö.
Thomas, F. N. (2010b). Semaphore, metaphor, two-by-four. In T. S. Nelson (Ed.), *Doing something different: Solution-focused brief therapy practices* (pp. 219–224). New York: Routledge.
Thomas, F. N. (2012a). Psychotherapist self-care: Resourcefulness across one's career. In H. Schemmel, & J. Schaller (Eds.), *Ressourcen: Ein Hand-und Lesebuch zur therapeutischen Arbeit* (2nd ed.). Tübingen, Germany: Dgvt-Verlag.
Thomas, F. N. (2012b). Solution focused supervision: Lessons from Insoo Kim Berg. In P. De Jong & I. K. Berg (Eds.), *Interviewing for solutions* (4th ed., pp. 345–354). Belmont: Thomson Brooks/Cole.
Thomas, F. N., & Nelson, T. S. (2007). Assumptions within the solution-focused brief therapy tradition. In T. S. Nelson & F. N. Thomas (Eds.), *Handbook of solution-focused brief therapy: Clinical applications* (pp. 3–24). Binghamton: Haworth.
Thomas, F. N., & Shappee, K. (2001). *Solution-focused supervision: The trainees' voices*. Workshop presented at the European Brief Therapy Association Conference, Dublin.
Thomas, F. N., Coffey, A., Scott, S., & Shappee, K. (2000a). (How) am I competent to supervise? In *Readings in family therapy supervision* (pp. 52–54). Washington, DC: AAMFT.
Thomas, F. N., Coffey, A., Scott, S., & Shappee, K. (2000b). *The other sides of the story: How trainees view supervision*. Workshop presented at the American Association for Marriage and Family Therapy conference, Denver.
Thomas, F. N., Wheeler, J., Lowe, R., Durrant, M., Fleckney, G., & Greaves, Y. (2002). *Searching for strengths in solution focused supervision*. Workshop presented at the European Brief Therapy Association Conference, Cardiff.
Todd, T. C., & Storm, C. L. (1997). *The complete systemic supervisor: Context, philosophy, and pragmatics*. Boston: Allyn & Bacon.
Todd, T. C. (1997a). Problems in supervision: Lessons from supervisees. In T. C. Todd & C. L. Storm (Eds.), *The complete systemic supervisor: Context, philosophy, and pragmatics* (pp. 241–252). Boston: Allyn & Bacon.
Todd, T. C. (1997b). Self-supervision as a universal supervisory goal. In T. C. Todd & C. L. Storm (Eds.), *The complete systemic supervisor: Context, philosophy, and pragmatics* (pp. 17–25). Boston: Allyn & Bacon.
Todd, T. A., Joanning, H., Enders, L., Mutchler, L., & Thomas, F. N. (1990). Using ethnographic interviews to create a more cooperative client therapist relationship. *Journal of Family Psychotherapy, 1*(3), 51–64.
Tognetti, S. S. (2002). Gregory Bateson. In P. Timmerman (Ed.), *Encyclopedia of global environmental change* (pp. 183–184). Chichester: Wiley.
Tomm, K. (1992). Ethical postures in therapy. *CONTEXT: A News Magazine of Family Therapy, 11*, 12–13.
Tomm, K., & Wright, L. (1982). Multilevel training and supervision in an outpatient service program. In R. Whiffen & J. Byng-Hall (Eds.), *Family therapy supervision* (pp. 211–227). New York: Grune & Stratton.
Tomm, K., Hoyt, M. F., & Madigan, S. P. (1998). Honoring our internalized others and the ethics of caring: A conversation with Karl Tomm. In M. F. Hoyt (Ed.), *The handbook of constructive therapies: Innovative approaches from leading practitioners* (pp. 198–218). San Francisco: Jossey-Bass.
Tomori, C., & Bavelas, J. B. (2007). Using microanalysis of communication to compare solution-focused and client-centered therapies. *Journal of Family Psychotherapy, 18*(3), 25–43.
Torti, P. (1997). *Supervision from a narrative perspective: The supervisee's experience*. Unpublished doctoral dissertation, Texas Woman's University.
Totro, T. (2007). Nykyisyys, menneisyys ja tulevaisuus työnojauksessa – teorianäköaloja (Present, past and future in supervision – theory perspectives). In Y. Ketonen & M. Korhonen (Eds.), *Työnohjaus (supervision)* (pp. 118–130). Oulu: Suomen Työnohjaajat ry.
Townsend, L. (2009). *Introduction to pastoral counseling*. Nashville: Abingdon Press.

Trenhaile, J. D. (2005). Solution-focused supervision: Returning the focus to client goals. *Journal of Family Psychotherapy, 16*(1/2), 223–228.
Triantafillou, N. (1997). A solution-focused approach to mental health supervision. *Journal of Systemic Therapies, 16*(4), 305–328.
Tromski-Klingshirn, D. M., & Davis, T. E. (2007). Supervisees' perceptions of their clinical supervision: A study of the dual role of clinical and administrative supervisor. *Counselor Education and Supervision, 46*, 294–304.
Turnell, A., & Edwards, S. (1999). *Signs of safety: A safety and solution oriented approach to child protection casework*. New York: Norton.
Turner, J., & Fine, M. (1995). Postmodern evaluation in family therapy supervision. *Journal of Systemic Therapies, 14*(2), 57–69.
Ueland, B. (1992). Tell me more: On the fine art of listening. *UTNE Reader*, November/December, 104–109.
Ungar, M. (2006). Practicing as a postmodern supervisor. *Journal of Marital and Family Therapy, 32*(1), 59–72.
Vargas, H. L., & Wilson, C. M. (2011). Managing worldview influences: Self-awareness and self-supervision in a cross-cultural therapeutic relationship. *Journal of Family Psychotherapy, 22*, 97–113.
Varttala, T. (2001). *Hedging in scientifically oriented discourse: Exploring variation according to discipline and intended audience*. Unpublished dissertation. Retrieved July 2, 2012 from www.helsinki.fi/englanti/elfa/ProGradu_Niina_Riekkinen.pdf
Visser, C. (2004). *Interview with Insoo Kim Berg*. Retrieved August 28, 2010 from http://interviewscoertvisser.blogspot.com/2007/11/interview-with-insoo-kim-berg.html, 5 pp.
von Bertalanffy, L. (1968). *General system theory: Foundations, development, applications*. New York: Norton.
von Foerster, H. (1976). The need of perception for the perception of needs. In K. Wilson (Ed.), *The collected works of the Biological Computer Laboratory*. Peoria: Illinois Blueprint Corporation.
von Foerster, H. (1984). On constructing a reality. *Observing systems* (2nd ed.). Seaside: Intersystems Publications.
von Foerster, H. (1990). Ethics and second-order cybernetics. *Systèmes, Éthique perspectives: En thérapie familiale. Textes issus des travaux du Congrès Système et thérapie familiale*, 4, 5, 6 Octobre 1990. Paris: ESF éditeur.
von Glasersfeld, E. (1995, 1986). *Radical constructivism: A way of knowing and learning*. London: RoutledgeFalmer.
Vygotsky, L. (1986). *Thought and language*. Cambridge, MA: MIT Press.
Wainwright, N. A. (2010). *The development of the Leeds Alliance in Supervision Scale (LASS): A brief sessional measure of the supervisory alliance*. Unpublished doctoral thesis, University of Leeds.
Walter, J. (2006). *Working with the mandated client (videorecording)*. Los Angeles: MastersWork.
Walter, J. L., & Peller, J. E. (2000). *Recreating brief therapy: Preferences and possibilities*. New York: W. W. Norton.
Wampold, B. E. (2001). *The great psychotherapy debate: Models, methods, and findings*. New York: Routledge.
Wampold, B. E., Imel, Z. E., & Miller, S. D. (2009). Barriers to the dissemination of empirically supported treatments: Matching messages to the evidence. *The Behavior Therapist, 32*(7), 144–155.
Waskett, C. (2006). The pluses of solution-focused supervision. *Counselling and Psychotherapy Journal, 6*(1), 9–11.
Watkins, C. E., Jr. (2011). Does psychotherapy supervision contribute to patient outcomes? Considering thirty years of research. *The Clinical Supervisor, 30*, 235–256.
Watzlawick, P., Weakland, J. H., & Fisch, R. (1974). *Change: Principles of problem formation and problem resolution*. New York: W. W. Norton.

Weatherford, R., O'Shaughnessy, T., Mori, Y., & Kaduvettoor, A. (2008). The new supervisee: Order from chaos. In A. K. Hess, K. D. Hess, & T. H. Hess (Eds.), *Psychotherapy supervision: Theory, research, and practice* (2nd ed., pp. 40–54). New York: Wiley.

Weiner-Davis, M. (1990). Divorce busters. In K. Tilley (Ed.), *Strengthening families: 1990 AAMFT annual conference monograph* (pp. 77–86). Washington, DC: AAMFT.

Weir, K. N. (2009). Countering the isomorphic study of isomorphism: Coercive, mimetic, and normative isomorphic trends in the training, supervision, and industry of marriage and family therapy. *Journal of Family Psychotherapy, 20*, 60–71.

Wetchler, J. (1990). Solution-focused supervision. *Family Therapy, 17*(2), 129–138.

Wheeler, J. (2007). Solution-focused supervision. In T. S. Nelson & F. N. Thomas (Eds.), *Handbook of solution-focused brief therapy: Clinical applications* (pp. 343–370). New York: Haworth.

Wheeler, S. (2007). What shall we do with the wounded healer? The supervisor's dilemma. *Psychodynamic Practice, 13*(3), 245–256.

Wheeler, J., & Greaves, Y. (2005). Solution-focused practice teaching in social work. *Journal of Family Psychotherapy, 16*(1/2), 263–276.

Wheeler, S., & Richards, K. (2007). The impact of clinical supervision on counsellors and therapists, their practice and their clients: A systematic review of the literature. *Counselling and Psychotherapy Research, 7*(1), 54–65.

White, M. (1994). Deconstruction and therapy. In S. Gilligan & R. Price (Eds.), *Therapeutic conversations* (pp. 22–61). New York: Norton.

White, M. (2007). *Maps of narrative practice*. New York: Norton.

White, S. (2010). *The last lie*. New York: Dutton.

White, M., & Epston, D. (1990). *Narrative means to therapeutic ends*. London: Norton.

White, M. B., & Russell, C. S. (1997). Examining the multifaceted notion of isomorphism in marriage and family therapy supervision: A quest for conceptual clarity. *Journal of Marital and Family Therapy, 23*(3), 315–333.

Wittgenstein, L. (1953). *Philosophical investigations* (trans: Anscombe, G. E. M.). Oxford: Basil Blackwell.

Wong, Y. J. (2006). Strength-centered therapy: A social constructionist, virtues-based psychotherapy. *Psychotherapy: Theory, Research, Practice, Training, 43*(2), 133–146.

Worthen, V. E., & Lambert, M. J. (2007). Outcome oriented supervision: Advantages of adding systematic client tracking to supportive consultations. *Counseling and Psychotherapy Research, 7*(1), 48–53.

Worthen, V., & McNeill, B. (1996). A phenomenological investigation of "good" supervision events. *Journal of Counseling Psychology, 43*, 25–34.

Zur, O. (2005). Dumbing down of psychology: Manufactured consent about the depravity of dual relationships in therapy. In R. H. Wright & N. A. Cummings (Eds.), *Destructive trends in mental health: The well-intentioned road to harm* (pp. 254–282). New York: Brunner-Routledge.

Author Index

A
Abidin, R.R., 191
Adams, J.F., 86, 165, 284
Ahn, H., 55
Ahola, T., 71, 102
Almstrom, C.M., 165
American Association for Marriage and Family Therapy (AAMFT), xvii, 33, 44, 214, 288, 291
Amundson, J., 12, 14, 15, 26, 56, 114
Andersen, T., xvii, 173, 205, 206, 213
Anderson, H., xvii, 12, 24, 25, 57, 188, 191, 272
Astin, A.W., 250, 251
Atkinson, B.J., 13, 54, 288
Aylott, H., 164

B
Baker, E.N., xi
Bambling, M., 165
Barnard, C.P., 86–89, 91, 125
Barnes, D., 12
Barnett, J.E., 277
Barrera, I., xi, 168
Barretta-Herman, A., 169
Bateson, G., 19, 32, 36, 47, 72, 77, 93, 118, 282
Bateson, M.C., 61, 284
Bavelas, J.B., xii, xix, 94, 127, 265, 283
Beach, A., 6, 48
Beck, A.T., 191
Becvar, D.S., 293
Becvar, R.J., 293
Benner, P., xiv, 79–81, 112, 293
Berg, I.K., xi, xii, xiv, 7–9, 12, 19, 24, 32, 33, 36, 38, 51, 59–75, 77, 84, 85, 88, 95, 97–102, 104, 108, 127, 128, 131, 147, 159, 161, 163, 167, 177, 189, 195, 222, 223, 243, 254–257, 259, 265, 267, 282
Bernard, J.M., xiv, 34, 47, 127, 162, 163, 165, 170
Berne, E., 189
Bertrando, P., 25, 36
Beutler, L.E., 188
Beyebach, M., 3, 101
Bidwell, D.R., xix, xx, xxvii, 33, 178–180, 186
Biever, J., 6, 49, 50, 123
Bliss, E.V., 3, 5, 9
Blumen, D.G., 86, 165, 284
Blumer, M., 54, 163
Bobele, M., xx, 6, 49, 50, 123
Bordin, E.S., 163, 166, 172
Borja, S.E., 165
Boscolo, L., 189
Bosk, C., 98
Bowman, D.C., 87, 162, 165
Bray, D., 3, 5, 9
Brickman, P., 21
Briggs, J.R., 6–8, 240
Brodsky, S.L., 196
Brossart, D.F., 3
Brown, G.K., 191
Bucknell, D., 6
Burnham, J., 273
Butcher, J.N., 191

C
Cade, B., xii, xv, xix, 9, 10, 32, 278, 279
Callahan, J.L., 165
Cantwell, P., viii, 27, 29, 62, 188, 313, 315
Cardin, S.A., 3

Carlisi, J., 12
Carlson, T.D., 6
Carrere, S., 21
Casemore, R., xi
Cecchin, G.-F., 189
Čepukienė, V., xi
Chang, J., xix, xxvii, 6, 187, 188
ChangingMinds.org, 35
Chenail, R.J., 167
Cheon, H.S., 54, 163
Chisholm, R.R., 87, 162, 165
Cigrand, D.L., 6
Cliffe, K., 54
Coates, D., 21
Coffey, A., 172, 283
Cohen, M.S., 169–171
Coleman, H.L.K., xiv
Conoley, C.W., 3
Constantine, J.A., 205
Cooper, R.J., 118
Cooper, S.J., xvii, 57
Corbett, M., 164
Corcoran, J., 96
Corcoran, K.B., xi, 173
Cornish, J.A.E., xi, 277
Corsiglia, V., 12, 13, 31, 54, 93, 218
Coward, R.L., 6, 48
Cox, H., xix, 296
Craig, M.C., 3
Cresswell, R., 6, 162
Crocket, K., 6, 162
Cronkright, A., xi, 6, 168, 173
Cullin, J., 36
Cunanan, E.D., xi, 5, 7, 168, 173, 284
Curtin, L.L., 118

D
Dahlstrom, W.G., 191
Dallos, R., 95
Davis, J., 168
Davis, R., 191
Davis, T.E., 164
De Jong, P., xi, xii, xix, 6–8, 12, 19, 24, 36, 38, 51, 59, 60, 62–71, 74, 75, 77, 84, 85, 95, 97, 98, 102, 104, 108, 127, 128, 131, 167, 168, 173, 177, 195, 222, 254, 255, 257, 259, 265
de Shazer, S., vii, xii, xiii, xx, 3, 9, 12, 32, 33, 38, 50, 60, 67, 95, 101, 108, 127, 128, 161, 162, 177, 189, 220, 252, 254, 256, 279, 280, 282
de Vries, M., 6, 162
Del Re, A.C., 27

Del Vento, A., 94, 127
Delworth, U., 230
Dishion, T.J., 190
D'Iuso, N., 162
Doherty, W.J., 279
Dolan, Y., xii, xix, 6–9, 33, 67, 108, 127, 189, 223
Dreyfus, H.L., 57, 79, 84, 110, 112, 123, 289
Dreyfus, S.E., 57, 79, 84, 110, 112, 123, 289
Dumont, F., 19
Duncan, B., 18, 85, 275, 278, 284
Durrant, M., xii, xix, 12, 108, 109

E
Echterling, L.G., 7
Edwards, S., 268, 269
Einstein, A., 61, 280
Ellis, A., 225
Ellis, J.M., 278
Ellis, M.V., 162, 164
Enders, L., 72, 87
Epstein, E.S., 284
Epstein, R.M., xii
Epston, D., 273
Erford, B.T., 188
Erickson Cornish, J.A.,
Erickson, M.J., 6
Ericsson, K.A., 79, 110
Etringer, B.D., 79

F
Falender, C.A., xiv, 85
Feit, S.S., 168
Fine, M., 6, 38, 40, 114, 123, 277, 279
Fisch, R., vii, 191
Fitzpatrick, H., 164
Fleckney, G., 109
Flemons, D.G., 277, 284, 293
Flückiger, C., 27
Fowers, B.J., 66
Frader, J., 98
Franklin, C., 6, 31, 55, 96, 276
Freitas, G.J., 161, 162, 165, 167
Frels, R.K., 235
Friedlander, M.L., 13, 163, 168, 170
Friedman, E., 62
Furman, B., 71, 102

G
Gadamer, H.G., 188
Gallagher, D., 32

Gantt, E., 55
Gardner, G., 6, 12, 23, 24, 49, 50, 123
Garza, Y., 235
Gazzola, N., 169, 170, 283
Gehart, D.R., 57, 188, 191
George, E., 102
Gerard, A.B., 191
Gergen, K.J., 19, 20, 25, 41, 67, 272
Gershenson, J., 169–171
Gingerich, W.J., 32, 55, 276
Godard, G.J., 30
Goldberg, P.D., 112
Gonzales, L., 60
Goodyear, R.K., xi, xiv, 34, 47, 127, 162, 163, 165, 170, 277
Goolishian, H., 24, 272
Gorsuch, N., 3, 187
Gottman, J.M., 21, 230
Gracie, J., 162
Graham, J.M., 3
Graham, J.R., 191
Graham, J.T., 55, 276
Gray, L.A., 13
Greaves, Y., xii, 6–8, 27, 109, 165, 174, 283
Green, S.K., 277
Greenleaf, R.K., 229
Grigg, K., xix, 304
Grossman, S., 191
Groth-Marnat, G., 188
Grus, C., xi
Gullestad, S., 164
Guy, G., 6–8, 117, 283

H
Haber, R., 284
Haley, J., vii, 32, 47
Halgin, R.P., 164
Halperin, M., 189
Halstead, J.L., 87, 162, 165
Hanna, F.J., 224
Hansen, B., 164
Harwood, T.M., 188
Hawkins, E.J., 166
Hayden, E.C.,
Heath, A.W., 13, 27, 29, 54, 169, 170, 283
Heath, C., 275
Heath, C.J., 165
Heath, D., 275
Heilemann, J., 189
Henden, J., 41
Henderson, P., xiv
Hendricson, S., 196
Hernandez, L., 284

Herrero, M., 3
Hess, A.K., 168
Heylighen, F., 60, 293
Hill, C.E., 164
Hillerbrand, E., 79
Hoffman, L., 25
Hofstadter, D.R., 47
Holloway, E., 165
Holmes, S., viii, 27, 29, 62, 188, 313, 315
Homrich, A.M., 7, 8
Hooks, B., 30
Horsfall, D., 30
Horvath, A.O., 27
Hoyt, M.F., 3, 30, 254
Hsu, W.S., xi, xix, xxvii, 6–8, 95, 166, 168, 197, 198, 200, 283
Hubble, M.A., 18, 57, 278, 284
Hundert, E.M., xii
Hunt, W.P., 224
Hyland, K., 98

I
Imel, Z.E., 55
Inman, A.G., xiv, 162–165, 169
Iveson, C., 51, 73, 102

J
Jackson, D.D., 32
Jackson, P.Z., 33, 35, 63
Jacobsen, C., 164
James, E.L., 275
James, I., 162
Janoff-Bulman, R., 21
Jennings, L., 57, 79
Joanning, H., xx, 72, 87
Joiner, T.E., 282
Jolly, B.C., 163, 288
Jones, C., 6–8, 24, 26, 93, 95
Jordan, A.E., 115
Juhnke, G.A., 6–8, 231

K
Kaduvettoor, A., 164
Kaemmer, B., 191
Kahneman, D., 79
Keeney, B.P., xx, 23, 41, 73, 293
Keeney, H., 36, 293
Kelly, S., 60
Keyes, R., 45
Kilminster, S.M., 163, 288
Kimball, T.G., 168

King, R., 165
Kisler, T.S., 86, 165, 284
Kitchener, K.S., 29, 276
Klein, G., 79
Klinger, R.S., 164
Knight, C., 6–8
Koltz, R.L., 168
Koob, J.J., xi, 7, 8, 166–168, 283
Korinek, A.W., 168
Korman, H., xii, xix, 9, 33, 61, 67, 73, 75, 101, 108, 127, 189, 265, 285
Krampe, R.T., 79
Kuehl, B.P., 32, 33, 86–89, 91, 125
Kulp, L.E., 164
Kuo, B., xix, xxvii, 95, 166, 197

L

Ladany, N., xiv, 13, 123–125, 162–165, 168, 169, 171, 283, 288, 289
Lakoff, G., 98
Lambert, M.J., 85, 86, 166, 288
Lambert, W., 165
Lane, D., xix, xxvii, 88, 100, 204, 207, 208, 212
Lee, M.Y., 36
LeGoullon, M., 54
Lehrman-Waterman, D.E., 123–125, 163, 164, 168, 171, 283, 288, 289
Levenson, E.A., 163
Levenson, R.W., 230
Lichtenberg, J.W., 166, 277
Liddle, H.A., 47, 62
Lipchik, E., 32, 181, 270
Lloyd, H., 95
Locke, L.D., 112
London, S., 6
Loos, V.E., 284
Lowe, R., 6–8, 109, 117–121, 283

M

Macdonald, A.J., 55, 95
Madanes, C., vii
Madigan, S.P., 30
Malinen, T., xvii, 57
Marek, L.I., 6–8, 48
Marovic, S., 36
Maturana, H.R., 30
McCarron, M.C.E., 277
McCollum, E.E., xi, 5, 7, 9, 18, 32, 33, 55, 67, 93, 94, 108, 112, 127, 168, 173, 189, 276, 284
McDermott, I., 38
McDowell, T., 213

McEwen, M.K., 251
McGee, D., 94, 108, 127
McKee, J.E., 7
McKergow, M., 31, 33, 35, 61
McLellan, A.T., 191
McNamee, S., 272
McNeill, B.W., xiv, 34, 79, 127, 162, 163, 172, 230
Meara, N.M., 115
Mee-Lee, D., 191
Metcalf, L., 18
Miller, G., xiii, 3, 6–9, 12, 31–33, 240, 279
Miller, S.D., 18, 55, 57, 85–87, 101, 123, 124, 191, 246, 247, 265, 267, 275, 278, 284, 289
Millon, C., 191
Millon, T., 191
Mills, S.D., 36
Milne, D., 162, 164, 166
Monk, G., 117–120, 123
Morgan, M.M., xii, 33, 170, 277
Mori, Y., 164
Murphy, M.J., 54, 164
Mutchler, L., 72, 87

N

Nardone, G., 170
Nash, J., 6–8
Nelson, M.L., 13, 163, 168, 170
Nelson, T.S., ix, xxi, xvii, xix, 9, 31, 61, 96, 101, 170
Neu, T., 31
Neufeldt, S., 165
Nims, D.R., 234
Norcross, J.C., 86, 164
Norman, H., xi, 8, 12, 201
Norsworthy, L.A., 87, 162, 165
Nowicki, J., 96
Nunnally, E., 243
Nutt, L., 164
Nyland, D., 12, 13, 31, 54, 93, 218

O

O'Connell, B., 6–8, 24, 26, 93, 95
O'Connor, J., 38, 294
Odegard, M.A., 168
O'Donoghue, K., 164, 171
O'Hanlon, W., 38, 116, 234, 278
Olk, M.E., 170
O'Pry, A., 3
OQ Measures, 87
O'Shaughnessy, T., 164

P

Paice, C., 6, 162
Pakrosnis, R., xi
Parker, I., 191
Parker, R.I., 3
Parry, A., 277
Patterson, V., 54
Pearce, J., 188
Pearson, Q.M., xi
Peller, J.E., 244
Pentecost, M., 6, 162
Peterik, J.M., 12
Pettifor, J., 277, 284
Pettit, J., 282
Pezzot-Pearce, T., 188
Philp, K., 6, 117
Pichot, T., xix, xxvii, 6–8, 110, 112, 215, 223
Pilkington, J., 162
Poerksen, B., 30
Pond, C., 117
Pope-Davis, D.B., xiv
Powers, W.T., 285
Prata, G., 189
Pratt, J., xix, xxvii, 224
Presbury, J., 7, 8, 27
Prince, E.F., 98
Protinsky, H.O., 6, 48
Provost, K., 168
Pyle, N.R., 97

R

Rambo, A., 277, 284
Ratner, H., 102, 108, 252
Raue, P., 165
Ray, W.A., xix, 170
Reese, R.J., 87, 162, 165
Reichelt, S., 164
Richards, K., 54, 162, 165, 166, 168
Roe v. Wade, 45
Roffman, M.S., xii, 7, 8, 172
Rogers, C., 27
Rønnestad, M., 57, 79, 164
Rosen, K.H., 112
Rosenthal, R., 126
Ross, L.R., 190
Rowlands, S.R., 87, 162, 165
Rudes, J., xii, xiv, xix, 7, 32, 36, 60–62, 65, 68, 73, 77, 98, 99, 101, 128, 129, 167, 168
Russell, C.S., 47, 48

S

Saba, G.W., 47
Sandifer, D.M., 6, 48
Sato, M., 54, 164
Schoepp, G., 277
Schröder, T., 168
Schweitzer, R., 165
Scott, M., 196
Scott, S., 172, 283
Sebold, J., 36
Selekman, M.D., 6–8, 28, 93
Selvini-Palazzoli, M., 189
Shafranske, E.P., xiv, 85
Shappee, K., xii, 54, 168, 170, 172, 174, 283
Sheldon, K.M., 282
Shih, A.T., 54, 164
Shilts, L., xii, 7, 32, 60, 77, 167, 284
Shotter, J., 188
Sinclair, S.L., 117–120, 123
Skjerve, J., 164
Skott-Myhre, H.A., 159
Skovholt, T.M., 57, 79–82, 84, 123
Slife, B.D., 55, 276
Sluzki, C.E., 114
Smith, J.D., 19
Smith, T., 168
Smock, S.A., 32
Snyder, C.R., 96
Snyders, F., 36
Söderquist, M., 9, 73, 75, 101
Solution-Focused Brief Therapy Association (SFBTA) Board, xii, xix, 5, 88
Sommers-Flanagan, J., 276
Sparks, J., 85, 86, 165, 276, 284, 288
Sparrer, I., 33
Sperry, L., 192
Spiegel, A., 19
Sprenkle, D.H., xii, 33, 36, 170, 277
Stark, C., 277
Stark, M., viii, xix, xxvii, 230, 235
Steer, R.A., 191
Steinhelber, J., 54
Stevenson, M.L., 32
Stewart, D., 277
Stewart, K., 12, 14, 15, 25, 56, 114, 120
Stith, S.M., 112
Stoltenberg, C.xiv, 34, 79, 127, 162, 230, 233, 234, 236
Storm, C.L., 33, 213
Stormshak, E.A., 190
Streeter, C.L., 6, 31, 96

Strong, T., xii, 7, 97, 120
Sun, S.-T.M., xi, 166, 168, 283
Sundman, P., xix, xxvii, 239, 240
Sutherland, O., 97
Sutherland, T., 213
Swift, J.K., 165
Symonds, D., 27
Szabó, P., 74, 223

T
Tarasoff v. Regents of the University of California, 45
Tarragona, M., 6
Taylor, E., xii, xix, xxvii, 225, 250
Taylor, L., 201
Tellegen, A., 191
Tesch-Römer, C., 79
*Texas Family Code Chapter*261, 113
Tharp, L., 27, 29, 169, 170, 283
Tharpar v. Zezulka, 45
Theriault, A., 169, 170, 283
Thomas, F.N., viii, xii, xiv, xv, xvii, xxvii, 6–9, 18, 23–25, 27–29, 31, 41, 48, 50, 54, 57, 60, 61, 72, 79, 81, 82, 86–88, 93, 96, 100–102, 109–111, 114, 117, 121, 168, 170, 172, 174, 204, 213, 225, 226, 283, 294
Tjeltveit, A.C., 66
Todd, T.A., 72, 87
Todd, T.C., 6–8, 28, 33, 62, 93, 117–119, 164, 213
Tognetti, S.S., 36
Tollestrup, D., 6, 162
Tomm, K., 30, 81, 206, 272
Tomori, C., 127
Torgersen, A., 164
Torti, P., 170, 172
Totro, T., 239
Townsend, L., 178
Trenhaile, J.D., xii, xix, xxvii, 8, 168, 250, 252, 283
Trepper, T.S., 9, 33, 55, 67, 108, 127, 189, 276
Triantafillou, N., xii, 7, 8, 32, 164, 165, 167, 168, 170, 283
Tromski-Klingshirn, D.M., 164
Tsai, S.L., xi, 6, 166, 168, 198, 283
Turnell, A., xx, 268, 269
Turner, J., 6, 38, 40, 114, 123, 277, 279

U
Ueland, B., 25
Uken, A., 36
Ungar, M., 6, 54, 56–58, 123
Usher, E.L., 87, 162, 165

V
Valentine, L., 12
Vargas, H.L., 117
Varttala, T., 98
Visser, C., 67
von Bertalanffy, L., vii
von Foerster, H., 23, 25, 34, 41, 45, 176, 285
von Glasersfeld, E., 41, 125
Vygotsky, L., 272

W
Wainwright, N.A., 123, 124, 163, 289
Walter, J., 32, 36, 244
Wampold, B.E., 27, 55, 81
Waskett, C., 7, 8, 24, 27
Watkins, C.E., 165
Watzlawick, P., vii, 191
Weakland, J.H., vii, 32, 71, 191
Weatherford, R., 164
Weiner-Davis, M., 23, 38, 234
Weir, K.N., 54, 55
Wetchler, J., 6–8, 18, 23, 27, 31, 48, 82, 93, 94
Wheeler, J., xii, xix, xxvii, 6–8, 27, 30, 75, 93, 95, 109, 110, 113, 165, 174, 260, 263, 283
Wheeler, S., 54, 162, 165, 166, 168
White, M., xvii, 120, 272, 273
White, M.B., 47, 48
White, S., 171
Wiggins, B.J., 55, 276
Wilk, J., 116
Williams, G., 282
Wilson, C.M., 117
Wittgenstein, L., xv, 189
Wolfe, R., 6, 162
Wong, Y.J., 280
Wood, S.M., 6
Worthen, V.E., 85, 86, 163, 166, 172, 288
Wright, L., 81, 206

Z
Zur, O., 118

Subject Index

A
AAMFT. *See* American Association for Marriage and Family Therapy (AAMFT)
Academic actions, 257–260
American Association for Marriage and Family Therapy (AAMFT), vii, xvii, 33, 44, 214, 288, 291
Amplification, 7, 51–53
Amplify, 8, 51, 53, 90, 167, 194–196
Assumptions, 66–67
    SF supervision, 35, 129, 147, 166
    therapist, 37, 253

B
Brief Family Therapy Center of Milwaukee (BFTC), vii, xii, xiii, xix, 32, 38, 60, 69, 78

C
Caring, 29–30, 171
Caring curiosity, 25–26
Case management, 44, 79, 81, 82, 90, 109, 119, 122, 289, 295, 296, 304
Cautions, 50, 215, 278–282, 306
Certainty, temporary, 14, 15, 25, 56, 121, 152, 185
Change, 5, 7
    amplify, 51
    assumed, 7
    identify, 270
Client
    outcomes, 44, 48, 50, 55, 77, 85, 87, 162, 165–168, 283
    perspectives, 68–69, 137, 284
Co-learning, 61, 75

Collaboration, 10, 25, 27–28, 35, 36, 44, 48, 49, 52, 53, 63–65, 74, 78, 92, 101, 103, 110, 111, 133, 137, 141, 143, 145, 146, 165, 168, 174–176, 205–209, 214, 217, 221, 254, 290
College student affair professional (CSAP), 250–257, 259, 260
Competence, enhancing, 240
Complimenting, 70, 109, 145, 182, 248
    direct, 102–104
    indirect, 104–106
    self-compliment, 107–108
Compliments, supervisor, 102, 104, 145, 175, 208, 214, 215, 236, 237, 248
Context, viii, xii, xiv, 3, 5–7, 12, 13, 19–26, 28, 31–48, 50, 51, 56, 58, 61, 63, 67, 68, 70–72, 77–84, 87, 88, 92, 96, 97, 100, 102, 104, 105, 109, 110, 113, 114, 116–119, 123, 124, 129, 146, 147, 167, 176–180, 186–189, 191, 197, 201, 205–207, 224, 228, 239, 247, 250, 251, 253–255, 269, 272, 277–279, 282, 296, 305, 313
Court, 36, 40, 45, 187–196, 279, 290
CSAP. *See* College student affair professional (CSAP)
Curiosity, 24–26, 51–54, 75, 146
    caring, 25–26, 29, 51

D
Deconstruction, 120
Delusions of certainty, 278–279
Dilemma talk, 114–116
Dyads, 166, 205
Dynamic tension, 14, 276

E

EBTA. *See* European Brief Therapy Association (EBTA)
Education, xi, xvii, xx, 13, 14, 23, 28, 29, 34, 39, 42, 48, 50, 55, 57, 63, 65–66, 75, 82, 84, 108, 119, 122, 128, 132, 134–137, 139, 140, 142, 144–146, 163, 166, 177, 182, 225, 228, 237, 250, 251, 257, 261, 276, 278, 291, 296, 304
Emergence, 33, 35, 38, 81
Ending rituals, 248
Epistemology, 31, 46, 96
Ethics, xiv, 6, 14, 22, 29, 40, 56, 75, 78, 89, 111, 115–118, 122, 155, 178, 205, 236, 253, 272, 276–277, 284, 288, 290, 291
European Brief Therapy Association (EBTA), 3, 252
Evaluation of goals, 18, 78, 82, 89, 122, 165, 174, 175, 236, 253, 282, 288, 289, 295
Exceptions, xi, 3–5, 7–10, 12–13, 26, 32, 41, 50–53, 61, 63, 64, 70, 82, 90–97, 101, 104–106, 135, 141, 144, 149–151, 155–157, 159, 160, 165, 166, 174, 193, 196, 198, 200, 207, 223, 232–234, 238, 254–256, 258, 264, 266, 279, 299, 306
Expert knowledge, 26, 78, 137, 138, 146

F

Family court
    case conceptualization, 192
    knowledge of court proceedings, 194
    knowledge of legal system, 190
    psychological testing, 58, 115, 191
    report writing, 191–193, 195
    testifying, 192
Family intervention, worker, 260–273
Feedback
    formal from therapists, 123
    less formal from therapists, 123–125
    supervisor/therapist/client, 39, 49, 85–89
Field supervision, 237
Future focus, 5, 67, 83, 108–110, 121–122, 157, 238, 280

G

Goaling, 239, 244, 246, 250
Goal orientation, 63
Goal-setting, xix, 5, 7, 8, 11, 17, 18, 49, 51, 52, 57, 58, 63, 78–92, 96, 97, 103, 106, 109, 119, 122, 124, 128, 150, 154, 157, 159, 163, 164, 166, 168, 171, 175, 231–232, 245, 253, 277, 288, 289, 295–310
    case management, 44, 79, 81, 82, 90, 109, 119, 122, 289, 295, 296, 304
    conceptual, 90, 238, 295, 299, 305
    participatory, 79, 81, 82, 296, 300, 306
    perceptual, 79, 82, 295, 298, 305
    policies, 42, 82

H

Hedging, 68, 73–74, 98–101, 132–138, 140, 141, 143, 144, 146, 155–157, 167, 314
Hierarchy, flattening, 28, 35, 43, 48, 55, 57, 61–62, 100, 167, 168

I

If it's not broken, don't fix it, 9
If it's not working, do something different, 9, 267
If it works, do more of it, 9, 181, 183, 265, 279
Imposition without permission, 121, 279
Indirect to direct, 153, 291
Informed consent, 10, 11, 49, 81, 205, 277, 287–292
Integrative developmental model, 34
In vivo supervisory dialogue, xiv
Isomorphism, 47–58
    coercive, 54–56
    hierarch, 49
    mimetic, 54–56
    normative, 54–56

J

Joint responsibility for clients, 290
Judicial conversations, 254, 255, 260

L

Labeling, pejorative, 19–21
Language, xiii, xv, 5–9, 12, 17, 19, 20, 35, 61, 67–68, 74, 78, 97, 100, 110, 152, 156, 167, 188, 189, 191, 192, 201, 220, 265, 272, 285, 299, 313, 314
LASS. *See* Leeds Alliance in Supervision Scale (LASS)
Leading from one step behind, viii, 27, 29, 62–63, 136, 160, 188, 313

Leeds Alliance in Supervision Scale (LASS), 123, 124, 289
Limitations of explanation, 14–16
Linear causality, 35

M

Medical model, 19
Mental Research Institute (MRI), vii, 9, 32, 33, 71, 143
Mentoring, 70, 97, 116, 170, 175, 205, 214, 307
Metaphor, 4, 19, 27, 40, 47, 51, 62, 79, 100, 110–114, 248, 278, 282
Minimalism, 279–280, 284
MRI. *See* Mental Research Institute (MRI)
Mutual causality, 35
Mutual respect, 26–28, 65, 170

N

Nonpathology, labeling, 18–21
Nosologies, 45
Not knowing, viii, 24–25, 63, 68, 73, 98, 100, 102, 104, 110, 135, 181, 188, 191, 192, 207, 216, 225, 228, 257, 258, 300, 309

O

Outcome rating scale (ORS), 86, 87, 247

P

Parallel process, 47, 55, 59, 168, 238
Parenting evaluations, 187–196
Participatory skill building, 152
Pastoral counseling, xvii, 178–187, 214
Pathologizing labels, 3
Paying attention to 'how,' 18, 103, 243
Perspectives
    clients, 137, 284
    therapists, 217
Postmodern, xv, 4, 6, 14, 20, 21, 28, 29, 33, 36, 41, 48, 56–58, 61, 64, 68, 71, 73, 102, 114, 117, 182, 198, 205, 275, 277, 285
Practices
    being indirect, 71–72, 100
    complimenting, 70
    direct, 85, 102–104
    indirect, 71, 104–106, 141, 142, 148, 212
    self-compliments, 5, 71, 102, 107–108, 111, 119, 133, 145, 148, 169
    consulting the client/therapist relationship, 58, 72

dilemma talk, 114–116
exceptions, 70, 193, 232–233
future focus, 5, 67, 83, 108–110, 121–122, 157, 238, 280
goal-setting
    challenging to therapist, 82, 84–85
    initial goals, 17, 89, 97, 295, 296, 304
    interactive, 34, 78, 82–84
    recalibrating goals, 89–92
    responsive to clients, 82, 85–89
    responsive to other systems, 82, 85–89
    re-visioning goals, 89
    and supervisor/therapist/client feedback process, 85–89
hedging, 73, 98, 100, 146
highlighting exceptions, 70, 92–95, 151, 157
highlighting successes, 70
indirect-direct spectrum, 71, 110–114
scaling, 70, 95, 219
self-supervision, 113, 118–122
using silence, 73
using "suppose", 74
using "you must have good reasons to", 67, 74–75
Practicum, vii, 6, 10, 11, 13, 20, 48, 54, 57, 58, 89, 119, 123, 225, 228, 230–239, 252, 296, 297, 299, 301–304, 307–309, 311
Pragmatic emphasis, xv, 5, 284
Pragmatism, 9–12, 125
Presuppositional questioning, 108, 111
Psychopharmacological intervention, 41

Q

Questions
    miracle, viii, ix, 3–5, 8, 99, 108, 128–131, 134, 135, 139, 144–146, 193, 222, 231, 234, 244, 266, 306
    relationship, 5, 8, 38, 63–65, 69, 70, 72, 95, 129, 132, 139, 146, 148, 193, 216, 223, 224, 235, 255
    scaling, 8, 64, 95, 97, 110, 193, 206, 209, 231, 233–234, 236, 238, 256, 259, 266, 272, 273, 306, 315

R

Reflection, ix, xii, 10, 23, 29, 32, 74, 79, 92–94, 107, 118–120, 122, 123, 141, 163, 167, 174, 180, 201–206, 209–210, 213, 237, 248–250, 259, 284
Reflective questions, 94, 237, 249
Reification of deficit, 19, 20

Research
  general supervision, xiii, 58, 165, 168, 283
  supervisees' perspectives, 169–175
    non-SF research, 169–175
    SF research, 3, 168
  supervision alliance, 162–165, 169
  supervision and client outcomes, 85, 162, 165–168, 283
Resources, 3, 5, 23–24, 35, 37, 56, 60, 61, 65, 66, 109, 120, 122, 159, 167, 178, 180, 198, 199, 204, 219, 232, 245, 247, 254, 257, 259, 277, 288
Respect, 25–30
  caring, 29, 30
  collaboration, 27, 28
  cooperation, 28, 29
  flexibility, 28–29
Ripple effect, 31, 35, 38, 53
Risk-goal chart, 311–312

S

Scaling, 4, 51, 63, 70, 95–98, 110, 124, 130, 193, 206, 207, 210, 219, 223, 234, 241, 256, 257, 266
Self-efficacy of therapist, 166–168, 171, 283
Self-supervision, 2, 12, 116–122, 168, 174, 179
Self-supervision practices
  contributing without imposing, 121
  deconstructing, 120
  goal-setting, 119
  highlighting competence, 119–120
  identifying challenges, 120
  identifying resources, 120
  keeping a future focus, 121–122
  skills, 122
  teaching, 122
  temporary certainty, 120–121
Semaphore, 100, 110–114
Session rating scale (SRS), 86, 123, 246
SFBT. *See* Solution-focused brief therapy (SFBT)
SF supervision
  addictions, 224–230
  evaluator role, 188, 189, 233, 236–237
  group, 199–201
  practicum, 230–239
  safety, 68, 73, 171, 221–222, 269
  school counselors in Taiwan, 197–204
  Taiwan, 197–204
  team, 57, 72, 88, 127, 128, 215–223
  team case conference, 201–204
  techniques,
    fast forwarding, 234–235
    sandtray, 235–236
  tools, 221–223
Simplify, 60–61, 97
Small steps, 9, 200, 203, 235, 272
Snowballing, 38, 96
Social construction, 33, 36, 117, 188–189,
Social constructionist theory, 6, 33, 67, 117, 188, 205
Solution-building skills, 66
Solution-focused brief therapy (SFBT), viii, ix, xii, xvii, xix, 4, 5, 9, 32, 36, 48, 54, 55, 57, 61, 65, 89–91, 108, 112, 127, 128, 167, 173, 174, 188, 189, 191, 193, 196–204, 215, 216, 219, 221, 224, 234, 237–239, 275, 276, 279, 280, 282, 283, 295
Solution-forced, 51, 54, 218–219
Solution-problem disconnect, 162
Spiritual, 178–181, 183, 184, 186, 187
SRS. *See* Session Rating Scale (SRS),
Stance, viii, xii, 9, 36, 46, 48, 54, 58–60, 67, 74, 98, 100, 102, 118, 120, 125, 126, 133–135, 145, 146, 167, 168, 172, 175, 179, 190, 205, 208, 210, 216, 218, 220, 221, 223, 228, 257–259, 261, 277, 309
Strengths, 3, 7, 17, 20, 23–24, 28, 37, 38, 48, 54, 56, 60, 65, 66, 82, 86, 124, 146, 164, 167, 172–175, 193, 194, 198, 200–202, 205, 208, 224, 231, 233, 236, 237, 239, 240, 246, 254–257, 259, 260, 266, 269, 288, 296, 302, 303, 309
  and resources, 3, 7, 37, 56, 60, 167, 257, 259, 288
Success, focus on, 70
Supervision
  alliance, 162–165, 169
  college student affair professional (CSAPs), 250–257, 259, 260
  continuous, 239, 241, 243–245, 247–250
  contract, 40, 62, 84, 105, 124, 125, 207, 241–245, 249, 287, 290, 291
  family court, 187–196
  informed consent, 10, 11, 49, 81, 205, 277, 287–292
  postmodern, xv, 4, 6, 14, 20, 21, 28, 29, 33, 36, 41, 48, 56–58, 61, 64, 68, 71, 73, 102, 114, 117, 182, 198, 205, 275, 277, 285

Subject Index 345

practicum, vii, 6, 10, 11, 13, 20, 48, 54, 57, 58, 89, 119, 123, 225, 228, 230–239, 252, 296, 297, 299, 301–304, 307–309, 311
  as therapy-once-removed, 62, 167, 280–282
Supervision-of-supervision (mentoring)
  collaboration, 206–209
  roles and rules, 205–206
Supervisor, stance, 1–30, 49, 51, 54, 58–60, 98, 100, 118, 125, 126, 145, 146, 161, 167, 168, 172, 179, 205, 208, 210, 216, 218, 228, 257, 277, 284
Systems
  ideas, 32, 34–38, 69, 112
  interactional view, 34–36
  multiple, 38–47
  mutual influence, 38–47
  paradigm, 31–33
  readings, 293–294
  thinking, 31, 216–218
Systems ideas
  context, 36–38
  emergence, 38
  interaction, 34–36

T
Teaching, viii, xiii, xvii, xx, 13, 26, 27, 62, 65–66, 95, 116, 117, 122, 134, 137, 146, 173, 175, 179, 195, 196, 200, 229–233, 236, 238, 253, 259, 305, 309, 313, 315
Teleology, 192
Tentativeness, 9, 12–18, 73, 125
Therapeutic impasse, 65
Therapist self-efficacy, 166–168, 171, 283
Therapy by proxy, 62
Therapy-once-removed, 62, 167, 280–282
Transitional nature
  of goal development, 17
  of problem/change experiences, 17
Transparency, 10, 43, 49–51, 101, 164, 277
Two-by-four, 100, 110–114

U
Unilateral causality, 35

W
Wow and how technique, 234

Printed in Great Britain
by Amazon